T0250124

Taking Intelligence Analysis to the Next Level

Taking Intelligence Analysis to the Next Level: Advanced Intelligence Analysis Methodologies Using Real-World Business, Crime, Military, and Terrorism Examples examines intelligence gathering and analysis and the significance of these programs. Coverage assumes a basic understanding of the intelligence cycle and processes, and this book builds upon the author's previous text, *Intelligence Analysis Fundamentals* – also published by CRC Press – to further address various types of intelligence, the function and increasing usage of intelligence in both the private and public sectors, and the consumption of intelligence products to inform strategic decision-making.

Developed for a classroom environment, chapters are packed with multiple examples, visuals, and practical exercises tailored for the intelligence community (IC), military intelligence analyst, criminal analyst, or business analyst alike. The text begins with a chapter on Analytical Ethics, an important topic that sets the tone for those to follow that address intelligence-gathering analytical techniques. The author utilizes multiple instructive learning approaches to build on the student's existing analytical skills gained from other training resources, their experience, or some other combination.

While topics covered are germane to all intelligence analysis fields including military, national, political, criminal, as well as business-specific chapters and sections. Most instructional examples, scenarios, exercises, and learning activities focus on the Homeland Security Mission and the associated problem sets. The training presentation methods and instructional approaches are the product of much thought, research, and discussion, and a variety of U.S. government and commercial analytical training methodologies are presented. This book closes with a final chapter looking at future trends in intelligence analysis.

Key Features:

- Provides tools to challenge intelligence assessments systematically and objectively, a prerequisite to vetted intelligence conclusions
- Outlines diagnostic techniques to explain events or data sets, anticipate potential outcomes, predict future trends, and make decisions for optimal outcomes
- Details how to conduct research to effectively write, edit, format, and disseminate reports to best effect

Ancillaries including PowerPoint lecture slides, as well as the Instructor's Guide with Test Bank, are available for qualified course adopters.

Taking Intelligence Analysis to the Next Level

Advanced Intelligence Analysis Methodologies Using Real-World Business, Crime, Military, and Terrorism Examples

Patrick McGlynn

CRC Press
Taylor & Francis Group
Boca Raton London New York

CRC Press is an imprint of the
Taylor & Francis Group, an **informa** business

The views expressed in this text are the author's and do not imply endorsement by the Office of the National Geospatial-Intelligence Agency (NGA) or any other U.S. Government agency. In addition, the manuscript has been reviewed by the proper government entities and has been determined to not contain any information deemed classified.

First edition published 2023
by CRC Press
6000 Broken Sound Parkway NW, Suite 300, Boca Raton, FL 33487-2742

and by CRC Press
4 Park Square, Milton Park, Abingdon, Oxon, OX14 4RN

CRC Press is an imprint of Taylor & Francis Group, LLC

Library of Congress Cataloging-in-Publication Data
Names: McGlynn, Patrick, 1960– author.
Title: Taking intelligence analysis to the next level: advanced intelligence analysis methodologies
using real-world business, crime, military, and terrorism examples/Patrick McGlynn.
Identifiers: LCCN 2021058883 (print) | LCCN 2021058884 (ebook) | ISBN 9781032136769 (hardback) |
ISBN 9781032136738 (paperback) | ISBN 9781003241195 (ebook)
Subjects: LCSH: Business intelligence. | Military intelligence. | Intelligence service.
Classification: LCC HD38.7 .M384 2022 (print) | LCC HD38.7 (ebook) |
DDC 658.4/72–dc23/eng/20220225
LC record available at https://lccn.loc.gov/2021058883
LC ebook record available at https://lccn.loc.gov/2021

ISBN: 9781032136769 (hbk)
ISBN: 9781032136738 (pbk)
ISBN: 9781003241195 (ebk)

DOI: 10.4324/9781003241195

Typeset in Minion Pro
by Newgen Publishing UK

Support material is available for this title at www.routledge.com/9781032136769.

Contents

Foreword

Intelligence gathering and analysis, at its optimal, is a highly sophisticated and complicated process. Many men and women spend their entire professional career trying to master the art/science, but only a handful ever genuinely do. Those who reach mastery often accomplish this by accident more than hard work.

However, the intellectual dichotomy related to this conundrum is, at its core, simple. Of course, the descriptor 'simple' is exceptionally relative and utterly dependent on one's interpretation or viewpoint. That said, all who have ever mastered an art or science have experienced a tendency to look back on the process and muse, 'that wasn't as hard as I thought it would be,' or 'I wish I had known that it was as simple as that.'

A few years ago, the author (and co-author) opened *Intelligence Analysis Fundamentals*, the precursor of this text, and published it through *CRC Press, Taylor & Francis Group*. The overall goal was to offer the concept and study of Intelligence Analysis to students intent on pursuing careers in the field of Intelligence in its purest form. The original text was well received and adopted by many colleges and universities in the United States and the United Kingdom.

We both spent much of our professional lives working in the Intelligence field, of course, and in the classroom as professional educators and trainers. Early in this teaching career, we learned a lesson every successful educator must master; learning on the student's part occurs in tiny increments over a lengthy period of time. Skills and capabilities are rarely inculcated, as epiphanies. As such, seemingly complicated theories and concepts must be offered up in bits and pieces, which are easily digestible and incorporated to become 'second nature.' The process must be spread out over time to build the necessary foundations. Mastery of the basics was the focus of our first text. This follow-on text to take the student to the next step.

Taking Intelligence Analysis to the Next Level builds on the groundwork of those first lessons, assume that students have incorporated some if not all of the basics and are ready to move into more complex material.

As stated earlier, intelligence gathering and analysis, at its core, is simple. Simple things, however, are rarely of a great deal of value unless they can be organized and categorized using the appropriate tools. Otherwise, the disorganized 'simple' thing is nothing more than a useless 'exercise.'

The famed, fictional character Sherlock Holmes would say, 'elementary, my dear Watson,' as he shaped the simple into something more practical and applied it to the complex issue at hand. Sir Arthur Conan Doyle, creator of the 'Holmes' character, was trained as a surgeon in real life. His mentor and professor would often guide him to observe the mundane and trivial and apply them to the more complex problem, giving him the impetus for the character and novel series.

The Cuban missile crisis in 1962, for example, began and fortunately ended peacefully with a somewhat regular scheduled U2 aerial recon photo mission providing visual proof of the buildup. An aerial reconnaissance photo, highly routine and simplistic, documented the evidence America had long suspected of a Soviet missile buildup in the island nation.

Another example of the 'simple' and somewhat lesser in terms of importance is the 2006 discovery of the most wanted terrorist leader Abu Musab al-Zarqawi's location. The founder of ISIS and leader of Al Qaeda in Iraq, Abu Musab al-Zarqawi stands apart from his peers in that he was particularly heinous. During the Iraq war, Zarqawi was responsible for thousands of deaths, and of those, most were fellow Muslims.

American special task force, TF-145, had searched for approximately three years for Zarqawi. One analyst involved in the years-long hunt for Zarqawi knew, like most other religious radicals, Zarqawi relied heavily on the endorsement of a spiritual advisor (or Mullah) to sanction his acts of extreme brutality. In early June 2006, it was observed through predator surveillance that Zarqawi's newest and most trusted religious advisor had left his home and proceeded with much fanfare and security in convoy to a seemingly obscure location in the country. This simple observation led to the killing of the terror leader, Abu Musab al-Zarqawi, on June 7, thus ending the Task Force's mission.*

Source: The Guardian, London, Iraq terrorist leader Zarqawi 'eliminated', June 8, 2006.

The processing of often trivial and mundane information and data, the information we rarely realize we receive routinely, and taking steps to turn the 'simple' and meaningless into the amazingly substantial and understandable, is a journey that has to be undertaken over time. It is a thoughtful excursion that periodically necessitates exposure to incrementally more guidance and detailed knowledge. Pat McGlynn provided the roadmap for this trip with *Intelligence Analysis Fundamentals*. McGlynn lays out the subsequent portion of the roadmap for this journey with *Taking Intelligence Analysis to the Next Level*.

The Foreword was provided by

Dr. Godfrey Garner PhD,

Author, Soldier, Lawman, Scholar,

my colleague and friend.

Preface

Taking Intelligence Analysis to the Next Level builds upon the preceding lessons as laid out in the text, *Intelligence Analysis Fundamentals*, also published by CRC Press. Like its predecessor, *Taking Intelligence Analysis to the Next Level* is constructed for the classroom environment, packed with multiple examples, visuals, and practical exercises tailored for the intelligence community (IC), military intelligence analyst, criminal analyst, or business analyst alike.

The text begins with Analytical Ethics in the first chapter and ends with Trends in Intelligence Analysis in the last. These two chapters and all the ones between utilize multiple instructive learning approaches to build on the student's existing analytical skills gained from the first text, other training resources, their experience, or some other combination. The first chapter, Analytical Ethics, assumes the student has had some analytical experience to appreciate better the requisite need for professional ethics from a more learned perspective.

As in the previous text, most topics covered are germane to all intelligence analysis fields (i.e., military, national, political, criminal, and business). However, specific chapters and sections and most instructional examples, scenarios, exercises, and learning activities focus on the Homeland Security Mission and the associated problem sets. The Department of Homeland Security mission statement is as follows:

> *The vision of homeland security is to ensure a homeland that is safe, secure, and resilient against terrorism and other hazards.*

Three key concepts form the foundation of our national homeland security strategy designed to achieve this vision are:

- Security;
- Resilience; and
- Customs and Exchange.[1]

The training presentation methods and instructional approaches embodied within the lesson material are the product of much thought, research, and discussion. Many US government and commercial analytical training methodologies are presented.

The Instructor's Guide (companion to this text) contains the same practical exercises as those found in the student text, as well as facilitator's guides, practical exercise solutions, discussion points, sample test questions, and answer keys, to include other websites that can provide additional instructional content.

---

1   United States Department of Homeland Security website, 2015, www.dhs.gov/our-mission.

About the Author

Patrick McGlynn is a retired Army Intelligence Officer. He holds a master's degree in Adult Education and Industrial Technology from Georgia Southern University. He has authored multiple authoritative strategic-level intelligence reports addressing terrorism, irregular warfare, WMD, and information operations (IO) during his career. His military career has included assignments with the U.S. Defense Intelligence Agency (DIA), military and civilian contractor tours in Afghanistan, Iraq, and other Middle East locations serving in various senior theater-level staff intelligence positions. He has developed analytical training courses for Counter-Improvised Explosive Devices (C-IED), Counter Insurgency Operation (COIN), Analytical Tradecraft, Terrorism, Information Operations, Collection Management, and Network Analysis. Since retiring from the military in 2007, Patrick McGlynn has authored numerous technical papers and articles for law enforcement and various intelligence professional periodicals, as well as co-authoring the textbook *Intelligence Analysis Fundamentals* (CRC Press).

CHAPTER 1

Analytical Ethics

INTRODUCTION

Analytical Ethics is the title for the first chapter of this text, and its placement as the first chapter is indicatative of the underlying importance associated with the subject matter. One might argue that the business of 'spying' implies a lack of ethics. However, this is not the case. On the contrary, there is an even greater imperative to be objective and truthful in one's analytical judgments. Pause for a moment and consider the consequences of potentially unethical behavior by an intelligence (military, business, national, or criminal) analyst. The intelligence community's (IC) sources and methods could be compromised, battles or wars lost, loss of market share or bankruptcy, criminals remain free or innocent people go to jail, the list of possibilities goes on.

Whatever your occupation and often without realizing it, many face daunting ethical choices each day. A single parent with limited income selects which child they send to college. A child caught up in a nasty divorce may have to pick which parent they want to live with. An emergency room nurse decides the priority that dozens of critically injured victims of a horrific city bus accident get desperately needed medical care. A geneticist chooses to modify a DNA strain and potentially creates a 'super-soldier' or a deformed human embryo. Combat veterans suffering from post-traumatic stress and deep depression ponder taking another life, and this time it might be their own. These are all real-world value-based decisions (or at least they should be).

Unlike some of the more recognizable professions (e.g., physician, judge, or scientist), the foundational ethics associated with intelligence analysis are, at best, complicated. All seasoned intelligence analysts have faced the dilemma of telling their supervisor or intelligence consumer what the collected *distressing data patterns suggest* and what they *believe to be the truth instead of telling them just what they want to hear.* It is understandable for one to get a bit nervous and uneasy because they may have to face questioning and possible ridicule from supervisors, peers, policymakers, and sometimes all three. It is no accident that the intelligence profession should be concerned about the ethical standards of its members. Intelligence consumers relentlessly demand answers to their questions. As a result, it becomes increasingly challenging for entry-level and the more experienced analysts to respond with, 'I just don't know.'

One of the *essential aspects* of making ethical decisions is recognizing that a situation requires an ethical decision-making. Also, to prepare for the moment of trial, intelligence professionals must work in advance to arm themselves with the necessary foundational ethical value set, have a valid, ethical decision-making process, and have the willpower to use these tools when faced with an ethical dilemma.

Dilemma is a word passed down from the Greeks, meaning 'double proposition' or choice. When applied to analytical ethics, it implies that analytic judgments are made based upon weighing

DOI: 10.4324/9781003241195-1

moral alternatives rather than merely following supervisory direction, standardized procedure, or unquestioned observed indicators when required.

Read the following fictional scenario for an example of how an analytical, ethical dilemma might transpire.

EXAMPLE

Friendly forces report three Lilliputian enemy tanks making an incursion into the bordering nation of Blefuscu, and multiple independent sources confirm the report. A Blefuscu intelligence analyst interprets this incursion as an 'armed invasion' and probable 'act of war' and assesses it as such in a report to higher. The Blefuscu intelligence analyst making the assessment holds a deep hatred for the Lilliputian military and does not disclose this fact before making the sensational and alarming assessment. Sometime later, it is determined that the incursion resulted from outdated maps and poor land navigation during a Lilliputian military exercise. Once recognized, the error report flows up the Lilliputian chain of command and diplomatic channels to the Blefuscu State Department. Relations between the two countries suffer from the confusion, but escalating rhetoric begins to fade, and a shaky peace prevails. In the aftermath, the whole episode is treated as a big mistake or understandable human error rather than punish the analyst for the ethical transgression. Of course, this is a make-believe example taken from the Gulliver's Travels storyline; however, real life is much more terrifying (see Author's Note).

The first obstacle in teaching analysts to make ethical choices is that not everyone's values, mores, or principles are aligned. The next hurdle is that analysts generally do not recognize the ethical dilemmas when they present themselves during the analytical process. Therefore, the unrecognized ethical choices come and go unnoticed, and the resulting consequences fall as they may.*

*Source: https://www.cia.gov/static/c053b4680f58a4b88c9863201c90e6a0/Integrity-Ethics-the-CIA. pdf, Retrieved May 16, 2022.

Author's Note: In 1983, NATO forces were conducting maneuvers, the exercise code-named: Autumn Forge. The Pentagon described the operation as a 'large military exercise.' However, Soviets intelligence misinterpreted the exercise as a prelude to war. Adding to the tension, on September 26, 1983, the Soviet ballistic missile early warning system erroneously reported twice that US ballistic missiles had been launched. At the time, Lt. Colonel Stanislav Petrov, the watch officer in the Soviet Air Defense Forces' command bunker, made an insightful and ethical call that the launch warnings were likely a sensor malfunction. (LTC Petrov argued, 'if the Americans truly were initiating a nuclear strike, they would fire more than two missiles.') It was later determined the warnings were caused by the way the sun bounced off high-altitude clouds. If LTC Petrov had followed the strike warning procedures in place, Yury Andropov (Head of the Soviet) would have been alerted to the erroneous nuclear launch, and an immediate Soviet ICBM strike would have been ordered...and WWIII begins. (This is not a fictional story!!!)**

** Source: BBC News, Stanislav Petrov: The man who may have saved the world, Pavel Aksenov, https://www.bbc.com/news/world-europe-24280831, September 26, 2013, Downloaded May 16, 2022.....and Wikipedia, 1983 Soviet nuclear false alarm incident, https://en.wikipedia. org/wiki/1983_Soviet_nuclear_false_alarm_incident, Retrieved May 16, 2022.

Intelligence analysts should be professional enough to adhere to a code of ethics and not hide behind the usual excuses for unprincipled behavior (e.g., human error, unforeseeable consequences, and so on). Regardless of the amount of training, organizational ethics may remain blurred in the individual analyst's eyes when ethical considerations conflict with mission accomplishment. No organization's training curriculum can adequately address all ethical issues and situations. Therefore, an ethical code must be institutionalized and ingrained early and often into each analyst's character.

This chapter endeavors to provide intelligence analysts, intelligence professionals, and their parent organizations' valuable guidance and a basis for recognizing ethical questions and effectively dealing with these analytical, ethical challenges. It also provides direction on institutionalizing ethics into the analytical processes of larger intelligence organizations.

WHAT 'CORE VALUES' ARE ASSOCIATED WITH INTELLIGENCE ANALYSIS, AND CAN THEY BE TAUGHT?

The often-presented argument of 'how can a spy be ethical, they are spies?' uses a fundamentally flawed and inaccurate premise. To begin with, spies (or confidential informants/sources), whether they work for law enforcement, marketing firms, or the IC, for the most part, are not analysts. 'Spies' are field operatives who may take cover identities and work overtly or covertly to collect information and then report it through channels to higher authorities to be analyzed and combined with and compared to other information. 'Analysts' perform 'analysis.' Analysts may become an operative at some point in their careers. Still, field operatives and intelligence analysts have different roles, dissimilar training, and follow starkly different codes of conduct.

This chapter focuses on the intelligence profession as a whole and, more specifically, on intelligence analysts. Field operatives also require a code of conduct. Due to the more nefarious requirements of an operative's job description, their ethical code of conduct would need to significantly deviate from the code that analysts and other intelligence professionals follow.

Intelligence Agency Core Values

The US intelligence agencies promulgate the core values of 'excellence,' 'courage,' 'respect,' and 'integrity.' These four core values are posted on the Office of the Director of National Intelligence (ODNI) website.[1] The core values, shown at right are presented just as displayed on the ODNI website (see Figure 1.1.)

Can Ethics Be Taught?

It is apparent that the IC values certain ethical priorities, but the question remains: Can ethics be taught?

The question has been debated for thousands of years. The philosopher Socrates argued that ethics could indeed be acquired through instruction. Simply put, Socrates' position was: 'Ethics consists of knowing what we ought to do, and such knowledge can be taught.'

Psychologists Say 'Yes.'

The contemporary psychologist, James Rest, would agree with Socrates. Modern psychological studies also indicate that formal curriculum used to influence awareness of moral problems and the reasoning or judgment process has effectively instilled ethical values. These same studies indicate that a person's behavior influences their moral perception and moral judgments.[2]

---

1   Office of the Director of National Intelligence (ODNI), *Mission, Vision & Values* page, www.dni.gov/index.php/who-we-are/mission-vision

2   Lawrence Erlbaum Associates, *Postconventional Moral Thinking: A Neo-Kohlbergian Approach*, By J.R. Rest, D. Narvaez, D., M. & T. Bebeau, 1999.

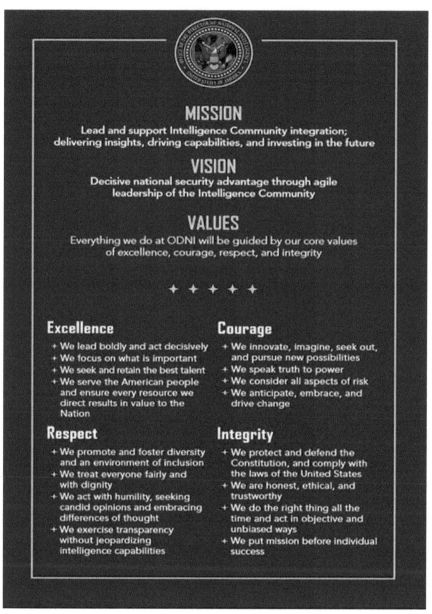

MISSION
Lead and support Intelligence Community integration;
delivering insights, driving capabilities, and investing in the future

VISION
Decisive national security advantage through agile
leadership of the Intelligence Community

VALUES
Everything we do at ODNI will be guided by our core values
of excellence, courage, respect, and integrity

✦ ✦ ✦ ✦ ✦

Excellence
+ We lead boldly and act decisively
+ We focus on what is important
+ We seek and retain the best talent
+ We serve the American people and ensure every resource we direct results in value to the Nation

Courage
+ We innovate, imagine, seek out, and pursue new possibilities
+ We speak truth to power
+ We consider all aspects of risk
+ We anticipate, embrace, and drive change

Respect
+ We promote and foster diversity and an environment of inclusion
+ We treat everyone fairly and with dignity
+ We act with humility, seeking candid opinions and embracing differences of thought
+ We exercise transparency without jeopardizing intelligence capabilities

Integrity
+ We protect and defend the Constitution, and comply with the laws of the United States
+ We are honest, ethical, and trustworthy
+ We do the right thing all the time and act in objective and unbiased ways
+ We put mission before individual success

Figure 1.1   ODNI Mission, Vision, Core Values.

Ethics Training Is Essential

Therefore, all intelligence organizations should have analytical ethics training as an essential element of the qualification curriculum at the entry-level and professional continuing education studies. That said, this section's discussion concludes with the following imperative, intelligence *analysts require a code of ethics to perform their professional duties properly,* and those *ethical values can be acquired through instruction.*

BEING ETHICAL IS NOT EASY; HOWEVER, IT IS REQUIRED

The well-worn adage, 'don't shoot the messenger,' is a phrase reaching back into antiquity to the Chinese Waring States period (around 450 BC, during the Eastern Zhoa dynasty). The expression refers to an unwritten code of martial conduct. Then as now, military commanders expected adversaries to receive and return emissaries or diplomatic envoys sent by the enemy unharmed. This chivalric and ethical concept also made good sense in that it prevented the executions of messengers sent by opposing sides and ensured a line of communication with one's adversary.

No One Wants to Be the Bearer of Bad News, but…

Intelligence analysts would undoubtedly desire to have their analytical judgments received as good news, preferably 'great news,' by their superiors and other intelligence customers. However, this is often not the case. Common sense dictates that no one wants bad news associated with their name or face. Given that the intelligence profession exists to find and forewarn leadership of potentially bad news, intelligence professionals understand that there is no avoiding the 'messenger of bad news' predicament.

From an ethical perspective, analysts should be prepared to deliver the 'bad news' message when required. However, the intelligence consumer very likely needs that unwanted 'bad news' message as soon as possible. Providing early warning of 'bad news' affords the intelligence consumer time to prepare and possibly mitigate the message's projected adverse consequences. Experienced analysts routinely point out that bad news does not improve over time. Bad news needs to be disseminated early, and the sources used in the assessment must be presently clearly for review.

USING ETHICAL STANDARDS TO RECOGNIZE ETHICAL QUESTIONS

Analytical judgments can be perplexing because all the available options may be similar and less than attractive, and therefore, the correct choice is not apparent. Often, the ethical quandary stems from the choice is not a matter of 'right-versus- wrong,' but instead, it is a case of 'right-versus-right.'

Right-versus-Wrong Is Easy, Right-versus-Right, Not so Much…

Right-versus-right choices are different from right-versus-wrong judgments. For instance, deciding what to do with satellite imagery depicting operational enemy ballistic missiles established in bases that threaten the continental United States is not an ethical dilemma between two right alternatives. The analyst's clear right choice is to report the information expeditiously up the leadership chain to higher authorities. The wrong choice is to hide, purposely misinterpret, or ignore the information.

However, the situation becomes somewhat more nuanced if, upon further inspection, it is determined that one of the missiles shown in the imagery appears to be a decoy (see Figures 1.2 and 1.3). Under these new circumstances, the assessment now evolves into an enigmatic quandary. New questions (and doubts) are introduced into the equation:

- *Are there more decoys? If so, how many more?*
- *Are they all decoys? If so, what is the purpose of the deception?*
- *Should one hold onto the intelligence report until more definitive information appears?*
- *What if more definitive reporting never materializes?*
- *How long should one wait?*

Figure 1.2   Right-versus-Wrong Judgment.

Open Source: Cuban missile crisis: 50 years on, Photo Title: An aerial view of one of the Cuban medium-range missile bases, taken October 1962, https://nly10.wordpress.com/2012/10/17/cuban-missile-crisis-50-years-on/, October 17, 2012, Retrieved 16 May, 2022.

Figure 1.3   Right-versus-Right Judgment.

Web page entitled: Cuban Missile Crisis, https://s3.amazonaws.com/s3.timetoast.com/public/uploads/photos/6781934/u2_photos_cuba.jpg, Viewed May 16, 2022.

USING ETHICAL VALUES AS A FRAMEWORK FOR ASSESSMENT

The following questions can be used as a framework for assessing ways to recognize and resolve right-versus-right analytical dilemmas:

1. Recognize that an ethical dilemma exists by asking yourself the following questions:
   • Is this a situation that can quickly be resolved with logic? *For example, identifying the enemy's location, strength, intent, and so on,...*

- Is the issue a clear 'right-versus-wrong' situation? *For example, stealing classified information, tipping a criminal organization under investigation, leaking proprietary information to a competitor...these situations are most likely not ethical dilemmas.*
- Are there ethical subtleties involved? *If there is more than one answer or more than one correct answer, it may well be an ethical dilemma. For instance, deciding what to do if you determine a friend has willingly shared their log-on password to a classified computer system and they want you to stay quiet or perhaps lie about it. This example presents a fuzzy ethical dilemma, as you must decide what is right and what is wrong, choose between 'loyalty or legality.'*

2. Then ask yourself: 'Which course of action does the most good and the least harm?' *For example, you receive a sensational report that space aliens have landed, and it is a single, uncorroborated report from an unreliable source.*
   The correct answer: *Faithfully pass the report on immediately as received. However, you should also flag that it is a 'single-source' report; the alien report's source is characterized as having reported 'unreliably in the past.' State that the report is being disseminated out of 'an abundance of caution.' Also, state that if new information changes the initial assessment, the report will be reissued, and the new supporting information included in a corrected/revised assessment. Military leaders and policymakers need the most accurate information available as quickly as possible and any subsequent changes equally as fast. Intelligence production delays reduce leadership effectiveness and hamper their opportunities for mission success.*

3. Finally, ask yourself: 'Which alternative best serves the mission purpose or information requirement?' *For example, your customer is a group of diplomats engaged with a rouge state. A single unverified report from a new source indicates that the rouge state is violating economic sanctions. Arguably, suppose the information is not reported immediately. In that case, the diplomatic mission (your customer) may continue to think that the rogue nation's diplomats are negotiating in good faith. Because of this misconception, the diplomatic exchange continues in an open and trusting environment, facilitating the parties involved to agree to terms potentially beneficial to both countries. Alternatively, the rogue nation takes advantage of the negotiations, the truth eventually comes out, and relations between the two countries are severely impaired. See the answer on the next page.*
   Answer: *Reporting economic sanction violations in a factual and timely manner best serves the mission requirements.*

Author's Note: With time, bruised aspirations and egos can mend. Getting the 75% solution out promptly is better than having the perfect answer too late. Conversely, delivering an assessment of 'no information available' also has value. In other words, tell the truth (as best as you can determine it, no embellishment or minimalizing) to your intelligence customer and do it as quickly as practical. Your job is not to worry about how your consumer handles the intelligence provided. Your job is to analyze and report. It is your customer's responsibility to deal with the intelligence appropriately provided.

INSTITUTIONALIZING ANALYTICAL ETHICS

Earlier in this chapter, it was determined that ethics could be taught, and it is an integral aspect of initial and continuing education for intelligence professionals. However, if one looks outside the ethics training as applied to specific analytical questions and more broadly at institutional integrity as a whole, the process of institutionalizing ethical values takes on a more productive focus. When one includes institutional programs and processes along with organizational management practices that lead to ethical dilemmas, the ethical fiber of the entire organization is addressed and thereby elevated. Suppose these institutional programs and processes are excluded or ignored. In that case, even the most well-intended analytical ethics program is destined to become disconnected from the overall management of the larger intelligence organization.

Indispensable, Come from Within, and Use Case Studies

Ethics training is an indispensable element of an overall strategy for institutional integrity. Intelligence is an inimitable profession with its unique ethical challenges and dilemmas. Subject matter experts (SMEs) on applying ethical principles and practices should be selected from the organization's ranks in which they serve. SMEs should be chosen based on their career records, selecting SMEs that best exemplify the ethical attributes most desired for the intelligence profession. These ethics SME-instructors could utilize lessons learned from multiple professions (medicine, scientific research, business, law, the military…). Intelligence professionals would be more open and less likely to evoke defensive responses if ethical case studies from other professions are used. The takeaway for students should be that all professional organizations follow an ethics code and professional ethics are an integral aspect of being an intelligence professional. These initial case studies should be followed up with more relevant examples of real-world ethical dilemmas. The ethics education program should gradually build toward more difficult case studies related to intelligence operations and analysis that illustrate the most problematic issues of right-versus-right situations or circumstances in which two or more strongly held values are in opposition. To the greatest extent practical, the case studies should outline the proper course for resolution and the cost of failure to the individual, the mission, and the institution as a whole.

Should Have Intrinsic Rewards, Not Legal Ramifications

Intelligence organizations' ethics training programs should appeal to the intrinsic rewards of following an ethical path. It may include rules, regulations, and legal aspects, but that should not be the priority. Ethical values should be a goal pursued out of self-interest rather than as a matter of legal compliance or as punishment for potential misdeeds. It should be deliberated as something that makes us better individuals, analysts, and intelligence professionals and a better and more effective organization.

Should Be All-Inclusive without Gray Areas

An institutional ethics program needs to be all-inclusive and reach and be understood by the entire organization. Separate ethical subcultures within the institution are not permissible. A clear understanding of ethical norms is a program imperative. Ethical norms for all job descriptions must be clearly defined and communicated, 'gray areas' cannot be allowed or tolerated.

Illustrations of 'what is allowed' and 'what is not allowed' must be presented in plain, unambiguous terms to analysts, field operatives, and uniformed officers. For example, lying is unethical, and lying is also the stock and trade of covert operatives. Therefore, it needs to be communicated and strongly and routinely reinforced that lying to criminals (or an adversary) is permitted and understood as a necessity of the job, but lying to supervisors or leadership is not permitted or condoned.

Available Forums for Discussion without Repercussion or Consequence

Some alternative forums that allow expression without repercussion or negative consequence should address situations not yet covered by the ethics curriculum. The venue should openly encourage entry-level employees and seasoned intelligence professionals to provide feedback, identify and debate ethical questions, and elevate points of confusion or newly uncovered gaps in the organization's established ethical norms. Organizational leadership and management need to oversee and participate in the ethics training curriculum. Senior leadership involvement in all aspects of an ethical training program keeps policymakers informed of possible ethical flaws in the organization and sends a clear message to all that ethical behavior is a priority from the top down.

Leadership Must Be the Program's Foremost Advocates

Separate from the ethics training, organizational leadership should praise those who exhibit the institution's ethical values. Those individuals, analysts, managers, field operatives, or uniform officers whose actions selflessly personify the ethical code should be publicly recognized and honored. In time, the ethical values become an ingrained code of conduct essential to the organization and its members, as valued as the bricks and mortar holding up the walls.

TIPS: 'ASPECTS OF AN EFFECTIVE INSTITUTIONALIZED ETHICS PROGRAM'

- *It is an integral aspect of initial and continuing education for all.*
- *The instruction should recount real-world ethical dilemmas.*
- *To the greatest extent practical, ethical training outlines the proper course for resolution and the cost of failure to the individual, the mission, and the institution as a whole.*
- *Training programs should appeal to the intrinsic rewards that come from following an ethical path.*
- *Need to be all-inclusive and reach and be understood by the entire organization.*
- *Should have a process that provides feedback, identifies and elevates points of confusion, and deals with situations not yet covered by the curriculum.*
- *Has management and senior leadership participation throughout all aspects of the program.*
- *Recognizes those members who exhibit the ethical values of the institution.*

CHAPTER SUMMARY

This chapter stressed the consequences of potentially unethical behavior by an intelligence (military, business, national, or criminal) analyst necessitating truth in one's analytical judgments. It pointed out the pressures from facing questioning and possible ridicule from supervisors, peers, or policymakers, and sometimes all three when trying to satisfy intelligence consumers' demands.

One of the *essential aspects* of making ethical decisions is recognizing that a situation requires an ethical decision-making. Also, to prepare for the moment of trial, intelligence professionals must work in advance to arm themselves with the necessary foundational ethical value set, have a valid, ethical decision-making process, and have the willpower to use these tools when faced with an ethical dilemma.

A '*dilemma*' is a word passed down from the Greeks, meaning '*double proposition*' or choice. When applied to analytical ethics, it implies that analytic judgments are made based upon weighing moral alternatives rather than merely following supervisory direction, standardized procedure, or unquestioned observed indicators when required.

The first obstacle in teaching analysts to make ethical choices is that not everyone's values, mores, or principles are aligned. The next hurdle is that analysts generally do not recognize the ethical dilemmas when they present themselves during the analytical process. Therefore, the unrecognized ethical choices come and go unnoticed, and the resulting consequences fall as they may.

Intelligence analysts should be professional enough to adhere to a code of ethics and not hide behind the usual excuses for unprincipled behavior, e.g., human error, unforeseeable consequences,…Regardless of the amount of training, organizational ethics may remain blurred in the eyes of the individual analyst when ethical considerations come into conflict with mission accomplishment. No organization's training curriculum can fully address all ethical issues and situations. Therefore, an ethical code must be institutionalized and ingrained early and often into each analyst's character.

This chapter endeavored to provide intelligence analysts, intelligence professionals, and their parent organizations' valuable guidance and a basis for recognizing ethical questions and effectively dealing with these ethical challenges. It also provided direction on institutionalizing ethics into the analytical processes of larger intelligence organizations.

WHAT 'CORE VALUES' ARE ASSOCIATED WITH INTELLIGENCE ANALYSIS, AND CAN THEY BE TAUGHT?

The often-presented argument of 'how can a spy be ethical, they are spies?' uses a fundamentally flawed and inaccurate premise. To begin with, spies (or confidential informants/sources), whether they work for law enforcement, marketing firms, or the intelligence community (IC), for the most part, are not analysts. 'Spies' are field operatives who may take cover identities and work overtly or covertly to collect information and report it through channels to higher authorities to be analyzed and combined with and compared to other information. 'Analysts' perform 'analysis.' Analysts may become an operative at some point in their careers. Still, field operatives and intelligence analysts have different roles, dissimilar training, and follow starkly different codes of conduct.

Ethics Can Be Taught

Modern psychological studies indicate that a formal curriculum used to influence awareness of moral problems that influence reasoning or judgment can instill ethical values. These same studies indicate that a person's behavior influences their moral perception and moral judgments.[3]

Ethics Training Is Essential

Therefore, all intelligence organizations should have analytical ethics training as an essential element of the qualification curriculum at the entry-level and professional continuing education studies. That said, this section's discussion concludes with the following imperative, intelligence *analysts require a code of ethics to perform their professional duties properly*, and those *ethical values can be acquired through instruction.*

BEING ETHICAL IS NOT EASY; HOWEVER, IT IS REQUIRED

The well-worn adage, 'don't shoot the messenger,' is a phrase reaching back into antiquity to the Chinese Waring States period (around 450 BC, during the Eastern Zhoa dynasty).

No One Wants to Be the Bearer of Bad News, but…

Intelligence analysts would undoubtedly desire to have their analytical judgments received as good news, preferably 'great news,' by their superiors and other intelligence customers. However, this is often not the case. Common sense dictates that no one wants bad news associated with their name or face. Given that the intelligence profession exists to find and forewarn leadership of potentially

---

3   Lawrence Erlbaum Associates, *Postconventional Moral Thinking: A Neo-Kohlbergian Approach*, By J.R. Rest, D. Narvaez, D., M. & T. Bebeau, 1999.

bad news, intelligence professionals understand that there is no avoiding the 'messenger of bad news' predicament.

USING ETHICAL STANDARDS TO RECOGNIZE ETHICAL QUESTIONS

Analytical judgments can be perplexing because all the available options may be similar and less than attractive, and therefore, the correct choice is not apparent. Often, the ethical quandary stems from the choice is not a matter of 'right versus wrong,' but instead, it is a case of 'right versus right.'

INSTITUTIONALIZING ANALYTICAL ETHICS

Earlier in this chapter, it was determined that ethics could be taught, and it is an integral aspect of initial and continuing education for intelligence professionals. However, if one looks outside the ethics training as applied to specific analytical questions and more broadly at institutional integrity as a whole, the process of institutionalizing ethical values takes on a more productive focus. When one includes institutional programs and processes along with organizational management practices that lead to ethical dilemmas, the ethical fiber of the entire organization is addressed and thereby elevated. Suppose these institutional programs and processes are excluded or ignored. In that case, even the most well-intended analytical ethics program is destined to become disconnected from the overall management of the larger intelligence organization.

Indispensable, Come from Within, and Use Case Studies

Ethics training is an indispensable element of an overall strategy for institutional integrity. Intelligence is an inimitable profession with its unique ethical challenges and dilemmas. Subject matter experts (SMEs) on applying ethical principles and practices should be selected from the organization's ranks in which they serve. SMEs should be chosen based on their career records, selecting SMEs that best exemplify the ethical attributes most desired for the intelligence profession. These ethics SME-instructors could utilize lessons learned from multiple professions (medicine, scientific research, business, law, the military,…). Intelligence professionals would be more open and less likely to evoke defensive responses if ethical case studies from other professions are used. The takeaway for students should be that all professional organizations follow an ethics code and professional ethics are an integral aspect of being an intelligence professional. These initial case studies should be followed up with more relevant examples of real-world ethical dilemmas. The ethics education program should gradually build toward more difficult case studies related to intelligence operations and analysis that illustrate the most problematic issues of right-versus-right situations or circumstances in which two or more strongly held values are in opposition. To the greatest extent practical, the case studies should outline the proper course for resolution and the cost of failure to the individual, the mission, and the institution as a whole.

Should Have Intrinsic Rewards, Not Legal Ramifications

Intelligence organizations' ethics training programs should appeal to the intrinsic rewards of following an ethical path. It may include rules, regulations, and legal aspects, but that should not be the priority. Ethical values should be a goal pursued out of self-interest rather than as a matter of legal compliance or as punishment for potential misdeeds. It should be deliberated as something that makes us better individuals, analysts, and intelligence professionals and a better and more effective organization.

Should Be All-Inclusive without Gray Areas

An institutional ethics program needs to be all-inclusive and reach and be understood by the entire organization. Separate ethical subcultures within the institution are not permissible. A clear understanding of ethical norms is a program imperative. Ethical norms for all job descriptions must be clearly defined and communicated, '*gray areas*' cannot be allowed or tolerated.

Illustrations of '*what is allowed*' and '*what is not allowed*' must be presented in plain, unambiguous terms to analysts, field operatives, and uniformed officers. For example, lying is unethical, and lying is also the stock and trade of covert operatives. Therefore, it needs to be communicated and strongly and routinely reinforced that lying to criminals (or an adversary) is permitted and understood as a necessity of the job, but lying to supervisors or leadership is not permitted or condoned.

Available Forums for Discussion without Repercussion or Consequence

Some alternative forums that allow expression without repercussion or negative consequence should address situations not yet covered by the ethics curriculum. The venue should openly encourage entry-level employees and seasoned intelligence professionals to provide feedback, identify and debate ethical questions, and elevate points of confusion or newly uncovered gaps in the organization's established ethical norms.

Leadership Must Be the Program's Foremost Advocates

Organizational leadership and management need to oversee and participate in the ethics training curriculum. Senior leadership involvement in all aspects of an ethical training program keeps policymakers informed of possible ethical flaws in the organization and sends a clear message to all that ethical behavior is a priority from the top down.

Separate from the ethics training, organizational leadership should praise those who exhibit the institution's ethical values. Those individuals, analysts, managers, field operatives, or uniform officers whose actions selflessly personify the ethical code should be publicly recognized and honored. In time, the ethical values become an ingrained code of conduct essential to the organization and its members, as valued as the bricks and mortar holding up the walls.

TIPS: 'ASPECTS OF AN EFFECTIVE INSTITUTIONALIZED ETHICS PROGRAM'

- *It is an integral aspect of initial and continuing education for all.*
- *The instruction should recount real-world ethical dilemmas.*
- *To the greatest extent practical, ethical training outlines the proper course for resolution and the cost of failure to the individual, the mission, and the institution as a whole.*
- *Training programs should appeal to the intrinsic rewards that come from following an ethical path.*
- *Need to be all-inclusive and reach and be understood by the entire organization.*
- *Should have a process that provides feedback, identifies and elevates points of confusion, and deals with situations not yet covered by the curriculum.*
- *Has management and senior leadership participation throughout all aspects of the program.*
- *Recognizes those members who exhibit the ethical values of the institution.*

PRACTICAL EXERCISE – PARTICIPANT'S GUIDE

ANALYTICAL PROBLEM/ETHICAL DECISION-MAKING

The practical exercise uses a scenario to practice ethical decision-making in an analytical environment. It allows participants to evaluate their ethical values and determine if they align with those required for a career in the intelligence profession. It is NOT a 'pass' or 'fail' exam. Look at it as an inventory of personal ethical values. If your values are not perfectly aligned, it does not mean you cannot be a good intelligence analyst. However, it should give you pause when making intelligence assessments to ensure your values are NOT adversely skewing your judgment.

AVAILABLE OPTIONS

- You can report both your relationship with the terror group and the improvised explosive device (IED) threat to your leadership, holding nothing back (Option 1), or not report either and wait for more information and withhold all reporting (Option 2)?
- Report your relationship with the terror group to your leadership and not report the IED threat (Option 3).
- Report the IED threat with your leadership and not report your relationship to the terror group (Option 4).

Now to analyze why one would make a particular choice? What personal value(s) is (are) guiding the decision?

Option 1: Concern for public welfare, selfless action, and desire for full disclosure and transparency

Option 2: Realistic concern for career and possible negative effect on family, desire to protect your old friends from having a police record, and potential physical harm

Option 3: Selfless action and desire for full disclosure and transparency, desire to protect your old friends from having a police record and potential physical harm

Option 4: Concern for public welfare, realistic concern for career, and possible negative effect on family

INSTRUCTIONS

Begin by reading the analytical problem *Scenario Setup* and *Scenario A* and select one (and only one) of the following four options and associated personal values that align with your values. Be prepared to share why you selected the particular option and value.

SCENARIO SETUP

Suppose that you are an intelligence analyst targeting a terror network. You submit an intelligence assessment that indicates that terrorists are operating within the continental United States (CONUS). The group has not committed any violent acts, yet substantial reporting exists that the situation is about to change. You notice that several group members are friends and acquaintances from your college days. You remember them as peaceful, decent folks who participated in a few student protests, but most students at your college were involved in some activist events. You have been following the group's activities, and they are supposed to take part in a legal assembly downtown today involving hundreds of people. You just received an unconfirmed report that an IED was allegedly transported downtown and detonated in the crowd.

SCENARIO B

The situation is the same as in Scenario A, but a recent evening news report spotlighted analysts/intelligence professionals' ill-treatment by organizational leadership. Over 300 whistleblower cases have been reported in the last decade in your organization, and all of the cases used proper reporting channels. In total, 75% of individuals who came forward have reported instances of supervisory harassment for their actions, problems with maintaining their security clearances, or losing their jobs. The news exposes uncovered information that most analysts and intelligence professionals in your organization already knew or firmly suspected.

SCENARIO C

Same as Scenario B, but this time you have received signals reporting via a wiretap transcript, and you are now 99% sure that the terror group did indeed build an IED and have admitted to testing a prototype of the same design they intend to place in the crowd.

Author's Note: An intelligence analyst/intelligence professional's life is not as glamorous as depicted in 007/ James Bond books and movies. This exercise is used to inform participants seeking a career in the field to understand better that individuals who value 'others before self' generally make better intelligence professionals. That said, 'selfless service often comes at a price.' That price usually affects family, personal life, and prosperity. These factors need to be given serious consideration before setting off on a career as an analyst/intelligence professional.

Not to imply that every intelligence professional's life is impoverished, has multiple failed marriages, or no family life. However, the intelligence profession (like many other professions) does take a personal toll. Therefore perspective intelligence analysts should come to terms with these potential (if not probable) realities before choosing to go into the field.

CHAPTER 2

CARVER and Other Criticality and Vulnerability Assessments

INTRODUCTION

CARVER analysis is an analytical tool that facilitates "criticality" and "vulnerability" assessments. Special Operations Forces (SOF) have long used CARVER analysis to aid them in targeting. Still, more recently, the Department of Energy (DOE), Department of State (DOS), and the Department of Homeland Security (DHS) have adopted the process for defensive purposes.

Analyzing criticality and vulnerability may seem an unsuitable topic to include in an intelligence textbook; however, it is highly appropriate information material from an analysis fundamental skills perspective. Analysis of criticality and vulnerability of an adversary's position and one's own situation is imperative in business, industry, governmental, law enforcement, and military institutions. Whether playing chess, launching a new business, securing a computer network, or preparing for war, making an exhaustive analysis of criticality and vulnerability of adversarial circumstances, as well as friendly positions, can be the deciding factor between success and failure. This chapter investigates the rationale for criticality and vulnerability analysis to include some of the federal government's analytical tools and methods used by the US military, state, and local authorities. As part of a more substantial CARVER analysis, the text uses CARVER analysis to assess criticality and vulnerability in offensive and defensive situations while providing examples of how to apply the analysis in business, information technology (IT), and Homeland Defense, as well as explaining the MSHARPP tool and how it relates to the CARVER analysis method. Additionally, this chapter introduces students to the US government's PSRAT tool for criticality and vulnerability of port facility assessment.

CARVER ANALYSIS

CARVER is an acronym that stands for 'criticality,' 'accessibility,' 'recoverability' (or recuperability), 'vulnerability,' 'effect,' and 'recognizability.' Its origins reach back to World War II and the Vietnam war. Developed during World War II, CARVER (then one letter shorter and known as CARVE). Initially, the US Army Air Corp developed it to identify and rank the most effective bombing targets. US Special Forces required a scaling tool to prioritize potential enemy targets in Vietnam. The US Special Forces revised CARVER analysis and further developed the CARVER matrix system to fulfill those needs. Offensively, knowing an adversary's critical weaknesses can provide a tactical and strategic military advantage, and having a tool that identifies and quantifies vulnerability is invaluable for the task. In other words, CARVER analysis is a reasonable and relatively objective approach to determining what one can do with what resources are available.

Table 2.1 Completed CARVER Matrix[1]

Potential targets	Electrical Power Plant Assets						
	C	A	R	V	E	R	TOTAL
Fuel tanks	8	9	3	8	5	6	39
Fuel pumps	8	6	2	10	5	3	34
Boilers	6	2	10	4	5	4	31
Turbines	8	6	10	7	5	9	45
Generators	4	6	10	7	5	9	41
Condensers	8	8	5	2	5	4	32
Feed pumps	3	8	5	8	5	6	35
Circulating water pumps	3	8	5	8	5	4	33
Generator step-up transformer	10	10	10	9	5	9	53

[1] Headquarters Department of the Army, *Police Intelligence Operations*, Field Manual, FM 3-19.50, July 2010.

CARVER MATRIX

US Special Forces and other US government agencies and branches of the military use the CARVER matrix primarily for offensive applications as an enemy target acquisition and prioritization tool and as a method of assessing one's defensive posture. The DHS, state and local law enforcement, and various commercial entities have also found the CARVER matrix beneficial to evaluate the facilities' defensive posture from an adversary's viewpoint.

CARVER analysis assumes the enemy's perspective to enable an analyst or assessment team to determine the hardness or softness of an adversary's targets or responsive actions to targeting. A CARVER matrix lists 'assets' in the left-hand column, and the columns contain the 'assessed variables' (see Table 2.1).

TIPS: 'ADAPTING THE CARVER MATRIX TO OTHER NONMILITARY APPLICATIONS'

Assuming that one was trying to defend against a cyber threat directed against office network servers. The CARVER matrix might look more like Table 2.2.

Table 2.2 Adapting the CARVER Matrix to Other Nonmilitary Applications

System	C	A	R	V	E	R	Total
SQL server	1	9	2	4	4	3	23
Application server	2	3	4	2	1	2	14
Email server	6	9	9	10	2	9	45
Web server	8	2	5	4	5	10	34
Email server	10	5	5	4	2	10	36

Note: The 'Email server', even though it is not the most 'critical' it is the 'vulnerable' one.

CARVER ANALYSIS CRITERIA

To use the CARVER method, analysts first develop an evaluation criteria matrix for each asset. The analyst then evaluates assets against evaluation criteria and records the results in a CARVER matrix. The results are then weighed, ranked, and compared. The analyst adapts the assessment criteria and manipulates the relative values as needed based on mission or operational needs (while maintaining consistency throughout the matrix). Table 2.1 and the companion Tips and Notes illustrate an example of completed CARVER matrixes for a generic bulk electrical power supply and a generic commercial Office Server Network.

Criticality

Criticality is usually the primary consideration. Criticality means target value (from either a friendly or adversarial perspective). A target is designated as 'critical' when its destruction or damage significantly impacts military, political, or economic operations. Assessing the value of a target is not always straightforward. Most would agree that a tank has more war-fighting (or martial) value than, for instance, a truck.

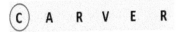

When considering the criticality criteria of any target subcomponent (using the bulk electrical power supply example), the analyst assigns a value of '10' if the asset's loss results in an immediate output halt or 100% curtailment. In other words, the target cannot function without the asset. Conversely, if the asset's loss would cause little or no change in operation, a value of '1' is assigned.

Using the 'fuel tanks' criticality rating of '8' (from Table 2.1) indicates that if the fuel tanks were lost, it might significantly affect operations, but other factors like an auxiliary or portable fuel tank might preclude total operational loss.

Author's Note: Taking the truck analogy a step farther. In most cases, the loss of an army truck may have less martial value than a tank, unless the armored company had many other tanks and only one truck, or the truck that was lost contained all the ammunition or fuel for the armored company. In this case, the martial value of the truck would increase drastically.

This is an overly simplistic example. In real-world situations, many other variables potentially could factor into the criticality assessment (e.g., time of year, whether or not the asset is currently operational or already out of service for maintenance, if there are multiple assets electric plants that could take up the slack).

Accessibility

Accessibility means many things depending on the targeting situation. Cyber analysts trying to secure a computer server reachable from the worldwide web would be determining how many exposed communication ports exist, the strength of passwords, or perhaps the firewalls' effectiveness. Alternatively, military analysts would likely use troops to infiltrate the target and identify potential obstacles and barriers (e.g., walls, guard towers, and checkpoints). If an adversary were using standoff weapons like bombs, artillery, or missiles, as an option, the analyst would evaluate radar coverage and other potential weapon countermeasures. An asset that is easily accessible with available resources would get a score of '10,' and an asset that is not accessible or only accessible with extreme difficulty would get a score of '1.'

Again, referring to the 'fuel tanks' example (see Table 2.1), assume that the asset is inside the facility perimeter wall but outdoors. If the fuel tanks were buried or hidden inside another structure, they would get a much lower accessibility score. Since the fuel tanks are considered *very accessible*, they are assigned a value of 8 for matrix scoring purposes. From a military viewpoint, a high accessibility score indicates troops could potentially engage the fuel tanks with one or more standoff weapons (e.g., mortar, rocket launcher) from outside the facility's perimeter wall.

Recoverability

Recoverability (also referred to as recuperability) measures the time required to restore function to the target (if an asset is disabled or destroyed), considering the availability of resources, parts, expertise, human resources, and available redundant assets or systems.

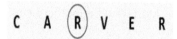

Analysts measure target recoverability in units of time; that is, how long will it take to replace, repair, or bypass the target damage. Recoverability varies with the sources and type of targeted components and spare parts availability. The following are lists of potential recoverability factors one might consider that are associated with some different target types (e.g., port facilities, IT, and railyards).

Port Facilities

- Vetted Operational Continuity Plan in place
- Availability of on hand equipment such as dock cranes, dry docks, and potential equipment cannibalization
- Potential restoration and substitution through redundancies
- Alternate navigable channels
- A skilled workforce is available to restore damaged facilities
- On hand spares
- Others....

Information Technology (IT) Facilities

- Vetted Operational Continuity Plan and IT Disaster Recovery Plan in place
- Availability of alternate/redundant hardware, software
- Availability of reconfigurable facilities that can run similar hardware and software applications, if needed
- Availability of skilled IT professionals to assess and execute recovery actions
- Vendors on contract to provide 'hot sites' for IT disaster recovery
- Others....

Rail Station/Rail Yards

- Vetted Operational Continuity Plan in place
- Availability of on hand equipment such as railroad cranes, repair facilities, rails, ties, on hand spares, and potential equipment cannibalization
- Availability of undamaged external switching facilities to reroute rail traffic
- A skilled workforce is on hand to restore damaged facilities
- Ability to redirect passengers and freight via alternate means (e.g., trucks, barges)
- Others....

Note: Common themes become apparent (e.g., continuity plans, spares, redundancy) when looking at the listed recoverability factors for various facilities presented above.

Vulnerability

Whether assessing a target as 'vulnerable,' from either attacker's or the defender's perspective, it all depends on whether the threat element has the means and expertise to attack the target successfully. When determining a target's vulnerability, the analyst measures the asset against the attacking element's capability, threatening it.

(Note: The ability of the potential attacking element can be found in the Threat Assessment.)

To assess vulnerability, analysts start with the threat assessment. The threat assessment determines the credibility and seriousness of a potential threat, as well as the probability that the threat becomes a reality.

For example, Homeland Security analysts assess the vulnerability of a CONUS target (e.g., a school) from an attack by an overseas terror organization that has publicly announced it has the desire to attack the target. Analysts would evaluate whether the terror organization has assets in-country to attack the target facility, the ability to bring assets in, or the ability to compel others to execute the terror attack in their stead. The threat assessment is critical to the vulnerability assessment. In other words, if there is no 'threat,' then there is no 'vulnerability.' However, even though the threat may not exist today, the requirement still exists to continuously monitor for all threats because the threat picture is constantly evolving. Therefore, vulnerability profiles are endlessly changing and must be repeatedly revised and updated.

Author's Note: This CARVER matrix is easily adapted to other nonmilitary or Homeland Security situations. For instance, assume that one is in charge of the electrical power facility used in Table 2.1 and was tasked with prioritizing limited plant maintenance resources.

Looking at the table, one would likely prioritize performing maintenance on the 'Generator Step-Up Transformer' over other components listed in the table. One makes this judgment because Generator Step-Up Transformer is the most essential and most challenging power plant component to replace.

Effect

The 'effect' of a targeted attack measures the possible military, political, economic, psychological, and sociological impacts at the target and beyond. When assessing a targeted asset's 'effect' aspect, the analyst uses differing standards based on its characteristic features and function. However, it is not always so obvious. For example, a military asset would likely be assessed based on its military value. Another illustration might be assessing a tech company's 'effect' aspect. In this case, one might ask, 'What is the effect on the company if the loss of the asset led to the company's competitors beating them to market with a product causing a loss of market share?' Although the probable military, political, and economic 'effect' components may be more apparent, it requires a much higher level of diligence to define the psychological and sociological aspects adequately.

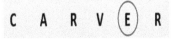

This CARVER assessment factor closely relates to measuring the target's criticality. Another illustration of the concept would be the 9/11 World Trade Center attack, multiple passenger jets crash, and the resulting fires and building collapse killing 2,801 people.

Figure 2.1   Aftermath of the World Trade Center Attack.

In the following days, millions of people in the metropolitan region were exposed to a combination of air pollution, dangerous work conditions, and psychological trauma. The attack also placed unprecedented demands on New York City's public health, health care, and social service systems.[1]

More than the physical damage and death toll associated with the World Trade Center attack, there was a significant psychological 'effect' on Americans and her allies, as well as Al Qaida and other terrorists. It was a statement to terrorists worldwide that even America was susceptible to a terror attack (see Figure 2.1).[2] Offensively, targeters evaluate the type and magnitude of given effects desired to assist planners select targets and target components for an attack. The *Effect* in this context addresses all significant subsequent outcomes, whether desired or not, that may result when attacking the selected asset. Traditionally, this element addresses the impact on the local population, but now (after 9/11), there are broader considerations.[3]

When considering the effect from a purely defensive (Homeland Security) perspective, factors other than human casualties, structures, facility equipment, operations downtime, and capital losses are measured. In today's hybrid (world/domestic terror and organized crime) environment, analysts must also weigh the total effect on the population. Analysts must ask themselves: 'What assets/targets would *(fill in the blank with criminal or terror organization's name)* want to attack and why?'

Author's Note: Referring to the 9/11 example, Al Qaida did not adequately calculate the effect on the American psyche. Bin Laden no doubt thought the attack would crush American resolve. Conversely, the attack not only did not cow the American public; instead, it unified them and instilled the necessary political and grassroots motivation to seek out the terror group and actively hunt them down for years to come. This is not to say one should encourage adversaries to attack targets with high population 'effect' values. I am sure Osama Bin Laden thought it would increase Al Qaida recruitment and rally Jihadist support, and it may very well have. However, I can reasonably argue that it did more harm to Al Qaeda's cause than good by killing thousands of innocents.

---

1   New York Times, *In Bereavement, Pioneers on a Lonely Trail*, Kirk Johnson, September 8, 2002, Retrieved December 31, 2019.

2   www.fbi.gov/image-repository/911-responders-world-trade-center-nyc-091101.jpg, Retrieved December 31, 2019.

3   Headquarters Department of the Army, *Special Forces Intelligence and Electronic Warfare Operations*, Field Manual, FM34-36, September 1991.

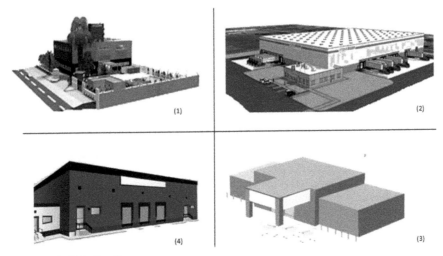

Figure 2.2   Hide-in-Plain-Site Figures.

Recognizability

A potential target's 'recognizability' is assessed by the degree to which it can be recognized by possible attackers and intelligence collection and reconnaissance assets under varying conditions. The weather has a distinct and significant impact on visibility. Being that rain, snow, and ground fog may obscure observation. Road segments with sparse vegetation and adjacent high ground provide excellent conditions for proper observation. Distance, light, and season variations are considerations for the assessment. Road maps, online mapping services (e.g., Mapquest® and Google Earth®), as well as road signs can also be tools that inadvertently lead an attacker to your location.

Other factors that influence recognition include the size and complexity of the target, distinctive target signatures, masking or camouflage, and the technical sophistication and training of the expected attackers.[4] 'Hiding-in-plain-sight' is an observational aspect often underestimated or overlooked by attackers and defenders. To hide in plain sight is to make something unnoticeable to an observer by staying visible in a setting that masks presence.

Recognizability Exercise

Observe the four building figures below and determine which figure (or figures) represent(s) a modern 'data center' (see Figure 2.2).

Notes:

- *First, take a moment to visualize just how a 'data center' looks in your mind.*
- *If you do not know, take out your cell phone and Google®'s data center buildings and see what comes up.*
- *Compare each figure below to your mental picture of a data center (or the images you found from your online search effort).*
- *Look for easily identifiable features associated with your mental picture of a data center (or the images you found from your online search effort) and look for those features in the four figures provided.*

---

4   Headquarters Department of the Army, *Special Forces Intelligence and Electronic Warfare Operations*, Field Manual, FM34-36, September 1991.

● *If an identifiable feature is missing from one of four figures, then try to rationalize 'Does the element have to be present (or some cases absent) to indicate that the image is indeed a data center?'*

TIPS: CONDENSED QUESTION LIST TO USE IN CREATING CARVER CRITERIA

C-Criticality: *How essential is the asset? Can they live without it?*

A-Accessibility: *How assessable is the asset? Are there walls, walls, or obstacles? Are there guards, CCTV, or alarms? How many, what types, where are they located? Is there a response force (e.g., QRF, police, off-site security responders?*

R-Recoverability: *How long will it take to get the asset's functions back to full operation by repair, bypass, or replacement?*

V-Vulnerability: *Does the threat have the capacity, either directly or indirectly, to reach out to the asset in such a way that it could damage or destroy it (e.g., sabotage, aerial bomb, mortar, rocket, cyber, and so on)? Are there defenses to these potential threats (e.g., guards, bunkers, armor plate, computer firewalls, and so on)?*

E-Effect on Population: *How many people work or reside inside or near the asset? If an attack occurred, how many people potentially would be injured or killed? Were there secondary effects from potential hazardous material release or fallout? Effect on the public psyche? Effect on world perception?*

R-Recognizability: *How easy is it for the threat to recognize the asset? (e.g., Does the school look like a school? Does the military base look like a military base? Etc.)*

(Go to the next page for discussion and answers.)

Recognizability Exercise – Discussion and Answers

Answer: All four figures could potentially be representations of data centers. It is standard industry practice to construct data centers to be low-profile buildings with physical security improvements that blend in with other modern industrial buildings. Table 2.3 follows with a CARVER analysis.

Discussion

Illustration 1 – Represents an oblique rear view of a modern data center from a standoff position outside the controlled perimeter.

Features:

A. *Controlled entrance*

B. *Backup generators*

C. *Perimeter barrier (fencing/wall)*

D. *Loading dock*

(1)

Illustration 2 – Represents an oblique front-side view of a modern data center from a standoff position inside the controlled perimeter.

Features:

A. *Perimeter barrier (fencing)*

B. *Loading dock*

(2)

Table 2.3 CARVER Analysis for the Facilities Case Example

CARVER Analysis Method

If tasked to perform a criticality and vulnerability assessment of a facility using the CARVER analysis process, the following assessment criteria can be used to guide your analysis. The criteria provided below come from the US Army's *Police Intelligence Operations Field Manual.*[1] *Assume the facility being assessed is a government facility in an overseas high-threat environment (e.g., A US Embassy or consulate). The analyst selects from the criteria below to create a CARVER Matrix to perform the assessment. Analysts should further assess items with high ratings (e.g., 8–10) to identify appropriate mitigation or contingency alternatives.*

Assessment Criteria (Note: Remember you are assessing the facility from an adversary's perspective.)	Rating Scale (1–10)
Criticality:	**Rating**
Immediate output halt or 100% curtailment. The target cannot function without the asset.	10
Halt less than one day or 75% curtailment in output, production, or service.	8
Halt less than one week or 50% curtailment in output, production, or service.	6
Halt in more than one week and less than 25% curtailment in output, production, or service.	4
No significant effect.	1
Accessibility:	
Standoff weapons can be deployed.	10
Inside the perimeter wall, but outdoors.	8
Inside of a building, but on the ground floor.	6
Inside a building, but on the second floor or in the basement. Climbing or lowering is required.	4
Not accessible or only accessible with extreme difficulty.	1
Recoverability (or Recuperability):	
Replacement, repair, or substitution requires 1 month or more.	10
Replacement, repair, or substitution requires 1 week to 1 month.	8
Replacement, repair, or substitution requires 72 hours to 1 week.	6
Replacement, repair, or substitution requires 24 hours to 72 hours.	4
Same-day replacement, repair, or substitution.	1
Vulnerability:	
Vulnerable to long-range target designation, small arms, or charges (weighing 5 pounds or less).	10
Vulnerable to light anti-armor weapons fire or charges (weighing 5–10 pounds).	8
Vulnerable to medium anti-armor weapons fire, bulk charges (weighing 10–30 pounds), or carefully placed smaller charges.	6
Vulnerable to heavy anti-armor weapons fire, bulk charges (weighing 30–50 pounds), or special weapons.	4
Invulnerable to all but the most extreme targeting measures.	1
Effect (on the local population):	
Overwhelming positive effects, but no significant negative effects (e.g., lots of innocent collateral damage and negative effects).	10
Moderately positive effects and few significant negative effects.	8
No significant effects and remains neutral.	6
Moderate negative effects and few significant positive effects.	4
Overwhelming negative effects and no significant positive effects (e.g., the local population would condemn and actively intervene to stop an attack and secure the facility/staff).	1

Table 2.3   Cont.

Recognizability:

Clearly recognizable under all conditions and from a distance and requires little or no personnel training for recognition.	10
Easily recognizable at small-arms range and requires little personnel training for recognition.	8
Difficult to recognize at night during inclement weather or might be confused with other targets or target components. Some personnel training is required for recognition.	6
Difficult to recognize at night or in inclement weather (even in small-arms range). The target can easily be confused with other targets or components and requires extensive personnel training for recognition.	4
The target cannot be recognized under any conditions, except by experts.	1

[1] Headquarters Department of the Army, *Police Intelligence Operations – Example of a CARVER Criteria Matrix,* Field Manual, FM 3-19.50, July 2010.

Illustration 3 – Represents an oblique front-side view of a modern data center from a position inside the controlled perimeter.

Feature:

A. Crash bollards along the edges of the building prevent free access to vehicular traffic

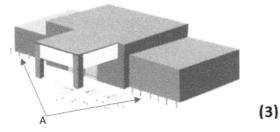

Illustration 4 – Represents an oblique rear-side view of a modern data center from a position inside the controlled perimeter.

Feature:

A. Loading dock

Note: Observe how hard it is to distinguish these buildings from other office buildings, warehouses,…

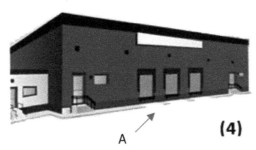

MSHARPP ASSESSMENT METHOD

The US government has created several criticality and vulnerability assessment tools that support the decision process. Another assessment tool is the MSHARPP assessment method. MSHARPP is an acronym for mission, symbolism, history, accessibility, recognizability, population, and proximity. Besides having a few different assessment criteria, MSHARPP differs from the CARVER method primarily in the analyst's assessment perspective. CARVER uses the adversary's (the

Table 2.4   Example of an MSHARPP Matrix

Target	M	S	H	A	R	P	P	Total	Threat Weapon
Headquarters building	5	4	5	1	3	4	1	23	4,000-pound, vehicle-borne improvised explosive device
Troop barracks	2	4	5	4	4	4	2	25	220-pound, vehicle-borne improvised explosive device
Communications center	5	4	2	3	5	3	1	23	4,000-pound, vehicle-borne improvised explosive device
Emergency operations center	3	3	2	4	4	4	2	22	50-pound satchel charge
Fuel storage facility	4	3	1	5	5	1	3	22	Small-arms ammunition and mortars
Airfield	5	5	3	2	5	5	4	29	Mortars and rocket-propelled grenades
Ammunition supply point	5	5	1	1	5	3	1	21	Small-arms ammunition and mortars
Water purification facility	5	2	3	5	5	0	4	24	Chemical, biological, and radiological contamination

attacker's) perspective, whereas the analyst using the MSHARPP method adopts the defender's viewpoint to perform the assessment.

SHARPP is a targeting tool to assess personnel vulnerabilities, but analysts also use it for facilities, units, or other assets. The analyst builds a MSHARPP matrix similar to the example shown below (see Table 2.4). Each asset is assigned a number (ranging from 1 through 5) corresponding to the applicable MSHARPP variable. The number 5 represents the greatest vulnerability or likelihood of attack; the number 1 represents the lowest vulnerability. The respective numerical values are totaled to provide a relative value as a target or the overall vulnerability level. See DOD 0-20012.H for an in-depth discussion of the use of MSHARPP.[5,6]

TIPS: CONDENSED QUESTION LIST TO USE IN CREATING MSHARPP CRITERIA

M-Mission: What does the asset do? What is its purpose?

S-Symbolism: Does the asset represent the government or have cultural significance (e.g., Eifel Tower, biggest bridge or tallest building in the land, Pentagon, and so on).

H-History: Has this type of asset been attacked before? How often? How recently?

A-Accessibility: How assessable is the asset? Are there walls, walls, or obstacles? Are there guards, CCTV, or alarms? How many, what types, where are they located? Is there a response force (e.g., QRF, police, off-site security responders)?

R-Recoverability: How long will it take to get the asset's functions back to full operation by repair, bypass, or replacement?

P-Population: How many people work or reside inside or near the asset? If an attack occurred, how many people potentially would be injured or killed? Were there secondary effects from potential hazardous material release or fallout? Were there secondary effects from potential hazardous material release or fallout? Effect on the public psyche? Effect on world perception?

P-Proximity: How many comparable or dissimilar assets are located nearby? Are there open fields or densely packed urban neighborhoods around the asset? If the asset were a refinery, are there schools, churches, or hospitals nearby?

---

5   Headquarters Department of the Army, *Police Intelligence Operations,* Field Manual, FM 3-19.50, July 2010.

6   Department of Defense, *DOD 0-2000.12-H-Protection and DOD Personnel and Activities against Acts of Terrorism and Political Turbulence,* https://commons.wikimedia.org/wiki/File:Protection_of_DoD_Personnel_and_Activities_against_Acts_of_Terrorism_and_Political_Turbulence.pdf, Retrieved January 1, 2020.

CHAPTER SUMMARY

CARVER analysis is an analytical tool that facilitates 'criticality' and 'vulnerability' assessments. SOF have long used CARVER analysis to aid them in targeting. Still, more recently, DOE, DOS, and DHS have adopted the process for defensive purposes.

CARVER ANALYSIS

CARVER is an acronym that stands for 'criticality,' 'accessibility,' 'recoverability' (or recuperability), 'vulnerability,' 'effect,' and 'recognizability.'[7] Its origins reach back to World War II and the Vietnam war. Developed during World War II, CARVER (then one letter shorter and known as CARVE). Offensively, knowing an adversary's critical weaknesses can provide a tactical and strategic military advantage. Having a tool that identifies and quantifies vulnerability is invaluable for the task. In other words, CARVER analysis is a reasonable and relatively objective approach to determining what one can do with what resources are available.

CARVER MATRIX

US Special Forces and other US government agencies and branches of the military use the CARVER matrix primarily for offensive applications as an enemy target acquisition and prioritization tool and as a method of assessing one's defensive posture. The DHS, state and local law enforcement, and various commercial entities have also found the CARVER matrix beneficial to evaluate the facilities' defensive posture from an adversary's viewpoint.

CARVER analysis assumes the enemy's perspective to enable an analyst or assessment team to determine the hardness or softness of an adversary's targets or responsive actions to targeting. A CARVER matrix lists 'assets' in the left-hand column, and the columns contain the 'assessed variables.'

CARVER ANALYSIS CRITERIA

To use the CARVER method, analysts first develop an evaluation criteria matrix for each asset. The analyst then evaluates assets against evaluation criteria and records the results in a CARVER matrix. The results are then weighed, ranked, and compared. The analyst tailors assessment criteria and manipulates the relative values as needed based on mission or operational needs (while maintaining consistency throughout the matrix). Table 2.1 and the companion Tips and Notes illustrate an example of completed CARVER matrixes for a generic bulk electrical power supply and a generic commercial Office Server Network.

Criticality

Criticality is usually the primary consideration. Criticality means target value (from either a friendly or adversarial perspective). A target is designated as 'critical' when its destruction or damage significantly impacts military, political, or economic operations.

Accessibility

Accessibility means many things depending on the targeting situation. Cyber analysts trying to secure a computer server reachable from the worldwide web would be determining how many exposed communication ports exist, the strength of passwords, or perhaps the firewalls' effectiveness. Alternatively, military analysts would likely use troops to infiltrate the target and identify potential obstacles and barriers (e.g., walls, guard towers, and checkpoints). If an adversary were

---

7   Headquarters Department of the Army, *Special Forces Intelligence and Electronic Warfare Operations*, Field Manual, FM34-36, September 1991.

using standoff weapons like bombs, artillery, or missiles, as an option, the analyst would evaluate radar coverage and other potential weapon countermeasures. An asset that is easily accessible with available resources would get a score of '10,' and an asset that is not accessible or only accessible with extreme difficulty would get a score of '1.'

Recoverability

Recoverability (also referred to as recuperability) measures the time required to restore function to target (if an asset is disabled or destroyed), considering the availability of resources, parts, expertise, human resources, and available redundant assets or systems.

Analysts measure target recoverability in units of time; that is, how long will it take to replace, repair, or bypass the target damage. Recoverability varies with the sources and type of targeted components and spare parts availability.

Vulnerability

Whether assessing a target as 'vulnerable,' from either attacker's or the defender's perspective, it all depends on whether the threat element has the means and expertise to attack the target successfully. When determining the vulnerability of a given target, the analyst measures the asset against the capability of the attacking element, which threatens it.

(Note: The ability of the potential attacking element is found in the Threat Assessment.)

To assess vulnerability, analysts start with the threat assessment. The threat assessment determines the credibility and seriousness of a potential threat, as well as the probability that the threat becomes a reality.[8]

Effect

The 'effect' of a targeted attack measures the possible military, political, economic, psychological, and sociological impacts at the target and beyond. When assessing a targeted asset's 'effect' aspect, the analyst uses differing standards based on its characteristic features and function. However, it is not always so obvious. For example, a military asset would likely be assessed based on its military value. Another illustration might be assessing a tech company's 'effect' aspect. In this case, one might ask 'What is the effect on the company if the loss of the asset led to the company's competitors beating them to market with a product causing a loss of market share?'

Although the probable military, political, economic, and effect components may be more apparent, the psychological and sociological aspects require much higher diligence to define adequately.

Recognizability

A potential target's 'recognizability' is assessed by the degree to which it can be recognized by possible attackers and intelligence collection and reconnaissance assets under varying conditions. The weather has a distinct and significant impact on visibility. Being that rain, snow, and ground fog may obscure observation. Road segments with sparse vegetation and adjacent high ground provide excellent conditions for good observation. Distance, light, and season variations are considerations to be factored into the assessment. Road maps, online mapping services (e.g., Mapquest® and Google Earth®), as well as road signs can also be tools that inadvertently lead an attacker to your location.

'Hiding-in-plain-sight' is an observational aspect often underestimated or overlooked by attackers and defenders. To hide-in-plain-sight is to make something unnoticeable to an observer by staying

---

8   National Association of School Psychologists, *Threat Assessment: Predicting and Preventing School Violence*, Retrieved October 16, 2014.

visible in a setting that masks presence. Other factors that influence recognizability include the size and complexity of the target, the existence of distinctive target signatures, the presence of masking or camouflage, and the technical sophistication and training of the expected attackers.[9]

'Hiding-in-plain-sight' is an observational aspect often underestimated or overlooked by attackers and defenders. To hide-in-plain-sight is to make something unnoticeable to an observer by staying visible in a setting that masks presence. Other factors that influence recognizability include the size and complexity of the target, the existence of distinctive target signatures, the presence of masking or camouflage, and the technical sophistication and training of the expected attackers.[10]

TIPS: CONDENSED QUESTION LIST TO USE IN CREATING CARVER CRITERIA

C-Criticality: How essential is the asset? Can they live without it?

A-Accessibility: How assessable is the asset? Are there walls, walls, or obstacles? Are there guards, CCTV, or alarms? How many, what types, where are they located? Is there a response force (e.g. QRF, police, off-site security responders)?

R-Recoverability: How long will it take to get the functions of the asset back to full operation by repair, bypass, or replacement?

V-Vulnerability: Does the threat have the capacity, either directly or indirectly, to reach out to the asset in such a way that it could damage or destroy it (e.g., sabotage, aerial bomb, mortar, rocket, cyber, etc.)? Are there defenses to these potential threats (e.g., guards, bunkers, armor plate, computer firewalls, etc.)?

E-Effect on Population: How many people work or reside inside or near the asset? If an attack occurred, how many people potentially would be injured or killed? Were there secondary effects from potential hazardous material release or fallout? Effect on the public psyche? Effect on world perception?

R-Recognizability: How easy is it for the threat to recognize the asset? (e.g., Does the school look like a school? Does the military base look like a military base? Etc.)

MSHARPP ASSESSMENT METHOD

The US government has created several criticality and vulnerability assessment tools that support the decision process. Another assessment tool is the MSHARPP assessment method. MSHARPP is an acronym for mission, symbolism, history, accessibility, recognizability, population, and proximity. Besides having a few different assessment criteria, MSHARPP differs from the CARVER method primarily in the analyst's assessment perspective. CARVER uses the adversary's (the attacker's) perspective, whereas the analyst using the MSHARPP method adopts the defender's viewpoint to perform the assessment.

SHARPP is a targeting tool to assess personnel vulnerabilities, but analysts also use it for facilities, units, or other assets. To perform the MSHARPP, first, build a MSHARPP matrix similar to the example shown below. Each asset is assigned a number (ranging from 1 through 5) corresponding to the applicable MSHARPP variable. The number 5 represents the greatest vulnerability or likelihood of attack; the number 1 represents the lowest vulnerability. The respective numerical values are totaled to provide a relative value as a target or the overall vulnerability level. See DoD's

---

9 Headquarters Department of the Army, *Special Forces Intelligence and Electronic Warfare Operations*, Field Manual, FM34-36, September 1991.

10 Headquarters Department of the Army, *Special Forces Intelligence and Electronic Warfare Operations*, Field Manual, FM34-36, September 1991.

Protection and DoD Personnel and Activities against Acts of Terrorism and Political Turbulence for a more in-depth discussion of the use of MSHARPP.[11,12]

TIPS: CONDENSED QUESTION LIST TO USE IN CREATING MSHARPP CRITERIA

M-Mission: *What does the asset do? What is its purpose?*
S-Symbolism: *Does the asset represent the government or have cultural significance (e.g., Eifel Tower, biggest bridge or tallest building in the land, Pentagon, and so on)*
H-History: *Has this type of asset been attacked before? How often? How recently?*
A-Accessibility: *How assessable is the asset? Are there walls, walls, or obstacles? Are there guards, CCTV, or alarms? How many, what types, where are they located? Is there a response force (e.g., QRF, police, off-site security responders)?*
R-Recoverability: *How long will it take to get the asset's functions back to full operation by repair, bypass, or replacement?*
P-Population: *How many people work or reside inside or near the asset? If an attack occurred, how many people potentially would be injured or killed? Were there secondary effects from potential hazardous material release or fallout? Were there secondary effects from potential hazardous material release or fallout? Effect on the public psyche? Effect on world perception?*
P-Proximity: *How many comparable or dissimilar assets are located nearby? Are there open fields or densely packed urban neighborhoods around the asset? If the asset were a refinery, are there schools, churches, or hospitals nearby?*

PRACTICAL EXERCISE – PARTICIPANT'S GUIDE

INSTRUCTIONS

Read the Task, Background, Scenario Setup, and Threat Assessment sections and complete the CARVER matrix. You may refer back to the text as needed.

BACKGROUND

For this case type, studies show that the most likely active shooter scenario profile is from an internal threat (student or former student). That being said, to date, there is no clear profile for the insider threat. The scenario used in the exercise is a hybrid using selected elements based upon the relatively common active shooter, violent extremist, and lone actor case studies.

It is kept at a more uncomplicated level to reinforce the fundamentals of CARVER analysis.

TASK

Using the criteria and other resources provided, perform a CARVER analysis, and complete the CARVER matrix at the end of the document. *Be prepared to discuss and defend your assessment.*

SCENARIO SETUP

You are the newly hired school district's emergency planning/safety officer. The county has two school districts, and you are only responsible for one. There are five schools scattered across the

---

11 Headquarters Department of the Army, *Police Intelligence Operations,* Field Manual, FM 3-19.50, July 2010.
12 Department of Defense, *DoD-0-2000.12H, Protection and DOD Personnel and Activities against Acts of Terrorism and Political Turbulence,* https://commons.wikimedia.org/wiki/File:Protection_of_DoD_Personnel_and_Activities_against_Acts_of_Terrorism_and_Political_Turbulence.pdf, Retrieved January 1, 2020.

district under your supervision (see the right half of Scenario Figure 1). While going about your assigned duties, you decide to review the district's emergency action plans (EAP). The district's EAP for active shooter events has a recovery standard that expects affected school(s) to reconvene classes on the next regularly scheduled school day with unaffected staff/students using vetted substitutes or redirect unaffected students to other educational facilities. It has a separate school transportation plan that can accommodate up to 150 students if a school closes for an extended period. Students need to be bused to another school inside (or outside) the district. As you examine the plans, there is a knock at the office door. It is the local sheriff.

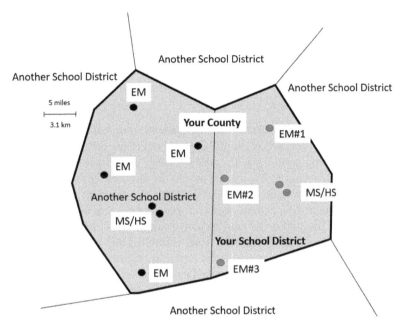

The sheriff introduces himself, and you offer him a chair. After exchanging greetings and pleasantries, the sheriff comes to the point of the visit. He states that he is making the rounds letting all the school security officers in the county know that the National Terrorism Advisory System (NTAS) had just sent out a bulletin. The NTAS bulletin states that an overseas terror group has issued a threat against public schools in our region. After the sheriff leaves, you decide to update the district's 'active shooter' emergency plans based on a CARVER analysis of the schools in your area of responsibility. You go to the file cabinets and collect the most recent facility inspection reports for each school in your district.

Author's Note: There is no profile for a student attacker. In the last 30 years in the United States, there have been male and female attackers, high-achieving students with good grades, and low performers. These acts of violence perpetrated over the last three decades were committed by students who were loners and socially isolated, as well as those who were well-liked and popular.

Note: For exercise purposes, a fictional threat scenario is employed that focuses on a foreign terror organization that can inspire unaffiliated or otherwise unconnected followers to take up arms and attack targets near where they live. Therefore, assume a lone actor for the practical exercise.

THREAT ASSESSMENT

Fictitious DHS Threat Assessment: An overseas radical terror/extremist organization Red Sword (fictitious name) has made a public threat to attack a public school in a Western Nation. The terror group claims that the 'attacks will demonstrate to the world their ability to strike their enemies where they live and least expect it.' The Red Sword is appealing to followers, supporters, and sympathizers, asking 'the willing and righteous to take up arms, enter the schools of the unbeliever, and strike them down.'

As of this date, there are no reports of Red Sword terror cells in your area. However, their propaganda is easily accessible on the web. There has been one individual [who resided 25 miles (≈ 40 km) from your school district] arrested and convicted of providing material support to the Red Sword terror organization two years prior. Red Sword has been successful three times in the past five years of inspiring unaffiliated individuals to commit acts of terror nationwide. No other specifically related Red Sword reporting was found.

SCHOOL BUILDING EAP INSPECTION REPORTS

The High School (Ages 14–18 Years)

The high school has a population of roughly 300 students (one-half capacity), and it is well maintained (see Scenario Figure 2). It is the only high school in the district. It has a ten-foot perimeter wall, which is challenging to scale. The wall runs only 50 yards from the building in some places. The school (built five years ago) is located next to the district's only middle school. Suppose the school is shut down for an extended period. In that case, an equivalent school facility is located in an adjacent district 20 miles (32.2 km) away to the west or collocates with the middle schoolers in the adjacent building. The staff performed an active shooter EAP drill three months ago that was satisfactory. The building has four ground-level controlled and observed access points. Per building security procedures, all access points are physically secured during and after classes are in session. The building has configurable alarm and CCTV monitoring systems to control access. Only one access point, used by the janitor to take the trash out, is vulnerable to unobserved or unmonitored entry when school is in session. However, the janitor's door is in the back of the building and is not visible from the building's street side (front). Access points are locked and alarmed at night. There is armed roving security present when the school is in session.

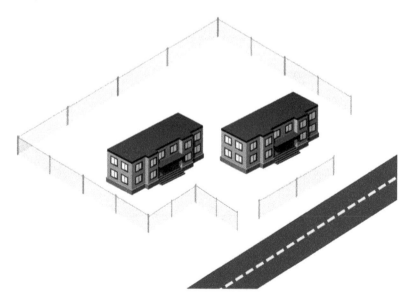

The Middle School (Ages 11–14 Years)

The middle school has a population of roughly 310 students (one-half capacity), and it is well maintained (see Scenario Figure 2). It shares the same ten-foot perimeter wall with the high school. The school is the district's only middle school. Suppose the school is shut down for an extended period. In that case, an equivalent school facility is located in an adjacent district 20 miles (32.2 km) away to the west or collocates with the high schoolers in the adjacent building. The staff performed an active shooter EAP drill two months ago that was satisfactory. The building has four ground-level controlled and observed access points. Per building security procedures, all access points are physically secured during and after classes are in session. The building has configurable alarm and CCTV monitoring systems to control access. Only one access point, used by the janitor to take the trash out, is vulnerable to unobserved or unmonitored entry when school is in session. However, the janitor's door is in the back of the building and is not visible from the street side (front) of the building. Access points are locked and alarmed at night. There is armed roving security present when the school is in session.

Elementary School #1 (Ages 5–11 Years)

Elementary school #1 has a population of roughly 100 students (full capacity), and it is well maintained (see Scenario Figure 3). Built two years ago, it is the newest of the district's three elementary schools. It has a six-foot perimeter wall on three sides that runs parallel from the building at least 52 yards on three sides. If the school is shut down for an extended period, an equivalent school facility is located in an adjacent district 15 miles (24.1 km) away to the west in a neighboring school district. The staff performed an active shooter EAP drill six months ago that was satisfactory. The building has four ground-level controlled and observed access points. Per building security procedures, all access points are physically secured during and after classes are in session. The building has configurable alarm and CCTV monitoring systems to control access. Only one access point, used by the janitor to take the trash out, is vulnerable to unobserved or unmonitored entry when school is in session. However, the janitor's door is in the back of the building and is not visible from the street side (front) of the building. Access points are locked and alarmed at night. There is armed roving security present when the school is in session.

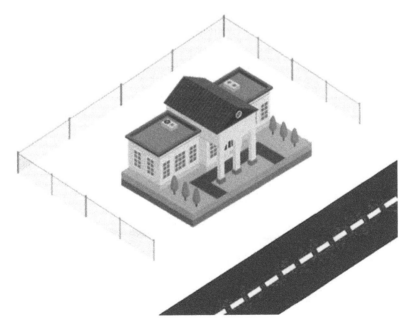

Elementary School #2 (Ages 5–11 Years)

Elementary school #2 has a population of roughly 105 students (full capacity), and it is well maintained (see Scenario Figure 4). Built 15 years ago, it is the second oldest of three elementary schools in the district. It has a six-foot perimeter wall on four sides with two openings in the front for pedestrian traffic. The wall runs parallel from the building at least 52 yards on all sides. If the school is shut down for an extended period, an equivalent school facility is located in an adjacent district 15 miles (24.1 km) away to the west in a neighboring school district. The staff performed an active shooter EAP drill five months ago that was unsatisfactory. There is no additional training or retesting scheduled as of this date. Per building security procedures, all access points are physically secured during and after classes are in session. The building has configurable alarm and CCTV monitoring systems to control access. Only one access point, used by the janitor to take the trash out, is vulnerable to unobserved or unmonitored entry when school is in session. However, the janitor's door is in the back of the building and is not visible from the street side (front) of the building. Access points are locked and alarmed at night. There is armed roving security present when the school is in session.

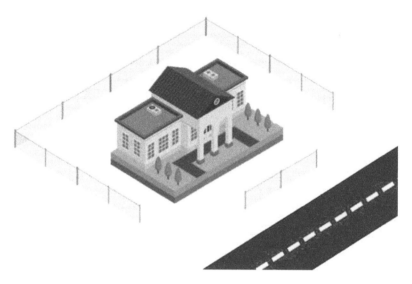

Elementary School #3 (Ages 5–11 Years)

Elementary school #3 has a population of roughly 125 students (overcrowded), and it is poorly maintained (see Scenario Figure 5). Built 25 years ago, it is the oldest of three elementary schools in the district. Funds typically directed toward school maintenance are being redirected to new construction. A larger replacement school is going up a few miles away but is one year behind schedule. The school has no perimeter wall, and one is not planned because the building it is scheduled to be condemned and abandoned soon.

The school has the only accredited special needs education program for ages 5 through 11. If the school shuts down for an extended period, there is no equivalent school facility located in an adjacent district or county for 50 miles (80.5 km) in any direction. The staff did not perform an active shooter EAP drill this year or the previous year, and there is no additional training or retesting scheduled as of this date. Per building security procedures, all access points are physically secured during and after classes are in session. The building has configurable alarm and CCTV monitoring systems to control access. However, the cameras for two of the four access points are unserviceable. Two access points, one regularly used by the janitor to take the trash out, are vulnerable to unobserved or unmonitored entry when school is in session. Access points are locked and alarmed at night, and there is armed roving security present when the school is in session.

Author's Note: On September 1, 2004, the first day of a new school year, Chechen terrorists enter a school (School #1) in southern Russia (town of Belsan) and take more than 1,000 children and adults hostage. Days later, rescue workers find hundreds of bodies in the debris of the burned-out former school gym. Nearly 340 people, about half of them children, died in the ensuing ordeal. More than 700 others are wounded. The portion of the school where the attack transpired is never reopened.

Years later, a new school was built opposite School #1, across the railway tracks where cows and goats graze. (Associated Press, 2004)

ASSESSMENT CRITERIA

	Relative Value Rating
Criticality:	
No school staff procedures exist for controlling the situation or ending the session for the day of the incident. No processes were identified to address the event. No other equivalent schools are available within reasonable travel distance, and schools may be closed indefinitely.	10
Untested/vetted school staff procedures exist for controlling the situation and ending the session on the day of the incident. May reconvene classes and repair/replace damaged facilities within a month with significant administrative assistance or redirect unaffected students to other educational facilities. An equivalent school is available within a reasonable travel distance. No indication that the staff is trained on associated plans and procedures.	8
Marginal Plans exist to support the school staff in controlling the situation and ending the session for the day of the incident. Can reconvene classes and repair/replace damaged facilities within two weeks with significant administrative assistance or redirect unaffected students to other educational facilities. Two other equivalent schools are available within a reasonable travel distance. No indication that the staff is trained on associated plans and procedures.	6
Adequate school staff procedures exist to control the situation and end the session for the day of the incident. Can reconvene classes within one week or (with some administrative assistance) redirect unaffected students to other educational facilities. More than two other equivalent schools are available within a reasonable travel distance. Staff is trained on all associated plans and procedures.	4

	Relative Value Rating
Adequate school staff procedures exist to control the situation and end the session for the day of the incident. Can reconvene on the next regularly scheduled school day or redirect unaffected students to other educational facilities. More than three other equivalent schools are available within a reasonable travel distance. Staff trains on all associated plans, procedures, and drills annually.	1

Accessibility:

No entry points are controlled or observed; some are not physically secured during and after classes are in session, and no perimeter wall exists. No building alarm system or CCTV monitoring system exists to control access.	10
There are multiple uncontrolled and unobserved entry points, but most are physically secured during and after classes are in session. A perimeter wall exists at the edge of school grounds, but it is easily scalable and only surrounds a portion of the school grounds. Some normally occupied buildings have an alarm system and/or CCTV monitoring system to control access.	8
Multiple entry points exist, half are uncontrolled and unobserved (by staff or security), but most are physically secured during and after classes are in session. A perimeter wall exists at the edge of school grounds, but it is easily scalable. Most normally occupied buildings have an alarm system and/or CCTV monitoring system to control access.	6
Multiple controlled and/or observed entry points exist. However, not all entry points are physically secured during and after classes are in session. A six-foot-high perimeter security wall exists at the edge of school grounds. The wall is located a minimum of 50 yards from occupied buildings or play areas. All normally occupied buildings have configurable alarm or CCTV monitoring systems to control access.	4
Multiple controlled and observed (by staff or security) entry points exist, and all are physically secured during and after classes are in session. A ten-foot-high perimeter security wall exists at the edge of school grounds. The wall stands a minimum of 100 yards from occupied buildings or play areas. All buildings have configurable alarm and CCTV monitoring systems to control access.	1

Recoverability:

No procedures exist to recover from the event. School may be closed indefinitely.	10
Procedures are in place to deal with the event, recover, and reconvene classes within a month with unaffected staff/students using substitutes or redirect unaffected students to other educational facilities. Adequate student transport resources can be obtained to relocate staff/students within a month.	8
Procedures are in place to deal with the event, recover, and reconvene classes within two weeks with unaffected staff/students using substitutes or redirect unaffected students to other educational facilities. To relocate staff/students within two weeks, adequate student transport resources can be obtained.	6

	Relative Value Rating
Adequate procedures are in place to deal with the event, recover, and reconvene classes within one week with unaffected staff/students using substitutes or redirect unaffected students to other educational facilities. Sufficient student transport resources can be obtained to relocate staff/students within one week. Staff trains on all associated plans, procedures, and drills annually.	4
Adequate procedures are in place to deal with the event, recover, and reconvene classes on the next regularly scheduled school day with unaffected staff/students using vetted substitutes or redirect unaffected students to other educational facilities. Adequate student transport resources are available to relocate staff/students. Staff trains on all associated plans, procedures, and drills annually.	1

Vulnerability:

All (100%) buildings are vulnerable to unobserved or unmonitored entry and no security personnel.	10
Vulnerable to unobserved or unmonitored entry to most (75%) of the ordinarily occupied buildings and all unoccupied buildings. Unarmed security is present when school is in session.	8
Vulnerable to unobserved or unmonitored entry to some (50%) of the typically occupied and all unoccupied buildings. Unarmed non-security personnel are present when the school is in session.	6
Few ($\leq$25%) access points are vulnerable to unobserved or unmonitored entry to normally unoccupied buildings. Some armed security personnel are present, but only when school is in session.	4
No (0%) access points are vulnerable to unobserved or unmonitored entry. Adequate armed security is present 24/7.	1

Effect (on population): *(Note: Remember this is from the adversary's perspective)*

Overwhelming positive effects, but no significant negative impact. (e.g., high student and staff casualties, considerable damage to the building(s), the school district goes bankrupt from lawsuits and cannot find replacement instructional facilities or alternatives for an indefinite period, praise for the attack by terror group supporters and followers resulting in higher recruitment and funding, international groups find justification for the attack resulting in little or no legal ramifications against the terror organizations by law enforcement or military.)	10
Moderately positive effects and few significant negative effects.	8
No significant effects and remains neutral.	6
Moderate negative effects and few significant positive impacts.	4
Overwhelming negative effects and no significant positive impact. (e.g., no, or few casualties, minimal interruption to school operations, the school district receives overwhelming positive praise, support, and recognition from the locality, national and international levels, international denunciation resulting in aggressive targeting operations by militaries, anti-terror organizations and law enforcement, terror group loses followers, supports, and funding.)	1

	Relative Value Rating
Recognizability:	
More than eight uncontrolled access points to the perimeter and buildings can be easily identified from a distance of 100 meters.	10
Five (or more) uncontrolled access points to the perimeter and buildings can be easily identified as such from a distance of 100 meters.	8
Three or more uncontrolled access points to the perimeter and buildings can be identified from a standoff position of 100 meters. Minimal or no surveillance is required to identify feasible unmonitored access.	6
One (or more) uncontrolled access point(s) to the perimeter and buildings can be identified as such from a standoff position of 100 meters. Unmonitored access to the school may require some surveillance or inside information.	4
No recognizable uncontrolled perimeter and building access points. Unmonitored access to the school would require significant surveillance or inside information.	1

Author's Note: When evaluating the Recognizability aspect as part of a CARVER analysis, it can be a straightforward exercise to assess a military facility. However, a school is nothing like a military facility. Localities make great efforts to make schools recognizable to the public (e.g., flagpoles, large street signs, children's crosswalks, crossing guards, reduced speed zones, and so on). Few of these accouterments can be removed or changed; some are required by law or local ordinance. Often the best result an analyst can achieve is to assess how recognizable the security weaknesses are that would make the school an easier, more accessible, or desirable target. Quite like a homeowner who puts a 'Beware of Dog' sign in the yard, even though their dog is downright tame. They are attempting to deter burglars by making their homes appear more secure.

PRACTICAL EXERCISE – CARVER MATRIX

District Schools							
Potential Targets	Criticality	Accessibility	Recoverability	Vulnerability	Effect	Recognizability	Total
High School							
Middle School							
Elementary School #1							
Elementary School #2							
Elementary School #3							

CHAPTER 3

Target-Focused Analysis

INTRODUCTION

Open up any intelligence trade magazine or intelligence-specific internet job site, and you are immediately confronted with advertisements for 'human-targeting officers' or some similar title or job description. The mid-range pay for these positions hovered around six figures when writing this book. The associated responsibilities commonly include:

- Reviewing operational traffic for intelligence leads;
- Drafting targeting packages;
- Writing, editing, formatting, and disseminating reports/message traffic;
- Conducting searches and traces on items, organizations, and entities, including persons of operational interest...

Without question, business, military, law enforcement, and especially the intelligence community (IC) all use a derivation of 'target-focused analysis.' The layperson may not immediately recognize it as such, but the target-focused analysis is a broadly used analysis approach.

Business, military, the IC, and law enforcement all value effective targeting skills. This chapter identifies, describes, compares, and contrasts target-focused analytical processes in each of these sectors. Since the military and the IC are very similar, they are both covered and discussed here. The following table describes a generic step-by-step targeting process model, and each step of the generic process is presented with its analogous counterparts aligned from left to right (see Table 3.1).

The first row of Table 3.1 begins with the Generic Targeting Model then displays three sectors (following three columns) that routinely conduct target operations. The last column (right) identifies the individual sectors' level of similarity compared to the Generic Targeting Model (far left). Looking at each model (shown in the vertical columns of Table 3.1), one quickly recognizes that most steps are similar and some are identical.

TARGETING CONCEPT

The concept of targeting is often misunderstood. The word 'target' usually congers visuals of multiple concentric circles forming the backdrop for the crosshairs of a riflescope reticle or, for spy novel fans, perhaps just a silhouette of a man in those crosshairs. However, targeting is a far more sophisticated concept.

DOI: 10.4324/9781003241195-3

Table 3.1 Targeting Process Steps

Generic Model	Business	Military/IC	Law Enforcement	Similarities
Identify target	Segmentation	Find	Identify	Similar
Locate	Target	Fix	Pursuit	Similar
Implement	Position	Finish	Apprehend	Similar
Observe effects	Customer survey	Exploit	Exploit/investigate	Very similar
Analyze	Analyze	Analyze	Analyze	Identical

Targeting Effects

One conducts targeting operations for many reasons, which may change with time and circumstances. These circumstances and varying parameters drive what is called 'target effects.' The military definition of 'target effects' is the cumulative results of actions taken to attack targets and systems by lethal and nonlethal means. These effects can be primary (*effects* that are the direct result of targeting actions) or secondary (effects that are indirectly the result of targeting). 'Nonlethal means' is insufficient terminology to describe a comprehensive and far-reaching task.

Lethal versus Nonlethal

Targeting actions can be extremely varied yet still fit under the category of 'less than lethal.' For example, most casually infer that international commodity trading is about making money. So, when a country sells a product (e.g., steel) far below the market value in another country, the purpose is objectively not to 'make money,' at least not in the short term or immediate time frame. In this case, the goal is more long term. The purpose is usually to take market share from existing competitors. This trade tactic is called 'dumping.' In this instance, a competitor sees an opportunity to 'target' a competitor's customers by dumping his product on that foreign market.

Author's Note: The trade-based targeting analogy was used to illustrate the point that targeting is not just about putting a bullet or bomb at the proper location.

To determine the best trade approach (dumping or competing with a higher quality product) would likely be based upon a cost analysis and other factors to determine which method would be most effective.

A target-focused intelligence analysis methodology attempts to align, or focus, all aspects of the intelligence process (e.g., Plan, Collect, Process, Analyze, Disseminate) toward one objective and, by doing so, optimize the entire process.

Referring to the commodity dumping scenario from earlier, the question is asked: 'Has non-lethal targeting transpired?' The answer is '*Yes*' and what makes this targeting operation so compelling is that the targeting action often goes unnoticed, sometimes for years. When finally recognized, it can be too late. The targeted competitor's industry is so damaged that recovery is impossible. In this analogy, the desired target effect was greater 'market share' (Figure 3.1).

The larger market share potentially could have been achieved by other competitive means. A market rival could have increased their product's quality in the customer's eyes, but that would likely expend significant funds for marketing surveys and research and design costs to improve the product. Once the product's quality has been improved upon, an advertising effort would be needed to communicate this fact to the consumer. If the customer does not recognize and accept the increased product value of increased quality, they are not likely to pay the higher price for the higher quality product. Since efforts to improve the product may or may not achieve the desired

The Market

Greater Market Share

Figure 3.1   Illustration of the Market Share Concept.

goal of gaining market share quickly and likely incur higher capital expenditure and production costs to improve its quality, nonlethal targeting measures become more appealing.

The following are three relatively straightforward example scenarios of targeting and targeting effects, which, upon closer observation, are perhaps not so straightforward.

EXAMPLE SCENARIOS

First Scenario – *Figure A at right displays a silhouette of a man being targeted by a sniper. Refer to example figure A.*

Discussion: *The figure appears to be a straightforward depiction of a man about to be assassinated. The target effect is likely 'lethal' in that the hypothetical sniper aims at the broadest part of the human body.*

(Note: Most countries' military sniper training teaches that the 'center of mass' (chest area) is the desired target area. The target area is based upon the assumption that a hit in this region, even if several inches off-center, most likely severely damages one or more vital organs causing instant death or death within a brief period after being struck.)

First Scenario – *Figure A shows a man's silhouette being targeted by a sniper. In this case, the center of mass is not the targeted area.*

Discussion: Again, the figure appears to be a straightforward depiction of a man about to be assassinated,...perhaps. In this case, the sniper has information that the mark is wearing ballistic armor under his jacket. So now, to still achieve a 'lethal' target effect, the sniper has chosen to move the desired strike point away from the center of mass to the head, a much smaller and more difficult shot.

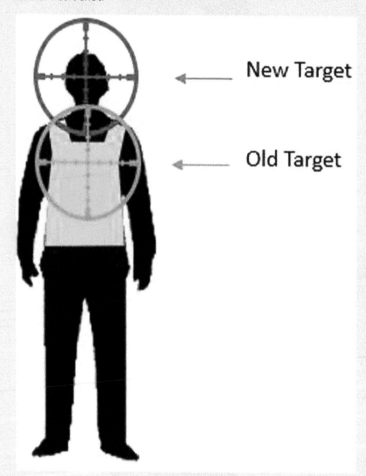

Second Scenario – Again, Figure B shows a man's silhouette targeted by a hypothetical sniper. However, this time, for some unknown reason, the desired target strike location is on the ground near (but not on) the silhouette.

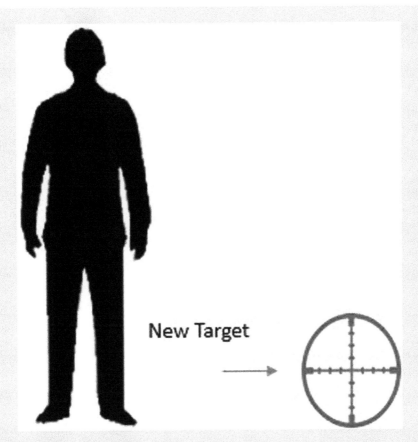

Discussion: *This would be another example of 'nonlethal effects' targeting. Potential motivations are:*

- *Harassment, just trying to scare the mark;*
- *Send a message, perhaps a warning that mark may, or may not, readily recognize;*
- *Fraud, the mark is the one who has engaged the sniper to stage the sniping event to convince others that his life is in danger and gain empathy and support;*
- *(Assuming the figure represents a politician making a speech in front of a crowd) Possible second-order effects include, but are not limited to:*
  - *The sniper only intends to frighten the politician (not kill or wound) to make him stop the speech or quit the political race, or*
  - *The sniper wants the politician to leave the podium or perhaps go to another location where there is an opportunity for a better shot,*
  - *Other potential second-order effects,…*

TARGETING (*GENERIC MODEL*)

In everyday terminology, targeting is a process of identifying an entity, group, or portion thereof, as possessing some aspect of a higher perceived value to the targeter. Some modest examples include hunting rabbits to eat or marketing a company's new product line. The targeting entity locates who/what is being targeted (them/it), directs a predefined effort toward (them/it), observes the effects, and analyzes the observed effects. Therefore, the process steps of the *Generic Targeting Model* include identifying the target, locating, implementing, observing effects, and analyzing. The following are a few simple examples explained in more detail.

Author's Note: Notice that once one gets into 'nonlethal effects' and 'second-order effects,' it is not difficult for the range of alternatives to expand exponentially.

Examples

EXAMPLE A

A hunter (targeter) hunting a rabbit (the target):

- *Decides he wants a rabbit for dinner (identifies).*
- *Tracks the rabbit through the woods (locates).*
- *Attempts to kill the rabbit (implements).*
- *Watches the rabbit die (observes).*
- *Assesses whether he should hunt a deer tomorrow because the rabbit was (or wasn't) enough to feed his family (analyzes).*

Author's Note: Just looking at Example 'A,' though it is overly simplified, it still exemplifies each step of the generic targeting model. Taking the analogy a step further, the hunter repeats the process at multiple levels by targeting where the rabbit lives to start stalking, targeting what part of the rabbit's body to aim his weapon to ensure a quick kill,....

Example 'B' is slightly more involved. Example B describes the 'S-T-P' marketing (targeting) process. The STP process is explained further in the next section.

EXAMPLE B

Product marketers (targeters) marketing a product in a targeted market:

- *Decide they want to sell a particular product to a specific market segment or segments (identifies).*
- *Determine where those market segments go to purchase the product, e.g., brick-and-mortar stores or online,...(locates).*
- *Place the advertising and/or the product itself such that the identified segment(s) encounter(s) the product (e.g., pop-ups advertising on a website, a can of beans moved to eye level on a store shelf (implements).*
- *Track sales figures (observes).*
- *Evaluate whether to adjust advertising and/or product placement (analyzes).*

BUSINESS TARGETING (*MARKETING*)

In business targeting (or marketing), the *generic model's implementation step* differs significantly from other sector targeting processes. Marketers strive to entice potential customers to purchase a product or service, in contrast to the target effects that other targeting sectors are trying to achieve, such as harassing, detaining, disrupting, destroying, neutralizing, apprehending, or any of the other more common targeting effects. Thus, the implementation step in marketing plans (also known as positioning/placement) tends to be far subtler, more nuanced, and often requires significant supporting research.

The business version of target-focused analysis is more commonly referred to as 'marketing analysis.' This type of target-focused analysis is often referred to as the *Segmented Approach* or the 'STP' marketing process. The Segmented Approach is a three-step marketing strategy where 'S' stands for segmenting, 'T' for targeting, and the 'P' for positioning. This process allows a business owner or advertisers/marketing professional to develop a marketing (*targeting*) strategy that ties company, brand, and product benefits to specific customer market segments. Postmarketing *customer surveys* and the analysis of those surveys are implied steps and generally are not called out as part of the STP process.

Segmentation Step of STP

The segmentation step involves finding out what kinds of customers might desire a product or service (or some specific aspect of a product or service). Typically, in military, IC, and law enforcement targeting operations, the *target characteristics* are predetermined or known (e.g., enemy concentrations, terrorists, criminals, and so on). However, in marketing, the *target* (segment) characteristics are undetermined. Therefore, since they often are not readily apparent or observable, they must be determined or discovered. For example, some years ago, Chattanooga, Tennessee, which draws significant revenue from drive-through tourism each year, tried to determine who the tourists were and why they came to their fair city, but for some unknown reason, only stayed the night.

Marketing surveys were conducted, and the answer surprised everyone. The primary reason had little to do with the amusements or attractions of the city or surrounding countryside; tourists came and stayed overnight in Chattanooga because it was roughly an eight-hour (one day) drive from Chattanooga, Tennessee, to Orlando, Florida (see Figure 3.2). For instance, if one were traveling

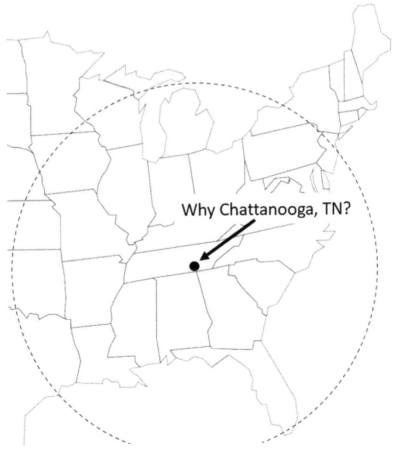

Figure 3.2 Why Chattanooga, TN.

by car to Orlando from approximately one-half of the continental US, Chattanooga would likely be a stopping point coming (or going) to the South Florida attractions (their destination). In this case, the *segment* the marketing professionals had identified was primarily families, with one or more children, who commonly traveled around eight hours per day and would likely be interested in amusements and entertainment complementing those found in Orlando.

> *Author's Note: In the city of Chattanooga example, it was determined that tourists were stopping in their town for purely logistical reasons. This revelation is quite significant. By leveraging this advantage of 'geographical positioning,' business owners in the city could double their annual tourism revenue by just enticing travelers to extend their stays by 'one day.'*

Targeting Step of STP

In the next STP step, the decision of whether to target one or more segments is made. The choice of segment(s) should be based upon multiple factors (e.g., cost, customer needs/desires, logistical considerations, and so on).

Usually, the first consideration is how well other suppliers serve existing segments? This step determines the targeting environment. If existing providers can adequately satisfy all segments, it is more difficult to draw them toward a different or unknown product or service.

EXAMPLE

Refer to Figure 3.3 as the STP marketing (Targeting) model's targeting step is discussed. A new hair restoration product/service is used in the example to demonstrate the Targeting step of STP.

The breakdown of the market segments of customers that used the product/service includes the following:

- *Used effective treatments that were expensive – 10%;*
- *Used ineffective treatments that were expensive – 30%;*
- *Used ineffective treatments that were expensive – 20%;*
- *Used ineffective treatments that were inexpensive – 30%; and*
- *Used effective treatments that were inexpensive – 10%.*

Therefore, only 20% of the existing market uses an <u>effective</u> *hair restoration treatment, and only half of those (10%) appear to care about the expense.*

Therefore, using the given data and assuming the new hair restoration product/service is both 'effective and inexpensive,' 90% of market segments are potentially available for targeting.

Positioning Step of STP

Positioning (also referred to as *placement*) involves implementing what was determined during the targeting step. This step works out how to best compete in the selected market segments. The marketing analyst identifies how to position their products/services. As it is likely that there are already competitive offerings in the market, the firm needs to work out how to win market share from established players. As mentioned previously, this process tends to be far subtler, more nuanced. Typically, this is achieved by being perceived by consumers as different, unique, superior, or providing superior value.

Figure 3.3   Identifying Targetable Market Segments.

Using the previous example of 'new hair restoration product/service,' the analyst has an easy task; they only have to demonstrate that their product 'works' and is 'reasonably priced.' However, some research may still be required to determine the media/advertising mechanism that best presents the intended message to the desired audience(s).

Author's Note: The marketing examples provided are minimal and cursory explanations and were purposely used in the Business Targeting (Marketing) section of this chapter. The examples were used only to illustrate basic concepts and compare and contrast business targeting processes with those used in other professional sectors.

I am a program management professional (PMP), certified manager. Over the years, I have worked as a program manager for several large government service contracts. This experience provides one with some understanding; however, I claim no great marketing analysis expertise. That said, there are many publicly available marketing analysis texts available, and I suggest those as more appropriate sources of in-depth insight into the subject of targeted-marketing analysis.

Along those same thought lines, my expertise in military/IC targeting processes, some would say, is quite noteworthy. Therefore, the military/IC explanations, targeting specimens, and elaboration presented in the text are more comprehensive and reflect decades of real-world application.

Customer Survey (*Feedback*)

The customer survey step is where marketers observe and collect the feedback from their marketing efforts. The customer survey design should fully evaluate and capture the effects/desired outcomes of the targeting effort. The survey can be administered online, by telephone, fax, or in person.

Analyze

This is the most critical aspect of any marketing/targeting exercise. In this step, one determines what was achieved. Does the targeted segment appreciate your product or service? Is it valued enough to purchase again or recommend to another? Did the customer feel that they paid too much? The answer to these questions and many other typical survey inquiries should be present in the market sector analysis results in an organized fashion to be easily understood.

> **TIPS**
>
> *The analysis step fails if one has to repeat the targeting/marketing process because the proper analysis did not adequately present the results captured from the survey step.*

MILITARY/IC TARGETING

The concept of analysis in support of targeting (or target analysis) has been around in military circles for many years, and the IC also uses it extensively. There is little difference between the military and IC models in many cases. The most significant difference is that the military has a broader range of target-focused analytical processes.

Principles of Targeting

The US military adheres to a targeting doctrine based upon four principles throughout the targeting cycle. These principles create desired target effects while diminishing undesired second-order and collateral effects. These principles are focused, effects based, interdisciplinary, and systematic.

Focused

Focused targeting efficiently achieves the objectives through target engagement within operational planning parameters, the operational limitations within the plans and orders, the rules of engagement (ROE), the law of war, and agreements concerning the sovereignty of national territories. Every target nominated should contribute to attaining those set objectives.

Effects Based

In military targeting, targeting *effects* are designed to satisfy the commander's objectives. Targeting is concerned with creating specific desired effects through target engagement. Target analysis considers all possible means to create desired effects, drawing from all available capabilities. The art and science of targeting seek to create desired effects with the least risk and least expenditure of time and resources.

Interdisciplinary

Joint targeting is a command function that requires the participation of many disciplines. It entails participation from all commanders' staff, component commanders' staff, other agencies, departments, organizations, and multinational partners.

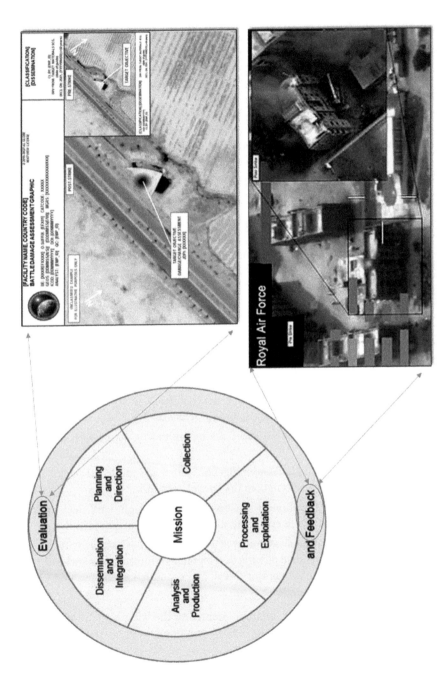

Figure 3.4   US Military Intelligence Cycle Graphic (Source: Joint Pub 2.0).

Systematic

The joint targeting cycle is designed to create effects systematically. It is a rational and iterative process that methodically analyzes, prioritizes, and assigns assets against targets systematically. Targets should be reconsidered for re-targeting if the desired effects are not observed.[1]

Intelligence Cycle

In conventional military terms, the analysis process (*a subset of the Intelligence Cycle, see Figure 3.4*) generally contains the tasks of identifying, locating, and planning the desired target effects (e.g., harass, disrupt, destroy) of target engagements of large military targets (e.g., railroads, industrial complexes, military troop assembly areas, and so on), then performing an after-action assessment, often referred to as the battle damage assessment (BDA). Based upon the BDA, a determination is made to increase the effect, repeat, decrease, or desist. Traditional military target analysis (e.g., determining where to drop bombs or strike with guided missiles) is still prevalent today. Even though the IC may occasionally utilize a drone strike to neutralize high-value targets (HVTs), they generally perform more focused targeting of critical groups, networks, and individuals (instead of larger strategic/tactical targets). In recent years, this HVT-focused type of analysis has truly come into its own.

Author's Note: The US military's analysis process was introduced as part of the Intelligence Cycle (shown in Figure 3.4), in Chapter 2 of the previous text, Intelligence Analysis Fundamentals. The military version of target-focused analysis, presently used by Special-Forces elements, is known by the acronym 'F3EA' or find, fix, finish, exploit, and analyze.

F3EA

Special Operations integrates and leverages 'analyze' and 'exploit' aspects into their operations process through an operational methodology. The F3EA process is inherent in executing all special operations (see Figure 3.5[2]). A general description of F3EA steps includes:

- **Find** – Identifies and locates all aspects of networks (threat/friendly) by synchronizing all intelligence disciplines, analyst-driven operations, and surveillance.
- **Fix** – Determination of precise location and tracking entities of the network or threat and limiting its options.
- **Finish** – Unilateral, bilateral, coalition, and indigenous lethal and nonlethal actions to disrupt and defeat the threat network and strengthen the friendly network.
- **Exploit** – Execution of a combination of sensitive-site exploitation, battlefield exploitation, technical exploitation, and document exploitation of the network (threat/friendly).
- **Analyze** – Methodical and detailed assessment of post-operation or post-activity intelligence, expansion of the common operational picture, development of future operations and activities, determination of impacts on the network or threat, and examination and evaluation of information of the network or threat.[3]

Even though the F3EA style of targeting appears oriented to the 'kill people' and 'break things' mentality, which without question is the mainstay of military operations, this is not always the case.

Find

The 'Find' step varies across the analytical spectrum (e.g., HUMINT, SIGINT, IMINT, and so on). HUMINTers (human intelligence analysts), may use the HUMINT 'screening process.' Like all

---

1   Department of Defense (DoD), Joint Publication 3-60, *Joint Targeting.*
2   Army Doctrine Reference Publication, 3-05, *Special Operations.*
3   Army Doctrine Reference Publication, 3-05, *Special Operations.*

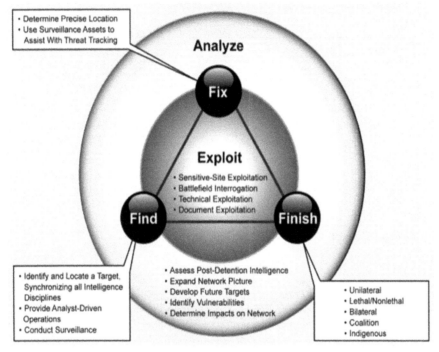

- Determine Precise Location
- Use Surveillance Assets to Assist With Threat Tracking

Analyze

Fix

Exploit
- Sensitive-Site Exploitation
- Battlefield Interrogation
- Technical Exploitation
- Document Exploitation

Find

Finish

- Identify and Locate a Target, Synchronizing all Intelligence Disciplines
- Provide Analyst-Driven Operations
- Conduct Surveillance

- Assess Post-Detention Intelligence
- Expand Network Picture
- Develop Future Targets
- Identify Vulnerabilities
- Determine Impacts on Network

- Unilateral
- Lethal/Nonlethal
- Bilateral
- Coalition
- Indigenous

Figure 3.5   Find, Fix, Finish, Exploit, and Analyze Process (Army Doctrine Reference Publication, 3-05).

intelligence operations, human source screening operations are focused on specific 'higher value' targets (HVTs). This definition of human sources includes local indigenous populations, refugees, travelers in the area, and detainees (including enemy prisoners of war or EPWs). Similar to the earlier business marketing 'segmentation' step, only selected potential targets (market segments) are likely to meet the desired targeting characteristics (e.g., ones who possess desired information, critical network hubs, group/organizational leader, and so on). The following is just such a HUMINT example.

EXAMPLE

A total of 60 EPWs were captured in a group. One could, if time allowed, interrogate all 60. In most cases, actionable intelligence is perishable, and it might take weeks, months, or even years to thoroughly interrogate all the EPWs. The military has developed an objective selection process that filters groups of potential sources to expedite the process.

By performing a brief screening exercise of the EPW group based upon the collected pocket litter, identification papers, uniform insignia, and using a few choice questions and then ranking the results (using the two provided tables, Source Screen Codes and Knowledgeability levels shown at right), the analyst can quickly and efficiently prioritize who in the group should be prioritized for interrogation[4] (see Figure 3.6).

For SIGINTers (signal intelligence analysts), if they have one (or more) signal selector(s) to search for (e.g., a cell phone number) and the appropriate system to search with, the 'Find' step is greatly simplified by shrinking the search area to a tiny perimeter. That is, provided the target is still using the identified selector.

---

4   Department of the Army, *Human Intelligence Collection Operations*, Field Manual, FM 2-22.3, 2006.

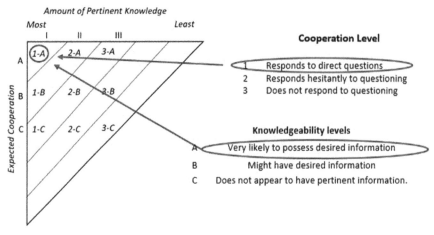

Figure 3.6   Interrogation Priority Chart.

Author's Note: Observing the Priority Chart (see Figure 3.6), observe that the EPWs most likely to have the desired information (the 'A' group), and who are also the most cooperative, are debriefed first, then the less cooperative EPWs follow. Following this process would likely yield more considerable amounts of the desired information more efficiently and expeditiously.

IMINTers (imagery intelligence analysts) often called 'geospatial analysts,' would use aerial imagery and fuse it using multiple layers of other geolocated intelligence to create a picture of the most probable target location(s).

Fix

The F3EA targeting process explains fixing the target by *determining the specific location and tracking elements* of the network or threat, thus limiting its options.[5] This explanation is accurate and, at the same time, inadequate. Determining the precise location of a terrorist HVT involves multiple factors that deter the 'fix' aspect of the F3EA process.

To illustrate the concept by using a fictitious example, it would be when a target, where the desired target effect is to arrest or detain, is located in a country that the US government has no extradition agreement. In such a case, one would think the 'fix' step is complete because the target's location is known. In reality, the fix step is not complete, and 'fixing the target' has only become more complex. Now 'determination' may entail enticing the target to relocate to another country, one the US does have an extradition agreement.

The following fictitious scenario describes just such a situation and discusses possible solutions.

EXAMPLE

Scenario: An international terrorist, Bilbo Abu Khan, has gone into hiding in the Quristan capital city of Ozbek. The US State Department is currently conducting sensitive trade negotiations with Quristan for precious rare earth metals needed for use in several classified National Security-related defense projects. The United States (US) has no extradition agreement with Quristan, but the neighboring Republic of Pithuainia does have friendly relations and a long-standing extradition agreement with the US (see Figure 3.7).

---

5   Army Doctrine Reference Publication, Field Manual, FM 3-05, *Special Operations*.

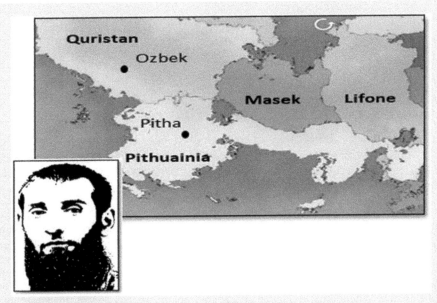

Figure 3.7 Fictitious Human-Targeting Scenario.

Discussion:

- *Option 1, the US (despite not having a formal extradition agreement) tries to extradite Bilbo legally, but should that effort fail, the US may covertly (or publicly) tip off Bilbo that efforts to extradite him are in progress. Not knowing if those extradition efforts may succeed, Bilbo may try to escape to some other unknown location.*
- *Option 2, the US could covertly try to kidnap Bilbo from his hiding spot in Ozbek, but it could damage or even scuttle trade negotiations if the operation become public knowledge.*
- *Option 3, the US could send a covert operative to approach Bilbo and gain his confidence. Then use this relationship to entice Bilbo to either accompany or travel separately to Pithuainia, where authorities are waiting to take him into custody.*

Note: In the third scenario, the targeting analyst 'determines' the target's location by having the target travel to another (preferred) location. This new location is one that facilitates the desired target effects (arrest/detain).

Author's Note: For years I have regretted having to explain the F3EA process and repeatedly spending more time on the 'Finish' step than any other.

Even the name for this step (Finish) is misleading. Using the term 'execute,' 'just do it,' or perhaps even 'finish what you started' would be more fitting.

It is unfortunate that the US military was obviously trying to create a snappy acronym (F3EA) and they could not conger up another more fitting word that starts with 'F' for this step.

Seriously, the 'Finish' step is the third step of a five-step process, one can hardly say that they are finished.

Finish

The F3EA definition for the 'Finish' step is network oriented; it uses stilted language to say 'use whatever and whoever needed to execute the planned targeting solution on the threat network to achieve the desired result.' The exact language is as follows:

Table 3.2 Targeting Process Steps (Excerpt)

Generic Model	Business	Military/IC	Law Enforcement
Implement	Position	Finish	Apprehend

Finish: Unilateral, bilateral, coalition, and indigenous lethal and nonlethal actions to disrupt and defeat the threat network and <u>strengthen the friendly network</u>.

That said, this definition highlights one aspect often overlooked or just assumed in the generic, business, and law enforcement versions. That overlooked aspect is <u>underlined</u> above. Whenever possible, efficient and effective targeting should positively assist friendly efforts, not just adversely affect enemy efforts.

The excerpt from Table 3.2 presents the 'Finish' step aligned with comparable steps in the generic model and other sectors. Only the F3EA and the law enforcement models consider the concept of 'strengthening of friendly networks.' (*Note: the law enforcement model has yet to be discussed in detail.*)

The fact that F3EA and law enforcement models include this aspect may be attributed to the gravity of this step. When lethal/nonlethal effects are implemented as part of this targeting step, the targeting actions taken, whether a drone strike or fugitive apprehension, may have life or death consequences for the military operators (or police) who implement them.

The business marketing model, by implication, is oriented toward strengthening the product's market position. That is not to say that possible 'negative effects' of product placement are not considered part of the business targeting model. However, little thought is often given to possible adverse effects or unforeseen ramifications of one's marketing/business actions. Citing a classic example of where possible adverse secondary effects were ignored is the long-standing competition between Coca-Cola and Pepsi.

In 1886, John S. Pemberton developed the original recipe for Coke, and 13 years later, Pepsi was created by a pharmacist, Caleb Bradham. This hard-fought soft drink market competition rages on to this day, but did you know that Pepsi went bankrupt twice, once in 1923 and again just before World War II, in 1938? Because of Pepsi's stumbling early business decisions and the depression, Coke had an opportunity three times to buy Pepsi out and remove the competition forever.[6] Coca-Cola's management declined both times to buy Pepsi out, thinking that Pepsi would go away on their own and they would not have to spend anything. History has vividly proven that was a mistake. This example demonstrates that not all business targeting/marketing actions deal strictly with 'advertising' or 'placement/position' of product/service ads in magazines or other media. As explained in the 'dumping scenario' of the Targeting Concept section, business targeting deals with targeting competitors.

Exploit

The exploitation phase of the F3EA model is defined as the 'execution of a combination of sensitive-site exploitation, battlefield exploitation, technical exploitation, and document exploitation of the network (threat/friendly).' The products from these exploitations feed the analytical/intelligence process to determine if the target must be targeted again (because the target was missed) or target others (based upon clues yielded from the exploited site/materials).

Again, the military's F3EA definition is accurate but lacking. There is so much more to this phase. The conventional military breaks the 'exploit' step down into a detailed six-step target assessment phase. The targeting assessment phase is common to both deliberate and dynamic targeting

---

6   *Basic Books, For God, Country and Coca-Cola, Mark Pendergrast, 2000.*

of the joint targeting process and thoroughly examines the target engagement results. Effective post-targeting assessments require detailed, continuous inputs from the earlier phases of the joint targeting process to include:

- End states, objectives, tasks, effects, measures of effectiveness (MOEs),[7] and measures of performance (MOPs).[8]
- Target materials to include characteristics, critical elements, and functional linkages.
- Target vulnerability, weaponeering solutions, and collateral damage estimates.
- Tasking orders, weapon/delivery platform, and delivery tactics.
- Intelligence collection supports the commander's critical information requirements, mission details, and mission reporting.

The outputs are BDA, munitions effectiveness assessment (MEA), collateral damage assessment (CDA), and reattack recommendations.[9]

Analyze

The 'analyze' step of the F3EA process involves a methodical and detailed assessment of post-operation or post-activity intelligence, expansion of the common operational picture, development of future operations and activities, determination of impacts on the network or threat, and examination and evaluation of information on the network or threat.

> **TIPS:**
>
> The military/IC targeting process varies based upon operations tempo (optempo). It has to be scalable from low-level low-intensity insurgent/terrorist optempos to the target-rich high OPTEMPO of theater-level war engagements. At all optempo levels, a decision process is used to determine which 'high payoff' targets are prioritized to the top of the target list. The target list yielded from the decision process occurs before the F3EA process begins and is adjusted and repeated as targets are serviced, and operations levels change.

The remainder of this chapter (and another book) could be dedicated to the 'analyze phase' and not scratch the subject's surface. It all depends upon what can be collected in the time allowed and the collection mechanisms available. Often after a drone strike, smoke obscures the target area, persistent ground or possible surface-to-air threats are present, and fuel considerations are all factors that combine to limit target assessment to a short window. Sending-in ground collection elements may be deemed too 'high risk,' leaving only a short window to loiter and collect some video to assess target effects. Whereas on other occasions, there may be more opportunities to conduct target site exploitation and collect materials for the 'analyze' step. For example, the documents (470,000), hard drives, cell phones, and other materials collected during the Bin Laden raid of May 2, 2011, took years to analyze appropriately.[10]

Therefore, the law enforcement targeting model (Figure 3.8) is a hybrid based on the US military police doctrine and federal, state, and municipal law enforcement literature research. As cited earlier, the law enforcement targeting process consists of the following steps: *Identify, Pursuit, Apprehend, Exploit/Investigate*, and *Analyze*.

---

7 Department of Defense (DoD), Joint Publication 5-0, *Joint Planning*.
8 Department of Defense (DoD), Joint Publication 5-0, *Joint Planning*.
9 Department of Defense (DoD), Joint Publication 3-60, *Joint Targeting*.
10 www.cia.gov/news-information/press-releases-statements/2017-press-releases-statements/cia-releases-additional-files-recovered-in-ubl-compound-raid.html

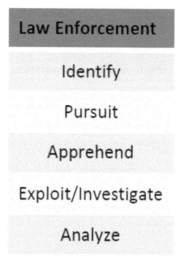

Figure 3.8   Law Enforcement Targeting Model.

LAW ENFORCEMENT TARGETING

Although criminal investigative analysis has become a more comprehensive investigative tool, no collective or agreed-upon definition describing this process exists, either in law enforcement or in academic literature.[11]

The law enforcement targeting process usually uses synonymous terms such as 'manhunt' or 'fugitive pursuit.' Still, the targeting process's process and intent essentially mirror the military/IC model, except the target effects are usually all nonlethal, such as to either gather enough evidence/information to meet the standard (or criteria needed) to warrant further investigation or apprehension arrest of a suspect (or target).

Similar to the F3EA targeting process, law enforcement targeting involves selecting and prioritizing targets (specifically criminals and criminal organizations) and matching the appropriate response to them, considering operational requirements and capabilities.

There is no consensus for how law enforcement prioritizes crimes and criminals because politics, public outcry, as well as law enforcement budget considerations often influence decisions regarding what crimes are prosecuted and in what priority. Also, that mixture of eclectic drivers is different at the federal, state, and local levels. To better illustrate the diverse influences that drive law enforcement priorities, observe the results of a recent CATO Institute public opinion survey. Only 19% of participants consider traffic law enforcement a top priority (see Figure 3.9).[12]

However, without question, small town or a big city, as a public revenue generator, traffic tickets are a local treasury's *bread and butter*. The recent introduction of traffic cameras has only made politicians greedier. Since FY 2007, the District of Columbia has issued 5.4 million speed camera tickets. From that single revenue stream derived more than a half-billion dollars, $535,712,457, including for the first time nearly $100 million in 2017 in speed camera revenue.[13] However, according to the DC.gov, Metropolitan Police Department's webpage of statistics, in 2018, there were 160 murders; the District's homicide stats ranked it 19th in the nation for metropolitan areas[14] (see Figure 3.10).

---

11 US Department of Justice, J. Amber Scherer, M.A., and John P. Jarvis, Ph.D., *Criminal Investigative Analysis (Practitioner Perspectives)*, 2014.

12 CATO Institute, *Americans Want Police to Prioritize Fighting Violent, Property Crime, but Few Prioritize Drug War*, 2017, www.cato.org/blog/americans-want-police-prioritize-fighting-violent-property-crime-few-prioritize-drug-war

13 AAA Mid-Atlantic, *District Issues Nearly 1 M Speed Camera Tickets*, 2017, https://midatlantic.aaa.com/public-affairs/press-release/?Id=f5ac8905-43f9-4374-9203-e2eb92e8504c#

14 DC.Gov, *Metropolitan Police Department*, Statistics webpage, https://mpdc.dc.gov/page/homicide-closure-rates

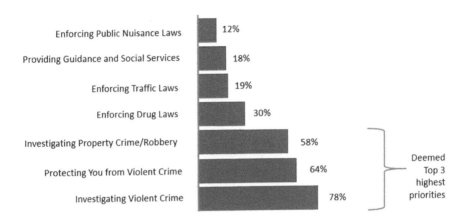

Figure 3.9   Top Three Priorities for Law Enforcement (Adapted from Cato Institute/YouGov 2016 Criminal Justice Survey).

District Crime Data			
Offense	2017	2018	Percent Change
Homicide	116	160	38%

Figure 3.10   Metropolitan Police Department's (MPD) Annual Report.

One can easily see that it only requires a simple order, suggestion, or word, from the top to the rank and file for traffic enforcement to be stepped up, and other law enforcement efforts shift to a lower priority. There is never a shortage of violations and violators. If there are complaints, politicians defend their actions by hiding behind the shielded position of '*it is being done to keep our streets safe for families and children.*'

Therefore, since no consensus exists on how civil law enforcement decides what crimes/criminals to investigate/prosecute for academic purposes and practical exercises, assume that you are in military law enforcement. Your supervision has made the hypothetical decision to prioritize the investigation and prosecution of violent crime. Therefore, as a military law enforcement targeter, please take the targeting step to *identify* a violent criminal or criminal organization.

The US military does have a well-defined doctrine for targeting crimes and criminals. Military police use what is referred to as the D3A methodology (Decide, Detect, Deliver, Assess). Military police, military command staff, and police intelligence provide inputs to targeting by:

- Deciding which targets to engage
- Detecting those targets
- Deliver (conduct the appropriate engagement operation)
- Assess the effects of the engagement.[15]

---

15 Army Doctrine Reference Publication, *Police Intelligence Operations*, Field Manual, FM 3-19.5, 2010.

Since crime analysts (civil or military) are most concerned with the second bullet of the D3A model, the text focuses the discussion on 'detecting targets.'

Detecting the Target

In modern times, the US, state, and local law enforcement organizations (LEOs) expend substantial effort, resources, and training to teach officers how to detect crimes. This training may include observing pickpockets and street drug dealers in their element or allowing more junior officers to ride along on actual surveillance operations (stakeouts) or arrests. In areas where law enforcement may have limited knowledge or skill sets, they may hire consultants (e.g., psychologists, auditors, cyber experts). Occasionally, they go so far as to 'hire the criminals' (e.g., white-collar criminals, con men, computer hackers.)[16,17] However, as helpful as this professional assistance and on-the-job training may be, unless law enforcement (or surveillance device) observes the criminal act and can apprehend and arrest the perpetrator(s) on the spot (or use photographic identification means), the identity of the criminal remains unknown. Not knowing the criminal's identity is where the real investigative work begins.

Identifying the Target

Some initial analysis (or investigation) is performed to identify the target(s). There may be iterations of this analysis exercised throughout the targeting process to confirm that the target being pursued is the correct one. The investigation may start with a witness statement, security camera photo, or an artist's rendering of the suspect. Once a suspect is apprehended, this preliminary identification is validated by multiple means.

Author's Note: To better illustrate the need to determine the target's true identity, let us look at the notorious Al Qaeda terrorist, Abu Musab al-Zarqawi.

In early 2006, I was a military intelligence officer stationed in Iraq. While following Zarqawi's terrorist propaganda efforts, I found over 25 aliases that Zarqawi had used over the years. I was quite pleased with my efforts and the extensive network analysis chart I had developed for him. However, my deployment ended, and I rotated back to the US, and some months later, Zarqawi was killed in a well-planned bombing strike.

Caption: **Abu Musab al-Zarqari (True name: Ahmad Fadeel al-Nazal al-Khalayleh).**

---

16 PC Magazine, *7 Hackers Who Got Legit Jobs from Their Exploits,* Sara Yin, June 28, 2011.
17 Broadway Paperbacks, *Catch Me If You Can,* Frank Abagnale, 2000.

Shortly afterward, I learned that the team targeting Zarqawi had uncovered over 100 aliases he had used.

By comparison, one could arguably say that I was only looking at 25% of the available informa-tion associated with this particular targeted individual. It was a humbling lesson that reinforced in me that the step of identifying the target never ends. To this day, convicted individuals are exonerated and set free due to misidentification.

Even in our modern high-tech computer age, often when an arrest is made at the scene of the crime, the suspect's true identity may not be known for several days, sometimes weeks. Fingerprints must be run through multiple databases inside and outside the state; outstanding warrants must be searched for and located. These processes, despite many being partially automated, take time.

Criminals who understand the wheels of justice can turn slowly are sometimes willing to take advantage. Repeat offenders may have outstanding warrants and criminal records in other states and jurisdictions. Taking advantage of this scattered records situation, repeat offenders realize that their chances of getting released by posting bail or other means would be adversely affected if they are held long enough to be correctly identified.

Career felons (and occasionally underage drinkers who just are not thinking) may be willing to risk getting caught and providing false identification to arresting officers. It gets much notoriety when someone is falsely accused because of misidentification. Matters are made worse when the innocent misidentified individual is convicted and serves time in prison. Books and movies have been written about the subject. Still, the other, and somewhat uncomfortable, aspect of misidentification is when real criminals are mistakenly released from custody. A clerk misspells a name, a criminal records check is run incorrectly, or not at all. It is not difficult to find examples of misidentified criminals.[18] However, when real criminals are mistakenly released from custody, they may again prey upon society.

The ability to get a 'true name' early on in the investigation/analysis process is key to effective targeting. With a valid name, law enforcement can find out where an individual resides, who family members are, discover friends, associates, possible accomplices, and can gain access to criminal records as well as to public records.

TIPS/NOTES:

'Possessing a positive ID for a suspect' cannot be stressed enough! In addition to all the individual-specific public records that become available, having a suspect's true identity allows investigators to follow a 'money trail.' Credit cards, money transfers, and old bank accounts can now be flagged and placed under surveillance. Fugitives invariably circle back and make a withdrawal from a bank account thought to be dormant or abandoned if they think no one is watching or if they find themselves willing to take the risk out of desperation for funds.

The identity of the target allows a myriad of search paths. This section provides a methodology for hunting an individual. The human-targeting methodology is based upon multiple sources and some years of practical experience.

Use of Biometrics in Identifying the Target

Recent developments in biometric technology (e.g., DNA, trace evidence), the introduction of formalized evidence collection and examination at incident/crime scenes, exploitation of unlawful use of social networks, tracking of cell phones, and the sharing of collected evidentiary material

---

18 Twin Cities Pioneer Press, *Sioux Falls Prisoner Accidentally Released Turns Himself In*, www.twincities.com, July 27, 2018.

Figure 3.11   FBI Wanted Poster/Mug Shot (Courtesy of www.FBI.gov).

and criminal information databases in other policed municipalities across and outside the US have greatly improved the effectiveness of law enforcement targeting efforts.

One of the higher-profile examples of this improvement is the Golden State Killer, Joseph James DeAngelo. DeAngelo killed 12 people and raped 45 women in California for ten years from 1976 to 1986 (see Figure 3.11). DeAngelo avoided suspicion for years and undoubtedly used his training, professional skills, and knowledge to avoid capture. DeAngelo was employed as a police officer from 1971 to 1979.[19] His law enforcement career ended with an arrest and conviction for shoplifting. He was linked to at least 45 rapes, and in 1979, DeAngelo attempted his first murder.[20] He would go on to commit 12 murders over the next decade.[21] The Golden State Killer case was cold and had been cold for decades when DeAngelo was identified, arrested, and convicted based upon DNA evidence matched against a relative found in a DNA database. DNA linked him to eight of the murders.

Pursuit

The pursuit generally begins after there is at least a partial identification of the target/suspect (e.g., photo, name(s), physical description, and so on); basically, the description should be definitive enough to allow pursuers to know that the suspect has been located with enough confidence that searches/pursuits of other leads are no longer required.

The pursuit is a situational exercise of resources and constraints: for the pursuit forces and the pursued.

Pursuit Forces

The resources brought to bear in the pursuit of a suspect may include all types of cutting-edge electronic surveillance and potentially unlimited numbers of law enforcement personnel. Simultaneously, these same pursuit forces may also be constrained by jurisdictional and legal limitations, asset availability, cost restrictions, bureaucratic strings, cultural barriers, rough terrain, even the weather may play a detrimental role in restraining the pursuit effort.

Pursued

Besides whatever personal advantages a fugitive may have (e.g., false identification papers, on hand funds, an escape vehicle, and other factors, and so on), the pursued may also be aided by their ability to blend into the terrain of a country providing safe haven by using a shared culture, ethnicity, local friends, family, and ideological support networks. These same support networks may be lost if they have to be abandoned traveling from one point to another. The following is one such example.

---

19 *Visalia Times-Delta, May 11, 1976, Anti-Burglary Funds Okayed, www.reddit.com.*

20 *Goleta Valley News, Sheriff's Blotter Section, October 10, 1979. Archived (PDF) from the Original on January 6, 2018.* Retrieved from archives, University of California, Santa Barbara, Santa Barbara, CA, 2018.

21 *Cold Case Killer, Help Us Catch the East Area Rapist, June 15, 2016, www.fbi.gov/news/stories/help-us-catch-the-east-area-rapist*

EXAMPLE

Suspect: *Eric Rudolph was wanted for detonating bombs in multiple states (see Figure 3.12).*

FBI TEN MOST WANTED FUGITIVE

MALICIOUSLY DAMAGED, BY MEANS OF AN EXPLOSIVE DEVICE, BUILDINGS AND PROPERTY AFFECTING INTERSTATE COMMERCE WHICH RESULTED IN DEATH AND INJURY

ERIC ROBERT RUDOLPH

Captured **Captured** **Captured**

Date of photograph unknown Date of photograph unknown Date of Sketch July 1998

Aliases: Bob Randolph, Robert Randolph, Bob Rudolph, Eric Rudolph and Eric R. Rudolph

Figure 3.12 FBI Wanted Poster for Eric Robert Rudolph.

Scenario: *These attacks included a crowded Centennial Olympic Park, a gay bar, an abortion clinic in Atlanta, Georgia, and an abortion clinic in Birmingham, Alabama. These attacks killed two and injured over a hundred people. The pursuit lasted from 1996 to 2003.*

According to Rudolph's personal accounts, he was at home in the wilderness. He had survival skills, which he used during his years as a fugitive by using empty cabins and camping in the Pisgah National Forest near Transylvania County, North Carolina. He foraged through the wild mountain terrain, gathering nuts and lizards, stealing vegetables from backyard gardens and grain from storage silos. He raided restaurant and grocery store dumpsters nearby when other food sources were inadequate. Leaving his safe haven (the backcountry of the National Forrest) and entering the town left him exposed.

On May 31, 2003, police officer J.S. Postell arrested Eric Rudolph while he was rummaging through a trash bin behind a rural grocery store in Murphy, North Carolina.[22]

Apprehend

Many would consider a suspects' apprehension by law enforcement to be generally straightforward, following standardized operational procedures that involve minimal analytics, and they would be correct,…*most of the time.* The suspect (target) is alleged to have committed a crime; they are identified, pursued, and apprehended. The variance to this given scenario is highlighted by the decision

---

22 Federal Bureau of Investigation, *Famous Cases -Eric Rudolph*, website: www.fbi.gov/history/famous-cases/eric-rudolph

of 'who' is selected for apprehension. An example of when apprehension is not as straightforward is when law enforcement chooses not to arrest a confidential informant (CI). If the CI were to be arrested and taken out of their criminal environment, it is apparent that they could no longer provide information. Therefore, another criminal is selected, preferably one whose removal from the organization leaves an opening that may potentially provide a path for the CI to move further up the criminal organization ladder.

Author's Note: As mentioned earlier in the F3EA military targeting process, 'actions to disrupt and defeat the threat network and strengthens the friendly network.'

The example chosen to describe selecting who is selected for apprehension does precisely that. Not arresting the CI allows them to continue reporting on the criminal organization. Arresting another, more valuable to the organization, is more detrimental to the threat network, while it strengthens the friendly network.

al-Zarqawi was killed in a well-planned bombing strike. Shortly afterward, I learned that the team targeting al-Zarqawi had uncovered over 100 aliases he had used.

By comparison, one could arguably say that I was only looking at 25% of the available information associated with this particular targeted individual. It was a humbling lesson that reinforced in me that the step of identifying the target never ends. To this day, convicted criminals are exonerated and set free due to misidentification.

Another example would be that law enforcement cannot hope to apprehend and prosecute every criminal with limited policing resources. Therefore, they preferentially select the ones that can do the most harm to society (e.g., organized crime figures, violent offenders, and others).

Exploit/Investigate

After an apprehension, the target/suspect is detained and interrogated. The suspect's collected biometrics (e.g., mug shot, fingerprints, DNA) and all of their pocket litter and belongings are cataloged into evidence. Law enforcement also exploits (searches) the suspect and scene for clues or items which may be introduced as evidence in prosecuting the alleged crimes.

TIPS:

The scene that is exploited for evidence may be a vehicle, perhaps a residence, or some other location identified after the suspect is taken into detention.

Analyze

Everything collected and all information gathered to this point (provided it is considered admissible in court) is analyzed and used to prosecute the suspect. The analysis is used to prosecute the apprehended suspect and any other suspects that may already be detained or still be at large.

The analysis may be repeated based upon the prosecuting authority demands, evidence inadmissibility, or further analysis may be performed due to possibly exculpatory evidence provided by the suspect's defense counsel. For instance, should a piece of evidence be thrown out of the court proceedings, other evidence may be introduced and analyzed to obtain a successful conviction.

CHAPTER SUMMARY

This chapter described business, military, the intelligence community (IC), and law enforcement value-effective targeting skills, and all use a derivation of 'target-focused analysis.' The text identified, described, compared, and contrasted target-focused analytical processes in each of these professional sectors that use target-focused analysis.

TARGETING CONCEPT

The concept of targeting is often misunderstood. The word 'target' usually congers visuals of multiple concentric circles forming the backdrop for the crosshairs of a riflescope reticle or, for spy novel fans, perhaps just a silhouette of a man in those crosshairs. However, targeting is a far more sophisticated concept.

Targeting Effects

One conducts targeting operations for many reasons, which may change with time and circumstances. These circumstances and varying parameters drive what is called 'target effects.' The military definition of 'target effects' is the cumulative results of actions taken to attack targets and systems by lethal and nonlethal means. These effects can be primary (effects that are the direct result of targeting actions) or secondary (effects that are indirectly the result of targeting). 'Nonlethal means' is insufficient terminology to describe a comprehensive and far-reaching task.

Lethal versus Nonlethal

Targeting actions can be extremely varied yet still fit under the category of 'less than lethal.' For example, most casually infer that international commodity trading is about making money. So, when a country sells a product (e.g., steel) far below the market value in another country, the purpose is objectively not to 'make money,' at least not in the short term or immediate time frame. In this case, the goal is more long term. The purpose is usually to take market share from existing competitors. This trade tactic is called 'dumping.' In this instance, a competitor sees an opportunity to 'target' a competitor's customers by dumping his product on that foreign market.

A target-focused intelligence analysis methodology attempts to align, or focus, all aspects of the intelligence process (e.g., Plan, Collect, Process, Analyze, Disseminate) toward one objective and, by doing so, optimize the entire process.

TARGETING (*GENERIC MODEL*)

In everyday terminology, targeting is a process of identifying an entity, group, or portion thereof, as possessing some aspect which has greater perceived value than other entities (groups, or portions thereof), locating it/them, directing predefined effort toward it/them, observing the effects, and analyzing the observed effects.

BUSINESS TARGETING (*MARKETING*)

In business targeting (or marketing), the *implementation* step of the generic model differs significantly from other sector targeting processes in that marketers are striving to entice potential customers to purchase a product or service as opposed to harassing, detaining, disrupting, destroying, neutralizing, apprehending, or any of the other more common targeting effects. Thus, the implementation step in marketing plans (also known as positioning/placement) tends to be far subtler, more nuanced, and often requires significant support research.

The business version of target-focused analysis is more commonly referred to as 'marketing analysis.' This type of target-focused analysis is often referred to as the 'segmented' approach or the 'STP' marketing process. It is a three-step approach where 'S' stands for segmenting, 'T' for targeting, and the 'P' for positioning. This process allows a business owner or advertisers/marketing professional to develop a marketing (*targeting*) strategy that ties company, brand, and product benefits to specific customer market segments. Postmarketing 'customer surveys' and 'analysis' of those surveys are implied steps and generally are not called out as part of the STP process.

Segmentation Step

The segmentation step involves finding out what kinds of customers might desire a product or service (or some specific aspect of a product or service). In military, IC, and law enforcement targeting, typically, but not always, the 'target' characteristics are predetermined or known (e.g., enemy concentrations, terrorists, criminals, and so on). However, the 'target' (segment) characteristics in marketing are undetermined.

Targeting Step

In the next step, the decision to target one or more segments is made. The choice of segment(s) should be based upon multiple factors (e.g., cost, customer needs/desires, logistical considerations, and so on).

Usually, the first consideration is how well other suppliers serve existing segments? This step determines the targeting environment. If existing providers serve all segments well, it is more challenging to draw them toward a different or unknown product or service.

Positioning Step

Positioning (also referred to as *placement*) involves implementing what was determined during the targeting step. This step, works out how to best compete in the selected market segments. The marketing analyst identifies how to position their products/services. As it is likely that there are already competitive offerings in the market, the firm needs to work out how to win market share from established players. As mentioned previously, this process tends to be far subtler, more nuanced. Typically, this is achieved by being perceived by consumers as different, unique, superior, or providing greater value.

Customer Survey (*Feedback*)

The customer survey step is where marketers observe and collect the feedback from their marketing efforts. The customer survey should fully evaluate and capture the effects/desired outcomes of the targeting effort. The survey can be administered online, by telephone, fax, or in person.

Analyze

This is the most critical aspect of any marketing/targeting exercise. In this step, one determines what was achieved. *Does the targeted segment appreciate your product or service? Is it valued enough to purchase again or recommend to another? Did the customer feel that they paid too much?* The answer to these and many other typical survey questions should be present in the analysis results and presented easily understood.

MILITARY/IC TARGETING

The concept of analysis in support of targeting (or target analysis) has been around in military circles for many years, and the IC also uses it extensively. There is little difference between the military and IC models in many cases. The most significant difference is that the military has a broader range of target-focused analytical processes.

Principles of Targeting

The US military adheres to a targeting doctrine based upon four principles throughout the targeting cycle. These principles create desired target effects while diminishing undesired second-order and collateral effects. These principles are focused, effects based, interdisciplinary, and systematic.

Focused

Focused targeting efficiently achieves the objectives through target engagement within operational planning parameters, the operational limitations within the plans and orders, the rules of engagement (ROE), the law of war, and agreements concerning the sovereignty of national territories. Every target nominated should contribute to attaining those set objectives.

Effects Based

Effects-based targeting is concerned with how targeting contributes to achieving the commander's objectives and creating specific desired effects through target engagement. Target analysis considers all possible means to create desired effects, drawing from all available capabilities. The art of targeting seeks to create desired effects with the least risk and least expenditure of time and resources.

Interdisciplinary

Joint targeting is a command function that requires the participation of many disciplines. It entails participation from all elements of the commander's staff, component commanders' staffs, other agencies, departments, organizations, and multinational partners.

Systematic

The joint targeting cycle is designed to create effects systematically. It is a rational and iterative process that methodically analyzes, prioritizes, and assigns assets against targets systematically. Targets should be reconsidered for re-targeting if the desired effects are not created.[23]

Intelligence Cycle

In conventional military terms, the analysis process (a *subset of the Intelligence Cycle*) generally contains the tasks of identifying, locating, and planning the desired target effects (e.g., harass, disrupt, destroy) of target engagements of large military targets (e.g., railroads, industrial complexes, military troop assembly areas, and so on), then performing an after-action assessment, often referred to as the battle damage assessment (BDA). Based upon the BDA, a determination is made to increase the effect, repeat, decrease, or desist. Traditional military target analysis is still prevalent today. Even though the IC may occasionally utilize a drone strike to neutralize high-value targets (HVTs), they generally perform more focused targeting of key groups, networks, and individuals (instead of larger strategic/tactical targets). In recent years, this HVT-focused type analysis has truly come into its own.

F3EA

Special Operations integrates and leverages 'analyze' and 'exploit' aspects into their operations process through an operational methodology. The F3EA process is inherent in executing of all special operations (see Figure 2[24]). A general description of F3EA steps includes:

- **Find** – Identifies and locates all aspects of networks (threat/friendly) bu synchronizing all intelligence disciplines, analyst-driven operations, and surveillance.
- **Fix** – Determination of precise location and tracking entities of the network or threat and limiting its options.
- **Finish** – Unilateral, bilateral, coalition, and indigenous lethal and nonlethal actions to disrupt and defeat the threat network and strengthen the friendly network.
- **Exploit** – Execution of a combination of sensitive-site exploitation, battlefield exploitation, technical exploitation, and document exploitation of the network (threat/friendly).

---

23 Department of Defense (DoD), Joint Publication 3-60, *Joint Targeting.*
24 Army Doctrine Reference Publication, 3-05, *Special Operations.*

- **Analyze** – Methodical and detailed assessment of post-operation or post-activity intelligence, expansion of the common operational picture, development of future operations and activities, determination of impacts on the network or threat, and examination and evaluation of information of the network or threat.[25]

Even though the F3EA style of targeting appears oriented to the 'kill people' and 'break things' mentality, which without question is the mainstay of military operations, this is not always the case.

Find

The 'Find' step varies across the analytical spectrum (e.g., HUMINT, SIGINT, IMINT, and so on). For HUMINTers (human intelligence analysts), it may involve the HUMINT 'screening process.' Like all intelligence operations, human source screening operations are focused on specific 'higher value' targets. This definition of human sources includes local indigenous populations, refugees, travelers in the area, and detainees (including enemy prisoners of war or EPWs). Like the earlier business marketing 'segmentation' step, only certain ones are likely to meet the desired targeting characteristics (e.g., possess the desired information).

For SIGINTers (signal intelligence analysts), if they have one (or more) signal selector(s) to search for (e.g., a cell phone number) and the appropriate system to search with, the 'Find' step is greatly simplified by shrinking the search area to a tiny perimeter. That is, provided the target is still using the identified selector.

Fix

The F3EA targeting process explains fixing the target as 'determination of precise location and tracking entities of the network or threat and limiting its options.'[26] This explanation is accurate and, at the same time, inadequate. Determining the precise location of a terrorist HVT involves multiple factors that deter the 'fix' aspect of the F3EA process.

Finish

The F3EA definition for the 'Finish' step is network oriented. It uses stilted language to say, 'use whatever and whoever needed to execute the planned targeting solution on the threat network to achieve the desired result.'

Whenever possible, efficient and effective targeting should positively assist friendly efforts, not just adversely affect enemy efforts.

Exploit

The exploitation phase of the F3EA model is defined as the 'execution of a combination of sensitive-site exploitation, battlefield exploitation, technical exploitation, and document exploitation of the network (threat/friendly).' The products from these exploitations feed the analytical/intelligence process to determine if the target must be targeted again (because the target was missed) or target others (based upon clues yielded from the exploited site/materials).

Again, the military's F3EA definition is accurate but lacking. The conventional military goes through a detailed six-step target assessment phase. The targeting assessment phase is common to both deliberate and dynamic targeting of the joint targeting process and examines the post-target engagement results.

The outputs are battle damage assessment (BDA), munitions effectiveness assessment (MEA), collateral damage assessment (CDA), and reattack recommendations.[27]

---

25 Army Doctrine Reference Publication, 3-05, *Special Operations*.
26 Army Doctrine Reference Publication, Field Manual, FM 3-05, *Special Operations*.
27 Department of Defense (DoD), Joint Publication 3-60, *Joint Targeting*.

Analyze

The 'analyze' step of the F3EA process involves a methodical and detailed assessment of post-operation or post-activity intelligence, expansion of the common operational picture, development of future operations and activities, determination of impacts on the network or threat, and examination and evaluation of information on the network or threat.

LAW ENFORCEMENT TARGETING

Although criminal investigative analysis has become a more comprehensive investigative tool, no collective or agreed-upon definition describing this process exists, either in law enforcement or academic literature.[28]

Therefore, the law enforcement targeting model is a hybrid based upon the US military police doctrine, federal, state, and municipal law enforcement literature research. As cited earlier, the law enforcement targeting process consists of the following steps: identify, pursuit, apprehend, exploit/investigate, and analyze.

The law enforcement targeting process usually uses synonymous terms such as 'manhunt' or 'fugitive pursuit.' Still, the targeting process's method and intent essentially mirror the military/IC model, except the target effects are usually all nonlethal in an effort to either gather enough evidence/information to meet the standard/criteria to warrant further investigation apprehension and arrest of a suspect/target.

Similar to the F3EA targeting process, law enforcement targeting involves selecting and prioritizing targets (specifically criminals and criminal organizations) and matching the appropriate response to them, considering operational requirements and capabilities.

There is no consensus for how law enforcement prioritizes crimes and criminals because politics, public outcry, as well as law enforcement budget considerations often influence decisions regarding what crimes to be prosecuted and in what priority and that mixture of eclectic drivers are different at the federal, state, and local levels.

The US military does have a well-defined doctrine for targeting crimes and criminals. Military police use what is referred to as the D3A methodology (Decide, Detect, Deliver, Assess). Military police, military command staff, and police intelligence provide inputs to targeting by:

- Deciding which targets to engage;
- Detecting those targets;
- Deliver (conduct the appropriate engagement operation);
- Assess the effects of the engagement.[29]

Since crime analysts (civil or military) are most concerned with the second bullet of the D3A model.

Detecting the Target

In modern times, the US, state, and local law enforcement organizations (LEOs) expend substantial effort, resources, and training to teach officers how to detect crimes. This training may include observing pickpockets and street drug dealers in their element or allowing more junior officers to ride along on actual surveillance operations (stakeouts) or arrests. In areas where law enforcement may have limited knowledge or skill sets, they may hire consultants (e.g., psychologists, auditors, cyber experts). Occasionally, they go so far as to 'hire the criminals' (e.g., white-collar criminals,

---

28 US Department of Justice, J. Amber Scherer, M.A., and John P. Jarvis, Ph.D., *Criminal Investigative Analysis (Practitioner Perspectives)*, 2014.

29 Army Doctrine Reference Publication, *Police Intelligence Operations*, Field Manual, FM 3-19.5, 2010.

con men, computer hackers.)[3031] However, as helpful as this professional assistance and on-the-job training may be, unless law enforcement (or surveillance device) observes the criminal act and can apprehend and arrest the perpetrator(s) on the spot (or use photographic identification means), the identity of the criminal remains unknown. Not knowing the criminal's identity where the real investigative work begins.

Identifying the Target

Some initial analysis (or investigation) is performed to identify the target(s). There may be iterations of this analysis exercised throughout the targeting process to confirm that the target being pursued is the correct one. The investigation may start with a witness statement, security camera photo, or an artist's rendering of the suspect. Once a suspect is apprehended, this preliminary identification is validated by multiple means. Even in our modern high-tech computer age, often when an arrest is made at the scene of the crime, the suspect's true identity may not be known for several days, sometimes weeks.

Career felons (and occasionally underage drinkers who just are not thinking) may be willing to risk getting caught and providing false identification to arresting officers. However, when real criminals are mistakenly released from custody, they may again prey upon society.

The ability to get a 'true name' early on in the investigation/analysis process is key to effective targeting. With a valid name, law enforcement can find out where an individual resides, who family members are, discover friends, associates, possible accomplices, and can gain access to criminal records as well as to public records.

The identity of the target allows a myriad of search paths. This section provides a methodology for hunting an individual. The human-targeting methodology is based upon multiple sources and some years of practical experience.

Use of Biometrics in Identifying the Target

Recent developments in biometric technology (e.g., DNA, trace evidence), the introduction of formalized evidence collection and examination at incident/crime scenes, exploitation of unlawful use of social networks, tracking of cell phones, and the sharing of collected evidentiary material and criminal information databases in other policed municipalities across and outside the US have improved the effectiveness of law enforcement targeting efforts.

Pursuit

The pursuit generally begins after there is at least a partial identification of the target/suspect (e.g., photo, name(s), physical description, and so on); basically, the description should be definitive enough to allow pursuers to know that the suspect has been located with enough confidence that searches/pursuits of other leads are no longer required.

The pursuit is a situational exercise of resources and constraints; for the pursuit forces and the pursued.

Pursuit Forces

The resources brought to bear in the pursuit of a suspect may include all types of cutting-edge electronic surveillance and potentially unlimited numbers of law enforcement personnel. Simultaneously, these same pursuit forces may also be constrained by jurisdictional and legal limitations, asset availability, cost restrictions, bureaucratic strings, cultural barriers, rough terrain, even the weather may play a detrimental role in restraining the pursuit effort.

---

30 PC Magazine, *7 Hackers Who Got Legit Jobs from Their Exploits,* Sara Yin, June 28, 2011.
31 Broadway Paperbacks, *Catch Me If You Can,* Frank Abagnale, 2000.

Pursued

Besides whatever personal advantages a fugitive may have (e.g., false identification papers, on hand funds, an escape vehicle, and so on), the pursued may be aided by their ability to blend into the terrain of a country providing safe haven by using a shared culture, ethnicity, local friends, family, and ideological support networks. These same support networks may be lost if they have to be abandoned traveling from one point to another.

Apprehend

Many would consider suspects' apprehension by law enforcement to be generally straightforward, following standardized operational procedures that involve minimal analytics, and they would be correct,…most of the time. The suspect (target) is alleged to have committed a crime; they are identified, pursued, and apprehended. The variance to this given scenario is highlighted by the decision of 'who' is selected for apprehension.

Exploit/Investigate

After an apprehension, the target/suspect is detained and interrogated. The suspect's collected biometrics (e.g., mug shot, fingerprints, DNA) and all of their pocket litter and belongings are cataloged into evidence. Law enforcement also exploits (searches) the suspect and scene for clues or items which may be introduced as evidence in court for prosecuting the alleged crimes.

Analyze

Everything collected and all information gathered to this point (provided it is considered admissible in court) is analyzed and used to prosecute the suspect. The analysis is used to prosecute the apprehended suspect and any other suspects that may already be detained or still at large.

The analysis may be repeated based upon the prosecuting authority demands, evidence inadmissibility, or further analysis may be performed due to possibly exculpatory evidence provided by the suspect's defense counsel. For instance, should a piece of evidence be thrown out of the court proceedings, other evidence may be introduced and analyzed to obtain a successful conviction.

PRACTICAL EXERCISE – PARTICIPANT'S GUIDE

TARGETING SCENARIO

Task: Given a specific target, collection of open-source and various other intelligence reports, as well as probative questions, develop leads in pursuit of a fugitive.

(NOTE: This targeting scenario is fictitious, developed for training purposes only. Some data are taken from open sources and blended with fiction to provide some level of realism; any correlation to factual information, names, and locations are coincidental.)

BACKGROUND INFORMATION

Open-Source News Article: *On the Trail of the Black Scorpion,*

The Arrest of Abu the Assassin, By Pat McGlynn *(Metropolitan Gazette, June 15th)*

One afternoon last December, an assassin on board an Air Arabia flight from Kuwait City arrived at Amsterdam's Schiphol Airport. The assassin's arrival was for tourism and pleasure, not business. The killer, aged 33, liked to travel and often documented his journeys around Europe on Instagram. He wore designer clothes and, on his right hand, a gold ring in the shape of a scimitar and a scorpion embossed upon it. His left hand was missing a pinky and an adjacent finger. The consequence of a faulty blasting cap. His passport was false, but it was a high-quality fake, one that only someone with deep resources could procure. The passport had been used successfully in the past, but not this time. Dutch customs recognized the name and directed him to a secondary holding area where he was arrested. The US State Department had filed a Red Notice with Interpol (an international arrest warrant) and knew that he was coming. Only after the Dutch authorities had the man in custody did they learn his real identity: Umar Mohammed al Din al Haditha (aka Abu Hassan, aka the Assassin, aka Abu the Assassin), terrorist, sniper, bomber, and killer at large for the terror organization Black Scorpion.

Helmand Province

Abu the Assassin was wanted on three continents; he was a shared asset between subcontinent drug lords and terror organizations. The arrangement is a byproduct of lethal resources comingling, resulting from the deadly nexus of criminal cartels and terror groups becoming ever more common these days.

Abu was currently working for Muhammed Umar Al Duranni Ali Khan, a notorious Afghan drug lord linked to terrorism, and runs a multimillion heroin operation based in Helmand province, Afghanistan. In a country where only a quarter of the population is literate in any language, symbols are important. Khan is known as the *Black Scorpion*. The black scorpion is also a logo stamped on each brick of red-tar opium or processed heroin produced by his drug organization. In Helmand province, the Black Scorpion is synonymous with drugs, violence, influence, and power.

In southern provinces of Afghanistan, the followers and foot soldiers of the Black Scorpion are known in Pashtu as (هر خای) or 'head khtah' (*Translation:* 'Everywhere'). Some of the Black Scorpion's minions can be identified by an irregular scorpion tattoo on an exposed part of their body; others may wear a piece of jewelry exhibiting the likeness of a scorpion. Whether they openly display the logo or not, enough of the population is affiliated with the organization to personify the name. Those who are not part of the group fear it.

There are no known authenticated photos of the Black Scorpion. Reports describe Khan as being in his late50s, graying hair with a full-graying beard and dark weathered skin. He is known to wear a traditional Pashtu dress, the perahan tunban, also known as a salwar kameez. The perahan tunban is an ensemble of a loose-fitting and lightweight, long shirt and oversized pants. Khan usually wears a pakol or turban, the traditional Afghan flat hat.

Artist's Rendition
(Based Upon Reports)

Obsessively secretive, Khan runs his multibillion-dollar drug enterprise from a remote compound hidden in Helmand, a remote southwestern province where he was born. The Black Scorpion exports industrial volumes of red-tar opium and heroin to Europe, Asia, and Africa; it is thought to be responsible for half the illegal narcotics that cross the border every year. The US Treasury Department has characterized Khan as 'one of the world's most powerful drug traffickers.' After Osama bin Laden's killing some years ago, he has become perhaps the most wanted fugitive on the planet. Afghan politicians promise to bring him to justice, and the US has offered a ten-million-dollar reward for information leading to his capture. But part of Khan's fame stems from the perception that he is uncatchable. He continues to thrive, consolidating the control of crucial smuggling routes and extending his operation into new markets in Europe, Asia, Africa, and Australia. According to one study, the Black Scorpion organization is active in more than 40 countries.

Purportedly, Khan was raised by his father as a subsistence farmer in the Now Zad district, Helmand Province. In the early 1960s, and out of respect for his father, he is rumored to regularly maintain a small vegetable garden wherever he stays for any period of time. However, he has lived and fought all over Afghanistan throughout the years. First in the Soviet-Afghan War in the 1980s as part of the mujahideen, then with the Taliban against Ahmad Shah Massoud, 'the Lion of Panjshir,' of the Northern Alliance. Unlike most of his peers, Khan learned to read; this made him stand out and advance. Khan became more powerful and influential under Taliban rule, moving back to Helmand, turning away from being a warlord and becoming a drug lord and regional tyrant. When NATO came to Afghanistan, Khan saw the Coalition Forces as too big of an enemy to face on the battlefield. Thereby, *'discretion became the better part of valor,'* and he quietly moved up into the 'Kush' (Hindu Kush Mountains). In the Kush, Khan is rumored to be invisible and all-powerful. It is said that Khan has multiple wives of various ages, but only a handful, which probably means five, or less. The Black Scorpion is said to have a second in command and heir apparent. However, little is known about Khan's adult son, other than he does not live with Khan in the Kush because he prefers a more western lifestyle.

Khan continues to quietly rule the northern districts of Helmand, despite the previously independent Afghan government, and now the Taliban, growing and processing opium, collecting taxes as a Taliban shadow governor, and for most of a generation existing as the undisputed ruler of northern Helmand.

NATO drew down its forces during the Obama and Trump administrations. Simultaneously, the Taliban became more aggressive in the southern regions of Afghanistan. With continued weakness emanating from the Afghan central government in Kabul and the new US administration showing minimal interest in moving significant troops back into Afghanistan, Helmand Province and likely all of southern Afghanistan reverted to complete Taliban control. In that power vacuum, the Black Scorpion and his drug/terror organization thrive and will likely become a significant threat to the region and perhaps the world.

Note: The targeting scenario is fictitious, developed for training purposes only.

OPEN-SOURCE UN REPORT

International Security Assistance Force (ISAF) Helmand Opium Report for 2019, Executive Summary (Excerpts)

Helmand Province is believed to be one of the world's largest opium-producing regions, responsible for around 42% of its total production. The Kajaki district produces more than any other district in Helmand Province….

Afghan government-led eradication remains negligible and getting worse; in 2018, only 406 hectares of opium poppy were eradicated in the whole, out of a total of 263,000 hectares in four provinces, compared to 750 hectares in 14 provinces, in 2017…

In Helmand, farmers *viewed this campaign differently and saw it as further evidence of a govern-*ment *campaign of violence against them. They did not recognize the claims of 'a narco-insurgency' or the suggestion that the drugs business is somehow part of an insurgency's objectives, as suggested by US special operations commanders….*

Conclusion

Although the area under cultivation decreased and Afghanistan produced less opium, the 2018 levels only decreased slightly from 2017 scores, the highest since 1994. The drought severely affected production and yields in the north and west. In the country's opium production power-house, Helmand, lower prices last year appear to have reduced the incentive for some farmers to sow poppy this year. As to counter-narcotics strategies, those by the government were only symbolic. , According to Mansfield, the US-led counter-narcotics air campaign has not dented production but has 'stirred up a hornet's nest. 'Farmers were quick to blame the lab strikes' for the decrease in prices, he said. In reality, there were other factors at work dampening demand and prices; he said, 'Continued high levels of production and the devaluation of the [Iranian] *toman* only leads to a lot of market uncertainty and a hesitancy amongst cross-border traders.'

The most worrying outcome of this year's decrease in opium prices for the rest of the world is that it may trigger a decrease in heroin prices on the world's illegal markets. An abundance of high-quality, low-cost heroin only results in cheap heroin on the streets and more people using the drug globally.

Note: The targeting scenario is fictitious, developed for training purposes only.

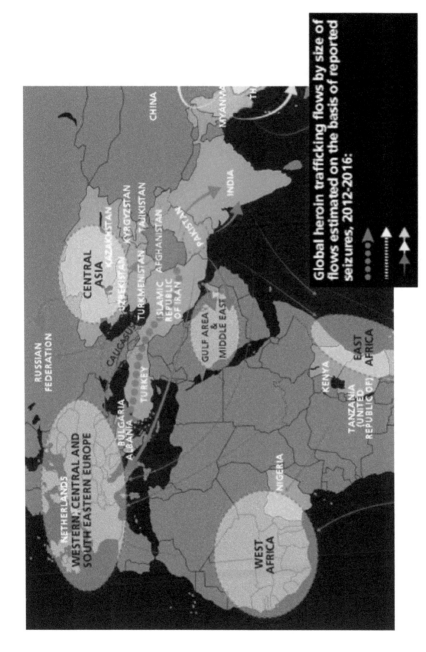

Main Heroin Trafficking Flows: 2016-2018

Interpol Intelligence/Interrogation Report Excerpt:

Name: Umar Mohammed al Din al Haditha *(Subject)*

Aliases: Abu Hassan, the Assassin, Abu the Assassin

Circumstances of Detention:

Detainee Number: #325822

Date: 11 December

Personal Belongings/Pocket Litter Recovered:

- *Found on Person:*
  - Rolex Watch, gold
  - Ring, signet, gold, scorpion, and scimitar embossed
  - Shoes, black, leather, Gucci
  - Belt, black, leather, Gucci
  - Cufflinks, gold, Gucci
  - Suit, tailored, black, Armani
  - Shirt, fitted, white, Eton
  - Socks, black, off-brand
- *Pocket Litter:*
  - Cell phone (Smartphone) w/ charger
  - Cash: €550 Euro, $2000 USD, ؋5050 Afs
- *Small Checked Bag:*
  - Russian-made, Makarov, 9x18mm semiautomatic pistol, Serial # ТД 3224 (*Note: disassembled and scattered to avoid detection, no ammunition found*)
  - Alarm Clock
  - 2 cell phones (*new and unused*)
  - 4 pair socks
  - 4 pair underwear
  - 2 new shirts (*still in packaging*)
  - 2 new ties (*still in packaging*)
  - Shaving Kit (*assorted personal hygiene items*)

Physical Data: (In English Standard Units)

   Height: 5'–9"

   Weight: 170 lbs

   Eyes: Brown

   Hair: Brown

   Skin: Olive/Tanned

   Scars/Marks/Tattoos: Black Scorpion tattoo on the upper chest

Debriefing Notes: Officer Dimitri Ustinov performed the interrogation in Russian and Pashtu. Assisted by Officer Serena Pashwri.

- *Question:* About the firearm in his luggage. *Subject:* Said it was not his bag. (*Field Comment: Subject was lying, fingerprints on contents matched his. Baggage claim ticket belonged to Subject.*)
- *Question:* About his purpose for travel. *Subject:* Had no answer.
- *Question:* About his association with the Black Scorpion. *Subject:* Threatened officers with violence, threatened Interpol, threatened officers' families.
- *Question:* About his future travel plans and informed that he would not be able to hide from Interpol and international partners in the War on Terror. *Subject:* We are easy to find, for we are 'head khtah' (translation: everywhere).
- *Question:* Again, about his purpose for travel. *Subject:* Had no answer….

(*Field Comment: After ½ hr, Subject stopped responding, and debriefing ended.*)

Subject's Demeanor: Argumentative, threatening, uncooperative.

Note: The targeting scenario is fictitious, developed for training purposes only.

Interpol Intelligence Report Excerpt:

Phone Owner (Name): Umar Mohammed al Din al Haditha *(Subject)*

Detainee Number: #325822

Date: 17 December

Cell Phone Exploitation Data: Make/Model: Chinese Knockoff/Clone of a Samsung Galaxy S8 Smartphone

*IMSI:*460001367924683 (Subscriber # traced to China)

IMEI: 358654630766659 (Equipment ID # traced to a stolen phone)

Phone #: +93 +70 455-6789 (Afghanistan Cell phone #)

Numbers found in Contacts on the phone:

- Afghan Mobile Phone #s: (70) 455–1234, (70) 455–1335, (70) 455–2238 and (70) 455–4577
- Pakistan Mobile Phone #: +92 (30) 671-3594 *(Comment: registered to a Karachi import/export company, Saladin LTD., owned by Ali Khan Mohammad al Washir)*

Four photos were recovered from the device's erased memory:

1. Unknown, late middle-aged male (50s), dark full beard, wearing traditional Pashtu attire, sitting, talking on a cell phone (comment: likely right-handed)
2. Unknown, middle-aged male (40s), standing against an urban backdrop, wearing a dark western cut lightweight suit, dark mustache, talking on a cell phone (comment: likely right-handed)
3. Unknown, middle-aged male (30s), dark full beard, wearing traditional Pashtu attire, sitting, talking on a cell phone, watch on the right hand (comment: likely left-handed)

4. Mid-day photo of a village, at the base of a barren mountain, with an arid plain below containing dry scrub trees in the foreground beyond the village. *(Analyst Comment: Computer analysis of the photo indicates the picture is of a northern section of Musa Qal'ah village, Musa Qal'ah District, Helmand Province, Afghanistan, with the Hindu Kush mountains as the backdrop, to the north.)* The depicted village is a collection of concrete block buildings and Conex containers, some with tarps over them to provide shade/shelter.

Note: The targeting scenario is fictitious, developed for training purposes only.

Interpol Intelligence/Ballistics Report Excerpt:

1. Makarov, 9 × 18 mm semiautomatic pistol, Serial # ТД 3224, matched a pistol reported stolen from an Afghan National Police (ANP) armory in Musa Qal'ah on February 2014.

2. Since 2014, the ballistics signature has been matched to six homicides. In four countries, two were in Afghanistan (May 2, 2015), one in Pakistan (June 7, 2015), one in Germany (April 9, 2016), two in France (February 22, 2017).

3. 9 × 18 mm shell casings found at each crime scene were traced to local suppliers.

Note: The targeting scenario is fictitious, developed for training purposes only.

Targeting Planning

(NOTE: This targeting scenario is fictitious, developed for training purposes only. Some data are taken from open sources and blended with fiction in order to provide some level of realism; any correlation to factual information, names, and locations is coincidental.)

Task: Using the information and handouts provided, following any specific (or combination) of the targeting models discussed in class, develop a targeting plan, citing potential leads to locate the target. Be prepared to compare and discuss your plans with the class.

Given a specific target, collection of open-source and various other intelligence reports (as background information), as well as probative questions to aid in your analysis.

Standard: (1) Develop workable leads (at least 4) in order to pursue the fugitive. (2) Provide/describe recommendations for how best to pursue each developed lead. (3) Briefly describe the process used to develop the lead.

Note: The purpose of pursuit is to apprehend the target in order to stand trial in an international court for multiple crimes, from human/drug trafficking to terrorism. Therefore, the targeting effects specified are 'nonlethal.' However, lethal force is authorized if fired upon or life is threatened.

Suspect/Target Name: Muhammed Umar Al Duranni Ali Khan (aka Hajji Muhammed, aka the Black Scorpion)

Question 1: Describe all the associations/relationships the target has (e.g., familial, tribal, business, and so on)?

- *For each association identified, specify the date and place the association began.*
- *Specify if associations intersect/overlap (e.g., business associate and tribal member or both attend the same house of worship and served time in prison together)*

Associations:

- *Prison*

- *Business/Crime*

- *Family*

- *Religion*

- *Ethnic/Tribal/Cultural/Language*

- *Political*

- *Education*

- *Military Service*

- *Personal Interest*

- *Areas/Regions Target Lived and Traveled*

Identify the Target's Regional Safe Areas Zones:

Identify the Target's Support Resources:

Identify the Target's Support Network:

Target Limitations/Constraints:

Targeting Plan

1. **Lead:**

   How might this lead potentially be exploited/pursued?

2. **Lead:**

   How might this lead potentially be exploited/pursued?

3. **Lead:**

   How might this lead potentially be exploited/pursued?

4. **Lead:**

   How might this lead potentially be exploited/pursued?

5. **Lead:**

   How might this lead potentially be exploited/pursued?

6. **Lead:**

   How might this lead potentially be exploited/pursued?

CHAPTER 4

Alternatives Analysis

INTRODUCTION

Alternatives analysis is a diagnostic technique that uses a rigorous analysis of alternatives to explain events or data sets, select the best option, anticipate potential outcomes, or predict future trends. To accomplish the task correctly, alternatives analysis requires multiple inputs. Therefore, one must first generate those inputs using some other process (e.g., brainstorming, star-bursting, and so on) if the inputs are not already available. This chapter describes the alternatives analysis's concept explains situations where it is most useful, some of the advantages and pitfalls, and potential roadblocks to practical usage.

In a continually changing, ever more complex world, trying to stay ahead of one's adversary (or business competitor) becomes increasingly difficult. Because enemies do not always come from the direction or in the form that one expects, or attacks using weapons and tactics that defense forces have trained and prepared for, analysts must always be able to provide policymakers and military leaders the intelligence needed to avoid 'surprise.' Many believe that avoiding tactical (or strategic) surprise has evolved into an insurmountable task. There are no guarantees which eliminate surprise. Yet, analytical processes aid in foreseeing and measuring the threat and providing critical forewarning. Therefore, to comprehend complex, multifaceted international threats (e.g., narco-terrorism, civil insurgencies, state-sponsored terror groups, national adversaries, hybrid threats, and so on), analysts require a more methodical, thorough, and structured approach.

Alternatives analysis (also known in the business world as *Analysis of Alternatives or 'AoA'*) is not just a tool of the intelligence community (IC). It can also be employed to evaluate multiple vendors' contracting proposals. Application of the AoA process is considered an integral part of good project management. The US government, and in most cases state governments, require a rigorous AoA to be performed and reviewed to award contracts above a specified value. Both the business and IC versions of alternatives analysis share the common goal of reaching the best (and preferably) correct answer/outcome. The business process varies from its intelligence counterparts only in the nature and number of steps. However, alternatives analysis is not always appropriate because it takes more time and resources than traditional methods.

PURPOSE OF ALTERNATIVES ANALYSIS

So, what is the purpose of an alternatives analysis exercise, and why is it valued? Let us start with purpose. The purpose is to identify a reasonable number of possible and plausible alternatives and evaluate each one methodically, thoughtfully, and objectively. If successful, the outcome

DOI: 10.4324/9781003241195-4

analytically assessed to be the most logical is, at the very least, the 'most appropriate,' and all being well, also the 'correct' result.

VALUE OF ALTERNATIVES ANALYSIS

Suppose traditional intelligence analysis produces predictions or explanations based on a rational assessment of available evidence. Following that train of thought, alternatives analysis strives to assist analysts and policymakers in critically evaluating assumptions and accepted perceptions by challenging these more familiar mindsets and expanding the range of possible outcomes considered. By its nature, an alternatives analysis is a more organized process than more traditional intelligence analysis approaches. It encourages thoughtful consideration of additional possibilities, variables, and previously unevaluated aspects that would generally result from analytical assessments based upon just the available and collected data. The desired outcome of alternatives analysis is that the analyst identifies, includes, and assesses the correct one by considering many alternatives.

Examples of Alternatives Analysis

Multiple Structured Analytic Techniques (SATs) are used to perform an alternatives analysis. The ones we cover in this section are:

- Anal of Competing Hypotheses (ACH)
- Evaluation of Indicators
- Alternate Futures Analysis (AFA)

ANALYSIS OF COMPETING HYPOTHESES (ACH)

The first example of alternatives analysis is ACH. ACH was introduced in Chapter 10, *Analytical Tradecraft*; the predecessor to this text, *Intelligence Analysis Fundamentals*. The ACH is an SAT that identifies, defines, and assesses alternative hypotheses by systematically listing them in a matrix and then evaluating all evidence associated, focusing on what rejects rather than confirms hypotheses.

When to Use

ACH has proven to be a highly effective method for ingesting and evaluating large amounts of data. Although a single analyst can use ACH, it is best performed with a small team of peers that can challenge each other's evaluation of the evidence. ACH is more useful when three or more possible answers are being evaluated. The collected evidence/data supports more than one hypothesis. Developing a matrix (or table) of hypotheses and loading collected information into the table can be achieved in a few days. If performing ACH for the first time, it is best to use an ACH experienced analyst as a facilitator to lead new analysts through this process. If the data must be reconstructed, the initial phases of the ACH process may require additional time.

ACH is particularly suitable for contentious issues when analysts want transparency and provide a record that demonstrates what theories they considered and how they arrived at their assessments. Developing the ACH matrix (table) allows others (e.g., analysts, intelligence end-users, and so on) to review their analysis and identify agreement and disagreement areas. Evidence can also be examined more systematically. Documenting the ACH process provides an excellent process for determining if deception and denial methods have been employed.[1]

---

1   US Government, Central Intelligence Agency (CIA), *A Tradecraft Primer: Structured Analytic Techniques for Improving Intelligence Analysis,* March 2009.

METHOD

ACH demands that analysts explicitly identify all the reasonable alternative hypotheses, then array the evidence against each hypothesis, rather than evaluate each hypothesis's plausibility one at a time. To be effective initially, the analyst must:

- Ensure equal treatment or weight when considering each hypothesis and evaluate all the information and argumentation.
- Deter the analyst from premature closure on a particular explanation or hypothesis.
- Protect the analyst against their innate tendencies (biases) to ignore or discount data that do not fit comfortably with the preferred answer. The following process should be followed to accomplish this task:
  1. Determine what is/are the essential question(s) needing to be answered.
  2. Brainstorm among analysts/peers with different perspectives to identify all possible hypotheses which answer the question(s).
  3. List all significant arguments and evidence pertinent to all the hypotheses.
  4. Prepare a matrix (or table) with hypotheses across the top and each piece of data/evidence to the side.*
  5. Each piece of evidence must be determined to be consistent, inconsistent, or not applicable to each hypothesis.
  6. Refine the matrix (table) and reconsider the hypotheses in some cases; analysts need to add new hypotheses and reexamine the evidence on hand.
  7. Focus on disproving hypotheses rather than proving one.
  8. Use a rating scheme to score the consistent and inconsistent evidence associated with each hypothesis to determine the strongest and weakest explanations.
  9. Determine the sensitivity of the ACH results by removing a few critical pieces of evidence; should those items be proven wrong, misleading, or subject to deception, how would it affect an assessment's authenticity?
  10. Question what evidence is not observed that is expected for a given hypothesis to be valid. Is there a possibility that denial and deception have been employed?
  11. Report all the determinations, including the conclusions associated with weaker hypotheses. All hypotheses should be monitored as new evidence develops.
  12. Determine the relative likelihood for each hypothesis and list all the assumptions and conclusions, including ones associated with the weaker hypotheses.
  13. Identify and monitor indicators that would be consistent o inconsistent with each hypothesis. Explore what could account for inconsistent data.

Note*: The 'diagnostic value' of the evidence emerges as analysts determine whether a piece of evidence is found to be consistent with only one hypothesis or could support more than one or indeed all hypotheses. In the latter case, the evidence is considered unimportant in determining which hypothesis is more likely to be correct.

EVALUATION OF INDICATORS

Rather than reviewing the available evidence, evaluating indicators in analytical terms is the process of creating a model that yields observables that can provide analysts a relatively objective method to validate or disprove a hypothesis, course of action (CoA), and/or/or specific data. For example, an analyst may use the indicator of 'rapidly rising river levels' as confirmation that an upstream dam had been compromised or broken (Figure 4.1). Granted, others may argue that *rapidly rising river levels* are not a very good indicator in that it does not provide much in the way of early warning. That said, it is an indicator. Few indicators stand alone, but the goal is to know the correct number of appropriate indicators that answer the key analytical questions, provide early warning, and confirm or refute hypotheses.

Figure 4.1   A Broken Dam as an Example.

Author's Note: Real-World Example of Evaluation of Indicators In WWII, allied strategic bombing raids had great difficulty finding their designated targets in Germany's heartland. However, after studying hundreds of targets, imagery analysts started developing target models and identifying specific questions or indicators to validate their targets and provide a mechanism for bomber crews to locate those targets.

At the time, there were modern highways in Europe, heavy equipment and material were moved by rail. Truck, tank, artillery, and other weapons-related war factories required these railways to bring raw materials and ship finished war materials out to the troops.

Using those same railways, imagery analysts would locate an easy-to-find major city or landmark near the designated target factory and follow the rails as they lead from the city to the factory.

Bomber crews only had to find the major city (a relatively simple task) then follow the train tracks (verifying type indicator) to their target (see accompanying figure).

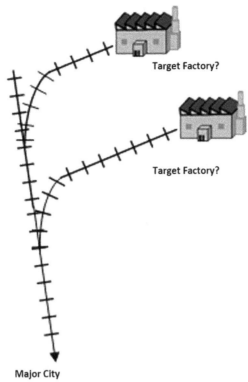

Target Factory?

Target Factory?

Major City

The track spurs generally led to a factory (of some type). The question now becomes, 'What factory?' Additional indicators must be identified to determine which is the 'target factory?'

When to Use ACH

When the analytical inputs are not available, an analysis of alternatives is needed. The need to per-form an ACH may happen when monitoring multiple enemy/adversary CoAs or just confirming a specific piece of data. It is particularly handy when looking for early warning indicators when the present environment is relatively static. The output of the process should be used to develop a collection plan.

An example of a *CoA* might be if an analyst were looking to corroborate the hypothesis/CoA that *the enemy was about to invade the country of Whatsistan,* they would determine *how things might appear when the situation is normal,* then <u>contrast</u> what might be observed *in a military buildup to invasion.* To further refine their model into multiple, they would break the indicators into more specific CoA, such as invasion by air, land, sea, or some combination, or invasion from the north, south, west.….

Another example of identifying indicators may well include confirming a *specific piece of data*, such as *proving a terror suspect resided at a particular location*. In this example, the analyst has an address but does not know if the terrorist is at the location. He could surveil the location and hopefully observe the target, use informants, or other more technical means. In Usama Bin Laden's case, US intelligence forces rented a home in Abbottabad, Pakistan, from which a team staked out and observed the compound over several months. The team also used informants and a fake polio vaccination program to collect DNA on local neighborhood residents to find Bin Laden's immediate family members.*

* Source: DIA Public Affairs, This Week in DIA History: DIA and the Abbottabad Raid, https://www. dia.mil/News-Features/Articles/Article-View/Article/1843144/this-week-in-dia-history-dia-and-the-abbottabad-raid, Retrieved May 16, 2022.

METHOD

Once an analyst has identified multiple alternative scenarios, the next step is to identify or develop indicators that would only present themselves should a particular scenario materialize.

- To the greatest extent, possible selected indicators need to confirm or deny each scenario.
- Indicators can overlap scenarios, but minimizing overlap aids in making the decision process more conclusive.
- Analysts need to assign numerical ratings representing the given *indicator's actual value*** for a specific scenario's assessment process to assess indicators properly.
- For each scenario, determine values that would represent a graduated probability scale (e.g., *Highly Unlikely, Unlikely, Neutral, Likely, and Highly Likely*)
- Ratings need to be tweaked also.

After an adequate number of indicators are identified/developed, array the indicators in a display that visually represents the data to be collected (e.g., chart, dynamic spreadsheet, or static matrix). The analyst(s) then need(s) to exercise the process by plugging in notional data sets and assessing and refining the results. Once satisfied with process outputs, a collection plan is developed and implemented to monitor each indicator (Tables 4.1 and 4.2 for example).

Note**: The 'indicator's actual value' varies from scenario to scenario.

Author's Note: Observe how to interpret the data displayed in the generic example above:

- *Indicators 'B,' 'C,' and 'D' do not apply to some scenarios.*
- *Even though Indicator 'A' affects all scenarios, the weighted values vary.*
- *Scenario #2 has the highest numerical value, but Scenario #4 is the 'Most Likely' since it's >7, the value which equates to the 'Highly Likely' assessment specific to that scenario.*
- *The 'Total' column in this example is a numerical sum. However, the calculation(s) selected to display real-world data should be appropriate to the given scenario (see Table 4.2).*

Table 4.1   Generic Example of an Evaluation of Indicators Matrix

	Indicator A	Indicator B	Indicator C	Indicator D	Total	Highly Unlikely	Highly Likely
Scenario 1	4	4	2	2	8	7	11
Scenario 2	5	N/A	4	N/A	9	9	12
Scenario 3	2	1	N/A	3	6	6	9
Scenario 4	3	2	1	2	8	2	7
Scenario 5	1	N/A	2	N/A	3	3	7

Table 4.2   More Specific Example of an Evaluation of Indicators Matrix

	Exhausts Observed from Stacks	Trains Bringing Supplies	Trains with Tanks Coming In	Trains with Tanks Going Out	Total	Highly Unlikely	Highly Likely
Generic operational military factory	2	3	N/A	N/A	5	7	11
Operational tank repair factory	5	3	4	3	15	9	12
Operational tank factory	2	3	N/A	0	5	6	9

Author's Note: In the 'More Specific Example' above, three different WWII German Military Factories are illustrated. The results of a tailored collection plan that uses on-the-ground observations and surveillance imagery have been entered into the chart. This process has allowed the identification of three distinct target types.

TIPS:

- *Indicators with the highest/lowest values are generally the most discriminating.*
- *This is a dynamic process; regularly appraise and adjust assigned ratings.*
- *Don't be afraid to discard indicators that are neutral or provide little value.*
- *The output of the process should be used to develop a collection plan.*

ALTERNATE FUTURES ANALYSIS (AFA)

Whereas the previous two alternatives analysis assessment techniques are more focused on the present or the near future, AFA is a set of techniques used to explore different, more futuristic states developed by varying a set of critical trends, indicators, drivers, and/or conditions. AFA systematically explores multiple ways a situation can develop when high complexity and uncertainty are present (Figure 4.2).

When to Use

AFA is most useful when a situation is viewed as too complicated or the outcomes as too uncertain about trusting a single outcome assessment. Examples include, but are not limited to when assessing the effectiveness of a proposed policy in different possible futures or perhaps predicting the potential effects of given fields of research.

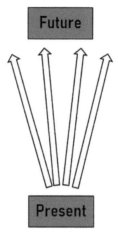

Figure 4.2   Alternate Futures Analysis.

METHOD

There are three general steps: identify the level of uncertainty, recognize the need to consider a broad range of aspects/factors, and explore potential future outcomes.

First, analysts must identify those aspects causing high uncertainty surrounding the matter in question.

Next, they must recognize that a need exists, which necessitates considering a broad range of aspects that might bear on the question.

Finally, methodically and systematically develop the potential future outcomes.* One common approach is as follows:

- Identify one 'central issue' by interviewing subject matter experts (SMEs) on the topic.
- Assemble the experts to brainstorm the possible forces and factors affecting the issue.
- Choose by consensus the two most critical and uncertain forces. Array the two identified 'forces' as perpendicular continuous vectors (axes) on a chart with the most appropriate endpoints labeled.
- The resulting quadrants provide the basis for characterizing the alternative futures. Indicators and milestones can then be developed.
- These indicators are arranged to represent the proper progression/regressions based upon changing variables. The final chart can be used to monitor for indications of the likelihood of a particular future.

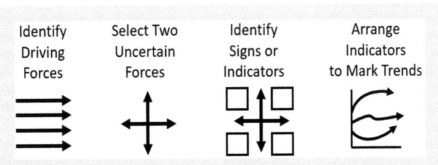

Note*: Analysts must be ready to explore a range of potential outcomes, and one must take caution; these outcomes should not be preconceived. If the results are predetermined, then analysts may short circuit the discovery process, and it all ends up being an exercise of finding support for one's analytical bias. Depending on how intricate the futures exercise is, the effort can represent a considerable time/money investment and analytic resource expenditure.

Simplified AFA Example

Figure 4.3 is a simplified AFA example. The topic is some foreign country conflict. The US military is involved on one side of the conflict, and a coalition of foreign military powers is on the other side. The two major uncertainties are 'will the US stay or go?' and 'will the foreign coalition stay or go?' Notional signs and indicators are arrayed in each of the four quadrants.

TIPS:

- AFA avoids the drawbacks of 'single point prediction.'
- Aids analyst to consider factors that would yield differing outcomes.
- Not an exact science; it should be weighed against other predictive analytical approaches.
- Use AFA to identify opportunities to drive policies that avoid potentially adverse outcomes.

Figure 4.3   A Simplified AFA Example.

Note: Another more detailed example of alternate futures analysis, authored by Brian Nichiporuk, can be found online at the Rand Corporation website. Refer to the footnote at the end of the page.[1]

1   Rand Corporation, *Alternative Futures and Army Force Planning, Implications for the Future Force Era,* Brian Nichiporuk, www.rand.org/pubs/monographs/MG219.html

CHAPTER SUMMARY

Alternatives analysis is a diagnostic technique that uses a rigorous analysis of alternatives, executed to explain events or data sets, select the best option, anticipate potential outcomes, or predict future trends. If multiple inputs are not already available, alternatives analysis requires that analysts first generate those inputs using another process (e.g., brainstorming, star-bursting, other methods, and so on). The text described the concept of alternatives analysis, and it also described the most useful applications and explained some advantages, pitfalls, and potential roadblocks to effective usage.

Alternatives analysis (also known in the business world as *Analysis of Alternatives or 'AoA'*) is not just a tool of the intelligence community (IC); it can also evaluate multiple vendors' contracting proposals. Application of the AoA process is considered an integral part of good project management.

PURPOSE OF ALTERNATIVES ANALYSIS

So, what is the purpose of an alternatives analysis exercise, and why is it valued? Let us start with the purpose. The purpose is to identify a reasonable number of possible and plausible alternatives and then methodically, thoughtfully, and objectively evaluate each one. If successful, the outcome analytically assessed to be the most logical is, at the very least, the 'most appropriate,' and all being well, also the 'correct' result.

VALUE OF ALTERNATIVES ANALYSIS

If traditional intelligence analysis produces predictions or explanations based on a rational assessment of available evidence, alternatives analysis strives to assist analysts and policymakers to critically evaluate assumptions and accepted perceptions by challenging these more familiar mindsets and thereby expanding the range of possible outcomes considered. By its nature, an alternatives analysis is a more organized process than more traditional intelligence analysis approaches. It encourages thoughtful consideration of additional possibilities, variables, and previously unevaluated aspects that would generally result from analytical assessments based upon just the available and collected data. The desired outcome is that the analyst identifies, includes, and assesses the correct alternative by considering many alternatives.

Examples of Alternatives Analysis

Multiple Structured Analytic Techniques (SATs) are used to perform alternatives analysis. The ones that were covered in this section are:

- Analysis of Competing Hypotheses (ACH)
- Evaluation of Indicators
- Alternate Futures Analysis (AFA)

ANALYSIS OF COMPETING HYPOTHESES (ACH)

The first example of alternatives analysis is ACH. ACH was introduced in Chapter 10, *Analytical Tradecraft,* from the book *Intelligence Analysis Fundamentals,* the predecessor to this text. The ACH is an SAT that identifies, defines, and assesses alternative hypotheses by systematically listing them in a matrix and then evaluating all evidence associated, focusing on what rejects rather than confirms hypotheses.

When to Use

ACH has proven to be a highly effective method for ingesting and evaluating large amounts of data. While an individual analyst can use ACH, it is best performed with a small team of peers that can challenge each other's evaluation of the evidence. ACH is more useful when three or more possible answers are being evaluated. The collected evidence/data supports more than one hypothesis. Developing a matrix (or table) of hypotheses and loading collected information into the table can be achieved in a few days. If performing ACH for the first time, it is best to use an ACH experienced analyst as a facilitator to lead new analysts through this process. If the data must be reconstructed, the initial phases of the ACH process may require additional time.

ACH is particularly suitable for contentious issues when analysts want transparency and provide a record that demonstrates what theories they considered and how they arrived at their assessments. Developing the ACH matrix (table) allows others (e.g., analysts, intelligence end-users, and so on) to review their analysis and identify agreement and disagreement areas. Evidence can also be examined more systematically. Documenting the ACH process provides an excellent process for determining if deception and denial methods have been employed.[2]

EVALUATION OF INDICATORS

Rather than reviewing the available evidence, evaluation of indicators in analytical terms is the process of creating a model that yields observables that can provide analysts a relatively objective method to validate or disprove a hypothesis, course of action (CoA), and/or specific data. For example, an analyst may use the indicator of 'rapidly rising river levels' as confirmation that an upstream dam had been compromised or broken. Other analysts might argue that *rapidly rising river levels* are not a good indicator in that it does not provide much early warning. That said, it 'IS' an indicator and should be considered. Few indicators stand alone, and the goal is to know the correct number of appropriate indicators that can answer the key analytical questions, provide early warning, and confirm or refute hypotheses.

When to Use ACH

When the analytical inputs are not available and alternatives analysis is needed. ACH is handy when looking for early warning indicators when the present environment is relatively static. The output of the process should be used to develop a collection plan.

ALTERNATE FUTURES ANALYSIS (AFA)

Whereas the previous two alternatives analysis assessment techniques are more focused on the present or the near future, AFA is a set of techniques used to explore different, more futuristic states developed by varying a set of critical trends, indicators, drivers, and/or conditions. AFA systematically explores multiple ways a situation can develop under highly complex and uncertain conditions.

When to Use AFA

AFA is most useful when a situation is viewed as too complicated or the outcomes as too uncertain about trusting a single outcome assessment. Examples include, but are not limited to when assessing the effectiveness of a proposed policy in different possible futures or predicting the potential effects of given research fields.

---

2   US Government, Central Intelligence Agency (CIA), *A Tradecraft Primer: Structured Analytic Techniques for Improving Intelligence Analysis,* March 2009.

PRACTICAL EXERCISE – PARTICIPANT GUIDE

CRIME ALTERNATIVES ANALYSIS SCENARIO

Note: Because crime analysis is typically not just performed by the military or IC members, this exercise is more directed at those aspiring to be crime analysts or criminologists.

TIPS/RULES/ASSUMPTIONS FOR THE PRACTICAL EXERCISE (PE):

Tips:

- ACH works best with three or more hypotheses but less than seven, so we need to reduce the number of alternatives to a reasonable value.
- As in real life, you have been provided a limited number of facts (evidence) for your teams to use.
- To assist in getting the critical answers, you should prioritize the most critical questions and answer them first.

Rules:

- There has been at least one crime committed (maybe more).
- The culprit can only be one (or more) of the five people listed above.
- There is adequate evidence presented to answer all the questions.

Assumptions:

- Somebody (or somebodies) is (are) guilty of something.
- Your team may not find all the answers, just as analysts (investigators) rarely do in the real world.

CRIME ACH SCENARIO

The instructor/facilitator provides a handout for this small group ACH exercise. The participants are broken into at least two (or more) groups of similar. However, the team size should be no larger than five so that everyone has a better opportunity to participate. Using the scenario provided, perform an Analysis of Competing Hypothesis (ACH). Take no more than one hour to conduct the ACH. Document your analysis using the matrix provided. Be prepared to present your assessment clearly and succinctly. Your team's assessment should include the following:

- What crime(s) was (were) committed (if any);
- Identify who is (are) the culprit(s) (if any);
- Based upon the evidence, explain logically how the victim was killed; pointing out:
  - Motive;
  - Means;
  - Opportunity; and
- Defend your team's analysis to the whole class.

Your team may use the internet, if it is available, to perform research.

Five hypotheses are provided, and they are as follows:

1. The butler did it, and the crime was _____

2. The wife did it, and the crime was _____

3. The victim's brother did it, and the crime was _____

4. The mistress did it, and the crime was _____

5. The victim did it, and the crime was _____

Notes/Hints: To limit the number of alternatives to a reasonable number. We have also provided a fixed number of suspects and prepared sets of facts for your teams to use. The culprit(s) can only be one (or more) of the five people listed above. Somebody (or somebodies) is (are) guilty. There also has been at least one crime committed (maybe more). There is an adequate amount of evidence presented to answer all the questions. Your team may not get all the answers, and analysts rarely do. However, it would be best to prioritize the most important questions and answer them first. Utilize the matrix below to better assist your team in analyzing the competing hypotheses.

TIPS/RULES/ASSUMPTIONS FOR THE PE:

Tips:

- ACH works best with three or more hypotheses but less than seven, so we need to reduce the number of alternatives to a reasonable value.
- As in real life, you have been provided a limited number of facts (evidence) for your teams to use.
- To help find critical answers, you should prioritize the most critical questions and answer them first.

Rules:

- There has been at least one crime committed (maybe more).
- The culprit can only be one (or more) of the five people listed above.
- There is adequate evidence presented to answer all the questions.

Assumptions:

- Somebody (or somebodies) is (are) guilty of something.
- Your team may not find all the answers, just as analysts (investigators) rarely do in the real world.

BLANK MATRIX

Evidence	Hypothesis #1 Victim Billionaire	Hypothesis #2 Suspect Mistress	Hypothesis #3 Suspect Spouse	Hypothesis #4 Suspect Butler	Hypothesis #5 Suspect Brother
Means					
Motive					
Opportunity					
Stab wounds in front/back with the right hand					
In the will					
Insurance policy					

Author's Note: Feel free to add to the matrix provided. The example provided is notional. You should use what works best for you and your group.

BACKGROUND

You are discovering everything as seen through the eyes of a grizzled metropolitan police homicide detective, and you just arrived in the middle of the night at the crime scene. But first, you must push your way past dozens of the news media, all scrambling to ask you questions. A few patrol officers hold the paparazzi at bay while you lift the yellow crime scene perimeter tape and walk up to and inside an unbelievably colossal mansion.

Inside the foyer, you ask the first patrol officer you approach, 'Who the hell lives here?' She responds: 'none other than the reclusive billionaire Steve Bobs!' She goes on to say, 'He is also the victim,' adding, 'he was found dead on the floor in the kitchen in a puddle of his own blood.' A CSI technician breaks into the conversation and introduces himself. Expounding on what was already shared, the tech explained: 'he was found lying face down by the butler with a knife sticking out of his back. Besides the butler, the only other people in the house at the time were the victim's brother and the victim's mistress.'

EVIDENCE

Suspect's Statements/Detective's Notes/Observations

The first interview was with the butler. He had found the body and made the 911 call. At the moment, he seemed to be the one with the most answers.

Face-to-Face Interview with the Butler: The butler reportedly was a loyal 15-year employee. I found him in his housecoat and pajamas, but neither the coat nor pajamas appeared wrinkled. He looked to be in his fifties but extremely fit. One might have thought he was once a bodybuilder. His combed hair and manicured beard were graying but well-kept. He was very calm when he explained that he found the body while going to the kitchen to get a midnight snack and immediately called the police. His calm, professional demeanor was odd for someone that had just found his employer's corpse in a puddle of blood. He matter-of-factly stated that he did not see anyone else in the kitchen with the body, nor did he see anyone enter or leave the house until the police arrived. He stated that Mr. Bobs' wife also lived there but was presently overseas vacationing in Europe. I asked if it were unusual for Bobs to have a live-in mistress while his wife was away. The butler explained he could not say and that it was not his place to speculate on that subject.

When asked if anyone hated Mr. Bobs enough to kill him, he denied that he knew of anyone, and he made a point of including himself in that group.

Detective's Note: Based upon later conversations with the spouse, brother, and others, when it came to employer-employee relations, the victim had always been somewhat patronizing in tone with his employees and staff. Yet lately, Bobs had become even more short-tempered, moody, and demanding, especially in the last few months. They also pointed out that Bobs had not given the butler a raise in years. Bottom-line, there was no love to be lost between Bobs and his servant. Even though they both agreed that the butler was poorly treated, the wife and brother believed he would never try to harm Bobs. The consensus of everyone interviewed was that the butler was always a consummate professional.

A quick background check on the butler revealed that he had previously been a sniper in the British army and had received an honorable separation from the service. According to his military jacket, he had survived three tours in Afghanistan (if being severely wounded twice is considered 'surviving') and had been highly decorated multiple times for his service. The file did not say how many 'kills' he had on his sniper's record; the number was classified and redacted.

Detective's Note: I surmised that there were likely to have been more than a few to earn the Victory Cross. At that point, the thought came to me that, from the butler's perspective, after going through that much combat had hardened him just a bit, and maybe finding a bloody corpse wasn't such a big deal after all.

The following logical interviews were with others who shared the residence: the mistress and the brother.

Face-to-Face Interview with the Victim's Brother: The victim's brother was dressed in his pajamas. His demeanor was slightly agitated. He claims he was upstairs and asleep and did not hear anything. Then he blurted out, 'Who could have done this?' Followed by 'do you think they are still in the house?' I placated him with, 'You are perfectly safe, Sir.' 'There have to be at least twenty police officers on the premises.' I then continued with my questions. When asked about his relationship with his brother, he said, 'we were once bitter rivals, but that was years ago.' He recounted how his brother took his girlfriend in college and married her. After saying that, he snickered and said, 'didn't his butler tell you about that little piece of history? I guess not. That guy is not very big on sharing gossip.'

When asked if anyone hated Mr. Bobs enough to kill him. He denied it by saying that he did not and pointed out he could not think of anyone who would. Then I asked if there was a will? He recounted that there was one and begrudgingly admitted that he and Bobs' wife also stood to gain handsomely if his brother were to pass away. At which time, he closed off the discussion by saying, 'if you have any other questions, you need to speak to my lawyer.'

Face-to-Face Interview with the Mistress: The mistress was young, beautiful, and completely blind. I was informed that her name was Shantal Monique Simpson. She said she was also upstairs in bed, and like the brother, claims she was asleep and did not hear anything. I asked if there might be a reason someone would want Bobs dead? She said 'no' while sobbing. I then asked if she might have a reason? At that point, she broke into tears and denied it, saying, 'no, I truly loved him.' The mistress was crying off and on for a bit and appeared to be visibly shaken. The butler physically supported her to keep her from collapsing to the floor. After a few minutes, she collected herself. She paused and sputtered. Finally getting it out, she said Bobs had once shared with her that she was not in the will, but she would be provided for in a separate life insurance policy, that is should something happen to him. She said she did not know the amount, only that she would 'be provided for.' Then she said, 'I guess that could be interpreted as a reason.' Then after a few more moments, she asked, 'have you spoken to his doctor?' I asked why I should. She said she could not explain, and Shantal only knew that when they first met, Bobs had been taking daily meds several months ago, and Shantal could not recall what for, but he had stopped, or at least she had not seen him take any for some time.

At which point, I decided she wasn't going to be of much more assistance tonight, and I would have to come back later if I had more questions. The next day, I confirmed with the ACME Insurance Company that she was the sole beneficiary of a multimillion-dollar life insurance policy Bobs had purchased roughly two months before his death. ACME asked how I knew about the policy and then explained that the Bobs obtained the policy, and he requested the existence of the policy be held with the utmost discretion.

Teleconference Interview with the Spouse: Although she was not present on the evening of Bobs' demise, she had a motive, and her alibi needed to be verified.

Detective's Note: Being out of the country did not eliminate the spouse as a suspect. She was rich, and she could have hired someone else to kill her husband. It would not be the first time a wife's paramour or paid assassin took out a rich husband, and I was just as confident that it would not be last if it turns out to be what happened in this case.

As the video teleconference started, I noticed that the victim's spouse, a middle-aged but gorgeous blonde, was sitting with her back to her hotel room window. Her room has a magnificent view of the Paris skyline with the Eiffel Tower in the background. I started asking a lot of the same questions I had asked the others. She said she knew about the mistress, which was the primary reason why she was on vacation. She explained that her husband and herself had an 'open' marriage. An open marriage was her way of saying that neither wanted a public fight in a divorce court. She acknowledged that the will's existence and that she, like her brother-in-law, stood to gain substantially. When asked if anyone hated Mr. Bobs enough to kill him. She also denied knowing anyone wanting Bobs dead and said she could not think of anyone who would. There was a pregnant pause, and then asked, 'Have you questioned his brother?' She stated the victim's brother is an irresponsible spendthrift playboy who could not be trusted with finances. He and her husband were once rivals, yet, despite any possible animosity between the victim and his brother, Mr. Bobs was the proverbial 'goose that laid the golden eggs.' She laughed as she said: 'With my dear husband confirmed dead, his brother has to start working for a living.' At that point, the screen got staticky and went suddenly went blank, and the interview ended. An IT technician explained that they had lost the signal.

At this point, it was late and time to get some sleep. Since the mistress suggested that Bobs may have been under a doctor's care for some reason and the brother came right out and directed my questions to his legal counsel, I planned on paying both a visit in the morning and possibly to tie up a few loose ends.

Face-to-Face Interview with the Lawyer: The brother's lawyer turned out to also be the victim's attorney. He was a short, balding man who had a craven appearance. The attorney stated that Mr. Bobs' last will and testament was 'iron-clad.' He went on to say that 'it is always possible that someone could contest it, but it was doubtful it could be overturned during the probate process.' The will clearly states that the wife and brother split the estate evenly, and no others stood to inherit anything. This fact annoyed the attorney since he also seemed to desire a piece of Mr. Bobs' fortune. His constant complaining during the interview reinforced this observation. To be safe, I asked him where he was last night, and he was quick to demonstrate that he had a solid alibi. He was the primary speaker at a political fundraiser in another state and just got back this morning. He volunteered that literally thousands of witnesses were present that could attest to his whereabouts to include the governor and corroborating video from the local evening news station.

Detective's Note: 'Do not like that guy.' Had the lawyer had means, motive, opportunity, or anything that pointed in his direction, I would have put him at the top of my list of suspects.

The lawyer said he personally knew everyone present at the mansion at the time of Bobs' death, and he did not believe that any of them, particularly the butler, wife, or brother (even though he felt they despised Mr. Bobs), would try to harm him. He said the brother and Bobs' spouse understood well enough that neither could run the company without Steve's 'genius' at the helm, and they were both quite happy to let him run it. At the same time, Bobs' was content to let them spend his money, provided they just left him alone.

Face-to-Face Interview with the Doctor: Mr. Bobs' doctor was an elderly and mild-mannered man. His office wall was decorated with awards and diplomas from several prominent universities. When asked, he stated that Mr. Bobs was generally in good health. He had excellent vision, hearing, and balance for a 62-year old male. However, he had suffered for years from major depressive disorder (MDD). Still, he was being treated for the condition with pharmaceuticals, specifically 2 milligrams of brexpiprazole daily. His MDD symptoms appeared to be under control based on the medical file and his clinical observations from Bobs's last examination. He said it was at least 3 months since the last office visit when asked how long it had been since he had examined Mr. Bobs. However, he had no reason to be concerned because Mr. Bobs' symptoms had been under control for over a year, and after his last appointment, he had provided him with a 90-day supply of his MDD meds.

CORONER'S REPORT

1. The coroner's report indicates multiple stab wounds to the front torso and one in the back. Details are as follows:

   - There were a total of four 3-inch deep puncture wounds to the front torso *(though painful, these were not likely to be immediately fatal)*; and

   - One 5-inch deep puncture wound in the back *(most likely the fatal wound)*.

   - The back-torso wound punctured the victim's right atrium and caused a one-inch opening in the heart, resulting in the victim quickly losing consciousness and bleeding out.

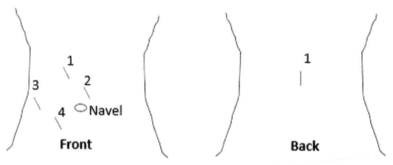

2. The frontal torso wounds all displayed roughly the same angle of attack and penetration depth, consistent with being from the same individual.

3. The murder weapon was determined to be the kitchen knife found protruding out of the single stab wound in the victim's back. There was a horizontal crack in the middle of the knife handle running across the width of the handle.

4. *Coroner's Observations:* The frontal stab wounds could have been performed by a left-handed assailant (approximately the same height as the victim) or conceivably self-inflicted by the victim's right hand. However, it is unlikely that the victim could have stabbed himself in the back because he could not have reached that far and achieved the angle of entry observed. *(Comment: It was impossible to determine the assailant's dominant hand for the single back-torso stab wound because the knife's protrusion angle from the victim's back was almost perpendicular in both vertical and horizontal planes.)*

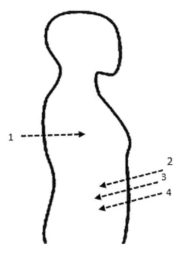

5. All stab wounds were consistent with what has been determined to be the murder weapon.

6. Toxicology scans found trace results for the antidepressant brexpiprazole. However, it appears that Mr. Bobs had not taken the drug in several days.

7. There were no defensive lacerations found on the victim's hands. *(Comment: Which implies the victim did not try to defend himself; reason unknown, either because he couldn't or wouldn't.)*

8. The time of death was no more than 30 minutes before the butler's 911 call.

CSI REPORT AND FIRST RESPONDERS REPORT

1. The body was lying face down with the murder weapon protruding from the back just a few steps inside the kitchen doorway. There were no tracks through the blood found other than the victim's.

2. There were no indications of a struggle, and nothing appeared to be stolen. The only thing that was noticed as out of place in the kitchen was the murder weapon.

Murder·Weapon

3. A small amount of blood was found on the inside door handles of the French doors which accessed the kitchen. The bloody fingerprints found on the door handles belonged to the victim.

4. The body was fully clothed when law enforcement arrived at the scene. The victim had his wallet on his person with $450 cash and several credit cards. Bobs wore an exclusive Brietling™ watch on his left arm and an expensive diamond-encrusted wedding ring. It did not appear as if any jewelry, credit cards, or money were missing.

5. It was observed that it was likely that the victim had not rolled in the puddle of blood and died where he fell. This observation was noted because clothing on the body's underside was soaked with blood, and there was a lack of blood on all other clothing areas where there were no stab wounds.

6. There were no indications that the body was relocated. The victim likely was stabbed, bled out, and died from his wounds in the kitchen.

7. Blood spatter analysis indicated that all stab wounds likely occurred in the kitchen inside the French doors' glass windowpanes. The glass doors would make it reasonable to assume that the victim would have seen his assailant before the attack. Further, he also likely knew the assailant and did not have reason to fear.

8. The murder weapon was a kitchen knife taken from the countertop stand of the victim's kitchen. The knife handle was damaged, and it had a horizontal straight-line indention or crease running around it about midway down the handle. As if something had clamped down on it. None of the other knives in the countertop stand displayed similar damage.

9. The fingerprints lifted off the murder weapon matched the butler, the victim's brother, and the victim (Mr. Bobs). No other fingerprints were found. *(Detective's Comment: It was not strange to find the butler's, victim's brother, and the victim's prints on the knife since they all lived in the same house and had legitimate reasons to handle the knife. It is also plausible that the assailant could have had gloves on. Prints were taken from the other knives in the countertop stand, and they also had similar but not identical results. Therefore, finding any of the suspect's fingerprints on the murder weapon has a neutral weight on the assessment of the available evidence.)*

Victim   Brother   Butler

10. All the fingerprints lifted from the crime scene belonged to someone who lived in the mansion.

11. The mansion had a security system that included perimeter alarms and exterior surveillance cameras. The system appeared to have been 'on' at the time of death and was in good working order. The butler only turned it off to allow the police and first responders into the premises. A review of security logs and camera footage did not show that there had been an intruder after the perimeter security had been turned on hours earlier at sunset. According to the butler, that was the usual procedure; alarm system 'on at sundown' and 'off at sunrise.' The security system logs corroborated his statement.

12. A perimeter sweep provided no indications of a break-in or attempted forced entry.

13. Forensics swipes of the mansion outside the kitchen did not find any of the victim's blood outside the immediate area around and near the body.

14. A search of the home discovered nothing out of the ordinary. A bottle of pills in Bobs' medicine cabinet was identified as a half-empty prescription for the antidepressant brexpiprazole; the dosage was 2 mg daily.

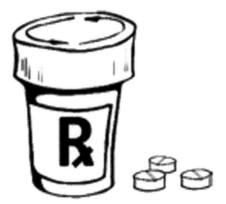

PRACTICAL EXERCISE RESULTS

Use this section to record your team's ACH results.

The culprit(s)

Explanation

Motive:

Means:

Opportunity:

Crime(s) Committed

Explanation

CHAPTER 5

Challenging Assumptions

INTRODUCTION

This chapter describes analytic techniques for challenging assumptions, including the key assumptions check (KAC) and linchpin analysis. The KAC is most effective when performed early in the analytical process. However, linchpin analysis is generally performed much later, often after the fact. It is a forensic exercise to determine what went wrong identify critical lessons to avoid future failures. This chapter explores the analytical methods used to perform the KAC and linchpin analysis, also covered are recent examples, advantages and disadvantages, and when to use each process.

LINCHPIN ANALYSIS

A dictionary-style definition would refer to a pin passed through the end of an axle to keep a wheel in position, or perhaps it would mention that a 'linchpin' is a person or thing vital to an enterprise. However, in the context of our lesson, linchpin analysis is a structured analytical technique (SAT) based upon known data or information (or data with at least a high probability of certainty), which anchors the analytical argument.

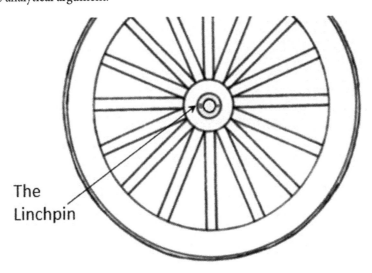

The Linchpin

DOI: 10.4324/9781003241195-5

Figure 5.1   Perceived Intelligence Failures.

Background

By the mid-1990s, America was being attacked at home, their interests were threatened overseas, and no one seemed to have the ability to see what was next coming consistently. This genuine need to discover why we missed it' gave birth to *linchpin analysis.*

As the 1980s passed and the 1990s began, intelligence analysts expressed a need for a more proactive approach that would question their assumptions, arguing that failures occur when faulty assumptions go unchallenged.[1]

Some of those failures include the:

- Beirut Marine Barracks, 1983
- USS Stark, 1987
- Iraq's Invasion of Kuwait, 1990
- 1st World Trade Center, 1993; and
- Oklahoma City, 1995 (see Figure 5.1).

Looking at one instance from the previous list, *Iraq's invasion of Kuwait*, we can more aptly see the need for a better method to challenge the basis for existing intelligence assumptions.

The failure to provide strategic warning during the months before Iraq invaded Kuwait generated recommendations for revamping the intelligence community (IC)'s warning analysis mechanisms. The consensus of the IC was that 'Iraq was unlikely to initiate warfare in the near term.' This flawed perception was widely held and rarely critically examined. Though flawed, it was issued repeatedly in the year before the assault on Kuwait. The assessment's underlying logical basis was the cited assumption that 'Iraq needed several years to recover from the military and economic devastation of its long war with Iran.'[2] However, that assumption was fundamentally flawed.

---

1   The Sherman Kent Center for Intelligence Analysis, *Occasional Papers: Volume 1, Number 1,* www.cia.gov/library/kent-center-occasional-papers/pdf/OPNo1.pdf

2   The Sherman Kent Center for Intelligence Analysis, *Occasional Papers: Volume 1, Number 1,* www.cia.gov/library/kent-center-occasional-papers/pdf/OPNo1.pdf

By the mid-1990s, America was being attacked at home, and their interests were threatened overseas, and no one seemed to see what was coming consistently. This requirement to discover 'why we missed it' gave birth to *linchpin analysis.*

How It Is Used

Linchpin analysis's basis sits upon using verified data or information (or data with a high probability of certainty). By starting from 'knowns' (and eliminating all impossibilities), the analyst has a powerful technique for showing intelligence consumers, peers, and higher-ups that a problem has both been thoroughly studied and constrained within the bounds of reality.

Linchpin analysis is a flexible, structured method intended to minimize mistakes and promote clarity even with complex issues containing multiple variables and uncertainty. The analyst's assumptions drive it, but these assumptions need to be as near to the facts as possible. That said, these assumptions are selected judiciously and are considered most likely to drive and determine the outcome. The predictions yielded from this logic exercise generally produce a higher degree of confidence.[3]

METHOD

Linchpin analysis starts by limiting the basis of the analysis by providing checkpoints. It then forces the development of the pre-drafted checkpoints (listed below) to produce the resulting product.

Pre-Drafted Checkpoints:

1. Identify the main indefinite factors or key variables judged likely to drive the issue's outcome, forcing systematic attention to the range of relationships among factors at play.
2. Determine the linchpin premises or analytic assumptions about the drivers. How you collect and assemble the findings and the logical reasoning used to defend the linchpins form the final assessment basis. This encourages testing key subordinate findings that hold the final analytical assessment together. The poor organization of the findings leaves the final assessment open to debate and error.
3. Explain the circumstances under which unanticipated developments could occur. Identify indicators or patterns of development that could emerge to signal that the linchpins were unreliable.
    a. List the causative factors or dramatic internal and external events that could reverse the expected trend.[4]
4. Now test your analysis results by plugging them back into your argument and determining if it indeed changes the outcome.

Author's Note: To better understand the linchpin analysis process, two graphic analogies are provided to assist in envisioning the 'linchpin' concept:

1. *Visualize 'linchpins' as the aspects upon which an argument balances. Other contributing factors weigh toward one outcome (or the other). In comparison, the 'linchpins' (drivers) have a far more significant effect by moving the argument's fulcrum decidedly toward one outcome.*

---

3   The Sherman Kent Center for Intelligence Analysis, *Occasional Papers: Volume 1, Number 1,* www.cia.gov/library/kent-center-occasional-papers/pdf/OPNo1.pdf

4   The Sherman Kent Center for Intelligence Analysis, *Occasional Papers: Volume 1, Number 1,* www.cia.gov/library/kent-center-occasional-papers/pdf/OPNo1.pdf

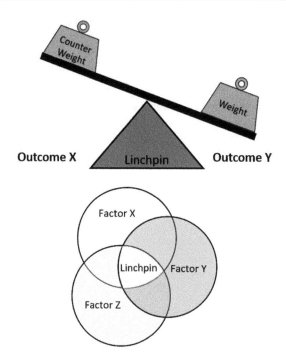

2. *Next, using a Venn diagram, look at all factors under consideration. The linchpin is the common area that interfaces with all (or most) other factors.*

SIMPLIFIED LINCHPIN EXAMPLE/DISCUSSION/ANALYSIS/ ASSESSMENT AND EXPLANATION

The following exercise is used to explain linchpin analysis. Using General George Custer's defeat at the Little Bighorn (see Figure 5.2), first list the main indefinite factors or key variables that contributed to the battle's outcome.

Contributing factors leading to Outcome Y (Custer's defeat at the Battle of the Little Bighorn)

A. *The enemy (Sioux) had overwhelming superior numbers.*

B. *Custer split his force in the face of a superior enemy and engaged.*

C. *The Sioux knew the lay of the land.*

D. *Custer had left the Gatling guns in the rear.*

E. *Custer had placed his supply train at a position where it could not have easily provided support.*

F. *Custer's hubris convinced him that he could overcome the Sioux on the battlefield, no matter the odds.*

Figure 5.2   Custer's Photograph Courtesy of the Library of Congress.

Author's Note: There are multiple other contributing factors (e.g., fighting experience of the various elements, numbers, types of firearms, and so on) that may have contributed to the outcome that was not listed for expediency reasons.

Also, it is worth noting that due to revisionist history and the deft lobbying skills of his wife, Elizabeth (Libbie) Custer, Custer's defeat was mislabeled as an intelligence failure for decades. Most historians did not challenge the assessment because, after all, what commander, in their right mind, would purposely engage a force four to five times superior in size to their own?

Discussion/Analysis: (Now determine the linchpin premises or analytic assumptions about the drivers.)

The major contributing factors to Custer's defeat are listed above (A through F). Review each one to determine which were the real 'drivers.' Some are 'key,' some are just contributing.

A. *The enemy (Sioux) had overwhelming superior numbers. (Estimates from Custer's native Crow scouts were from 1,500 to 2,500 Sioux. Custer's entire force totaled less than 600. The US military academy at West Point taught that force ratios of 2 or 3:1 superiority are needed to ensure success in the attack. Even if Custer had kept his element intact, he still would have been severely outnumbered.)*

B. *Custer split his force in the face of a superior enemy and engaged. (Custer only had 210 men with him when he engaged the Sioux, splitting his force was just making a bad situation far worse.)*

C. *The Sioux knew the lay of the land. [Note: The Sioux likely did have a better understanding of the terrain, but the intended engagement area had been scouted, and Custer had been briefed as to the size and disposition of the enemy before deciding to attack. This knowledge convinced Custer that, along with the fact that Custer had the initiative (he was on the attack), likely diminished this advantage for the Sioux significantly.]*

D. Custer had left the Gatling guns in the rear. The two Gatling guns that Custer left behind would have provided needed firepower. However, Custer's tactics at the Little Bighorn were to move fast and initiate the Sioux attack using a combination of fire and maneuver. Custer left the guns behind because, in his opinion, they were primarily defensive weapons, and they 'would slow him down.'

E. Custer had placed his supply train at a position where it could not easily have provided support. (This situation is an extension of Custer's decision in Factor 'B.' Custer split his force (Reno's 350 men) and put the pack mule trains in Reno's column so they would not hinder Custer's ability to maneuver.)

F. _Custer's hubris convinced him that he could overcome the Sioux on the battlefield, no matter the odds._ (This is likely the 'linchpin.' Custer had overconfident to the point of recklessness his entire life. He graduated ranked last in his class from West Point in 1861 with over 700 demerits on his file, one of the worst academic records in the school's history. Custer's overconfidence in fighting the Plains Indians was based primarily on his experience fighting the Sioux. Custer had few engagements (less than five) with small Sioux war parties. His forces always heavily outnumbered the Sioux. Therefore, the Sioux showed reasonable tactical competence when he attacked them. They recognized the severe force ratio imbalance against them and fled the battlefield to fight another day.[5] Custer misinterpreted this otherwise practical and rational behavior (i.e., retreating in the face of superior numbers). In his mind, the Sioux's actions were nothing less than pure unadulterated fear. Custer's own experience convinced him that he and the 7th Calvary alone could defeat a significantly larger Sioux force. To that extent, he did not realize he was disregarding multiple logical and factual arguments that sharply conflicted with West Point tactical training, his scouts' reports, and his subordinates' recommendations.)

Assessment and Explanation

The following sections highlight the linchpin analysis's assessment result and explain how the assessment was derived.

Assessment

Linchpin – F. Custer's hubris is the 'linchpin.'

Explanation

A through E were all valid factors that could tip the scales, yet Custer's overconfidence overrode all other factors.

A. Custer knew the force was significantly larger – But he ignored the intelligence.

B. Custer knew that splitting his forces was tactically unsound – However, he likely considered it and decided it would not matter.

C. Custer did not trust the reports from his Crow scouts – This is evidenced by his disregarding the Crow scouts' reports. Custer only acknowledged the enemy's positions, not their numbers. Similar to Custer's low opinion of the Sioux, he likely viewed the Crow scouts as inferiors on the battlefield also, which is why he likely devalued their reports.

D. The year was 1876, Custer knew of the capabilities of Gatling guns; they had been used multiple times in the Civil War (1861–1865).[6] However, during the Civil War, the dozen or so times the guns were reported used, they were employed in a fixed configuration mounted on gunboats, or defensively in the trenches at the siege of Petersburg, Virginia – Custer had made his plan, and the Gatling guns (a fixed position-defensive weapon) were not part of it.

---

5   Evan S. Connell, *Son of the Morning Star*, New York: Harper Perennial, 1997.
6   Russ A. Pritchard Jr., *Civil War Weapons and Equipment*, September 2003.

E. Like Factor 'B,' Custer knew to have his supplies located out of his reach was tactically unsound – He likely considered it and decided it would not matter.

To test the assessment, assume that Custer had not had this overwhelming hubris. Would he have likely followed his West Point tactical training, heeded the reports of his scouts and his subordinates' recommendations, and likely not engaged when he did? In light of the disproportionate size of the enemy force, Custer more logically might well have delayed the battle. Instead, he would have requested reinforcements and continued to monitor the enemy's size and disposition until reinforcements arrived. Once they arrived, he would have gained a numerical and tactical advantage. (Outcome X)

Finally, using the pre-drafted checkpoints of the linchpin analysis, validate the final argument.

A. Identify the main indefinite factors/key variables judged likely to drive the outcome of the issue....

   ✓ These were items 'A' through 'F.'

B. Determine the linchpin premises or analytic assumptions about the drivers.

   ✓ Custer's hubris was demonstrated in all aspects of his life, on the battlefield, his school record, his interactions with subordinates.

C. Explain the circumstances under which unanticipated developments could occur.

   ✓ An indicator that linchpin is invalid would be if it could be shown anywhere leading up to the battle that Custer considered and heeded his tactical training or the scout's reports, warnings, or subordinates' recommendations.

Final Thoughts on Linchpin Analysis

Linchpin analysis is a method that analysts can demonstrate to managers and policymakers alike that all the alternatives are covered. It is a structured approach for forecasting, as well as figuring out what went wrong. It is an anchoring tool that seeks to reduce the hazard of self-inflicted intelligence errors and policymaker misinterpretation. At a minimum, the linchpin approach promotes thoroughness through a series of pre-drafting checkpoints. Analysts can also use it to organize and evaluate their analysis when dealing with issues of high uncertainty. Reviewing managers use linchpin analysis to ensure that the argument in such assessments is sound and clear.[7]

Note: If desired, desired readers can find online a more detailed example of a linchpin analysis of a narcotrafficker's ability to challenge the Mexican government's sovereignty (see footnote below).[8]

TIPS:

Linchpin analysis:

- Helps analysts to identify the key assumptions.
- Requires the analyst to think through and assess their assumptions, ensuring that alternative possibilities are considered.
- Helps analysts to identify the key assumptions that could make or break their view of a focal situation.
- Born of the need for a more proactive approach.

---

7 The Sherman Kent Center for Intelligence Analysis, *Occasional Papers: Volume 1, Number 1*, www.cia.gov/library/kent-center-occasional-papers/pdf/OPNo1.pdf

8 Linchpin Analysis Example, *Calderón likely to lose control of portions of Mexico to narcotraffickers*, https://vdocuments.mx/linchpin-analysis-example.html

Strengths and Advantages

Linchpin analysis is:

- *Valuable in challenging conventional wisdom.*
- *Beneficial when policymakers operate on false, outdated, or overly optimistic or pessimistic perceptions of the situation.*

Weaknesses and Limitations

- *Identifying key assumptions is difficult to do.*
- *Linchpin analysis does not lend itself well to situations that require a very timely turnaround.*
- *Linchpin analysis does not generate forecasts or predictions.*
- *Many analysts do not conduct linchpin analysis because they are apprehensive of having their analysis shown to be deficient.*
- *Often, decision-makers do not ask for it because they do not know it exists or do not understand it.*

THE KEY ASSUMPTIONS CHECK (KAC)

The KAC was introduced in Chapter 10, *Analytical Tradecraft*, from the text *Intelligence Analysis Fundamentals*, the predecessor to this text. This chapter demonstrates the KAC usage using realistic examples, noted earlier in the text. Further, it explores how to apply the KAC in various intelligence analysis venues (e.g., business, crime, others).

Background

Historically, US analysis of Soviet Warsaw Pact operations against NATO had to 'assume' a level of non-Soviet Warsaw Pact reliability (i.e., would war with the west broke out, would these forces fight?). For this example, there was a high degree of uncertainty. Depending on what level of reliability one assumed, the analyst could arrive at very different conclusions about a potential Soviet offensive operation. Additionally, when economists assess the prospects for foreign economic reforms, they may unconsciously assume a degree of political stability in those countries or regions that may or may not exist in the future. Likewise, political analysts reviewing a developing country's domestic stability might unconsciously assume stable oil prices when this fundamental determinant of economic performance and underlying social peace might fluctuate. These examples highlight that analysts often rely on stated and unstated assumptions to conduct their analysis. The goal is not to undermine or abandon key assumptions; instead, it is to make them explicit and identify what information or developments would demand reassessing.[9]

How It Is Used

The KAC is an SAT that lists and reviews the key working assumptions upon which fundamental analytical judgments rest. A key assumption is any hypothesis that analysts have accepted as accurate and forms the analytical assessment basis. For instance, military analysis focuses exclusively on analyzing key technical and military variables (sometimes called *doctrinal factors*). Therefore, a doctrinal analysis assumes that forces operate similarly based upon their size and configuration. In other words, Soviet-trained motorized rifle regiments or Peoples Liberation Army (PLA) brigades in a particular environment (e.g., in the desert, open plains, or arctic conditions) follow a specified doctrine (or playbook). Postulating other conditions or situations would employ other assumptions and may dramatically impact the analytical assessment.

---

9   US Government, Central Intelligence Agency (CIA), *A Tradecraft Primer: Structured Analytic Techniques for Improving Intelligence Analysis*, March 2009.

The 'key assumptions check' is most useful at the beginning of an analytic project. An individual analyst or a team can spend an hour or two articulating and reviewing the key assumptions. Reassessing assumptions may also be valuable at any time before finalizing judgments to ensure that the assessment does not rest on flawed premises. Identifying hidden assumptions can be one of the most difficult challenges an analyst faces, as the analyst often holds these assumptions subconsciously as factual. Therefore, the assumptions are seldom examined and rarely challenged.[10]

METHOD

Checking for key assumptions requires analysts to consider how their analysis depends on the validity of certain premises, which they do not routinely question or believe to be in doubt. A four-step process that helps analysts:

1. Review the current analytic line on just what the issue appears to be and write it down for all to see.
2. Articulate all the premises (both stated and unstated) which must be accepted in the finished intelligence as factual for this analytic line to be valid.
3. Challenge each assumption, asking why it 'must' be factual and whether it remains valid under all conditions.
4. Refine the list of key assumptions to contain only those that 'must be true' to sustain your analytic line; consider under what conditions or in the face of what information these assumptions might not hold.

KAC EXAMPLE/DISCUSSION AND EXPLANATION

The Case – The Beltway Sniper (aka D.C. Sniper) Investigation

In 2002, the Federal Bureau of Investigation (FBI) and local law enforcement in the Washington D.C. metropolitan area combined efforts to solve the Beltway Sniper case. This case provides excellent examples of how intelligence analysis and reliable police investigative techniques worked to catch the perpetrators. At the same time, there were significant lessons to be learned which should apply to future domestic terror cases. This example demonstrates the SAT, known as the KAC. This exercise demonstrates that if the KAC were used early in the investigation, it likely reduces confusion and prevents misdirection of investigative and analytical assets. The exercise also shows that the FBI's criminal profile was critically flawed and likely hindered more than helped the investigation. The Central Intelligence Agency (CIA) cites this particular criticism of the need for applying the KAC to the assumptions used in the Beltway Sniper case in a publication from 2009.[11]

TIPS:

Below are a few questions to ask one's self to assist in performing the KAC:

- *How much confidence exists that this assumption is correct?*
- *What explains the degree of confidence in the assumption?*
- *What circumstances or information might undermine this assumption?*
- *Is a key assumption more likely a key uncertainty or key factor?*
- *Could the assumption have been true in the past but less so now?*
- *If the assumption proves wrong, would it significantly alter the analytic line? How?*
- *Has this process identified new factors that need further analysis?*

---

10 US Government, Central Intelligence Agency (CIA), *A Tradecraft Primer: Structured Analytic Techniques for Improving Intelligence Analysis*, March 2009.

11 US Government, Central Intelligence Agency (CIA), *A Tradecraft Primer: Structured Analytic Techniques for Improving Intelligence Analysis*, March 2009.

Also, the exercise expands the CIA's observations as it makes a compelling argument that shows that if basic police investigative practices and methodical analysis of the available information had been applied (e.g., no FBI profile used), the task force potentially would have discovered the true identity of both snipers nearly two full weeks earlier than investigators uncovered their identities.

The Time Line

Begin by creating a timeline of events. Figure 5.3 is the FBI's timeline listed below displayed against a calendar of October 2002.

The Key Assumptions

Most Americans who followed the case during the fall of 2002 remember that after the initial outbreak of shootings on October 2, 3, and 4, the combined task force's operating assumptions were broadcast on every television station. These assumptions were that the shootings were the work of:

- *single, white male;*
- *having some military training; and*
- *driving a white van.*

These assumptions were included in most news articles and prominently placed and repeated in every televised media storyline and internet news website.

First Question: How Did They Arrive at These Assumptions?

So how did law enforcement arrive at these assumptions? After John Muhammed and Lee Malvo's arrests, several scathing critiques of the flawed taskforce assumptions appear in the public narrative. Years later, the FBI posted an account of the Beltway Sniper investigation on their official web-site, highlighting their successes, and merely mentioned but did not explain their errors in criminal profiling.

Below is an excerpt from the FBI's public website.

> *Within days, the FBI alone had some 400 agents around the country working the case. We'd set up a toll-free number to collect tips from the public, with teams of new agents in training helping to work the hotline. Our evidence experts were asked to map many of the evolving crime scenes*

October 2002						
Sunday	Monday	Tuesday	Wednesday	Thursday	Friday	Saturday
		1	**2** Man killed while crossing a parking lot in Wheaton, MD	**3** Five more murders, four in Maryland and one in D.C.	**4** Woman wounded while loading her van at Spotsylvania Mall	**5**
6	**7** 13-year-old-boy wounded at a school in Bowie, MD	**8**	**9** Man murdered near Manassas, Virginia, while pumping gas	**10**	**11** Man shot dead near Fredericksburg, VA, while pumping gas	**12**
13	**14** FBI analyst Linda Franklin killed near Falls Church, VA	**15**	**16**	**17**	**18**	**19** Man wounded outside a steakhouse in Ashland, VA
20	**21**	**22** A bus driver, the final victim, killed in Aspen Hill, MD	**23**	**24** Muhammad and Malvo arrested in Maryland	**25**	**26**

Figure 5.3   The FBI's Timeline on a Calendar for October 2002.

digitally, and <u>our behavioral analysts helped prepare a profile of the shooter</u> for investigators. We'd also set up a Joint Operations Center to help Montgomery County investigators run the case.[12]

A Byte Out of History, the Beltway Snipers, Part 2

Next Question: Why Go Public with the Assumptions?

So, why go public with the criminal profile? We can only speculate. From an analytical perspective, profiles help focus limited intelligence collection assets on potentially most effective areas. Investigative assets (e.g., detectives and patrol officers) are typically limited as a rule. Criminal profiles can help law enforcement direct investigative emphasis toward areas with the highest potential for success while simultaneously eliminating some of the Washington D.C. metro area's population from the prospective suspect pool.

Discussion

The purpose of this exercise is not to find fault in the FBI's production of an erroneous profile. Intelligence analysts and criminal investigators make mistakes every day, especially those under significant pressure. With attacks mounting, citizens were dying, and the public and government officials were demanding action. It would be hard to argue that the beltway sniper task force was not under considerable pressure. However, the pivotal error came when the task force did not validate its initial assumptions. So how does one validate their assumptions using a KAC?

The KAC can be performed at any time, but it is most useful at the beginning of an analytic project. The analyst(s) spend(s) an hour or two articulating and reviewing key assumptions. Having performed the KAC once does not prevent rechecking assumptions at any time before finalizing judgments to ensure that assessments do not rest on flawed premises.

Using KAC, let us review the FBI's initial assumptions and determine which, if any, are valid. Since anyone can appear 'all-knowing' using hindsight as their guide, the exercise uses only the information available at the time to validate the assumptions that started the investigation off in the wrong direction.

Breaking the assumptions down into single factoids yields the following list:

1. *Sniper is a male.*
2. *Sniper is acting alone.*
3. *Sniper is white.*
4. *Sniper has military training/experience.*
5. *Sniper is driving a white van.*

   Keep in mind that there was confusion from the beginning; the Beltway Sniper attacks fell into two overlapping criminal profiles, 'serial killers' and 'snipers.'

Starting with Assumption #1, 'the sniper is male.' According to statistics from the 2002 Uniform Crime Report (UCR), which the FBI drew upon heavily to produce the suspect profile, 97% of all known serial killers (of the 214 total) are male (see Figure 5.4). Using accepted intelligence assessment practices makes this assumption **highly likely** *(but not definite). So, what is the downside of using this assumption? Based on crime data, not much. Therefore, investigators would be taking a small (3%) risk by not looking for females.*

---

12 US Government, Federal Bureau of Investigation, website: www.fbi.gov/news/stories/2007/october/snipers_10240.

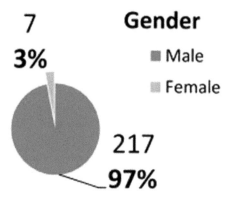

Figure 5.4   2002 Uniform Crime Report (UCR).

Assumption #2, 'the sniper is acting alone.' Once again, statistics for serial killers show it is **highly likely***, a 95% or higher likelihood based upon two decades of crime data, the sniper was working alone. Once more, what is the risk? Should the task force search for a lone shooter and discover others at the scene when detaining the initial suspect, then procedurally, law enforcement detains all involved for questioning. Only after the elimination of individuals as potential suspects would anyone be released. Therefore, even if the lone shooter assumption proves incorrect, only a minimal level of risk exists.*

Author's Note: Based upon US government sources, the Beltway Sniper case's FBI profile relied heavily on the 2002 UCR. The underlying data for the UCR is from 20 years of US law enforcement agencies contributing data. The UCR states that, from 1982 to 2001, there were 327 total incidents involving murder during a sniper attack in which the weapon was a firearm. Within those 327 incidents, there were 379 victims and 224 instances for which supplementary data (the age, sex, and race of the offender) exist. Using this information, it becomes quickly apparent that the data set the FBI used to construct its profile had significant flaws in that it was missing 31% of the supporting data. Therefore, the conclusions (or assumptions) would potentially have a built-in ±31% error factor.

Assumption #3, 'the sniper is white.' At best, there is only limited statistical support for Assumption #3. UCR data point to the shooter being white as **roughly even odds** *(45–55%), hardly a certainty given past patterns (see Figure 5.5). By using this assumption, the task force takes on significant risk by ruling out nonwhites from the suspect pool. Although the UCR data are comparable to the overall US population demographics, according to the 2000 census, in this instance, the US Census data are misleading. The data are misleading because the 2000 regional census data for the D.C. metro area showed the black population to be 60.1% (not 43%).*[13]

In the absence of hard evidence, the analyst/profiler should not have excluded any group unless statistical data indicates a high probability (at least an 80–95 percentile) preference toward a particular group, race, or ethnicity. Even then, performing a risk assessment to determine possible adverse effects of excluding the other group(s), in this case, possibly excluding up to 20% of the suspect population, is imperative.

Assumption #4, 'the sniper has military training/experience.' Assumption #4 was another instance where the data did not validate and, in fact, contradicted the basis of the assumption. The FBI's UCR does not include snipers/serial killers and military training data. However, a review of the available research located an independent Radford University study, which cites a figure of 22.4% for serial

---

13 US Government, Census Bureau, *The Black Population: 2000*, website: www.census.gov/prod/2001pubs/c2kbr01-5.pdf

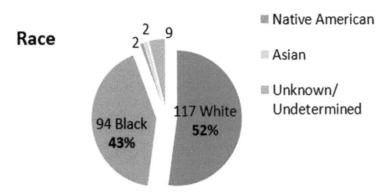

Figure 5.5   More FBI UCR Statistics.

killers that were prior military.[14] *Another independent source, Florida Gulf Coast University, cited a study of 354 American serial murders yielding only 25 (7%) with a military background.*[15] *Whether the actual number is closer to 7% or 22.4%, neither number merits excluding nonmilitary suspects or three quarters (or more) of the general population from consideration.*

Concluding with Assumption #5, 'the sniper is driving a white van.' Assumption #5 is the only assumption that stems from a single credible eyewitness report. Granted, the witness (the Guatemalan immigrant landscaper) was credible. He also had a reasonable view of the victim, and there existed excellent lighting and visibility at the crime scene (Attack #5, Sarah Ramos). However, federal, state, and local trial documents possess a litany of well-documented reliability issues associated with eyewitness accounts. Questionable reliability of witness statements aside, the fact that tens of thousands of white trucks registered to owners in the D.C. metropolitan area further complicates, rather than simplifies the issue. Also, there is no reason not to suspect there may have been more than one vehicle involved.

Citing the publication, A Tradecraft Primer, Structured Analytic Techniques for Improving Intelligence Analysis, documented the CIA's observations of the sniper task force investigation. Below is an excerpt.

> *Avoid jumping to conclusions (the sniper is white, has military training, and drives a white van) that did not hold up under scrutiny. By explicitly examining each assumption, officials could have avoided prematurely narrowing down the potential pool of suspects to a group that did not include the actual perpetrator. Similarly, they might have been more cautious about accepting that the sniper was driving a white van.*[16]

While not advocating that law enforcement should disregard eyewitness accounts, giving a single eyewitness account undue credence can (and did) misdirect observers and investigators just as quickly as it can lead law enforcement to suspects. On October 3, there was only one report of the infamous white box truck. Whereas the actual sniper vehicle, a Chevy Caprice, was spotted at three different attack sites (according to later court documents).[17]

So, How the Taskforce Should Have Solved This Case?

Many might argue that it is easy to criticize from the propitious perspective of hindsight. Then extend arguments and observations contending that at the time, the evidence and sage insights were just not available to the ones' doing the investigation (also known as 'Monday-morning quarterbacking').

14 Radford University, FGCU Serial Killer Database, website: maamodt.asp.radford.edu/Serial%20Killer%20Information%20Center/Serial%20Killer%20Statistics.pdf, November 23, 2015

15 Florida Gulf Coast University, Kristin Elink-Schuurman-Laura, *Serial Killers and the Military: Misconceptions and Statistical Facts*, website: skdb.fgcu.edu/public/Kristin%20Elink-Schuurman-Laura/Serial%20Killers%20and%20the%20Military%20Misconceptions%20and%20Statistical%20Facts.pdf

16 US Government, Central Intelligence Agency (CIA), *A Tradecraft Primer: Structured Analytic Techniques for Improving Intelligence Analysis*, March 2009.

17 Court Documents, Muhammad v. Commonwealth, 269, Virginia and 451, 611 S.E.2d 537, Virginia, 2005.

However, there was adequate evidence to investigators at the time available, and there was and is a better approach.

Using open-source reports from the early days of October 2001 and a methodical analysis of the facts available, we can show that the task force could have deduced the identity of the culprits within the first few days, specifically by October 5 (possibly October 3), as opposed to October 22, when Muhammed and Malvo were identified.

Why is identifying the suspects so significant? Criminal investigators (and intelligence targeters) point out that identifying suspects in a criminal inquiry is critical information. Once detectives have a name, it leads to other identifiers that feed the search, a solid description, a face, aliases, vehicle ID, make, model, vehicle color, an address, known associates, and family connections are integral to an investigation. Suspect identification precedes apprehension often within days, and in the Beltway Sniper case, identification preceded apprehension by just two days.

The Analytical Process

Starting with a walk around the crime scene, notice the location's physical features (see Figure 5.6[18]) are urban, modern streets, a collection of office structures, and businesses. Each is likely to possess surveillance cameras. Given that the traffic cameras and business CCTV may not have captured the actual attack, they potentially would have captured some of the vehicular and pedestrian traffic surrounding the time of the attack. Since there were several attacks in the first days, a comparison of vehicle descriptions at each crime scene very likely would have produced photos of and possibly a license plate from the getaway vehicle.

One asks, so what…you find a vehicle. You may even get a make, model, and license plate. How do you know the vehicle had anything to do with the sniper attacks? Again, the basic principles of criminal investigation (i.e., method, motive, and opportunity) require placing the suspect(s) at the scene of the crime.

Basic Pattern Analysis to Prove 'Opportunity'

Given that the attacks on October 3 were close to each other (see Figure 5.7) and searching through crime scene traffic photos may have produced several false positives from local cars coincidently near the area at the time of the attacks, might make the task of sorting fact from fiction too daunting. Noting

Figure 5.6   Attack #3 Location, Google Street View.

---

18 *Author's Note: Google Street View launched in 2007 and therefore was not available in 2002. Even if Street View had been available, since it does not continuously take pictures, it would not have been able to spot the sniper. However, it does provide a general visual understanding of the area surrounding the crime scenes.*

Basic Pattern Analysis

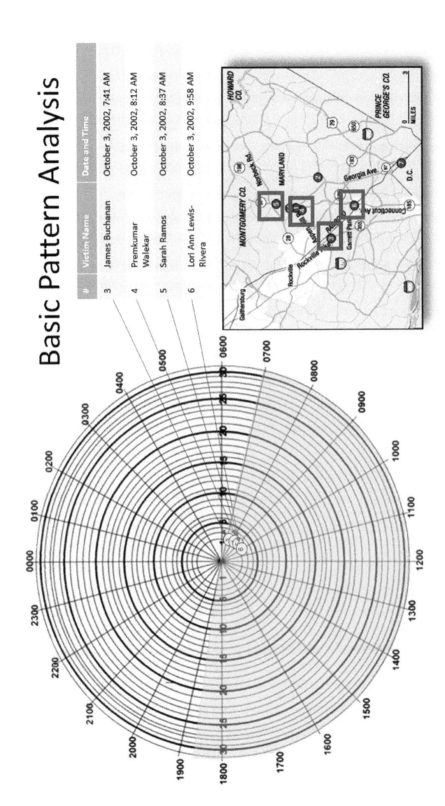

#	Victim Name	Date and Time
3	James Buchanan	October 3, 2002, 7:41 AM
4	Premkumar Walekar	October 3, 2002, 8:12 AM
5	Sarah Ramos	October 3, 2002, 8:37 AM
6	Lori Ann Lewis-Rivera	October 3, 2002, 9:58 AM

Figure 5.7 Proximity of October 3 Attacks.

the short period separating Attacks 3 through 6 and the rush-hour traffic congestion, only a vehicle following a planned and practiced route could have made it to all locations in time. Therefore, the number of false positives would be few, and due to the small number, quickly investigated, discounted, and eliminated.

Determining Involvement

From personal experience tracking improvised explosive device (IED) bombers overseas, it is common to find military-age males (MAMs) with cell phones at the scene of IED attacks. On one, or more, of these cell phones, there may be recently taken photos of the exact military vehicle hit by the IED. Still, that alone does not mean the MAMs with cell phones are guilty of anything. Just as Americans might slow down and 'rubber neck' at an unfortunate traffic accident, some of the more ghoulish might even snap a picture on the accident with their smartphone. The fact that the rubberneckers were at the scene does not mean they caused the accident (or detonated the IED).

Yet, if you look closer at that smartphone and find multiple pictures from different times and locations, all showing horrific car accidents, you might strongly suspect the photos are not so innocent, and perhaps they did have a hand in the accidents. For a moment, just think, what are the chances of someone happening upon multiple severe car accidents on different days, in dispersed locales, over a few days? When seen in those terms, the odds become convincing that the person with the smartphone filled with accident photos is somehow involved with the accidents. Using the same logic, if you could place a particular vehicle at more than one sniper crime scene, the connection becomes stiffer. However, it only circumstantially signifies that the vehicle occupants are somehow involved in the sniper attacks.

Analyzing the Shooter's Line of Sight (LOS)

Law enforcement knew a great deal about the shooters and their technique shortly after the October 3 killing spree (see Author's Note below). The next step is to build a crime scene model using LOS analysis to determine the sniper's most likely firing position(s).

Author's Note:

On 4 October 2002, even before final ballistics results were available, law enforcement officials had already linked all of the 3 October attacks…each victim killed by one .223 caliber bullet,…the shooter may have fired with skill at some distance, possibly from across nearby parking lots…all single shots.

Source: LA Times

LOS is an analysis tool commonly used by military imagery analysts where the analysts draw a line between two points, an origin, and a target, to determine whether the target is visible from the origin and, if it is not visible, where the view is obstructed (see Figure 5.8).

Using LOS analysis to help construct a crime scene model, along with the other information available, investigators would have quickly seen the shooters were likely firing from adjacent parking lots.

Further, modeling points to the 'concealed position' were most likely from the inside (or behind) a motor vehicle (e.g., a car, van, or truck) stationary and located in a parking lot. The parking lot was most likely adjacent to the target with few obstructions (e.g., no high traffic roads between shooter and target) (see Figure 5.9).

News reports also stated the sniper fired 'single shots' that were auditable only to a fraction of the witnesses. Postulating those witnesses hearing the shots were closest to the victim and the shooter (court records substantiate this assessment). Police reports from the time only state that the sniper shots came from 'some distance.' Estimating the distance to be roughly 50 yards (or less). To avoid lengthy explanation and supporting calculations, a condensed argument supporting the 50-yard (or less) estimate follows:

Attack #4, (3rd Beltway Victim)

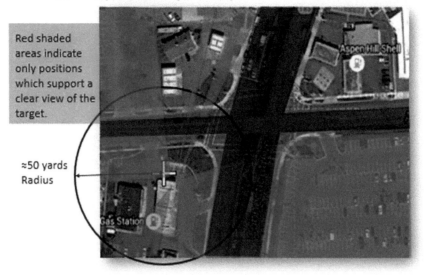

Red shaded areas indicate only positions which support a clear view of the target.

≈50 yards Radius

Figure 5.8   Third Victim Crime Scene for Representation of LOS Analysis.

Attack Modeling

Figure 5.9   Attack Modeling Obstructions.

- *Fact: Witnesses farther than 50 yards from the victim heard nothing.*
- *Conclusion: Had the shooter been at greater distances, rush-hour road noise would likely mask the sound of the gunshot.*
- *Assumption: 'Single-shot' mortal wounds imply close proximity (the shooter was so close that they could not miss).**
- *Fact: The bullets' flat trajectory implies close proximity to the target (longer shooter-to-target distance implies more obstacles in the LOS profile and necessitates the shooter to move to a higher elevation to engage the target).*

Author's Note: Some would argue the snipers could have also been 'excellent marksmen.' However, this was not the case when weighed with the other factors (the defendant's court statements also support this position).*

Attack Modeling

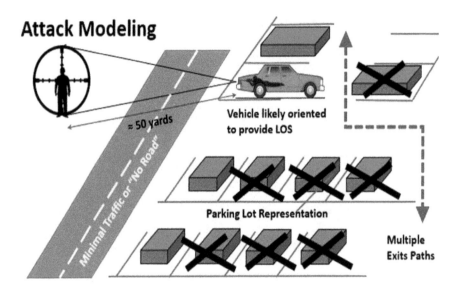

Figure 5.10 Final Model of the October 3 Attacks.

Attack #4, (3ʳᵈ Beltway Victim)

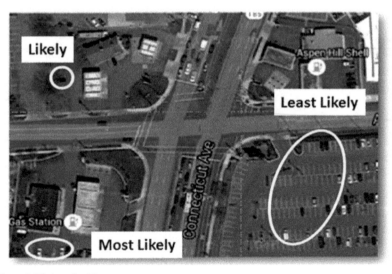

Figure 5.11 Potential Sniper Positions.

Pulling all the data together into the shooter's perspective yields a very probable representation or 'model' of the crime scenes of October 3, 2001. It also reveals the most likely parking spots used as shooting positions.

A layperson may wonder how this helps the investigator. These models assist detectives and patrol officers in focusing their investigations and questions. When law enforcement collects statements, they can give higher value to accounts from witnesses closest to the probable location of the sniper's position. LOS analysis also helps analysts sort through potentially hundreds of traffic cam clips, store surveillance photos, and CCTV videos to concentrate only on those areas most likely to be sniper perches and potential vehicle access and egress paths (see Figures 5.10 and 5.11).

Police did collect surveillance video and questioned bystanders at all six 3 October sniper attack sites.[19] Additionally, various witness accounts identified an older model Chevy Caprice at four of the October 3 sniper attack sites, and in Washington, D.C. on October 3, 2002, at approximately 7 PM, a police officer stopped the same Caprice for running two stop signs (this all according to court documents). The police officer testified that the Caprice's windows were heavily tinted and that he could not see anyone else in the car. The police officer gave John Muhammad a verbal warning and let him go.[20,21]

Therefore, the task force did have the needed information sources necessary to put out an all-points bulletin for an older model, 'dark-colored' or 'blue' Chevy Caprice. Had the bulletin gone out, there would have been a reasonable chance the snipers would have been stopped on the evening of October 3. If they had not been stopped on October 3, they would surely have been on October 8 or 9 because the sniper's Chevy Caprice was coincidently stopped, and the driver was also questioned by police on those days.[22]

CHAPTER SUMMARY

This chapter described analytic techniques for challenging assumptions, specifically, the key assumptions check (KAC) and linchpin analysis. The KAC is most effective when performed early in the analytical process. However, linchpin analysis is generally performed later in the process if performed at all. It is often done after the fact as a forensic exercise to learn what went wrong and determine how it could be best avoided in the future. This chapter explores the analytical methods used to perform the KAC and linchpin analysis, also covered are recent examples, advantages and disadvantages, and when to use each process.

LINCHPIN ANALYSIS

A dictionary-style definition would refer to a pin passed through the end of an axle to keep a wheel in position, or perhaps it would mention that a 'linchpin' is a person or thing vital to an enterprise. In the context of our lesson, linchpin analysis is a structured analytical technique (SAT) based upon known data or information (or data with at least a high probability of certainty), which anchors the analytical argument.

Background

The failure to provide strategic warning during the months before Iraq invaded Kuwait generated recommendations for revamping warning analysis. The IC's consensus that Iraq was unlikely to initiate warfare in the near term was widely held and rarely examined critically. This assessment was issued repeatedly in the year before the assault on Kuwait. The underlying logic of the assumption was that Iraq needed several years to recover from the military and economic devastation of its long war with Iran.[23]

By the mid-1990s, America was being attacked at home, and their interests were threatened overseas, and no one seemed to be able to see what was coming next consistently. This genuine need to discover why we missed it' gave birth to *linchpin analysis*.

How It Is Used

The basis of linchpin analysis sits upon using known data or information (or data with at least a high probability of certainty). By starting from 'knowns' (and eliminating all impossibilities), the

19 Chicago Tribune, October 4, 2002, 'Police canvassed the area questioning people at all six sites,…They are also collecting security videotapes from businesses near the shootings,' http://articles.chicagotribune.com/2002-10-04/news/0210040287_1_shootings-dealership-al-briggs

20 Court Documents, Muhammad v. Commonwealth, 269, Virginia and 451, 611 S.E.2d 537, Virginia, 2005.

21 *Author's Note: Court documents revealed that Mohammed's blue Chevy Caprice was stopped multiple times by police (October 3, 8, and 9) and identified by eyewitnesses at multiple crime scenes (October 3, 4, 5, 6, and 11).*

22 Court Documents, Muhammad v. State, 934 A.2d, 1059, Maryland App., 2007.

23 The Sherman Kent Center for Intelligence Analysis, *Occasional Papers: Volume 1, Number 1*, www.cia.gov/library/kent-center-occasional-papers/pdf/OPNo1.pdf

analyst has a powerful technique for showing intelligence consumers, peers, and higher-ups that a problem has both been thoroughly studied and constrained within the bounds of reality.

Linchpin analysis is a flexible, structured method intended to minimize mistakes and promote clarity even with complex issues containing multiple variables and uncertainty. The analyst's assumptions drive it, but these assumptions need to be as near to the facts as possible. That said, these assumptions are selected judiciously and are considered most likely to drive and determine the outcome. The predictions yielded from this logic exercise generally produce a higher degree of confidence.[24]

THE KEY ASSUMPTIONS CHECK (KAC)

The KAC was introduced in Chapter 10, *Analytical Tradecraft*, from the book *Intelligence Analysis Fundamentals*, the predecessor to this text. This chapter demonstrated the KAC usage by leveraging realistic examples and exploring how better to apply the KAC in various intelligence analysis venues (e.g., business and crime).

Background

Historically, US analysis of Soviet Warsaw Pact operations against NATO had to 'assume' a level of non-Soviet Warsaw Pact reliability (i.e., would war with the west broke out, would these forces fight?). For this example, there was a high degree of uncertainty. Depending on what level of reliability one assumed, the analyst could arrive at very different conclusions about a potential Soviet offensive operation. Additionally, when economists assess the prospects for foreign economic reforms, they may unconsciously assume a degree of political stability in those countries or regions that may or may not exist in the future. Likewise, political analysts reviewing a developing country's domestic stability might unconsciously assume stable oil prices when this key determinant of economic performance and underlying social peace might fluctuate. These examples highlight that analysts often rely on stated and unstated assumptions to conduct their analysis. The goal is not to undermine or abandon key assumptions; instead, it is to make them explicit and identify what information or developments would demand reassessing.[25]

How It Is Used

The KAC is an SAT that lists and reviews the key working assumptions upon which fundamental analytical judgments rest. A key assumption is any hypothesis that analysts have accepted to be accurate and forms the basis of the assessment. For instance, military analysis focuses exclusively on analyzing key technical and military variables (sometimes called *doctrinal factors*). Therefore, a doctrinal analysis assumes that forces operate similarly based upon their size and configuration. In other words, Soviet-trained motorized rifle regiments or Peoples Liberation Army (PLA) brigades in a particular environment (e.g., in the desert, open plains, or arctic conditions) follow a specified doctrine (or playbook). Postulating other conditions or situations would employ other assumptions that may dramatically impact the analytical assessment.

The 'key assumptions check' is most useful at the beginning of an analytic project. An individual analyst or a team can spend an hour or two articulating and reviewing the key assumptions. Reassessing assumptions may also be valuable at any time before finalizing judgments to ensure that the assessment does not rest on flawed premises. Identifying hidden assumptions can be one of the most difficult challenges an analyst faces, as the assumptions are often held subconsciously as factual and, therefore, seldom examined and rarely challenged.[26]

---

24 The Sherman Kent Center for Intelligence Analysis, *Occasional Papers: Volume 1, Number 1*, www.cia.gov/library/kent-center-occasional-papers/pdf/OPNo1.pdf

25 US Government, Central Intelligence Agency (CIA), *A Tradecraft Primer: Structured Analytic Techniques for Improving Intelligence Analysis*, March 2009.

26 US Government, Central Intelligence Agency (CIA), *A Tradecraft Primer: Structured Analytic Techniques for Improving Intelligence Analysis*, March 2009.

CHAPTER 6

Applications of Modeling in Analysis

INTRODUCTION

Whether for scientific, business, law enforcement, or military, creating models is critical for anyone doing research or analysis. Models enhance the understanding of their users. Models are often used to avoid real-world failures and the associated losses of time, capital, and other critical resources. Using models allows one to gain greater insight into a problem or process that might otherwise present, high risk, or may realistically be impossible to perform otherwise. For instance, the National Aeronautics and Space Administration (NASA) created a mind-numbing amount of models to support placing a man on the moon. See Figure 6.1 for an example of one of the myriad conceptual models produced for the Apollo space missions.[1]

Models are useful tools to help analysts understand or visualize processes and problem sets (e.g., military targets, business adversaries, criminal organizations, or science challenges), as well as presenting assessments or findings to intellectual peers, reviewers, or intelligence consumers.

This chapter describes characteristics common to all models; introduces the various types of models (e.g., conceptual, analytical, static, dynamic, and simulations); provides examples of models used by law enforcement, business, and the intelligence services; and describes how to construct conceptual and analytical models.

CHARACTERISTICS COMMON TO ALL MODELS

Rarely do models not use empirical (or historical) information for their basis. As a rule, it is best to build models based on empirical information. As a rule, empirical data causes the model to reflect real-world situations. Below are but a few of the characteristics common to all models:

- Provide documentation for information exchange or future reference
- Communicate critical details and factual material to those who need the information
- For its users, it advances understanding of the modeled subject or system
- Use empirical data whenever possible
- Affords a common understanding or reference point for people (e.g., analysts, researchers, designers, developers) to produce more detailed plans for actual processes or products or perhaps develop even more sophisticated models

---

1 US National Aeronautics and Space Administration, History Website, https://history.nasa.gov/afj/ap13fj/pics/premiss ion-trajectory.png, Retrieved May 9, 2020.

DOI: 10.4324/9781003241195-6

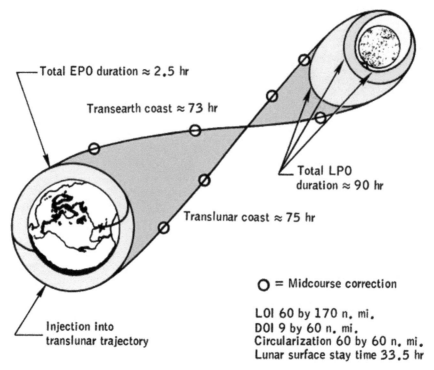

Figure 6.1   NASA Conceptual Model of the Apollo 13 Space Mission.

CONCEPTUAL MODELS

A conceptual model is an abstract creation of the mind that best integrates and takes advantage of an analyst's mental processes. A conceptual model is typically documented or reflected in some format that others can comprehend (e.g., physical replica, sculpture, or math equation). Conceptual models are not necessarily quantitative, requiring data or calculations to fulfill their purpose. Conceptual modeling offers a way of representing concepts that help one better understand that model's subject (e.g., a problem, process, or experiment). Often drawn as diagrams, conceptual models show relationships between factors and the flow of data or processes. See Figure 6.2 for a typical conceptual targeting model[2] and Figure 6.3 for a conceptual model describing the thought processes involved in law enforcement use of force situations.[3]

The following are key attributes or outcomes of a conceptual model:

- Simple, fast, less information required
- Not suited to data calculation
- Often less accurate than analytic models when forecasting
- Communicates critical details and factual material to those who need the information
- Typically, it is best to develop a conceptual framework before bringing math into the discussion.

---

2   Headquarters, Department of the Army, *Targeting – Army Techniques Publication,* ATP 3-60, May 7, 2015.
3   Philadelphia Police Department, *Use of Force Directive 10.01,* www.phillypolice.com/accountability/index.html, Retrieved May 10, 2020.

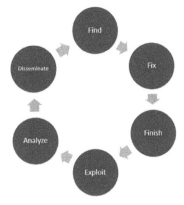

Figure 6.2   US Army High-Value Targeting (HVT) Model.

Figure 6.3   Philadelphia Police Department Use of Force Model.

Advantages

Conceptual models provide users with a powerful descriptive tool to support current situations' estimates and predict future circumstances. Models can present the modeled subject's qualitative (conceptual) or quantitative (data) aspects. However, process equations and algorithms used to represent the modeled subject may be confusing, particularly for the more visually disposed learner. Conceptual models promote understanding by providing a visualization of the subject.

Disadvantages

Since conceptual models only approximate their subjects, they are inherently inexact and can carry errors into the final assessment. Even mathematical-based models can be imperfect; the analysts' understanding of the subject can be complete (or completely wrong). The parameters used in conceptual models to represent actual processes are often uncertain or approximate because these parameters are empirically determined from small (or unrepresentative) samples or represent multiple processes. Additionally, a model's starting and boundary conditions may not be well understood.

Despite these shortfalls, conceptual models are practical representation tools. Conceptual models are often the only means available to generalize to broader applications or offer forecasting abilities.

Authors Note: *Most intelligence analysts eventually adopt one or two analytic approaches as their 'go-to' method when no other apparent analytical approach seems appropriate. It has been my experience that these 'go-to' methods are selected because they have proven effective in past circumstances.*

For myself, building conceptual models is that 'go-to' approach. Whether studying ballistic missile bunkers in Western Asia, starting a new business, or finding opium production laboratories in Afghanistan, starting with a solid conceptual model has always paid dividends.

As noted in the following firepower example, many researchers suspected some progressional relationship existed among weapon system performance parameters. However, for seven centuries, no one truly knew precisely what that relationship was until an analytical model was created to represent it.

CONSTRUCTING CONCEPTUAL MODELS

Sometimes it is advantageous to provide a representative example as one attempts to describe a somewhat abstract process or idea. Thus, an illustrated example of a conceptual model construction step-by-step process is presented in parallel with the explanation.

Conceptual models most commonly consist of three significant steps, and they are:

1. *Defining the Problem or Subject,*
2. *Collect, Organize, and Validate Requirements, and*
3. *Build the Model Based on the Requirements.*

Defining the Problem or Subject

Defining the problem (or subject) is a necessary and logical first step; defining the 'right' problem is even more critical because the intelligence end-user occasionally cannot articulate to the analyst specifically what information is essential and what is 'nice-to-know'. The time wasted chasing answers, other than the desired answers, is often time (and resources)that is unrecoverable.

The chosen problem set for illustration purposes comes from business and industry.

CONCEPTUAL MODEL EXAMPLE

Note: The provided business case example is purely instructional. Though it may provide some logistical and business insights, it should not be viewed as a 'perfect representation of how to expand a grocery store chain.'

Scenario: *The problem statement is: <u>How to determine where to best build the following stores of a major national grocery store chain?</u>*

Starting with a problem statement to be modeled. (Here are a few general questions one might ask.):

- ✓ *Is the problem definition adequate?*
- ✓ *Does it provide all the required information?*
- ✓ *Does it require further refinement or definition?*

A few more specific questions might be:

- ✓ *How many stores are required? If so, Why that number?*
- ✓ *Is there a general desired region for expansion?*
- ✓ <u>*Are there any logistical, resource, or scheduling restrictions?*</u>

After further discussion with stakeholders, new information becomes available:

- ✓ There is funding for 30 new stores?
- ✓ Additionally, the number '30' dovetails with the maximum number of stores reasonably supplied from one of the company's standardized warehouses.
- ✓ The marketing group has been advertising that the company plans to open stores in states 'A,' 'B,' 'C,' and 'D,' and marketing has set the public's expectations that it should happen in the next two years (Figure 6.4).

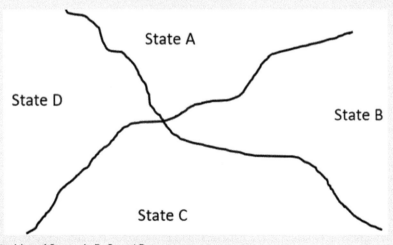

State A

State D

State B

State C

Figure 6.4   Map of States A, B, C, and D.

- ✓ Other stakeholders share that the company's rolling stock's maximum logistical radius can support a 200-mile travel radius hours (between the warehouse, hub, and the farthest most supplied store) or 3–3.5 hours of driving time. They also explained that they had experienced high turnover rates within the in-house truck driving staff due to qualified semi-drivers getting attractive salary offers from competitors.

Redefined Problem Statement: *The original problem statement is redefined based on the new stakeholder information to:*

- ✓ *How to determine where to best build the next 30 stores of a major national grocery store chain;*

    ✓ Within a specific four-state region;
    ✓ In the next two years;
    ✓ While ensuring not to exceed a 200-mile logistics radius with the warehouse; and
    ✓ Minimizing driver turnover?

Collect, Organize, and Validate Requirements

Based upon the redefined problem (or subject), collect pertinent requirements, and organize them into logical groups. Requirements (stated and implied) appear from concept inception through model construction and after completion. Since requirements unceasingly appear, it makes sense that there should be a mechanism to collect, validate, and correctly organize them.

Modeling requirements can be abstract, such as *How to represent the logistical radius?…or…To the more mundane, such as: …What is the model's budget?…or…What construction materials does the model require?…or…What other resources are needed to build the model? Returning to the Conceptual Model Example (the store chain expansion model),* collect, organize, and validate your requirements.

CONCEPTUAL MODEL EXAMPLE (CONTINUED)

Now take inventory of the requirements, validate, and organize the requirements.
1. Base Model Requirements (Resources need to construct the model)
   A. A 4 ft. Drafter's-grade color plotter and paper (for printing the final product)
   B. A Modeling Software license
   C. 40 hours of Drafter's time
   D. 60 hours Graphic Artist's Time
   E. 10 hours Logistics Consultant Time
   F. 10 hours Marketing Group's Time
   G. ….
2. Integral Logistical Requirement
   A. A 200-logistical radius from the warehouse (hub) or 3–3.5 of driving time (one way)
   B. Must use company trucks as much as possible
   C. …

> Author's Note: As you may have noticed, you have only gotten to the second step, and there is much jumping back and forth between steps.
>
> Finding another requirement may cause a redefinition of the 'problem statement' and subsequently cause a change to the model's purpose.
>
> Don't get concerned; it often happens, and it is normal. If it did not happen, the model would likely be incomplete or wrong because something was missed or integrated incorrectly.

3. Marketing Requirements
   A. Build stores within a specific four-state region
   B. Ensure there is a minimum of one store in each of the four specified states
   C. …
4. Human Resource Requirements
   A. Reduce company drive turnover
   B. …

5. *Schedule*
   A. *Build all 30 stores within two years*
   B. ...
6. *Cost...*
7. *Sales Dept. – one store for 25,000 population size*
8. ...

Build the Model Based on the Requirements

Some may view the Build Step of constructing the conceptual model as a natural and straightforward step. However, there is more to do than just assembling the pieces.

The actual construction of the model is an iterative process (Figure 6.5).

Now construct the conceptual model using the desired medium [e.g., a document, two-dimensional (2D) representation, three-dimensional (3D) sculpture, or any combination thereof].

Author's Note: If this is your first model and you notice it looks like something a first grader heavily glued together to get it done to collect their well-earned 'C-,' don't despair.

There is as much 'art' in modeling as in 'science.' The first model is a learning experience. Subsequent models tend to benefit from initial mistakes (and lessons learned) while constructing early modeling attempts.

Notice back in the previous example (Base Model Requirements), the model required more of the graphic artist's time than any other consultant. More of the graphic artist's time was needed because if the model looks like it was sketched hurriedly on the back of a napkin, few are going to want to look at it, and even fewer take it seriously.

Bottom line: If you want your model to be accepted as a 'professional product,' then put the time, resources, and effort into making it look 'professional.'

Figure 6.5   Construction of the Model Is an Iterative Process.

CONCEPTUAL MODEL EXAMPLE (CONTINUED)

Document all the information (and requirements) in some form or fashion.

It does not matter where one starts (e.g., problem statement, requirements).

Review the list of requirements and determine which is the most limiting. Once the most limiting requirement is satisfied, go to the next most limiting and so on.

It appears that the most limiting factor is the 200-mile logistical radius.

However, some unanswered questions remain:

- *Why is the high turnover rate among the company's truck drivers such a problem?*
- *What actions are the company taking to assuage the turnover problem, and were those actions effective in remedying the problem?*

You start asking these driver-related questions to the various stakeholders and discover that the HR, Operations, and Marketing groups have studied the problem and obtained the following supplementary information:

- *The company business model allows for a 10% maximum annual turnover rate. They determine that, for every driver, they lose above that turnover rate, results in a 50,000 dollar additional operating cost for each month the in-house position is unfilled.*
  - *Company truck drivers that distribute groceries from the hub warehouse to the stores and return the empty trailers require a Level 'A' commercial driver's license (CDL-A) to do their job.*
  - *On average, it takes about seven weeks to get your CDL-A when attending the company-approved full-time driver training program. (Training Cost is $10,000, provided they pass on the first try.)*
  - *Hiring temporary drivers and liberal use of overtime break the business labor-cost model.*
  - *Having a waiting list of potential hires only reduces the time the slot is open to two months.*
- *Operations endeavors to maintain driver staffing levels sufficient to support an eight-hour workday (with little or no overtime).*
- *It is cost-prohibitive to place the distribution warehouse in an urban environment, with a >100,000 population (compared to rural locations), due to local taxes, permitting, traffic and environmental considerations, real estate costs, labor costs, and many other related factors. Therefore, if possible, the company must position the warehouse in a rural setting.*
- *A labor force study of towns in the region under consideration found seven town populations of less than 50,000. Of the seven smaller towns, three towns (La Porte, Maggie, White Pines) had workforce demographics scores that showed that these towns had high education levels and low desire to work overtime or relocate. Hence, these workers were potentially less likely to leave the area once they finished the company driver's training to take higher-paying, out-of-the-area jobs.*
- *A real estate review of the region found that all of the region's towns have the municipal infrastructure (power, sewer, water, road access) adequate to support one or more company grocery stores. However, three of the seven smaller towns (Mayberry, Red Dog, and Roanoke) do not have sufficient support infrastructure for one of the standard company distribution warehouses.*

Start overlaying the information onto the model (see Figure 6.6). Begin by documenting as much as possible in the most instructive medium practical. Following the adage that a picture is worth a thousand words, use a map to depict the four-state region and overlay gathered information and requirements in the most instructive way possible.

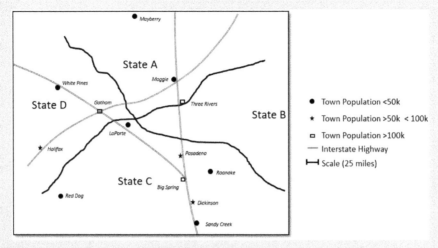

Figure 6.6   Initial Map of Four-State Region.

Next, overlay onto the map the following information:

- Annotate on the map the towns with inadequate infrastructure to support a standard-sized warehouse or populations >100,000 using an 'X.'
- Annotate the towns with the best workforce demographics using a '✓.'

The second figure is taking shape (Figure 6.7), and it provides a 2D model representing some of the more critical information required. The map now depicts all the unsuitable locations, and by default, one can also see the remaining more suitable locations for the warehouse.

Reviewing the problem statement: Determine where to best build the next 30 stores of a major national grocery store chain;

- Within a specific four-state region;
- In the next two years;
- While ensuring not to exceed a 200-mile logistics radius with the warehouse; and
- Minimizing driver turnover?

Using the developed model, now overlay a red circle that represents a 200-mile logistical radius. Moving the circle around the map while using various potential towns as the center of the circle, one gets La Porte (Figure 6.8a), Maggie (Figure 6.8b), and Pasadena (Figure 6.8c) on the next pages.

Observing that Figure 6.8a is the visibly best location of the three figures due to its central location (ability to reach the most towns in the region) and excellent workforce demographics.

Using Figure 6.8 validate the model by tentatively assigning stores based on the Sales Dept. limitation of '1 store for 25k population size.'

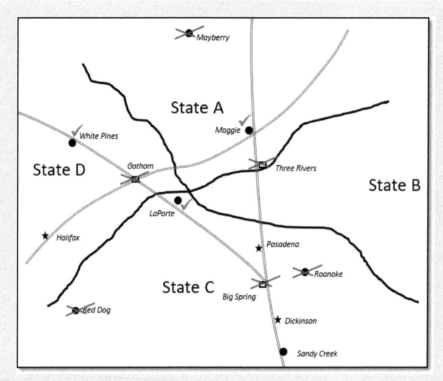

Figure 6.7 Map Depicting All Unsuitable Locations.

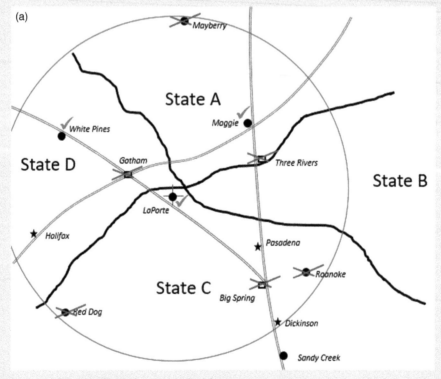

Figure 6.8 a–c The Map Overlaying Various Red Circles.

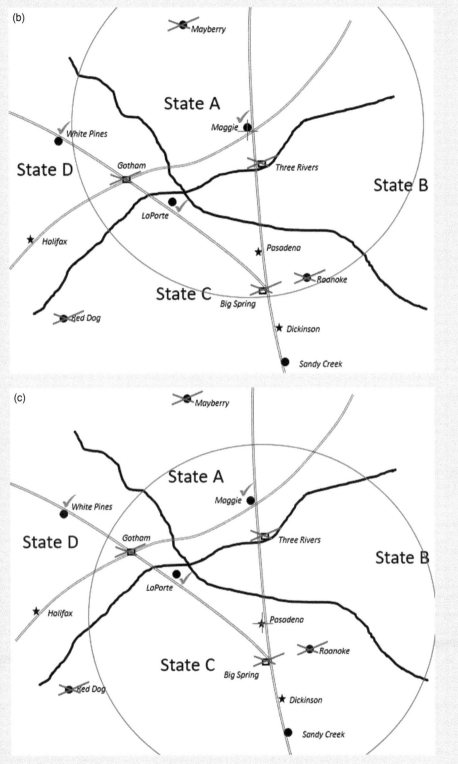

Figure 6.8 a–c Continued

The final figure (Figure 6.9) validates the model based upon the problem statement.

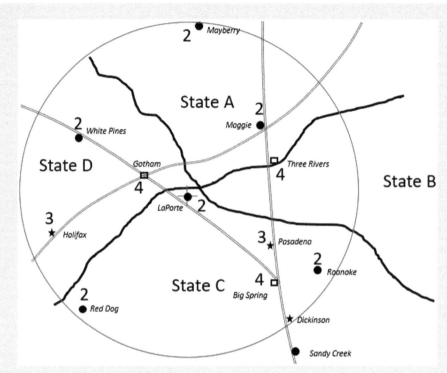

Figure 6.9   Final Map.

- *Count the numbers designating where to build stores (30 stores)* ☑
- *Store locations cover the entire four-state region?* ☑
- *Is the 200-mile logistics radius not exceeded?* ☑
- *Have steps been taken to minimize driver turnover?* ☑

Now, all that remains is to get the stores built within the allotted time: the next two years.

ANALYTICAL MODELS

Analytical models differ from conceptual models in that they are quantitative and are used to answer specific questions or make specific design decisions or predictions using data. Different analytical models are used to address the numerous aspects of a given network or problem set (e.g., evaluating a competitor's business model, an adversary's weapon system, or finding weaknesses in an organized crime network), such as its performance, reliability, or related properties. Analytical models require a level of precision to support formal analysis, which is typically performed by computer calculations. Model checkers need to confirm that analytical models are well developed to provide reliable outcomes. Next, two of the more common analytical models, static and dynamic, are explained.

The following *Analytic Model Example* displays the law-like progression of a series of measurable parameters common to military weapon systems over the centuries.

ANALYTIC MODEL EXAMPLE

The example presents two graphs from a study noting that when plotting a military systems' composite characteristic (a calculated weighted sum of logarithms) of mass, speed, effective range, crew, rate of fire, and projectile's kinetic energy, the data fall approximately on the same curve for a broad range of military weapon system types. Figures 6.10 and 6.11 display the associated graphs for the US Army Research Laboratory's Analytical Model.[4]

According to Dr. Alexander Kott, author of the study, 'In hindsight, this multi-century, multi-scale regularity may not be all that surprising, but somehow nobody noticed this previously.'

The graph at left shows that the ordinate is a weighted sum of logarithms of a <u>weapon system's rate of fire</u>, <u>projectile's kinetic energy</u>, <u>speed</u>, <u>effective range</u>, and <u>crew size</u>. The abscissa combines the logarithm of a system's mass and a piecewise linear function when the system appeared.

A composite characteristic is the weighted sum of logarithms of military systems' mass, speed, effective range, crew, rate of fire, and projectile's kinetic energy, which falls approximately on the same curve for a broad range of system types (Figure 6.10).

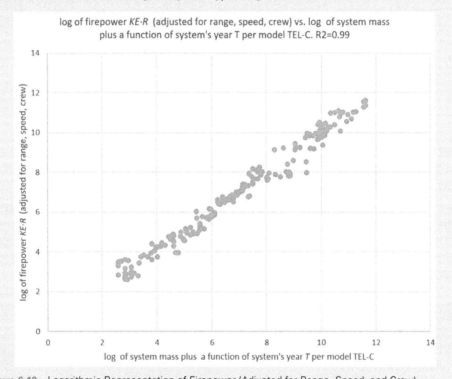

Figure 6.10   Logarithmic Representation of Firepower (Adjusted for Range, Speed, and Crew).

This steady progression occurs despite significant differences in the systems' physical scale and underlying technologies for over seven centuries, the plot inflecting up at the dawn of industrialization.

Figure 6.11 displays a composite character of widely differing military systems, from medieval archers to modern tanks. It falls approximately on a straight line over a wide range of physical scales and historical periods (1300–2015 ce).

---

4   US Army CCDC Army Research Laboratory, By Dr. Alexander Kott, *Army Research Uncovers Law-Like Progression of Weapons Technologies – From a Crossbowman to a Tank*, September 18, 2019.

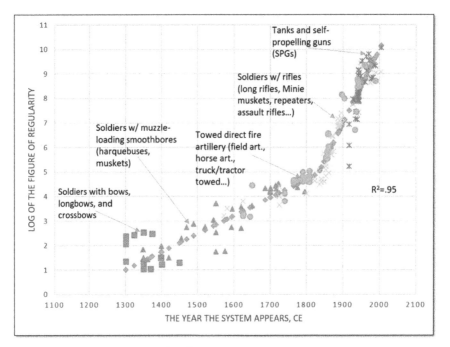

Figure 6.11　Weapon System Firepower Over Time.

Static Models

Static models are analytical models that characterize the properties of a system, independent of time (in other words, the characterization is *valid for a fixed point in time*). A representative illustration of how military analysts use static models would be to apply them to estimate the size and strength of an adversary's military units (see Figure 6.12).

Estimating unit size and strength is a limited and simplified analogy, but it does demonstrate the concept. Also, note that the associated equipment or staffing (*associated model parameters*) numbers may vary with time. Remember, the estimation is only considered accurate for a single (fixed) point in time. Knowing that the observations may have other deterministic parameters may include other associated probability distributions.

EXAMPLES OF STATIC MODELS

For demonstration purposes, the two static models to be used are a US Army armored company consisting of 14 M1 tanks…and a modern US Army light infantry platoon with 42 personnel (Figure 6.12).

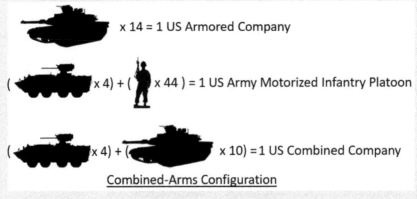

Figure 6.12　Examples of Static Models.

Scenario 1

An enemy scout counts the number of tanks located in a forward assembly area, and the scout also spots several dismounted infantry nearby. The tanks numbered 14, and the troops came to 42, respectively. By comparing the observations to the provided static models, it would be reasonable to assume that the scout is looking at an armored company and an infantry platoon, both at full strength.

Scenario 2

When estimating a tank company's strength, one uses other deterministic parameters (in this case, it is the organizational force structure). For instance, if the observer were to find only ten tanks the next day, one might say (based strictly upon the provided model definition) they observe an <u>understrength tank company</u>. However, if the tank company's total numbers were reduced by four (e.g., less than full strength) instead, one may need to reassess based upon other model parameters.

Conversely, suppose there were only ten tanks, but four armored personnel carriers were also present. In that case, it <u>may still be considered a full-strength tank company</u> (because of an added deterministic parameter). The scout is just observing a reorganized unit, and the new force structure is known as a tank-heavy company in a combined-arms configuration.

These static model examples could extend to descriptions of business supply chains, (mature) leadership models of organized crime networks, maintenance support units, and many other networks and organizations.

Dynamic Models

Dynamic models are analytical models representing the variable time aspect of the modeled subject, such as its velocity, acceleration, and position as a function of time. The most noticeable difference between static and dynamic models is that static models represent a fixed point with respect to time, whereas a dynamic model changes with time. Additionally, differential equations can only be used in dynamic models. Static models are in equilibrium (steady-state), and dynamic models continually change with time.

The type of question posed determines the selection of a dynamic model versus a static model. As shown previously, a dynamic model would be best suited to observe weapon system performance parameters over time (see Figure 6.8). However, a static model is more appropriate for determining whether one observes a squad, a platoon, or a company of infantry troops (see Figure 6.9).

SIMULATION MODELS

Simulation modeling is used to produce and analyze a physical model's mathematical-based prototypes to forecast system performance under varying parameters. Simulation models help intelligence analysts, researchers, designers, and engineers understand how systems perform over time or other varying stimuli or changing system parameters. A simulation model is composed of multiple other models (static or dynamic) operated by a simulation application using a set of predefined initial conditions.

Whether performing intelligence analysis for business, law enforcement, military, or homeland defense, one discovers that simulation modeling is more valuable due to its capacity to assess risk or validate proposed solutions. The following example comes from the AnyLogic company website's simulation model, developed by Purdue University.[5]

---

5   Purdue University, Purdue Homeland Security Institute, By Jae Yong Lee, Modeling the 1999 Columbine High School Shooting, Modeling the 1999 Columbine High School Shooting, https://cloud.anylogic.com/model/27e919e8-6d5f-4c08-8444-5fc504ab24df?mode=SETTINGS, Retrieved April 18, 2020.

EXAMPLE

As of 2020, the prevailing US government-advocated response to an active shooter situation is 'run, hide, fight.' The Purdue-developed computer model offers a method to test how well the 'run, hide, fight' protocol works during various active shooter scenarios. Using the Purdue computer model (see Figure 6.13), graduate students demonstrated possible alternatives to using the 'run, hide, fight' active shooter protocol. Furthermore, their research suggests that the protocol may be fundamentally flawed.[6]

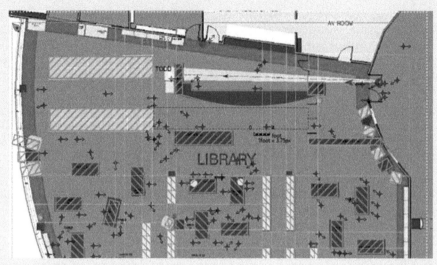

Figure 6.13   Any Logic Active Shooter Test Simulation.

Author's Note: Purdue University's Columbine Shooting: Active Shooter Mitigation Policies Simulation offers individuals an excellent opportunity to appreciate what a well-developed simulation can bring to understanding the essential workings of the modeled researched subject matter.

Students can go to the website listed below and run the simulation for themselves. You can even play with the variables to reach different outcomes. (Go to https://youtu.be/ODU4wdoqvKw)

HOW TO CONSTRUCT AN ANALYTICAL MODEL

This section guides students on how to construct a basic analytical model. Analytical models, as mentioned previously, differ from conceptual models in that they are quantitative; therefore, they require data and are used to answer specific questions. Analytical modeling construction steps are very similar to constructing a conceptual model. Both conceptual and analytical models are valuable tools for understanding complex problem sets. However, the inclusion of data enhances the model's ability to enumerate the outcomes in a way that conceptual models cannot.

Unlike conceptual models, consisting of three significant steps, analytical models can have a dozen or more steps (and sub-steps). Analytical models, with their many possible associated attributes

---

6   Purdue University, Purdue Homeland Security Institute, *Is 'Run, Hide, Fight' Effective in Shooter Situations? New Research Provides Insight*, By John O'Malley, July 31, 2019, https://polytechnic.purdue.edu/newsroom/run-hide-fight-effective-shooter-situations-new-research-provides-insight, Retrieved April 18, 2020.

(e.g., properties, labels, data types), can easily overcomplicate the model until it is so complex that it can only be processed by a computer.

However, for instructional purposes, this text describes a simplified and more generalized analytical model and only discusses four primary steps and those steps are:

1. *Define the Problem,*
2. *Selecting and Processing the Data,*
3. *Data Sampling, Review, and Processing, and*
4. *Building the Model.*

Define the Problem

Like conceptual modeling, analytical modeling begins with defining the problem. It is incumbent upon the analyst to inquire early on how information the intelligence consumer requires from the model. Additionally, the analyst must regularly exercise a well-lubricated information exchange with the intelligence consumer to ensure the model stays on track.

Selecting and Processing the Data

Construct and train the model using empirical (historical) data if possible. The data is usually dispersed across multiple sources and may require processing, validation, and formatting. The multisource aspect of prospective training data often streamlines the data validation step. Data may contain duplicate reports and possibly erroneous information, depending on analysis goals and modeling objective(s); some datasets may need omitting to avoid erroneously skewing model conclusions. Selected datasets may have gaps, require translation or transformation (e.g., foreign languages, mathematical manipulation, or weighting), and may be used to produce derived characteristics better predictive outcomes aligned with modeling objectives. In practice, the data quality drives the model's accuracy.

Data Sampling, Review, and Processing

Start by splitting the collected data into two sets: the training and the test data sets. The training data set builds the model, and the test data set verifies the model's accuracy. The collection of a sufficient amount of representative sampling data reduces the chances of underfitting the model, and there is a method to validate and accurately measure the model's performance. An underfitted model typically is missing functional terms or has gaps in its primary (training) data set, causing some output parameters or terms to appear incorrectly or not at all. Having adequate data in both training and the test data sets is also imperative. With inadequate amounts of test data run, one takes the chance of overfitting the model. Overfitting implies that the model may fail to fit additional data or predict future observations unreliably. The production of model outputs corresponding too closely or precisely to a particular data set (to the point that it picks all the characteristics, including the signal and the noise) indicates an overfitted model. Overfitted underperform on new data sets.

Assuming enough sampling data have been collected (for training and testing), one can now start the review process. Reviewing the data confirms the model's integrity by examining data to ensure it's complete, clean, and reliable. The review looks for and removes inconsistencies, assigns missing values, translates (if required), and processes the sample data to be integrated. Step 3 is critical to prevent including erroneous data, which can only provide erroneous outputs.

Building the Model

Analytic models have existed for many centuries, for as long as there has been mathematics and algebra. Rarely will one have to construct a model from nothing. Therefore constructing a new model is typically an exercise in selecting and adjusting existing algorithms and models to one's needs. However, often the collected data do not lend itself to a specific algorithm or existing model. Therefore, selecting a particular algorithm(s) or preexisting model(s) may not be as obvious. To facilitate the process, refer back to Step 2, *Selecting and Processing the Data,* and take the opportunity to run as many potential algorithms as practical and compare their outputs. Use these results to influence model selection. Occasionally, one can run a collection of models simultaneously on the same data and choose the final model by comparing their various outputs.

HOW TO CONSTRUCT AN ANALYTICAL MODEL – PRACTICAL EXERCISE

This section guides students on how to construct an analytical model. The steps are very similar to the steps for constructing a conceptual model. Both conceptual and analytical models are valuable tools for understanding complex problem sets. Analytical models, as mentioned previously, differ from conceptual models in that they are quantitative; therefore, they require data and are used to answer specific questions. Although the inclusion of data enhances the model's ability to enumerate the outcomes in a way that conceptual models cannot.

Define the Problem

Like conceptual modeling, analytical modeling begins with defining the problem. It is incumbent upon the analyst to inquire early on how information the intelligence consumer requires from the model. Additionally, the analyst must regularly exercise a well-lubricated information exchange with the intelligence consumer to ensure the model stays on track.

EXAMPLE

Using the grocery store scenario from the earlier example. Now a year has passed, and 20 stores are up and running, and the operations and sales groups have reached out and asked for a <u>predictive analytic model to forecast revenue numbers for all 30 stores for the next two years</u>.

Selecting and Processing the Data

Construct and train the model using empirical (historical) data if possible. The data is usually dispersed across multiple sources and may require processing, validation, and formatting. The multisource aspect of prospective training data often streamlines the data validation step. Data may contain duplicate reports and possibly erroneous information, depending on analysis goals and modeling objective(s); some data sets may need omitting to avoid erroneously skewing model conclusions. Selected data sets may have gaps, require translation or transformation (e.g., foreign languages, mathematical manipulation, or weighting), and may be used to produce derived characteristics better predictive outcomes aligned with modeling objectives. In practice, the data quality drives the model's accuracy.

The available empirical data collected is from the construction of the first 20 stores over one year (Figure 6.14).

Store #	Jan	Feb	Mar	Apr	May	Jun	Jul	Aug	Sep	Oct	Nov	Dec
1	$52,000	$75,400	$76,120	$76,840	$75,660	$76,380	$76,530	$76,680	$76,830	$76,980	$77,130	$77,280
2	$23,400	$76,890	$76,840	$77,230	$77,120	$77,343	$77,483	$77,623	$77,763	$77,903	$78,043	$78,183
3		$13,200	$70,530	$75,430	$76,380	$74,430	$75,900	$75,400	$75,346	$75,292	$75,238	$75,184
4			$25,280	$75,090	$77,107	$74,101	$76,008	$75,288	$75,162	$75,037	$74,912	$74,786
5				$68,200	$77,467	$73,126	$75,693	$74,648	$74,420	$74,193	$73,966	$73,738
6				$15,090	$74,123	$76,840	$79,557	$82,274	$84,991	$87,708	$90,425	$93,142
7					$6,200	$74,302	$77,849	$78,879	$80,478	$82,078	$83,677	$85,277
8						$18,970	$78,330	$79,978	$82,204	$84,429	$86,655	$88,881
9							$78,687	$80,728	$83,397	$86,066	$88,735	$91,404
10							$25,900	$81,044	$83,928	$86,812	$89,696	$92,580
11								$81,664	$84,923	$88,182	$91,440	$94,699
12								$82,284	$85,917	$89,551	$93,185	$96,818
13								$1,260	$81,044	$76,830	$76,980	$77,130
14									$81,664	$77,763	$77,903	$78,043
15									$8,970	$75,346	$75,292	$75,238
16										$75,162	$75,037	$74,912
17										$9,210	$76,980	$81,044
18											$77,903	$81,664
19											$78,910	$77,903
20												$14,680

Figure 6.14   Cumulative Revenue for Each Newly Constructed Store Over One Year.

Figure 6.14 shows the cumulative revenue for each newly constructed store over one year. The first two stores (Stores #1 and #2) were under construction three months earlier (beginning of October, in the previous year). However, neither of them was open and producing revenue until January.

Data Sampling, Review, and Processing

Start by splitting the collected data into two sets: the training and the test data sets. The training data set builds the model, and the test data set verifies the model's accuracy. The collection of a sufficient amount of representative sampling data reduces the chances of underfitting the model, and there is a method to validate and accurately measure the model's performance. An underfitted model typically is missing functional terms or has gaps in its primary (training) data set, causing some output parameters or terms to appear incorrectly or not at all. Having adequate data in both training and test data sets is also imperative. With inadequate amounts of test data run, one takes the chance of overfitting the model. Overfitting implies that the model may fail to fit additional data or predict future observations unreliably. The production of model outputs corresponding too closely or precisely to a particular data set (to the point that it picks all the characteristics, including the signal and the noise) indicates an overfitted model. Overfitted underperform on new data sets.

Assuming enough sampling data have been collected (for training and testing), one can now start the review process. Reviewing the data confirms the model's integrity by examining data to ensure it's complete, clean, and reliable. The review looks for and removes inconsistencies, assigns missing values, translates (if required), and processes the sample data to be integrated. Step 3 is critical to prevent including erroneous data, which can only provide erroneous outputs.

Using the first ten store's monthly revenue data (Figure 6.15) for training data and using linear regression to predict a dependent variable value (y, monthly revenue) based on a given independent variable (x, time in months) yields the equation and graph above.

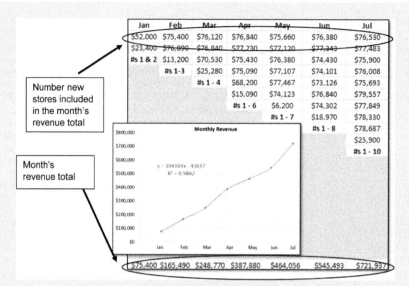

	Jan	Feb	Mar	Apr	May	Jun	Jul
	$52,000	$75,400	$76,120	$76,840	$75,660	$76,380	$76,530
	$23,400	$76,890	$76,840	$77,230	$77,120	$77,343	$77,483
#s 1 & 2	$13,200	$70,530	$75,430	$76,380	$74,430	$75,900
#s 1-3		$25,280	$75,090	$77,107	$74,101	$76,008
#s 1-4			$68,200	$77,467	$73,126	$75,693
				$15,090	$74,123	$76,840	$79,557
#s 1-6				$6,200	$74,302	$77,849
#s 1-7					$18,970	$78,330
#s 1-8						$78,687
						$25,900
#s 1-10						

Number new stores included in the month's revenue total

Month's revenue total

Monthly Revenue

y = 104104x - 43697
R² = 0.9882

$75,400 $165,490 $248,770 $387,880 $464,056 $545,493 $721,937

Figure 6.15 Using the First Ten Store's Monthly Revenue Data and a Linear Projection.

Using stores 11 through 20 monthly revenue data (Figure 6.16a) as test data and the equation developed confirms the model's accuracy, as shown in Figure 6.16b, thereby validating the model.

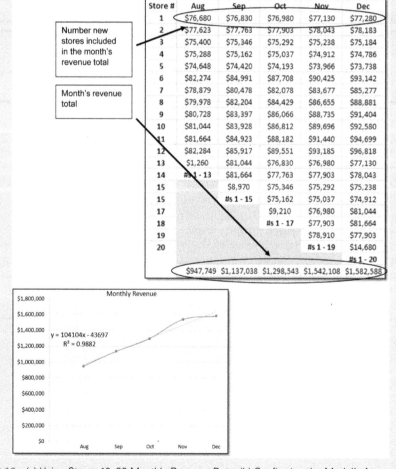

Store #	Aug	Sep	Oct	Nov	Dec
1	$76,680	$76,830	$76,980	$77,130	$77,280
2	$77,623	$77,763	$77,903	$78,043	$78,183
3	$75,400	$75,346	$75,292	$75,238	$75,184
4	$75,288	$75,162	$75,037	$74,912	$74,786
5	$74,648	$74,420	$74,193	$73,966	$73,738
6	$82,274	$84,991	$87,708	$90,425	$93,142
7	$78,879	$80,478	$82,078	$83,677	$85,277
8	$79,978	$82,204	$84,429	$86,655	$88,881
9	$80,728	$83,397	$86,066	$88,735	$91,404
10	$81,044	$83,928	$86,812	$89,696	$92,580
11	$81,664	$84,923	$88,182	$91,440	$94,699
12	$82,284	$85,917	$89,551	$93,185	$96,818
13	$1,260	$81,044	$76,830	$76,980	$77,130
14	#s 1-13	$81,664	$77,763	$77,903	$78,043
15		$8,970	$75,346	$75,292	$75,238
15		#s 1-15	$75,162	$75,037	$74,912
17			$9,210	$76,980	$81,044
18			#s 1-17	$77,903	$81,664
19				$78,910	$77,903
20				#s 1-19	$14,680
					#s 1-20

Number new stores included in the month's revenue total

Month's revenue total

$947,749 $1,137,038 $1,298,543 $1,542,108 $1,582,588

Monthly Revenue

y = 104104x - 43697
R² = 0.9882

Figure 6.16   (a) Using Stores 10–20 Monthly Revenue Data. (b) Confirming the Model's Accuracy.

Building the Model

Analytic models have existed for many centuries, for as long as there has been mathematics and algebra. Rarely will one have to construct a model from nothing. Therefore, constructing a new model is typically an exercise in selecting and adjusting existing algorithms and models to one's needs. However, often the collected data do not lend itself to a specific algorithm or existing model. Therefore, selecting a particular algorithm(s) or preexisting model(s) may not be as obvious. To facilitate the process, refer back to Step 2, Selecting and Processing the Data, and take the opportunity to run as many potential algorithms as practical and compare their outputs. Use these results to influence model selection. Occasionally one can run a collection of models simultaneously on the same data and choose the final model by comparing their various outputs.

Using the equation developed and tested in the previous steps:

$$y = 104104 \times -43697$$

$$R^2 = 0.9882$$

Recall that the model requirement was to 'forecast revenue numbers for all thirty stores for the next two years.' Substituting '30' for the 'x' variable in the equation above yields a result of '$3,079,423.' At a construction rate of ten stores per year, the '$3,079,423' monthly revenue figure is sustained for an additional 12 months (assuming no other operational stores added during the final year). Therefore, the model forecasts a final value of '$36,953,076.' Adding the revenue amount accumulated up to the three-year point.

$$(\$3,079,423 \times 12) + \$3,079,423 = \$40,032,499$$

The final model forecast number equates to $40,032,499 with an R^2 value of '0.9882.'

(Note: R^2 is a statistical measure of how close the data are to the fitted regression line. It is also known as the coefficient of determination.)

CHAPTER SUMMARY

Creating models is a critical skill for anyone doing research or analysis. Models are often used to avoid real-world failures and the associated losses of time, capital, and other critical resources. Using models allows one to gain greater insight into a problem or process that might otherwise present, high risk, or may realistically be impossible to perform otherwise.

This chapter describes characteristics common to all models, introduces the various types of models (e.g., conceptual, analytical, static, dynamic, and simulations), provides examples of models used by law enforcement, business, and the intelligence services, and describes how to construct conceptual and analytical models.

CHARACTERISTICS COMMON TO ALL MODELS

Rarely do models not use empirical (or historical) information for their basis. However, creating models, for whatever is the model's purpose is, it's best to build the model based on empirical information. The model's output will more likely reflect real-world situations if empirical data is used. Below are but a few of the characteristics common to all models:

- Provide documentation for information exchange or future reference
- Communicate critical details and factual material to those who need the information
- For its users, it advances understanding of the modeled subject or system
- Use empirical data whenever possible

- Affords a common understanding or reference point for people (e.g., analysts, researchers, designers, developers) to produce more detailed plans for actual processes or products or perhaps develop even more sophisticated models.

CONCEPTUAL MODELS

A conceptual model is an abstract creation of the mind that best integrates and takes advantage of an analyst's mental processes. A conceptual model is typically documented or reflected in some format that others can comprehend (e.g., physical replica, sculpture, or math equation). Conceptual models are not necessarily quantitative, requiring data or calculations to fulfill their purpose. Conceptual modeling offers a way of representing concepts that help one better understand that model's subject (e.g., a problem, process, or experiment). Often drawn as diagrams, conceptual models show relationships between factors and the flow of data or processes.

The following are key attributes or outcomes of a conceptual model:

- Simple, fast, less information required
- Not suited to data calculation
- Often less accurate than analytic models when forecasting
- Communicates necessary details and factual material to those who need the information
- Typically, it is best to develop a conceptual framework before bringing math into the discussion.

Advantages

Conceptual models promote understanding by providing a visualization of the subject. Conceptual models provide users with a powerful descriptive tool to support current situations' estimates and predict future circumstances. Conceptual models are more commonly used to present the modeled subject's qualitative (conceptual) aspects. However, process equations and algorithms used to represent the modeled subject may be confusing, particularly for the more visually disposed learner. In these cases, conceptual models can be employed (in a limited fashion) to optically present the process equations and algorithms (quantitative aspects) of the modeled subject.

Disadvantages

Since conceptual models only approximate their subjects, they are inherently inexact and can carry errors in the final assessment. Even mathematical-based models can be imperfect; the analysts' understanding of the subject can be incomplete (or completely wrong). The parameters used in conceptual models to represent actual processes are often uncertain or approximate because these parameters are empirically determined from small (or unrepresentative samples) or represent multiple processes. Another disadvantage of a conceptual model arises from constructing the model when boundary conditions are not well understood.

Despite these shortfalls, conceptual models are practical representation tools. Conceptual models are often the only means to generalize to broader applications or offer forecasting abilities.

CONSTRUCTING CONCEPTUAL MODELS

Sometimes, it is advantageous to provide a representative example as one attempts to describe a somewhat abstract process or idea. Thus, an illustrated example of a conceptual model construction step-by-step process is presented in parallel with the explanation.

Conceptual models most commonly consist of three significant steps, and they are:

1. *Defining the Problem or Subject,*
2. *Collect, Organize, and Validate Requirements, and*
3. *Build the Model Based on the Requirements.*

ANALYTICAL MODELS

Analytical models differ from conceptual models in that they are quantitative and are used to answer specific questions or make specific design decisions or predictions using data. Different analytical models are used to address the numerous aspects of a given network or problem set (e.g., evaluating a competitor's business model, an adversary's weapon system, or finding weaknesses in an organized crime network), such as its performance, reliability, or related properties. Analytical models require a level of precision to support formal analysis, which is typically performed by computer calculations. Model checkers need to confirm that analytical models are well developed to provide reliable outcomes. Next, two more common analytical models, static and dynamic, are explained.

Static Models

Static models are analytical models that characterize the properties of a system, independent of time (in other words, the characterization is *valid for a fixed point in time*). A representative illustration of how military analysts use static models would be applying them to estimate the size and strength of an adversary's military units.

Dynamic Models

Dynamic models are analytical models representing the variable time aspect of the modeled subject, such as its velocity, acceleration, and position as a function of time. The most noticeable difference between static and dynamic models is that static models represent a fixed point with respect to time, whereas a dynamic model changes with time. Additionally, differential equations can only be used in dynamic models. Static models are in equilibrium (steady-state), and dynamic models continually change with time.

SIMULATION MODELS

With simulation modeling, one produces and analyzes mathematical-based prototypes of a physical model to forecast system performance under varying parameters. Simulation models help intelligence analysts, researchers, designers, and engineers understand how systems perform over time or other varying stimuli or changing system parameters. A simulation model is composed of multiple other models (static or dynamic) operated by a simulation application using a set of predefined initial conditions.

HOW TO CONSTRUCT AN ANALYTICAL MODEL

Analytical modeling construction steps are similar to those used in constructing a conceptual model. Both conceptual and analytical models are valuable tools for understanding complex problem sets. Analytical models, as mentioned previously, differ from conceptual models in that they are quantitative; therefore, they require data and are used to answer specific questions. However, data inclusion enhances a model's ability to enumerate outcomes and provides opportunities for more granular analysis in a way that conceptual models cannot.

Unlike conceptual models, consisting of three significant steps, analytical models can have a dozen or more steps (and sub-steps). Analytical models, with their many possible associated attributes (e.g., properties, labels, data types, and so on), can easily overcomplicate the model until it is so complex that it can only be processed by a computer.

However, for instructional purposes, this text describes a simplified and more generalized analytical model and only discusses four primary steps and those steps are:

1. *Define the Problem,*
2. *Selecting and Processing the Data,*
3. *Data Sampling, Review, and Processing, and*
4. *Building the Model.*

Author's Note: When creating mathematically based models, one needs a certain amount of experience and domain expertise to identify the pertinent fixed and variable factors necessary data sources to construct the model. However, the proper algorithm to employ may be elusive. I recommend Colleen McCue's text, 'Data Mining and Predictive Analysis, Intelligence Gathering and Crime Analysis, for further information on models used for modeling analytical intelligence problem sets.'

TIPS/NOTES: MODEL TYPES CHARACTERISTICS AND ATTRIBUTES

Common to All Models
- Provide documentation for information exchange or future reference
- Communicate critical details and factual material to those who need the information
- For its users, it advances understanding of the modeled subject or system
- Use empirical data whenever possible
- Affords a common understanding or reference point for people (e.g., analysts, researchers, designers, developers) to produce more detailed plans or develop analytical models

Conceptual Models
- Simpler, faster, less information required
- Not suited to data calculation
- Often less accurate than analytic models when forecasting
- Communicates critical details and factual material to those who need the information.
- Typically, it is best to develop a conceptual framework for understanding before bringing math into the discussion

Advantages
- Provides users with a powerful descriptive tool
- Can present qualitative (conceptual) aspects of the modeled subject
- Also used (in a limited fashion) to present process equations and algorithms (quantitative aspects) used to represent the modeled subject that may be confusing, particularly for the more visually disposed observer
- Promotes understanding by providing a visualization of the subject

Disadvantages
- Only approximate their subjects and are inherently inexact
- Starting conditions and the boundary conditions may not be well understood

Characteristics of Various Models

Analytic Models
- Requires data
- Takes longer to set up, train, and validate data
- Often require significantly more information
- More predictive than conceptual models
- More accurate than conceptual models
- Can be static or dynamic

Static Model
- Type of analytical model that represents a 'fixed' point in time

Dynamic Models
- Type of analytical model that represents a factor(s) as it (they) change(s) with time

Simulations
- A more sophisticated version of a dynamic model

CHAPTER 7

Challenging the Assessment

INTRODUCTION

The ability to effectively challenge one's own assessment and the assessments of other intelligence professionals is an essential aspect of producing consistent and reliable intelligence. This topic's content provides analysts with tools to challenge intelligence assessments systematically and as objectively as possible.

A consistent shortfall identified by multiple US intelligence community (IC) lessons-learned reviews is analysts' failure to challenge well-established consensus assessments. The proponents of the existing

IC mindset or 'group think' position often silence those who dare question those consensus views. Post-9/11, the IC has dramatically increased emphasis on applying structured analytic techniques (SATs) to promote rigorous analysis, lessen the risk of intelligence failure, and make analysts' reasoning more transparent to consumers.

However, a recent Rand study of SATs used by analysts at the US Central Intelligence Agency (CIA) to improve the quality of their intelligence assessments yielded the following key finding:

> The US Intelligence Community does not systematically evaluate the effectiveness of structured analytic techniques, despite their increased use…[supporting this assertion] RAND reviewed 29 CIA IAs [see Glossary for information on 'IAs'] posted on the World Intelligence Review electronic (WIRe) [web]site during a two-week period in July 2014. The IA is the longest form of current intelligence the CIA publishes…Of the CIA IAs in our sample, 23 _showed no evidence of using SATs._[1]

Challenging the assessment can and should be a continuous process. Still, it is often delayed until after the intelligence product is drafted or never performed due to time and other resource constraints. In truth, when the analysis is in line with consensus judgment, often efforts to challenge

---

1 RAND Corporation, _Assessing the Value of Structured Analytic Techniques in the U.S. Intelligence Community,_ By Stephen Artner, Richard S. Girven, and James B. Bruce, 2016.

DOI: 10.4324/9781003241195-7

147

the assessment are not even attempted because analysts/reviewers (and their supervision) do not desire to cause conflicts with other agencies, groups, or higher-ups.

Multiple SATs were introduced in Chapter 10 of the previous text, *Intelligence Analysis Fundamentals*. In Chapters 4 and 5 of this text, several SATs were further discussed using *alternatives analysis and challenging assumptions*. *Alternatives analysis* provides different interpretations and multiple explanations of given events or collected data sets, thereby allowing the analyst to select the best assessment from numerous plausible alternatives. *Alternatives analysis* is generally done as a parallel analysis task.

Chapter 5 follows the SATs associated with, *Challenging Assumptions, a task done early in the analysis process. Challenging assumptions* use primarily two methods; *key assumptions check* (KAC) and *Linchpin Analysis*. Both KAC and lynchpin analysis methods question the basic precepts for the analytical basis arguments, which provide the fundamental drivers for the analysis.

Author's Note: Analysts/reviewers are regularly faced with the quandary: 'if the assessment matches the existing consensus, why challenge it?'

This chapter, *Challenging the Assessment*, can be performed at any time, yet it is most effective after all the data are collected, exploited, analyzed, and the final assessment is drafted. Moreover, it should be performed periodically as the assessment ages and becomes the IC's 'accepted' mindset.

A prime historical example would be the allied high command mindset before World War II, *Battle of the Bulge*. The allied high command assumed if there were to be a German counter-attack, it would be a small operation or highly unlikely, due to several reasons, to quote a US historian:

> *It may be phrased this way: the enemy can still do something, but he can't do much; he lacks the men, the planes, the tanks, the fuel, and the ammunition.*[2]
>
> Hugh Cole, U.S. Historian

This chapter identifies and describes various SATs used for challenging the analytical assessment, specifically Red Team Analysis, High Impact/Low Probability Analysis, Structured Self-Critique, and Devil's Advocacy. At the conclusion of this chapter, a table provides multiple analytic situational issues that align with one or more suitable SATs (see Table 7.1).

---

2   Center of Military History United States Army, *United States Army in World War II, The European Theater of Operations the Ardennes: Battle of the Bulge,* By Hugh M. Cole, Center of Military History United States Army, Washington, D.C., 1993.

Table 7.1 outlines various analytical issues/problems and the more appropriate analytical techniques analysts can select to resolve the issue.

Table 7.1   Analytical Issue/Problem and Associated Techniques for Solving

Analytical Issue/Problem	Devils Advocacy	High Impact/Low Probability	Red Team	Structured Self-Critique
Tactical and strategic operations planning and assessment	X	X	X	X
Weighing validity of source/information	X	X	X	X
Checking/rechecking key assumptions	X	X	X	X
The current situation in a short period of time			X	X
Trying to see a situation from the perspective of another individual or group	X	X	X	X
Political (or other competitive) environment surrounding a government (or criminal/terror) organizational entity			X	
Challenging a strong mindset that an event will NOT happen or confidently made forecast may NOT be justified		X		
Before making a critical decision to determine what could go wrong	X		X	
The possibility that the evidence available is fraudulent or deception is involved	X		X	X
There exist cultural or environmental aspects that are not being adequately evaluated			X	X

....

Author's Note: I recall a headline in USA Today which, at the time, gave me pause: 'Naive: President Trump disputes his own intelligence chiefs on Iran, North Korea.'[3]

There was also a highlighted quote which stated: 'intelligence people are trained professionals who serve our nation with honor and dignity every day, tweeted Michael Morell, the former acting and deputy director of the CIA. They don't play politics with national security – ever.'...

Having been an intelligence analyst and professional producing assessment products at the tactical and strategic levels for numerous administrations and military commanders, I must unequivocally disagree with Mr. Morell's assertion.

Whether conscious or subconscious, everyone has a bias. If one has read the previous text, Intelligence Analysis Fundamentals, and taken the practical exercise quiz associated with the chapter 'Perception and Deception,' there would be immediate recognition that this to be the case.

As long as humans produce intelligence products, those intelligence assessments will be tainted with the authoring analysts' biases and reviewers that produced them. It is the epitome of arrogance or ignorance to assume otherwise.

To further illustrate the point, the following listed instances below are but a few erroneous or woefully inadequate executive national security-related intelligence assessments which were very likely skewed (or severely flawed) due to having been negatively affected by an analysts' and reviewers' biases and then presented to their reader (policymakers and the President of the United States) as the best intelligence available.

_____

3   USA Today, *'Naive': President Trump Disputes His Own Intelligence Chiefs on Iran, North Korea,* By David Jackson, www.usatoday.com/story/news/politics/2019/01/30/donald-trump-intelligence-community-iran-north-korea-isis/2719280002/, January 30, 2019.

Figure 7.1   Khushab Plutonium Production Reactor, Pakistan.[a]

- *Pakistan's development of nuclear weapons (Figure 7.1);[b]*
- *India's development of nuclear weapons;[c]*
- *Soviet invasion of Afghanistan;[d]*
- *Iraq's invasion of Kuwait;[e]*
- *Iraq's possession of (or lack thereof) weapons of mass destruction;[f]*
- *North Korea's development of nuclear weapons;[g]*
- *Russian's incursions into Georgia (2008) and the Ukraine (2014);[h]*
- *Arab Spring;[i] others.*

Others could be listed, but these should be adequate to prove the point: analysts/intelligence reviewers must constantly 'challenge the assessment.'

[a] Photo – Khushab Plant and the Fissile Gap, webpage: http://www.allpakistaninews.com/khushab-plant-and-the-fissile-gap.html, October 29, 2010, Retrieved 16 May, 2022.

[b] Pakistan's development of nuclear weapons – https://www.nytimes.com/1998/05/13/world/nuclear-anxiety-the-blunders-us-blundered-on-intelligence-officials-admit.html,   Retrieved 16 May, 2022.

[c] India's development of nuclear weapons – https://www.nytimes.com/1998/05/13/world/nuclear-anxiety-the-blunders-us-blundered-on-intelligence-officials-admit.html, Retrieved 16 May, 2022.

[d] Soviet invasion of Afghanistan – www.cia.gov›static›e8fa84316547f220a8432d3e1d, Retrieved 16 May, 2022.

[e] Iraq's invasion of Kuwait – HYPERLINK "http://www.latimes.com/archives/la-xpm-2004-jun-17-fg-intel17-story.html"   www.latimes.com/archives/la-xpm-2004-jun-17-fg-intel17-story.html, Retrieved 16 May, 2022.

[f] Iraq's possession of (or lack thereof) weapons of mass destruction – https://discover.hubpages.com/politics/10-Biggest-Blunders-by-the-Central-Intelligence-Agency, Retrieved 16 May, 2022.

[g] North Korea's development of nuclear weapons – https://www.wral.com/u-s-intelligence-failed-to-foresee-north-korea-s-nuclear-strides/17238394, Retrieved 16 May, 2022.

h https://ebrary.net/84882/political_science/russian_incursions_georgia_ukraine, Retrieved 16 May, 2022.
i Arab Spring – https://foreignpolicy.com/2012/01/03/the-ten-biggest-american-intelligence-failures/

RED TEAM ANALYSIS

Red Teaming builds upon concepts gained in Chapter 4, *Alternatives Analysis*. It provides intelligence end-users an independent capability to fully explore alternatives in the context of a given environment and from the perspectives of partners, adversaries, and others.

Red Team Analysis is a contrarian analysis approach that performs three general types of tasks:

1. *Provides decision support,*
2. *Critically reviews existing plans/analyses, and*
3. *Provides a hypothetical Devil's Advocate (threat/adversary's) perspective.*

Red Team Analysis can be performed from an adversary's perspective or systematically/holistically, challenging the group or organization's plans, programs, or ideas at all levels. The text addresses the 'adversarial' method only.

Purpose of Red Team Analysis

The purpose of Red Team Analysis is to challenge or test a system plan or perspective through the eyes of an adversary, outsider, or competitor and, by doing so, understand options available to adversaries by generating plausible hypotheses of adversary behavior and countering adversary deception.

TIPS/NOTES: KEY POINTS

- *Provides a capability to explore alternatives from another's perspective fully;*
- *It is a contrarian analysis approach;*
- *Performs three general types of tasks:*
    1. *Provides decision support,*
    2. *Critically reviews plans/analysis, and*
    3. *Provides a hypothetical Devil's Advocate (threat) perspective;*
- *Analysis can be performed from an adversary's perspective or systematically/holistically, challenging the group or organization's plans, programs, or ideas at all levels.*

TIPS/NOTES: RED TEAM ANALYSIS

- *Present the most compelling arguments first*
- *Use strong, simple declarative statements*
- *Avoid equivocation and analogy*
- *You can use logical argument but try to find reporting that supports the logic*
- *Red teaming should contribute quality thinking rather than quantity*
- *Endeavor not to project personal biases onto the adversary*
- *Despite its many advantages, red teaming is not a silver bullet*
- *Product credibility depends upon the quality and experience of the team, the team's approach and toolset, the quality of the leadership, and the overall context of the effort*
- *Uninformed, overconfident, or culturally biased teams are less likely to add value and may be detrimental to the effort*

METHOD

Leadership should direct a Red Team Analysis performance when there is a potential challenge to a consensus assessment for a particular issue. Since organizational leadership likely has to defend the analysis (*to the corporate board, city hall, or the IC*), especially if the analysis results are contrarian, it is logical for leadership to be on board, willing, and knowledgeable stakeholders of the Read Teaming initiative.

1. Start by studying the adversary, e.g., their culture, history, how they have acted in the given situation in the past, and so on.
2. If possible, embedded cultural expertise into the Red Team, which aids in gaining a more appropriate analytical perspective (the perspective of an adversary).
3. The Red Team Analysis is most effective when it tests existing perceptions with a challenge built upon the strongest possible case. Weakly supported assessments are discounted and ignored.
4. Use role-playing to view the issue from the adversaries' perspective.
5. To avoid being caught in the intellectual ruts created by previous analytical arguments, endeavor to ignore earlier assessments, collect your own data sets, and perform an independent analysis.

(Note: The specific steps used in performing a hypothetical Devil's Advocate (threat) perspective analysis are covered under the section titled 'Devil's Advocacy Analysis' later in this chapter.)

Process Steps

1. Identify/define the Red Team problem – *A clearly defined problem is more likely to yield a more specific, well-articulated response (instead of a vague or overly broad assessment).*
2. Select the Red Team:
   * *The team must possess the right mix of skills and expertise to address the problem fully*
   * *Should be comprised of a combination of subject matter experts, critical and creative thinkers, analysts, cultural experts, and surrogate adversaries*
   * *Fit the tool to the task, assemble an appropriate red team, and ensure individuals have the right skills and experience to do the job*
   * *May require reaching outside the group/organization to call on experts (e.g., other military branches, academia, think-tank institutions, defense industries, and so on)*
3. Set the team objectives:
   * *Focus on key clearly defined issues*
   * *Poorly defined objectives lead to poorly conducted Red Teaming, which is pointless, may be misleading, and engender false confidence*
4. Determine how to use the outputs of the Red Teaming effort – *Knowing what products are to be generated from the Red Teaming process helps to ensure those products/outputs are appropriately addressed*

HIGH IMPACT/LOW PROBABILITY ANALYSIS

High Impact/Low Probability Analysis provides leadership and policy/decision-makers with an early warning that an event, perceived as unlikely, may potentially transpire, accompanied by significant negative consequences. An often-cited example of a high impact/low probability event would be an extinction-level event (ELE), such as a significant meteor impact, which would extinguish nearly all life on the planet as depicted at right[4] (see Figure 7.2). A few relatively recent

---

4   NASA, Artist's depiction of a collision between two planetary bodies, www.nasa.gov/multimedia/imagegallery/image_feature_1454.html, Retrieved April 5, 2019.

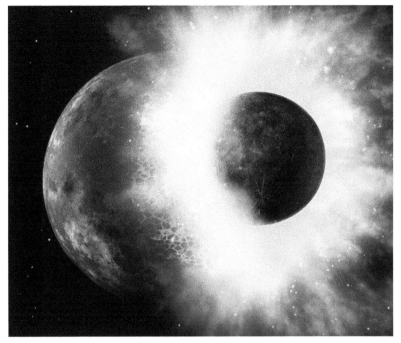

Figure 7.2   Artist's Depiction of a High Impact/Low Probability Event.[4]

examples of where High Impact/Low Probability Analysis would have been helpful are the fall of the Soviet Union, Arab Spring, and ISIS's use of chemical weapons.

> **TIPS/NOTES: KEY POINTS**
>
> *High Impact/Low Probability Analysis:*
>
> - *Provides leadership with an early warning that an event is perceived as unlikely but may transpire to alert leadership to the subsequent consequences.*
> - *Analysis requirement is triggered when indicators are identified, suggesting that the High Impact/Low Probability event may indeed transpire.*
> - *The analysis assumes that the event transpires as a fact, not a possibility, and focuses on consequences and potential mitigating factors.*

Purpose of High Impact/Low Probability Analysis

The purpose of High Impact/Low Probability Analysis is to forewarn policymakers of an improbable event. The impetus for conducting a High Impact/Low Probability Analysis is when some indicator appears in the reporting stream (oftentimes as a fragmentary report). It is recognized, thereby prompting intelligence organizations to suggest that a previously low-probability event is about to occur. The analysis identifies all the potential negative consequences ofo developed counter-actions and mitigation plans.[5]

---

5   Defense Intelligence Agency (DIA), Anonymous, *A Tradecraft Primer: Basic Structured Analytic Techniques*, 2nd ed., 2009.

METHOD

High Impact/Low Probability Analysis assumes that the high-impact event 'will happen,' allowing the analyst to explore potentially detrimental effects fully.

Process Steps

1. Select a group of analysts with broad experiences to brainstorm events.
2. Begin the process by clearly and accurately describing the event using understandable straightforward terminology – *A direct and concise description of a high-impact event provides leadership a distinct picture to better understand 'what is about to happen,' e.g.,*
   * *An improvised nuclear device is in transit to a US coastal port of entry, or*
   * *Terrorists possess a nerve agent that could kill everyone in a city of 100,000;*
   * *A cyber threat could potentially cause a blackout of the east coast, and they intend to or may have already crossed our southern border, and so on….*
3. Identify and list plausible and potentially unpredictable event triggers and outline plausible explanations for or 'scenarios' supporting the low probability outcome.
   * *Each scenario should be expressed as clearly as possible*
   * *Then identify for each scenario a set of indicators or 'observables' that would help you anticipate that events were beginning to play out this way*
   * *These indicators can be used for later monitoring, should the event timeline shift and the immediate threat subside*
4. Insert possible triggers or changes in momentum if appropriate. These can be natural disasters, loss of key national leaders, exacerbation of existing situations (e.g., droughts or famines), or new economic or political tremors that have occurred in the past or elsewhere in the world.
5. Identify potential factors that would reduce the impact(s) or encourage a positive outcome.
6. Outline a periodicity to report on whether any of the scenarios may (or may not) be developing.

STRUCTURED SELF-CRITIQUE

Structured Self-Critique is a systematic method used to identify weaknesses in ones' analysis. Analysts take a hypothetical critical position on their assessment and develop a list of questions. The list of questions should critique all aspects of the analysis to include information gaps, sources of uncertainty, analytic processes followed, and key assumptions used. The analysts then endeavor to respond to each question on the list.

Purpose of Structured Self-Critique

Begin by putting yourself in the shoes of an observer or critic. Imagine being graded on your ability to find weaknesses in your own analysis/assessment. Using the list of topics provided below, critic your analysis/assessment. Unnamed Figure Here

(Note: The list is not all-inclusive, additional topics can be added to the list.)

Analysis – *Was the analytical method appropriate to the data/material under evaluation? Are the results as expected? Was the analysis based on the data or personal bias? Is there a way to determine if the analysis was objective? Was the analysis systematic/methodical? Should another analytical model be used? Did it identify any key assumptions?*

Information Gaps – *Were there any gaps? Were the gaps significant? Do the gaps affect the assessment confidence? If so, how?*

Evidence/Data – *Is the data valid? Can it be validated/tested? Could the evidence/data be otherwise explained (alternative analysis)?*

Sources – *Were the information sources reliable? Were they contradictory or supportive?*

Deception/Diversion – *Is there a possibility that the evidence available is fraudulent? If so, is there a way to determine its authenticity? Is there some parameter or check that can be performed to determine if deception is involved? Is the item/situation under observation created to divert attention/intelligence, surveillance, and reconnaissance (ISR) assets away from something else?*

Inconsistent Evidence – *Was collected data/evidence inconsistent with the final analytical judgment? If so, can it be considered to be valid? Can it be otherwise explained?*

Key Assumptions – *Were there assumptions used? What was their basis? Was it valid? Can they be tested? What is the risk(s) if key assumptions are incorrect and used in the process?*

Cultural/Environmental Considerations – *Are cultural or environmental aspects being adequately evaluated?*

After answering and documenting each of these questions, reassume the analyst's perspective and objectively determine if the assessment should be revised and/or the confidence level adjusted.

The purpose of the Structured Self-Critique is to reassess the analytical assessment's overall confidence level by systematically evaluating all of the materials and processes used to create it.

Author's Note: An example of Cultural/Environmental Considerations: In Afghanistan, it was reported that certain locals were out at night digging near a road during a night aerial surveillance flyover. The initial assessment was that the activity was an exact match for insurgents laying improvised explosive devices (IEDs). Planning was immediately initiated to execute an interdiction mission. However, after further analysis and review, it was learned that local farmers work in their fields at night during the hotter months because of high daytime temperatures. Another surveillance mission was flown, and closer observation demonstrated that the farmers' field happened to be next to a military supply route, and the farmers were indeed tending their fields. An explosive ordnance disposal (EOD) team was sent out to confirm the road was clear, safe and the road surface undisturbed.*

*Source: Just Security, Hostile Intent and Civilian Protection: Lessons From Recent Conflicts, Bonnie Docherty, https://www.justsecurity.org/29871/hostile-intent-civilian-protection-lessons-conflicts, March 10, 2016, Retrieved May 16, 2022.

DEVIL'S ADVOCACY ANALYSIS

The *Advocatus Diaboli* is Latin for Devil's Advocate. The role of the Devil's Advocate is taken from the canonization process in the Roman Catholic Church. In 1587, Pope Sixtus V established a process involving a canon attorney who argued against the canonization (sainthood) to uncover any character flaws or misrepresented evidence favoring canonization.[6] In Devil's Advocacy Analysis, the analysis is best performed by an 'independent' agent (who is not part of the team which performed the original assessment). This analysis collects its own data/evidence, which may be duplicative so that it arrives at the assessment untainted by the initial analytical process.

---

6   Maupin House Publishing, *Exploring Idioms*, By Valeri R. Helterbran, January 1, 2008.

Purpose of Devil's Advocacy Analysis

Devil's Advocacy Analysis looks for what could go wrong and scrutinizes assumptions, data collected, and processes used. It does not need to (or necessarily should be) be adversarial or confrontational. Analytical management/supervision should decide when 'best' to use the technique so as to not create unneeded contention and unhealthy disputes among analysts. The Devil's Advocate can be helpful to keep analysts on track and at the same time assist in ensuring all evidence and perspectives are correctly considered.

Devil's Advocacy Analysis adds strength to the assessment; before being presented to leadership/policymakers in the sense that the assessment would have already successfully withstood the criticism of independent analysis.

TIPS/NOTES:

Devil's Advocacy is not a straightforward and rigid exercise. It can strengthen assessment results or potentially derail and turn the analytical process into a chaotic exercise pitting analysts against their peers.

- *When the advocate selects assumptions, the most vulnerable assumption is often the one with the least corroborating/supporting evidence.*
- *When the advocate reviews validity of supporting information and data used, if significant gaps exist, or if deception is possibly indicated, they can perform their task by asking a series of questions addressing the reliability and validity of the methods and sources used to arrive at the analytical assessment.*

Author's Note: When in the role of 'Devil's Advocate,' focus more effort on sharing alternative views than on arguing analytical positions to convince others.

The purpose of the exercise is to provide analysts with perspectives and facts that may have been missed by the original analysis, not instigate disharmony.

METHOD

The Devil's Advocacy approach used by this text differs from the historical method used by the Catholic Church, which uses an 'independent' advocate. For intelligence analysis purposes, the Devil's Advocate may be a designated member of the analysis team with little or no involvement in the initial analysis.

To challenge a completed analytical product/assessment or just the prevailing analytic line, the Devil's Advocate should:

- First, outline the principal judgment and key assumptions and characterize the collected data supporting evidence associated with the original analytic view/position.
- The advocate then selects one (or more) assumption(s) which appear the most vulnerable to analytical challenge.
- They then review the supporting information/data used to assess whether any is questionable, whether deception is possibly indicated, or whether significant gaps exist.
- The advocate should review cited information gaps and verify that no unidentified/uncited gaps exist.

- Examine any evidence that contradicts the stated assessment, ensure no omissions, and the rationale for why the evidence was discounted is reasonable and clearly explained.
- Verify the possibility that deception has been considered. If it is determined that no deception is involved, an explanation of what indicators were considered to arrive at the 'no deception' decision should be included in the final product.
- Identify alternative analytical methods used or considered, and if analytical outcomes differed using those methods, what were those outcomes, along with potential reasoning for why they differed or were unchanged.

PRACTICAL EXERCISE – DEVIL'S ADVOCACY

This practical exercise has participants performing an independent analysis/review of the canonization of Maid of Orléans (Figure 7.3). You are acting in the capacity of the *Advocatus Diaboli* (aka Devil's Advocate) for the candidate Joan of Arc in order to uncover any character flaws or misrepresentation of the evidence favoring canonization (sainthood). Your task is to take a skeptical view of the candidate's character, look for holes in the evidence, argue that any miracles attributed to the candidate were fraudulent, etc.

Figure 7.3   The Maid of Orléans.

Note: The instructor has to print out and distribute the handout for this exercise.

CHAPTER SUMMARY

The ability to effectively challenge one's own assessment and the assessments of other intelligence professionals is an essential aspect of producing consistent and reliable intelligence. This chapter has presented analytical approaches that analysts can use to challenge intelligence assessments systematically and objectively.

A consistent shortfall identified by multiple US intelligence community (IC) lessons-learned reviews fail to challenge well-established consensus assessments. Often the proponents of the existing IC mindset or 'group think' position tend to silence those who dare question those consensus views. Post-9/11, the IC has dramatically increased emphasis on structured analytic techniques (SATs) to promote rigorous analysis, lessen the risk of intelligence failure, and make analysts' reasoning more transparent to consumers.

However, a recent Rand study of SATs used by analysts at the US Central Intelligence Agency (CIA) suggests that much still needs to be done to institutionalize SAT processes further.

Challenging the assessment can and should be a continuous process. Still, it is often delayed until after the intelligence product is drafted or never performed due to time and other resource constraints. In truth, when the analysis is in line with consensus judgment, often efforts to challenge the assessment are not even attempted because analysts/reviewers (and their supervision) do not desire to cause conflicts with other agencies, groups, or higher-ups.

This chapter identifies and describes various SATs used for challenging the analytical assessment, specifically: Red Team Analysis, High Impact/Low Probability Analysis, Structured Self-Critique, and Devil's Advocacy.

RED TEAM ANALYSIS

Red Teaming builds upon concepts gained in Chapter 4, *Alternatives Analysis*. It provides intelligence end-users an independent capability to fully explore alternatives in the context of a given environment and from the perspectives of partners, adversaries, and others.

Red Team Analysis is a contrarian analysis approach that performs three general types of tasks: (1) provides decision support, (2) critically reviews existing plans/analysis, and (3) provides a hypothetical Devil's Advocate (threat/adversary's) perspective.

Red Team Analysis can be performed from an adversary's perspective or systematically/holistically, challenging the group or organization's plans, programs, or ideas at all levels. The text addresses the 'adversarial' method only.

Purpose of Red Team Analysis

The purpose of Red Team Analysis is to challenge or test a system plan or perspective through the eyes of an adversary, outsider, or competitor and, by doing so, understand options available to adversaries by generating plausible hypotheses of adversary behavior and countering adversary deception.

HIGH IMPACT/LOW PROBABILITY ANALYSIS

High Impact/Low Probability Analysis provides leadership and policy/decision-makers early warning that an event, perceived as unlikely, may transpire, accompanied by significant negative consequences. An often-cited example of a high impact/low probability event would be an extinction-level event (ELE), such as a giant meteor impact, which would nearly extinguish all life on the planet. A few relatively recent examples of where High Impact/Low Probability Analysis would have been helpful are the fall of the Soviet Union, Arab Spring, and ISIS' use of chemical weapons.

Purpose of High Impact/Low Probability Analysis

The purpose of High Impact/Low Probability Analysis is to forewarn policymakers of an improbable event, and the impetus for conducting High Impact/Low Probability Analysis is when some indicator appears in the reporting stream (oftentimes as a fragmentary report), prompting intelligence organizations to suggest that a previously low-probability event is about to occur. The analysis identifies the potential negative consequences in order to develop counter-actions and proper mitigation plans.[7]

---

7   Defense Intelligence Agency (DIA), Anonymous, *A Tradecraft Primer: Basic Structured Analytic Techniques*, 2nd ed., 2009.

STRUCTURED SELF-CRITIQUE

Structured Self-Critique is a systematic method used to identify weaknesses in ones' analysis. Analysts take a hypothetical critical position on their assessment and develop a list of questions. The list of questions should critique all aspects of the analysis to include information gaps, sources of uncertainty, analytic processes followed, and key assumptions used. The analysts then endeavor to respond to each question on the list. Unnamed Figure Here

Purpose of Structured Self-Critique

The purpose of the Structured Self-Critique is to reassess the analytical assessment's overall confidence level by systematically evaluating all of the materials and processes used to create it.

Devil's Advocacy Analysis

The *Advocatus Diaboli* is Latin for Devil's Advocate. The role of the Devil's advocate is taken from the canonization process in the Roman Catholic Church. In 1587, Pope Sixtus V established a process involving a canon attorney who argued against the canonization (sainthood) to uncover any character flaws or misrepresented evidence favoring canonization.[8]

In Devil's Advocacy Analysis, the analysis is best performed by an 'independent' agent (who is not part of the team which performed the original assessment). This analysis collects its own data/evidence, which may be duplicative so that it arrives at its own assessment untainted by the initial analytical process.

Purpose of Devil's Advocacy Analysis

Devil's Advocacy Analysis looks for what could go wrong and scrutinizes assumptions, data collected, and processes used. It does not need to (or necessarily should be) be adversarial or confrontational. Analytical management/supervision should decide when 'best' to use the technique so that it does not create unneeded contention and unhealthy disputes among analysts. The Devil's Advocate can be helpful to keep analysts on track and at the same time assist in ensuring all evidence and perspectives are appropriately considered.

Devil's Advocacy Analysis adds strength to the assessment; before being presented to leadership/policymakers, it has already successfully withstood the criticism of independent analysis.

---

8   Maupin House Publishing, *Exploring Idioms*, By Valeri R. Helterbran, January 1, 2008.

CHAPTER 8

Futures Analysis

INTRODUCTION

Throughout history, rulers, military leaders, and commoners have sought after those who claimed to foretell the future (Figure 8.1). Astrologers, seers, palm readers, and profits have tried their hands at telling the future. Humans have an innate desire to know what comes next, whether it is the next minute or years into the future. Humankind's desire to know the future could be natural curiosity or a real need to control risk or uncertainty.

In any case, analysts should understand that *controlling risk and uncertainty* are the two concepts central to forecasting. Additionally, of the fundamental processes essential to prediction and all aspects of analytical estimation, the most crucial aspect associated with these processes is *accuracy* to avoid inserting additional errors into the process. Using accurate data in intelligence assessments is always crucial. It is ever more critical when forecasting because one starts at a known point, the present, and moves into an ever-changing and unknown future. Therefore, the initial data sets used when forecasting must be as accurate and up to date as possible to avoid inserting additional errors into the process.

Author's Note: Multiple volumes exist that are wholly devoted to making stock market forecasts and predicting financial trends. These texts use a myriad of diverse available approaches. Since I have only achieved a modicum of success with my personal stock portfolio, I shall bow to my betters and direct readers to seek financial forecasting knowledge elsewhere. That said, some of the analytical processes and methods in this text can be adapted to financial or business applications. However, the analytical forecasting applications suggested and examples provided herein shall focus only on military, criminal, counterterrorism, and other more traditional intelligence matters and situations.

DOI: 10.4324/9781003241195-8

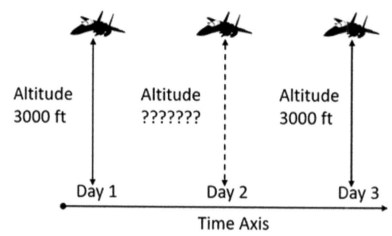

Figure 8.1   Interpolation Example.

This chapter's topic is futures analysis. Futures analysis is principally what the name implies, predicting the future following a defined process. At present, there are two dominant schools of thought; *forecasting* and *backcasting* both are built upon one's perspective. Although the business sector has a great demand for them, the text stays away from financial prediction methods.

Futures analysis discussions within this chapter shall be further confined to the concepts associated with predictive and anticipatory analysis processes and their differences. Predictive analytics employs key past event variables and significant trends that have triggered noteworthy events in the past and then uses the data to determine the probability of recurrence.

The underlying premise of predictive analytics is that past events and trends recur cyclically. In contrast, anticipatory analytic factors rise from the context of changing stakeholder or key player intent, potential reactions to an event or events, and, most significantly, differing alternative futures ranging from the most probable to outlier outcomes.

ANALYTICAL ESTIMATION FUNDAMENTALS

The two most fundamental quantifiable estimation methods used in the analysis are interpolation and extrapolation.

Interpolation

Interpolation is when one estimates a value situated within two known values in a sequence of values. For example, an adversary flies over a target and bombs it three times over three days. On days one and three, the attacking aircraft's altitude could be measured using targeting radar at 3,000 feet. Yet, the targeting radar malfunctioned on day two, and the altitude could not be measured (see Figure 8.1). Suppose the analyst estimated the altitude on day two to be '3,000 feet,' based upon the aircraft's altitude the day before and the day after. This type of estimation is called 'interpolation,' estimating a value situated within two known sequential values.

Extrapolation

Extrapolation is to infer or estimate by extending or projecting from known information or data point. To explain extrapolation, a slightly modified version of the previous example is used. Again, attacking planes engage over three days. Though, in this case, on days one and two, the attacking aircraft's altitude could be measured at 3,000 feet, then on day three, the altitude could not be

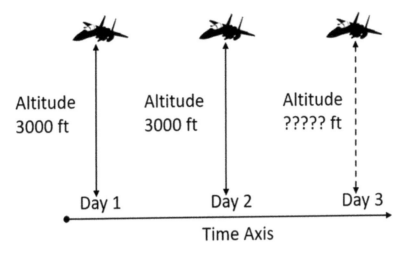

Figure 8.2   Extrapolation Example.

measured (see Figure 8.2). The estimate is still 3,000 feet, but the estimated unknown value is situated at the end of two known sequential values.

Empirical data shows that accuracy and reliability increase with the data set's accuracy and size, allowing for better trend analysis. However, experience shows that in most cases, extrapolation is less accurate than interpolation because with the last known value in the sequence, the likelihood that the data has changed increases. Similarly, accuracy suffers in interpolated data as the distance between known points increases. Estimation accuracy, risk, and uncertainty of extrapolated data increase as one progresses down the time axis away from the last 'known' data point (see Figure 8.3).

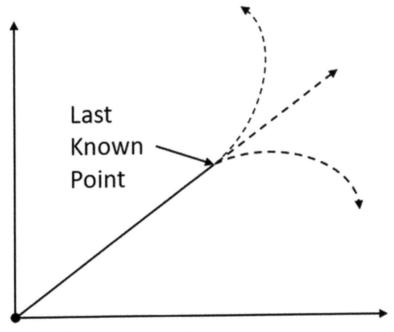

Figure 8.3   Accuracy Suffers Past the Last Known Point.

Forecasting

*Predict most
likely future*

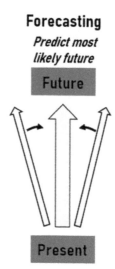

Figure 8.4   Forecasting.

FORECASTING

Forecasting is an objective estimation technique used to predict future data as a function of past known data (Figure 8.4). Forecasting is the process of making analytical estimates of the future based on past and present data and is most commonly performed by analyzing trends. There are multiple processes available for analysts to predict the future (more that deal with looking forward, then back) and, for apparent reasons, more that deal with finance and business than political or military situations. Forecasting is usually applied to short- or intermediate-range decisions and may be quantitative or qualitative.

Quantitative Forecasting

Quantitative forecasting models predict future data (or event cycles) by following past data (or event cycles). Quantitative forecasts are appropriate to use when past numerical data are available, and it is reasonable to assume that some of the data patterns are expected to continue.

TIPS/NOTES: QUANTITATIVE FORECASTING

Used

- When past numerical data **ARE** available, it is reasonable to assume that some of the data patterns are expected to continue
- Short- or intermediate-range decisions

Examples

- Regression analysis,
- Exponential smoothing, and
- Time series analysis

Quantitative forecasting methods are usually applied to short- or intermediate-range decisions. Examples of quantitative forecasting methods are regression analysis, exponential smoothing, time series analysis, prediction markets (PMs), and an analysis of alternate futures (AFA)/scenarios.

Qualitative Forecasting

Qualitative forecasting is a subjective technique based on consumers' and experts' opinions and judgment; it is most appropriate when *past numerical data is unavailable for estimation purposes*. Qualitative forecasting is usually applied to intermediate- or long-range decisions. Qualitative forecasting methods include informed opinion and judgment, the Delphi method, and various historical research types. Examples of qualitative forecasting methods include the Delphi method, PMs, and AFA/scenarios method.

> *Author's Note: A linear regression analysis is used in the Practical Exercise demonstrated in Chapter 6, Applications of Modeling in Analysis.*

Backcasting

Backcasting is the opposite of forecasting; it also involves making analytical estimates (Figure 8.5). Backcasting is an analytical process that defines a potential (desirable/undesirable) future (end-state). It is not concerned with predicting the future per se. The primary distinguishing characteristic of backcasting analyses is the concern, not with likely futures but with how desirable futures can be attained. Thus, it is explicitly normative, involving 'working backward' from a particular future endpoint to the present to determine what changes or series of events would be required to reach that future.

TIPS/NOTES: QUALITATIVE FORECASTING

Used

- *When past numerical data are **NOT** available for estimation purposes*
- *Intermediate- or long-range decisions*

Examples

- *Informed opinion and judgment,*
- *Delphi method, and*
- *Various other types of subject matter expert (SME)-based forecasting methods*

The analyst works backward to identify situations, policies, processes, and other events required to connect the postulated future to the present. The guiding question of backcasting asks: 'if we (or potential enemy) want to attain a particular goal or objective, then what actions must be taken to get there?' (see Figure 8.6). Backcasting is usually applied to intermediate- or long-range decisions.

> *Author's Note: Backcasting is more qualitative. However, PMs and the AFA/scenarios forecasting methods can be qualitative or quantitative, depending on the situation and the provided data.*

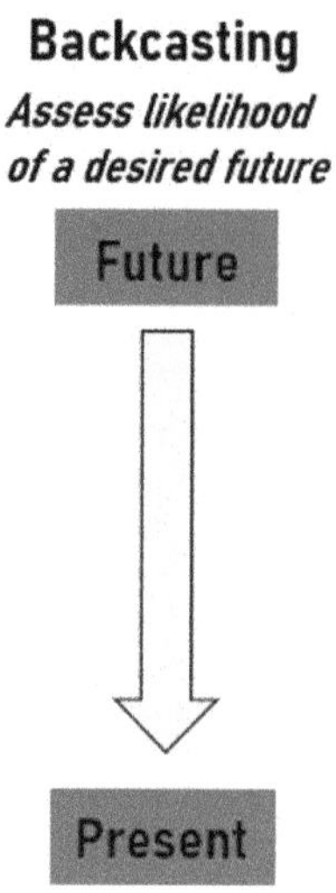

Backcasting

*Assess likelihood
of a desired future*

Future

↓

Present

Figure 8.5   Backcasting.

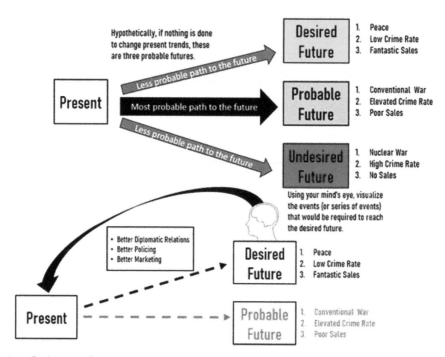

Figure 8.6   Backcasting Examples.

DELPHI METHOD

The Delphi method is a qualitative forecasting technique that uses a panel of experts who are given a situation and asked to provide initial predictions based on a prescribed questionnaire; these experts develop written opinions. These responses are analyzed, summarized, and submitted to the experts for further consideration. All these responses are anonymous so that others' opinions influence no member. This process is repeated until a consensus is obtained. Initially developed for forecasting military events, the Delphi method has also become a useful tool in other areas (see Figure 8.7).

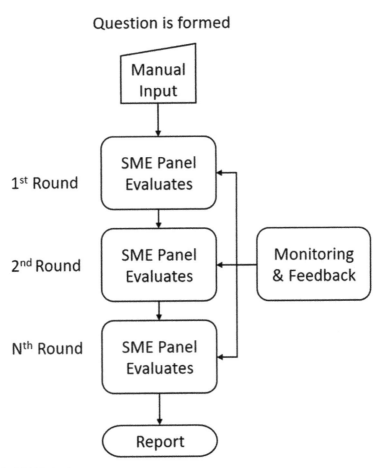

Figure 8.7   Delphi Method.

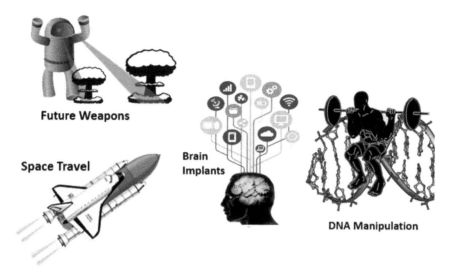

Figure 8.8 Future Technologies Assessed by the Delphi Method.

Background

The Delphi references the Oracle at Delphi in ancient Greece. The Delphi method was initially developed to answer military questions from the early Cold War. Since then, it has been used to assess modern weapons, space, and medical technologies' possible impacts on business and society (see Figure 8.8).

TIPS/NOTES: THE DELPHI METHOD

Advantages

- It can be used to bring geographically dispersed panel experts together (by use of surveys)
- Anonymity and confidentiality of responses
- Avoids direct confrontation of experts with one another
- Structured/organized group communication process (condenses experts' opinions into a few precise and clearly defined statements)
- Cost-effective and flexible/adaptable, fast, versatile.
- Does not require historical/empirical data to be useful.

Disadvantages

- No guidelines for determining consensus, sample size, and sampling techniques
- Requires time/participant commitment
- Time delays between rounds in the data collection process
- Concerns about the reliability of the technique.

TREND IMPACT ANALYSIS

Trend impact analysis (TIA) is a quantitative forecasting approach that extrapolates historical data into the future. Since quantitative methods are based on historical data, they disregard the effects of unprecedented future events. This problem applies to all quantitative methods that require historical data. TIA permits an analyst to systematically examine the effects of possible future events expected to affect the extrapolated trend. The events can include technological, social, economic, political, and value-oriented changes.

TIA is one of the most widely used future studies methods, which includes forecasting, contingency planning, political feasibility analysis, strategic planning, and scenario writing. TIA bases its forecast on quantitative processes but improves the initial forecast using experts' opinions about probable future events. The forecast is typically provided by the Delphi method.

TIA uses various statistical tools, all of which are accessible to intelligence/crime analysts (or business owners). At the most fundamental level, you can plot data points to visualize trends, clarify relationships between variables, and identify 'outliers' or random points that do not fit the pattern. Data points can then be transformed into moving averages to smooth random fluctuations. An analyst (or business owner) can use spreadsheet software to 'fit' trend lines on charted data or build regression models. These allow one to include more variables to predict sales more accurately and forecast the impact of rising interest rates and seasonal changes.

TIA provides a systematic means for combining mathematical extrapolations with an expert assessment of probabilities and impacts of specified future events.

Author's Note: In 1944, General Henry (Hap) Arnold ordered a US Army Air Corps report on future military technological capabilities. Different methods were tried, but the traditional forecasting methods were limited in that there was insufficient empirical data to support the existing forecasting methods became quickly apparent. Therefore, the RAND project developed the Delphi method during the 1950s and 1960s (1959) by Olaf Helmer, Norman Dalkey, and Nicholas Rescher. For years, the Delphi method was widely used outside the intelligence community (IC) (e.g., academia, research, and business). However, it has less application in the IC since many faster and more consistent forecasting methods are now available.

METHOD

1. A curve is fitted to the historical data to calculate the future trend (extrapolation), given no unanticipated future events.
2. Other similar event series and associated indicators are compared and contrasted to existing trends and indicators at hand.
3. Expert judgments are used to identify a set of future events that could cause deviations in the extrapolation of historical data if they were to occur.

EXAMPLE

Taking a topic straight from multiple financial periodicals: Is hyperinflation around the corner for America? First, let's start by defining the term hyperinflation. Hyperinflation is when the prices of goods and services rise more than 50% per month. While there can be several causes of high inflation (e.g., war, their aftermath, sociopolitical calamities, and so on). However, almost all hyperinflations have been caused by government budget deficits financed by an increased money supply. This extraordinary currency creation event happens when a country's government begins printing money to pay for its spending. As the government increases the money supply, prices rise as in regular inflation. An example of one such extraordinary currency event happened in the country of Zimbabwe in 2009 (see Figure 8.9).[1]

---

1   US Treasury, Dallas Branch, *Globalization and Money Policy*, Dated 2011, Retrieved February 13, 2021.

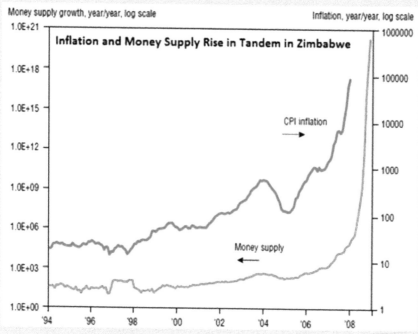

Figure 8.9   Zimbabwe Inflation versus Money Supply Chart.

Now to determine the possible economic trends that brought on hyperinflation in Zimbabwe. According to Figure 8.9, Zimbabwe's hyperinflation event gained significant momentum in 2009. Referring to Figure 8.10,[2] notice that in 2009, the hyperinflation event coincided with Zimbabwe's debt to gross domestic product (GDP) ratio reaching 150%.

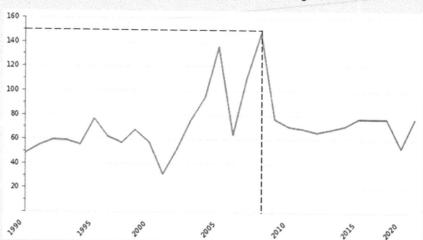

Figure 8.10   Percentage Zimbabwe Government Debt to GDP Ratio.

Figure 8.11 is a historical chart of the US debt to GDP ratio.[3] Assuming the Congressional Budget Office (CBO) budget projection holds and a 150% debt to GDP ratio triggers hyperinflation. For the exercise, assume you and your peers are economic experts. Determine when the US economy might experience hyperinflation?

---

2   Data published Yearly by Reserve Bank, *What Is Zimbabwe Government Debt to GDP Ratio?* https://take-profit.org/en/statistics/government-debt-to-gdp/zimbabwe/, Retrieved February 13, 2021.

3   US Congressional Budget Office, *Long-Term Budget Projections,* Dated January 2020.

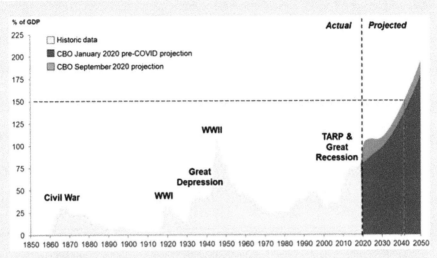

Figure 8.11   CBO Projection of US Dept to GDP Ratio.

TIPS/NOTES: TREND IMPACT ANALYSIS

Advantages:

- *With easy access to data and the computer's capability to process it, trend analysis applications seem almost limitless.*
- *Since trend analysis is based on verifiable data, it can easily be validated.*
- *The use of numbers makes the analysis less subjective.*
- *Trend analysis can be replicated, reviewed, updated, and refined when necessary.*

Disadvantages:

- *Historical data do not always provide an accurate picture of an underlying trend (e.g., outlier and spurious data can skew the trend).*
- *Trend analysis requires analysts to correctly identify the turning points in the data when dealing with short-term data sets.*

Figure 8.12 shows a straightforward generic example of TIA. The figure shows some given parameter 'X' as it progresses with time at a steady-state slope that is slightly positive (e.g., population size). Assume some change in government policy occurs (e.g., increased immigration). The expected result (impact) is that in the future, parameter X (e.g., population size), based upon expert judgment, is expected to grow at a higher rate, reach a peak (max) level, and then decrease to some new steady-state estimated positive value. Once again, there is a new equilibrium; for this example, the new steady state is likely to be positive…perhaps?

PREDICTION MARKETS

PMs (*also known as predictive markets, decision markets, information markets, or cloud sourcing*) are exchange-traded markets created for trading on the projected outcome of events. PMs) is a cutting-edge quantitative/qualitative analytical process that applies economic theory for the ideas behind prediction to tackle real-world issues, including intelligence analysis problem sets.

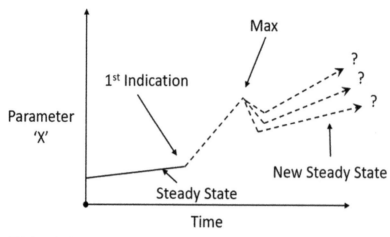

Figure 8.12 TIA Generic Example.

PMs are new and can more effectively anticipate future events better and more consistently than traditional prediction methods (e.g., Delphi method), yet it still has shortfalls. Like most qualitative prediction practices, it can be affected by bias.

> *Author's Note: Theodore J. Gordon first introduced PMs in the early 1970s. At the time, forecasting was done mainly by quantitative methods based on historical data and trend extrapolation. However, these types of methods ignored the impacts of unexpected future events.*

Using the old truism, 'two heads are better than one at solving problems,' PMs exercise this premise by using the collective intelligence of a large group of minds to find a solution. Individual analytical bias is reduced by using large groups and aggregating the bias across a much larger number, thereby diminishing the bias's impact.

Even though the answer may have come from a PM, the resulting answer is equally poor if the analytical question is poorly formulated. Just as in surveys, sampling error plays a role. Moreover, if outside elements pressure participants (e.g., the media, peers, and so on), it also adversely affects outcomes.

> *Author's Note: PMs are not as susceptible to bias, but they are still prone to error. Three conspicuous examples:*
>
> - *Multiple PMs got the 2016 and 2020 presidential elections wrong and in a big way; and*
> - *The 2016 World Series had the Cleveland Indians as the winners up until the next to last game.*
>
> *In the first case, the PMs were entirely off, and in the third case, they barely got it right.*

How It Works

PMs work best when focused on a binary event where something will or won't happen (e.g., an election, will a rocket launch on time, and so on). PMs make the result of this forecasted event tradeable. A financial example of a PM is when participants trade with contracts where the payoff varies depending on the future event's outcome.

Participants essentially are placing wagers on the probability of specific outcomes in certain situations, such as the potential sale of a company, elections, price fluctuations of stocks, or even changes in the weather. The value of a wager will, in most cases, reflect the probability of an outcome materializing.

FUTURES WHEEL

The futures wheel is a visual aid or tool that helps the analyst imagine and document the forecasting exercise (see Figure 8.13). It begins with a central term (event or trend) describing the change to evaluate. The initiating event is positioned in the center of the page (or drawing area). Then, subsequent events or consequences following directly from the initial event are positioned around it. Next, the (indirect) consequences stemming from the direct consequences are positioned around and outside the first-order consequences. The consequences are connected as nodes in a tree (or even a web). The levels often are marked by concentric circles.

Usage

A futures wheel is usually used to organize thoughts about a potential future event or trend. As one approaches the event or follows the trend, possible impacts are identified and put down in a structured way. The lines connecting the events as they progress make it possible to visualize interrelationships of the causes and resulting impacts. Futures wheels can help develop and extend estimations about possible future(s) and other analytical exercises such as 'what-if' analysis or supporting a brainstorming session. They can get analysts past the immediate implications and start the long-term thought process. The futures wheel, depicted in the text, only has four sectors; however, there is no limit on how many sectors an initiating event can have. Still, it becomes quite noticeable that things can get out of hand as the number of sectors approaches ten.

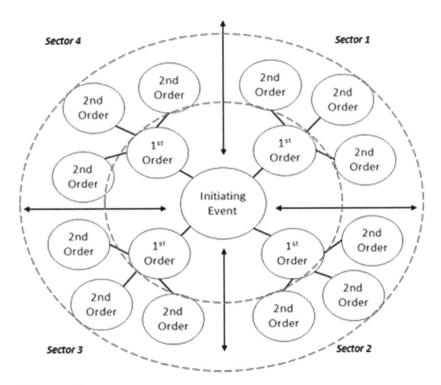

Figure 8.13   Futures Wheel.

TIPS/NOTES: FUTURES WHEEL

- *Don't worry about how it looks, as long as you understand what it says.*
- *Be methodical; take one branch to its end first, don't skip steps.*
- *Try to take it past the third order at a minimum.*
- *When first filling it out, there are no wrong answers.*
- *Cull out the implausible/irrelevant data only after filling out the wheel.*
- *Use the output of this exercise to complement other intelligence efforts.*

METHOD

To create a futures wheel, one only needs a piece of paper (whiteboard or butcher paper), something to write with, and your intellect(s) if more than one analyst is involved. The steps are as follows:

- Identify an event or trend. Discrete events generally make smaller wheels.
- Brainstorm what happens first (first-order):
  - Identify positive, negative, or neutral (*Note: nothing happening is usually a plausible option*)
  - Try to have at least a handful (*Note: more than ten quickly gets to be unmanageable*)
  - Use topics to expand the thought process (*e.g., economic, political, military*)
- Identify what comes next after the first set of outcomes (second-order).
  - There should be multiple branches off each event/impact, positive, neutral, and negative. However, there may be more (*Note: use color codes to make it more user-friendly*).
  - Events branches may have multiple applications (*e.g., forecasting friendly, enemy, allied, market competitor actions, and so on*).
- Repeat the process until events/impacts move beyond the obvious.
- Now identify and evaluate all the underlying assumptions (*see Figure 8.14*).
- Seek opportunities to encourage, mitigate, or deter outcomes as appropriate.
- Cross impacts – Identify and assess linked events/impacts between branches/sectors.
- Delayed impacts – Identify and assess linked delayed events/impacts between branches/sectors.
- Refine and modify the wheel to show what is plausible and relevant to the intelligence consumer/customer.

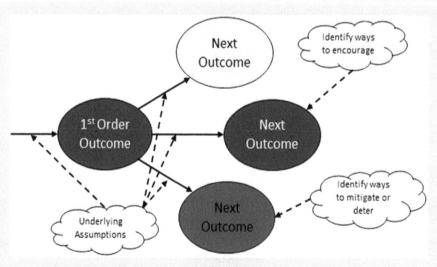

Figure 8.14   Identifying Underlying Assumptions, Ways to Encourage or Mitigate.

Author's Note:

- When using the futures wheel, avoid single-track thinking. Many unanticipated consequences occur when different but dependent branches interact in unintended and surprising ways.
- Futures wheels do not produce finished intelligence products. Indicators must be identified, and associated collection requirements developed, which reflect the results of the exercise.
- *From the analyst's perspective, the futures wheels' purpose is to stimulate thought and prod the analyst(s) to identify and evaluate Nth order outcomes/effects.*

PREDICTIVE ANALYTICS

Predictive analytics is an automated process that uses historical data/trends, machine learning (ML), data mining (DM), and modeling programs to predict the future. However, predictive analytics is somewhat limited in that the historical data/trends input is not comprehensive; as mentioned earlier, the basis of predictive analytics is the hypothesis that past events tend to recur cyclically (see Figure 8.15).

Using the information from predictive analytics can help government policymakers, scientists, law enforcement, military, and business leaders by suggesting actions that can affect positive operational changes (e.g., where to station patrol assets in higher density crime areas, which crops to plant, the enemy's most likely avenue of advance, and so on). Predictive analytics helps to foresee if a change helps them reduce risks by changing one's 'own' operations in order to change that outcome. However, it typically does not consider how a competitor's or adversary's potential actions (or reactions) in the future may affect outcomes.

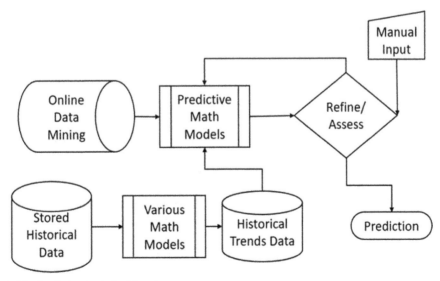

Figure 8.15 Predictive Analytics Flowchart.

METHOD

1. The intelligence consumer's question is fed into the automated process.
2. Historical data and other inputs are fed into a mathematical model that considers critical trends and patterns using the appropriate algorithms and math models.
3. The predictive model is then applied/compared to current minded data to predict what happens next (see Figure 8.16).
4. A feedback process either refines or modifies (or perhaps totally changes) the original question to ensure relevance to the consumer.*

Note: If results have a 10% probability of being correct looking out ten years, but a 70% probability of being correct looking out two years, one may desire to refine the scope to 'two' years.

TIPS/NOTES: PREDICTIVE ANALYTICS

Advantages:

- *Less effort than anticipatory intelligence, less computing power*
- *Identifies the most plausible and probable outcomes.*
- *Suggests changes to one's operations that could possibly modify forecasted outcomes.*

Disadvantages:

- *Does not consider all (or even most) historical events.*
- *Depends on the assumption that historical trends are cyclical.*
- *Doesn't consider effects of competitor's/adversary's potential actions (or reactions) on outcomes.*

Predictive ability is limited by the accuracy of the model and the input data.

ANTICIPATORY ANALYTICS

Anticipatory analytics is an automated systematic process that uses historical data/trends, ML, DM, and modeling programs (like predictive analytics).

A relatively new concept, anticipatory analytics is groundbreaking and is gaining prevalence as a forecasting methodology. It exceeds predictive analytics. It enables governments and private sector organizations to forecast future behaviors quicker than traditional predictive analytics by identifying trends, change, acceleration/deceleration dynamics, and potential adversary actions. However, anticipatory analytics (unlike predictive analytics) uses a robust and diverse data input and then folds this collected information into another algorithm that characterizes potential and imminent anomalies, identifies threats and opportunities, compares the result to trending events and critical events/potential catalysts. (*Refer to Figure 8.17 as each anticipatory analytic constituent process is discussed.*) The various functions that typically reside within anticipatory analytics software are Horizon Scanning, Future Framing, Normative Modeling, AFA, and Monitoring indicators.

Horizon Scanning – Horizon scanning is a technique for detecting early signs of potentially significant developments through a systematic inspection of potential threats and opportunities, emphasizing new technology and its effects on the issue at hand. The process calls for

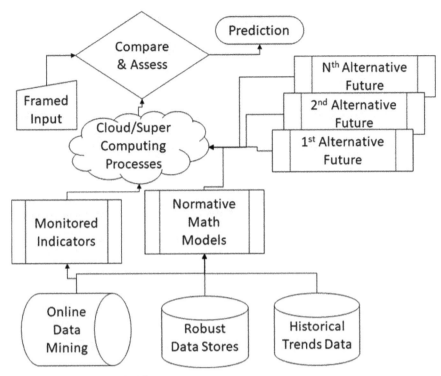

Figure 8.16   Anticipatory Analytical Process.

determining what is constant, what changes, and what continually changes. It explores novel and unexpected issues and persistent problems and trends, including matters at the margins of current thinking that challenge past assumptions. Horizon Scanning is discussed further in the AFA/Scenarios Method section.

Future Framing – Future Framing is the anticipatory analytical process where the analyst structures the question(s) such that all direct/indirect factors which impact current or future trajectories are identified and taken into account. Future Framing is also discussed further in the AFA/Scenarios Method section.

Normative Modeling – Normative Modeling is a process where observations of behaviors and activities are performed and collected; then, a normative model is created as the basis for judging deviations in behavior or predictions of future trends or potential outcomes.

AFA – AFA is a set of predictive techniques used to explore dissimilar, more futuristic states developed by varying a set of key trends, indicators, drivers, and/or conditions. AFA systematically explores multiple ways a situation can develop when there is high complexity and uncertainty. It is most useful when a situation is viewed as too complex or the outcomes as too uncertain to trust a single outcome assessment. AFA was introduced in Chapter 4, *Alternatives Analysis*, and this chapter provides greater detail and multiple examples of its use (see Figure 8.17).

Monitoring Indicators – The process of using the indicators generated by the AFA process and comparing them against anomalies and deviations in the normative models to identify early pointers to deviations in trends that may lead to predicted or unaccounted for outcomes. Analysts using AFA develop indicators or markers to flag increasing/decreasing confidence in any emerging or established trend.

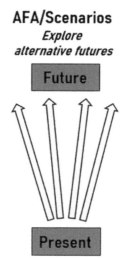

Figure 8.17   AFA/Scenarios Method.

ALTERNATE FUTURES (AFA)/SCENARIOS METHOD

AFA/scenario method handles a wider variety of variables or drivers as compared with other more traditional approaches. It operates in situations where there is high uncertainty because it uses weak indicator signals or even intermittent or missing data inputs.

Scenario generation is integral to the AFA process. Scenarios describe the possible futures. All AFA scenarios generally share a common past and present, yet each future scenario describes a different future. The scenarios are based upon a set of assumptions, knowns, and unknowns. The benefits of developing scenarios are that it allows analysts, by thinking through the process, to identify risks, intelligence gaps, the limits of our knowledge, and by doing so, provide insights into what is needed to prepare for each alternate future (see Figure 8.18).

Analysts build out the extrapolated future scenarios using various factors (or drivers) to support the underlying assumptions. As the various AFA scenarios are socialized, discussed, and argued, two circumstances generally manifest themselves 'spread' and 'collation.'

Author's Note: AFA was initially introduced in Chapter 4, Analyzing Alternatives. The following section briefly reviews what was covered in Chapter 4 and then takes it a step further.

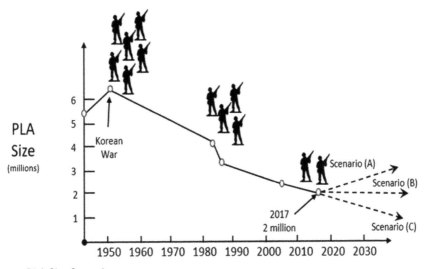

Figure 8.18   PLA Size Scenarios.

EXAMPLE

Refer to Figure 8.19. Illustrating the AFA concept, three future scenarios are depicted using the Chinese People's Liberation Army's (PLA) size as the AFA subject; the figure displays a manning spike upward of 6.3 million men, which coincides with the Korean War. However, for approximately 60 years, one sees a gradual shrinking of the force. Military force structure analysts who follow the PLA typically extrapolate the data for the next 10–20 years using multiple scenario endpoints and providing various supporting assumptions for each future scenario.

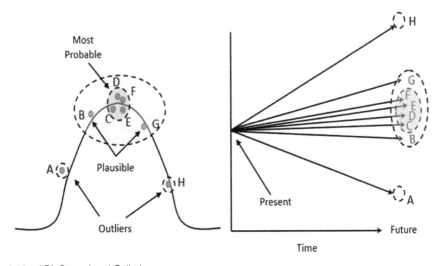

Figure 8.19   AFA Spread and Collation.

*Author's Note: **(Take a moment to have an informal classroom discussion.)** Referring to the example above, note that no scenario provides a more 'optimistic' trend (notice that the most optimistic scenario has the vector continuing with the same slope). Analytical best practices require analysts to provide 'all' plausible alternatives. In this case, the PLA force size has been on a negative slope for 60 years. So continuing at a more negative slope is obviously considered to be implausible.*

Therefore, isn't it more likely (or at least 'as likely') that the slope would continue to be negative moving into the future? That being said, what possibly could drive the PLA force size to shrink (or expand) at a faster rate than what has been observed historically?

Take a minute and hypothesize and discuss what factors might need to be in place to support Scenarios A, B, and C? What would be some of the potential observable indicators that would show that your hypothesis is correct or in error?

Spread

Spread reveals itself as the time axis advances into the future. The more extreme assumptions drive the scenarios to skew away from each other (more or less) based on the influential strength of the future scenarios' internal drivers (see Figure 8.20).

Collation

Collation shares the observable characteristic of 'spread' but to a lesser extent. The more extreme hypotheses become statistical outliers (Scenarios 'A' and 'H'), whereas the more plausible (and generally more supportable) hypotheses tend to group or collate (Scenarios 'B' through 'G'). The 'most probable' alternatives (Scenarios 'C' through 'F') become grouped within the 'plausible' subset, not necessarily in the precise center but generally within the plausible hypotheses' limits. Be aware that just because scenarios are considered the 'most plausible' and are generally easier to support, it does not necessarily mean they are correct, as shown in the example below (see Figure 8.21).

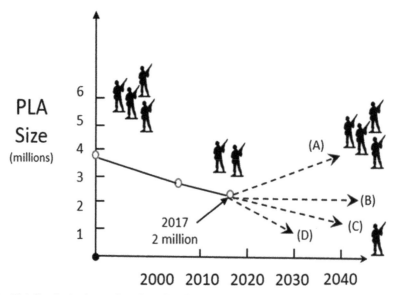

Figure 8.20   PLA Size Projections – Four Specific AFAs.

EXAMPLE

Extending on the previous AFA example using the projected size of the PLA, now four scenarios are provided. In the next 20 years,

 A. *PLA size increases to 1980s levels (roughly 4 million);*
 B. *PLA size stays the same (≈ 2 million);*
 C. *PLA size adheres to its historical slightly negative slope and decreases to about 1 million; and*
 D. *In the next ten years, PLA size decreases by half to about 1 million.*

Table 8.1 outlines basic assumptions, supporting indicators, possible options, and various mitigation activities dovetailed to each of the four AFA scenarios.

Author's Note: Looking back at the provided AFA scenario example for projecting the PLA force size, it should be noted that it is massively oversimplified and should NOT be considered to be definitive or realistic. The example provided only demonstrates the AFA/scenario development process.

Only a few scenarios are provided (enough for academic purposes), including a null option (e.g., 'things stay the same alternative') plus a couple of negative and positive alternatives. Increase, decrease, and unchanged would be considered the bare minimum cases one might consider. A much more robust and nuanced exercise would be more appropriate considering the significance of the topic and its potential influence on national policy decisions.

Next, observe that the necessary steps in developing AFA scenarios are demonstrated (e.g., underlying assumption/hypothesis, supporting indicators identified, options/opportunities, and possible deterring actions/mitigation provided). It does not need to be in a table or matrix. The data is displayed in the format provided merely for instructional purposes.

The AFA/scenario process can become much more complicated. Additional plausible scenarios can be (and typically are) added based upon multiple yet identified drivers (e.g., an unexpected change in leadership of the countries involved, such as China, Taiwan, India, and so on). Furthermore, though not demonstrated in the example provided, unknown (and sometimes overlapping) controlling factors may override the influencing factors/drivers called out at the beginning of the AFA/scenario process. For instance, no potential underlying economic factors were identified in the previous example. One economic factor not mentioned earlier is the ever-increasing per-unit cost of modern military equipment. This economic factor is represented by the production cost of the US Army main battle tank (MBT) from 1945 to 2017 listed below:

- M4 Sherman MBT cost $44,556 to $64,455 in 1945 dollars,[4] depending upon the variant, that equates to $608,000 to $879,000 in 2017 dollars;

- M60 Patton MBT cost $1.2 million in 1990 dollars,[5] which equates to $2.4 million in 2017 dollars;

- M1A2 Abrams MBT cost $8.92 million in 2016 dollars[6] (see Figure 8.22).

Without difficulty, one can observe that the per-unit cost of the US MBT is skyrocketing. At the present rate of increase, it can quickly become exponential and thereby unsustainable. The

---

4   Army Service Forces Catalog ORD 5-3-1, Dated August 9, 1945.
5   US Pricing Policy on the Sale of M60A3 Tanks, Hon. Lee H. Hamilton (Extension of Remarks, November 24, 1993).
6   *Department of Defense, Annual Report FY99.*

Table 8.1   Example AFA Scenarios and Supporting Factors/Drivers

	Assumptions	Indicator	Indicator	Options/Mitigation
A	Increasing regional and international tensions combine to recreate a conflict similar to the Korean War	Open conflict to manifest itself in the Spratly Islands, Taiwan, and/or Indian border dispute	A marked increase in PLA training exercises replicate large-scale combined-arms scenarios to support specific large-scale military operations	Increase open and covert support of regional militaries, new bases, possibly forming alliances, to deter outsider military action Demonstrate military superiority and a clear understanding of potential repercussions
B	Regional and international tensions remain the same or increase slightly, perhaps to a 'Cold War' level	Similar force numbers, missiles, and equipment based in the Spratly Islands, coastal areas facing Taiwan Straits, and/or along the Indian border	No significant change in PLA training operations tempo	Sustained support of regional militaries to deter military action, no new regional military bases
C	Regional and international tensions remain the same or gradually decrease	Gradually reduced force numbers, missiles, and equipment based in the Spratly Islands, coastal areas facing Taiwan Straits, and/or along the Indian border	An overall gradual reduction in PLA training operations tempo However, anticipatory analytics (unlike predictive analytics) uses a robust and diverse data input and then folds this collected information into another algorithm that characterizes potential and imminent anomalies, identifies threats and opportunities, compares the result to trending events and critical events/ potential catalysts.	Gradually reduce support of regional militaries, reduce regional bases, and encourage them to take a more significant role in their country's defense
D	Regional and international tensions decrease drastically	Marked reduction($\approx 1/2$) of force numbers, missiles, and equipment based in the Spratly Islands, coastal areas facing Taiwan Straits, and/or along the Indian border	Overall marked reduction in PLA training operations tempo	Markedly reduce support of regional militaries, leaving them to take a greater role in their country's defense

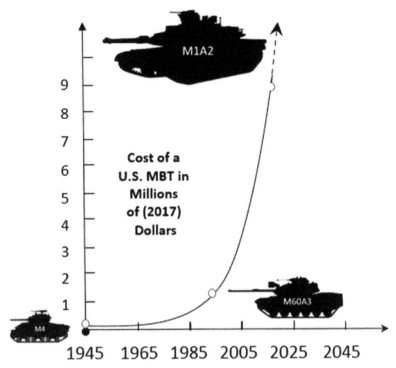

Figure 8.21   Increasing Cost of the US MBT.

US MBT cost curve can be replicated, with comparable results, for most frontline US combat systems, whether ships, submarines, fighter aircraft, or bombers. The phenomenon of ever-decreasing national military force size since the 1950s has manifested itself in most modern armies worldwide, driven primarily by the exorbitant per-unit cost of state-of-the-art modern military equipment.

Author's Note: The US MBT (as opposed to the PLA MBT) was used as the text's example for multiple reasons. The Type 59 MBT was the first indigenous Chinese-made tank, made in 1959, so there is no 1945 PLA MBT counterpart. Additionally, there exists no reliable unclassified PLA cost data available for academic purposes.

The Type 99A2 is the most modern version PLA MBT and has comparable size, modern armor, and weaponry. Therefore, it is logical to assume the 99A2 would have analogous manufacturing costs to the US MBT. Most military historians cite the US versus Soviet arms race of the late 1980s as the death knell that led to the dissolution of the Soviet Union, primarily because of the associated high military development and production costs and the inability of the Soviet economy to sustain the pace.

Therefore, using the logic presented, could the cost of modern military equipment be considered a possible 'unidentified' indirect yet controlling factor? Does it provide new opportunities? Final Question: Does a potential arms race benefit the United States or China, both or neither?

Horizon Scanning

Horizon Scanning detects early signs of potentially significant developments, mainly when dealing with new technologies and their effects on the issue(s) at hand.

Following that thought thread, a few technologies have emerged with potentially disruptive military implications in the last 20 years. Of note is unmanned aerial vehicle (UAV) technology, also known as 'drones.' Autonomous commercial drone technology is likely to expand in the near future to perhaps replace commercial train and truck transport. Drone technology has made a sobering impact in the field of military intelligence reconnaissance. Naval ship and submarine prototypes have also been built and tested, and autonomous tanks and other ground combat vehicles are forecasted to appear operationally on global battlefields.

Author's Note: **Food for thought:** Extending the 'PLA Force Size' example from earlier; 'How could drone technology (if adopted) potentially affect the size of the force?'

Future Framing

Future Framing was identified earlier as a process where the analyst structures the 'question(s)' such that all direct and indirect factors which impact current or future trajectories are identified and taken into account.

Analysts would work with SMEs to identify these questions at various scenario development stages to ensure that as many direct/indirect factors are included and accounted for in the AFA/scenarios.

Using the high trajectory of military expenditures as a plausible indirect factor impacting military force size's trajectory generates potential questions. *What is the impact of the greater scarcity of rare earth metals on state-of-the-art military electronics production? Will the scarcity of rare earth metals impact the trajectory of both the United States and China military force structures equally?*

FINAL THOUGHTS

This chapter has covered multiple approaches to futures analysis. All approaches use a structured process to deal with analytical bias and handle the uncertainty and risk levels that grow and expand as analysts probe further down the timeline into the future.

However, the future is ever-changing and evermore increasingly complex. The complexity of futures analytics is quite complicated and is becoming more so continuously as one extrapolates into the future and adds more variables to the analysis. Therefore, it should be apparent that modern predictive and anticipatory analytics are very dependent on machine analytics and artificial intelligence. The IC uses supercomputers and cloud computing networks for much of this type of analysis. Breakthroughs in artificial intelligence and futures analysis using these marvels of technology are coming into their own and forecasted to dominate the intelligence field soon.

CHAPTER SUMMARY

This chapter explained that the two most fundamental quantifiable estimation methods used in the analysis are interpolation and extrapolation. Then went on to the concepts of understanding and controlling risk and uncertainty; both are central to forecasting. Additionally, of the fundamental processes essential to prediction and all aspects of analytical estimation, the most crucial aspect associated with these processes is *accuracy.* Accuracy is crucial to avoid inserting additional errors into the process.

At present, futures analysis supports two major schools of thought: *forecasting* and *backcasting*, and both are built upon one's perspective. Some of the analytical processes and methods in this text can be adapted to financial or business applications.

Furthermore, futures analysis discussions within this chapter were confined to the concepts of the predictive and anticipatory analysis processes and their differences. Predictive analytics employs key past event variables and significant trends that triggered noteworthy events in the past and then uses the data to determine the probability of recurrence. The underlying premise of predictive analytics is that past events/trends recur cyclically. In contrast, anticipatory analytics factors into the solution, changing stakeholder/key player intent, potential reactions, and, most significantly, different alternative futures ranging from probable to outlier outcomes.

ANALYTICAL ESTIMATION FUNDAMENTALS

The two most fundamental quantifiable estimation methods used in the analysis are interpolation and extrapolation.

Interpolation

Interpolation is when one is estimates a value situated within two known values in a sequence of values.

Extrapolation

Extrapolation is to infer or estimate by extending or projecting from known information or data point.

FORECASTING

Forecasting is an objective estimation technique used to predict future data as a function of past known data. Forecasting is the process of making analytical estimates of the future based on past and present data and is most commonly performed by analyzing trends. Multiple processes are available for analysts to predict the future (more that deal with looking forward, then back).

Quantitative Forecasting

Quantitative forecasting models predict future data (or event cycles) by following past data (or event cycles). Quantitative forecasts are appropriate to use when past numerical data are available, and it is reasonable to assume that some of the data patterns are expected to continue.

Quantitative forecasting methods are usually applied to short- or intermediate-range decisions. Examples of quantitative forecasting methods are regression analysis, exponential smoothing, and time series analysis.

Qualitative Forecasting

Qualitative forecasting is a subjective technique based on consumers' and experts' opinions and judgment; it is most appropriate when *past numerical data is unavailable for estimation purposes*. Qualitative forecasting is usually applied to intermediate- or long-range decisions. Qualitative forecasting methods include informed opinion and judgment, the Delphi method, and various historical research types.

Backcasting

Backcasting is the opposite of forecasting; it also involves making analytical estimates. Backcasting is an analytical process that defines a potential (desirable/undesirable) future (end-state). It is not concerned with predicting the future per se. The primary distinguishing characteristic of backcasting analyses is the concern, not with likely futures but with how desirable futures can be attained. Thus, it is explicitly normative, involving 'working backward' from a particular future endpoint to the present to determine what changes or series of events would be required to reach that future.

The analyst works backward to identify situations, policies, processes, and other events required to connect the postulated future to the present. The guiding question of backcasting asks: 'if we (or potential enemy) want to attain a particular goal or objective, then what actions must be taken to get there?' Backcasting is usually applied to intermediate- or long-range decisions. Examples of qualitative forecasting methods include the Delphi method, PMs, and analysis of alternate futures (AFA)/scenarios method.

DELPHI METHOD

The Delphi method is a qualitative forecasting technique that uses a panel of experts who are given a situation and asked to provide initial predictions based on a prescribed questionnaire; these experts develop written opinions. These responses are analyzed, summarized, and submitted to the expert panel for further consideration. All these responses are anonymous so that others' opinions influence no member. This process is repeated until a consensus is obtained. Initially developed for forecasting military events, the Delphi method has also become a useful tool in other areas.

TREND IMPACT ANALYSIS

Trend impact analysis (TIA) is a quantitative forecasting approach that extrapolates historical data into the future. Since quantitative methods are based on historical data, they disregard the effects of unprecedented future events. This problem applies to all quantitative methods that require historical data. TIA permits an analyst to systematically examine the effects of possible future events expected to affect the extrapolated trend. The events can include technological, social, economic, political, and value-oriented changes.

TIA is one of the most widely used future studies methods, which include forecasting, contingency planning, political feasibility analysis, strategic planning, and scenario writing. TIA bases its forecast on quantitative processes but then tries to improve the initial forecast using experts' opinions about probable future events. The forecast is typically provided by the Delphi method.

TIA uses various statistical tools, all of which are accessible to intelligence/crime analysts (or business owners). At the most fundamental level, you can plot data points to visualize trends, clarify relationships between variables, and identify 'outliers' or random points that do not fit the pattern. Data points can then be transformed into moving averages to smooth random fluctuations. An analyst (or business owner) can use spreadsheet software to 'fit' trend lines on charted data or build regression models. These allow one to include more variables to predict sales more accurately and forecast the impact of rising interest rates and seasonal changes.

TIA provides a systematic means for combining mathematical extrapolations with an expert assessment of probabilities and impacts of specified future events.

METHOD

1. A curve is fitted to the historical data to calculate the future trend (extrapolation), given no unanticipated future events.
2. Other similar event series and associated indicators are compared and contrasted to existing trends and indicators at hand.
3. Expert judgments are used to identify a set of future events that could cause deviations in the extrapolation of historical data if they were to occur.

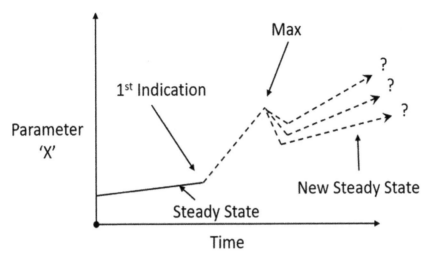

Figure 8.22 TIA Generic Example.

Figure 8.22 shows a straightforward generic example of TIA. Some given parameter 'X' progresses with time at a steady-state slope that is slightly positive (e.g., population size). Some change in government policy (e.g., immigration) occurs. The expected result (impact) is that in the future, parameter X (population size), based upon expert judgment, is expected to grow at a higher rate, reach a peak (max) level, and then decrease to some new steady-state estimated positive value. Once again, there is a new equilibrium; the new steady-state is likely to be positive…perhaps?

PREDICTION MARKETS

PMs (*also known as predictive markets, decision markets, information markets, or cloud sourcing*) are exchange-traded markets created for trading on the projected outcome of events. PM is a cutting-edge quantitative/qualitative analytical process that applies economic theory for the ideas behind prediction to tackle real-world issues, including intelligence analysis problem sets.

PM is new and can more effectively anticipate future events better and more consistently than the traditionally accepted prediction methods (e.g., Delphi method), yet it still has its shortfalls. Like most qualitative prediction practices, it can be affected by bias.

Using the old truism, 'two heads are better than one at solving problems,' PMs exercise this premise by using the collective intelligence of a large group of minds to find a solution. Individual analytical bias is reduced by using larger groups to aggregate the existing bias across a much larger number, thereby diminishing the bias's impact.

Even though the answer may have come from a PM, the resulting answer is equally poor if the analytical question is poorly formulated. Just as in surveys, sampling error plays a role. Moreover, if outside elements pressure participants (e.g., the media, peers, and so on), it also adversely affects outcomes.

How It Works

It works best when focused on a binary event where something will or won't happen (e.g., an election, will a rocket launch on time, others, and so on). A financial example of a PM is when participants trade with contracts where the payoff varies depending on the future event's outcome. PMs make the result of this forecasted event tradeable.

Participants essentially are placing wagers on the probability of specific outcomes in certain situations, such as the potential sale of a company, elections, price fluctuations of stocks, or even changes in the weather. The value of a wager will, in most cases, reflect the probability of an outcome materializing.

FUTURES WHEEL

The futures wheel is a visual aid or tool that helps the analyst imagine and document the forecasting exercise. It begins with a central term (event or trend) describing the change to evaluate. The initiating event is positioned in the center of the page (or drawing area). Then, subsequent events or consequences following directly from that initial event are positioned around it. Next, the (indirect) consequences stemming from the direct consequences are positioned around and outside the first-order consequences. The consequences are connected as nodes in a tree (or even a web). The levels often are marked by concentric circles.

Usage

A futures wheel is usually used to organize thoughts about a potential future event or trend. As one approaches the event or follows the trend, possible impacts are identified and put down in a structured way. The lines connecting the events as they progress make it possible to visualize interrelationships of the causes and resulting impacts. Futures wheels can help develop and extend estimations about possible future(s) and other analytical exercises such as 'what-if' analysis or supporting a brainstorming session. They can get analysts past the immediate implications and start the long-term thought process. The futures wheel, depicted in the text, only has four sectors; however, there is no limit on how many sectors an initiating event can have. Still, it becomes quite noticeable that things can get out of hand as the number of sectors approaches ten.

METHOD

To create a futures wheel, one only needs a piece of paper (whiteboard or butcher paper), something to write with, and your intellect(s) if more than one analyst is involved. The steps are as follows:

1. Identify an event or trend. Discrete events generally make smaller wheels.
2. Brainstorm what happens first (first-order):
   - Identify positive, negative, or neutral (Note: nothing happening is usually a plausible option)
   - Try to have at least a handful (Note: more than ten quickly gets to be unmanageable)
   - Use topics to expand the thought process (e.g., economic, political, military)
3. Identify what comes next after the first set of outcomes (second-order).
   - There should be multiple branches off each event/impact, positive and negative. However, there may be more (Note: use color codes to make it more user-friendly).
   - Events branches may have multiple applications.
4. Repeat the process until events/impacts move beyond the obvious.
5. Now identify and evaluate all the underlying assumptions.
6. Seek opportunities to encourage, mitigate, or deter outcomes as appropriate.
7. Cross impacts – Identify and assess linked events/impacts between branches/sectors.
8. Delayed impacts – Identify and assess linked delayed events/impacts between branches/sectors.
9. Refine and modify the wheel to show what is plausible and relevant to the intelligence consumer/customer.

PREDICTIVE ANALYTICS

Predictive analytics is an automated process that uses historical data/trends, machine learning (ML), data mining (DM), and modeling programs to predict the future. However, predictive analytics is somewhat limited in that the historical data/trends input is not comprehensive; as mentioned earlier, the basis of predictive analytics is the hypothesis that past events tend to recur cyclically.

Using the information from predictive analytics can help government policymakers, scientists, law enforcement, military, and business leaders by suggesting actions that can affect positive operational changes (e.g., where to station patrol assets in higher density crime areas, which crops to plant, the enemy's most likely avenue of advance, and so on). Predictive analytics helps to foresee if a change helps them reduce risks by changing one's 'own' operations in order to change that outcome. However, it typically does not consider how a competitor's or adversary's potential actions (or reactions) in the future may affect outcomes.

METHOD

1. The intelligence consumer's question is fed into the automated process.
2. Historical data and other inputs are fed into a mathematical model that considers critical trends and patterns in the data using appropriate algorithms and math models.
3. The predictive model is then applied/compared to current-minded data to predict what happens next. The feedback process either refines or modifies (or perhaps changes) the original question to ensure relevance to the consumer.*

Note: If results have a 10% probability of being correct looking out ten years, but a 70% probability of being correct looking out two years, one may desire to refine the scope 'two' years.

ANTICIPATORY ANALYTICS

Anticipatory analytics is an automated systematic process that uses historical data/trends, ML, DM, and modeling programs (like predictive analytics).

However, anticipatory analytics (unlike predictive analytics) also uses a very robust and diverse data input and then folds this collected information into another algorithm that characterizes potential and imminent anomalies, identifies threats and opportunities, compares the result to trending events, and critical events/potential catalysts. The various functions that typically reside within anticipatory analytics software are Horizon Scanning, Future Framing, Normative Modeling, AFA, and Monitoring indicators.

Horizon Scanning – Horizon scanning is a technique for detecting early signs of potentially significant developments through a systematic inspection of potential threats and opportunities, emphasizing new technology and its effects on the issue at hand. The process calls for determining what is constant, what changes, and what continually changes. It explores novel and unexpected issues and persistent problems and trends, including matters at the margins of current thinking that challenge past assumptions. Horizon Scanning is discussed further in the AFA/Scenarios Method section.

Future Framing – Future Framing is the anticipatory analytical process where the analyst structures the question(s) such that all direct/indirect factors which impact current or future trajectories are identified and taken into account. Future Framing is also discussed further in the AFA/Scenarios Method section.

Normative Modeling – Normative Modeling is a process where observations of behaviors and activities are performed and collected; then, a normative model is created as the basis for judging deviations in behavior or predictions of future trends or potential outcomes.

AFA – AFA is a set of predictive techniques used to explore dissimilar, more futuristic states developed by varying a set of key trends, indicators, drivers, and/or conditions. Systematically explores multiple ways a situation can develop when there is high complexity and uncertainty. Most useful when a situation is viewed as too complex or the outcomes as too uncertain to trust a single outcome assessment.

Monitoring Indicators – The process of using the indicators generated by the AFA process and comparing them against anomalies and deviations in the normative models to identify early pointers to deviations in trends that may lead to predicted or unaccounted for outcomes. Analysts using AFA develop indicators or markers to flag increasing/decreasing confidence in any emerging or established trend.

ALTERNATE FUTURES (AFA)/SCENARIOS METHOD

AFA/scenarios method handles a wider variety of variables or drivers as compared with other more traditional approaches. AFA/scenario operates in situations with high uncertainty because it uses weak indicator signals or even intermittent or missing data inputs.

Scenario generation is integral to the AFA process. Scenarios describe the possible futures. All AFA scenarios generally share a common past and present, yet each future scenario describes a different future. Each scenario is based upon a set of assumptions, knowns, and unknowns. The benefits of developing scenarios are that it allows analysts, by thinking through the process, to identify risks, intelligence gaps, and the limits of our knowledge and, by doing so, provide insights into what is needed to prepare for each alternate future.

Analysts build out the extrapolated future scenarios using various factors (or drivers) to support the underlying assumptions. As the various AFA scenarios are socialized, discussed, and argued, two circumstances generally manifest themselves 'spread' and 'collation.'

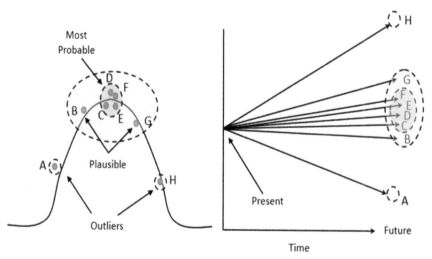

Figure 8.23   AFA Spread and Collation.

Spread

Spread reveals itself as the time axis advances into the future. The more extreme assumptions drive the scenarios to skew away from each other (more or less) based on the influential strength of the future scenarios' internal drivers.

Collation

Collation shares the observable characteristic of 'spread' but to a lesser extent. The more extreme hypotheses become statistical outliers (Scenarios 'A' and 'H'), whereas the more plausible (and generally more supportable) hypotheses tend to group or collate (Scenarios 'B' through 'G'). The 'most probable' alternatives (Scenarios 'C' through 'F') become grouped within the 'plausible' subset, not necessarily in the precise center, but generally within the plausible hypotheses' limits. Be aware that just because scenarios are considered the 'most plausible' are generally easier to support; it does not necessarily mean they are correct, as shown in the example above (see Figure 8.23).

The AFA/scenario process can become much more complicated. Additional plausible scenarios can be (and typically are) added based upon multiple yet identified drivers (e.g., an unexpected change in leadership of the countries involved; China, Taiwan, India, and so on). Furthermore, though not demonstrated in the example provided, an unknown (and sometimes overlapping) yet controlling factors may override the influencing factors/drivers called out in the initiating AFA/scenario process. For instance, no potential underlying economic factors were identified in the previous example. One economic factor not mentioned earlier is the ever-increasing per-unit cost of modern military equipment. This phenomenon represents the production cost of the US Army main battle tank (MBT) from 1945 to 2017.

One can without difficulty observe that the per-unit cost of the US MBT is skyrocketing. At the present rate of increase, it can quickly become exponential and thereby unsustainable. The US MBT cost curve can be replicated, with comparable results, for most frontline US combat systems, whether ships, submarines, fighter aircraft, or bombers. The phenomenon of ever-decreasing national military force size since the 1950s has manifested itself in modern armies across the globe, primarily due to the exorbitant per-unit cost of state-of-the-art modern military equipment.

Horizon Scanning

Horizon Scanning detects early signs of potentially significant developments, mainly when dealing with new technologies and their effects on the issue(s) at hand.

Following that thought thread, a few technologies have emerged with potentially disruptive military implications in the last 20 years. Of note is unmanned aerial vehicle (UAV) technology, also known as 'drones.' Autonomous drone technology may expand in the near future to perhaps replace commercial train and truck transport. Drone technology has made a sobering impact in the field of military intelligence reconnaissance. Naval ship and submarine prototypes have also been built and tested, and autonomous tanks and other ground combat vehicles are forecasted to soon appear operationally on the battlefield.

Future Framing

Future Framing was identified earlier as a process where the analyst structures the 'question(s)' such that all direct/indirect factors which impact current or future trajectories are identified and taken into account.

Table 8.2 When to Apply Forecasting Techniques.

Method \ Property	Quantitative	Qualitative	Forward Perspective	Backward Perspective	Past numerical data required	Past numerical data NOT required	Usage	Characteristics	Example(s)
Interpolation	X		X	X	X		Estimating a value situated within two known values in a sequence	Good for filling data set gaps	Inverse Distance Weighted (IDW) and Spline estimates
Extrapolation	X		X	X	X		Inferring or estimating by extending or projecting from known information or data point	Good for working with incomplete data sets	Linear, Polynomial, Conic, French curve
Forecasting	X	X	X		X		Broad usage	Can be quantitative or qualitative	Quantitative, Qualitative
Quantitative Forecasting	X		X		X		Short or intermediate-range decisions	Objective, less bias	Regression analysis, Exponential smoothing, and Time series analysis, Prediction Markets, Alternate Futures/Scenarios
Qualitative Forecasting		X	X			X	Intermediate or long-range decisions	Susceptible to bias	Delphi Method, Prediction Markets, Alternate Futures/Scenarios
Backcasting		X	X	X			Determining actions/events required to make a desired future more likely	Normative	Exercises directed at influencing or changing the future
Delphi Method		X	X			X	Assess modern weapons, space, and medical technologies' possible impacts on business and society	Expert opinions collected and shared in a structured iterative process	Impact of DNA manipulation, Space travel and mining. Use of hypersonic weapons and lasers by adversaries
Trend Impact Analysis (TIA)	X	X	X			X	Uses quantitative forecasting to extrapolate past trends into the future typically using the Delphi Method	Uses both quantitative and qualitative estimation processes	Contingency planning, political feasibility analysis, strategic planning, and scenario writing
Prediction Markets (PMs)	X	X	X			X	Applies economic theory to solve binary problem sets by using a wagering process	Uses both quantitative and qualitative estimation processes	Elections, stock markets, futures trading
Futures Wheel		X	X			X	Used to stimulate the imagination of analyst to identify Nth order consequences of an event	Stimulates the analytical process, not a final product	Brainstorming exercises, What if analysis, visualizing relationships

Table 8.2 Continued

Property / Method	Quantitative	Qualitative	Forward Perspective	Backward Perspective	Past numerical data required	Past numerical data NOT required	Usage	Characteristics	Example(s)
Predictive Analytics	X	X	X		X		Automated process that uses ML, DM, and modeling to perform quantitative forecasting to extrapolate past trends into the future	Uses predictive analytic algorithms has a feedback system, does not consider adversary actions/reactions	Used by policymakers, scientists, law enforcement, military, and business leaders by suggesting actions to effect positive operational changes
Anticipatory Analytics	X	X	X	X	X		Automated process that uses ML, DM, modelling, robust and diverse inputs, and cloud computing to perform quantitative forecasting to extrapolate past trends into the future	It exceeds predictive analytics by using Horizon Scanning, Future Framing, Normative Modeling, Alternate Futures Analysis, and monitoring indicators	It enables governments and private sector organizations to forecast future behaviors quicker than traditional predictive analytics by identifying trends, change, acceleration/deceleration dynamics, and potential adversary actions.
Horizon Scanning	X	X	X		X		Technique for detecting early signs of potentially significant developments through a systematic inspection to determine what is constant, what changes, and what continually changes	Explores novel and unexpected issues and persistent problems and trends	Aspect of Anticipatory Analytics, most useful for identifying the emergence of new technologies
Future Framing	X	X	X		X		Anticipatory analytical process that reveals the impact of current or future trajectories based upon predined input factors	Analyst defines direct/indirect factors to be into account	Aspect of Anticipatory Analytics. Useful for what if analysis and contingency planing
Alternate Futures Analysis	X	X	X	X	X		Predictive techniques used to explore dissimilar, more futuristic states developed by varying a set of key trends, indicators, drivers, and/or conditions	Systematically explores multiple ways a situation can develop when there is high complexity and uncertainty	Aspect of Anticipatory Analytics, most useful when a situation is viewed as too complex or the outcomes as too uncertain to trust a single outcome assessment
Normative Modeling	X	X	X		X		Process where observations of behaviors and activities are performed and collected; then, a standardized model is created as the basis for judging deviations in behavior or predictions of future trends or potential outcomes	Must have observations of behaviors and activities to use for a model to be effective, provides an input to monitoring indicators process	Aspect of Anticipatory Analytics, useful in behavioral analytics and Activity based intelligence
Monitoring Indicators	X	X	X		X		Process of using indicators and comparing them against anomalies and deviations in the normative models to identify early pointers to deviations in trends that may lead to predicted or unaccounted for outcomes	Uses AFA developed markers to flag increasing/decreasing confidence in emerging or established trends	Aspect of Anticipatory Analytics, uses the output (indicators) generated by the AFA process
Alternate Futures (AFA)/Scenarios	X	X	X		X		Uses generated scenarios, based upon a set of assumptions, knowns, and unknowns to describe the possible futures	Operates in situations where there is high uncertainty because it uses weak indicator signals or even intermittent or missing data inputs	Aspect of Anticipatory Analytics, allows analysts, by thinking through the process, to identify risks, intelligence gaps, the limits of our knowledge, and by doing so, provide insights into what is needed to prepare for each alternate future

Analysts would work with SMEs to identify these questions at various scenario development stages to ensure that as many direct/indirect factors are included and accounted for in the AFA/scenarios.

Using the high trajectory of military expenditures as a plausible indirect factor impacting military force size's trajectory generates potential questions. *What is the impact of the greater scarcity of rare earth metals on state-of-the-art military electronics production? Will the scarcity of rare earth metals impact the trajectory of both the US and China military force structures equally?*

PRACTICAL EXERCISE – PARTICIPANT GUIDE

This practical exercise utilizes the *futures wheel* as a visual aid/tool to help your team perform and document an abbreviated futures analysis session (Figure 8.25). You are tasked with choosing one of the three listed items below, which are associated with potentially disruptive technologies in the areas of artificial intelligence (AI), the human genome, and space exploration. Break up into groups of at least two, but no larger than five participants. Multiple groups can select the same bulleted item from the list to conduct the exercise.

Forecast the benefits and risks to humanity (or for our country) associated with:

- Development of artificial intelligence/superintelligence
- Genetic manipulation of the human genome
- Exploring our solar system

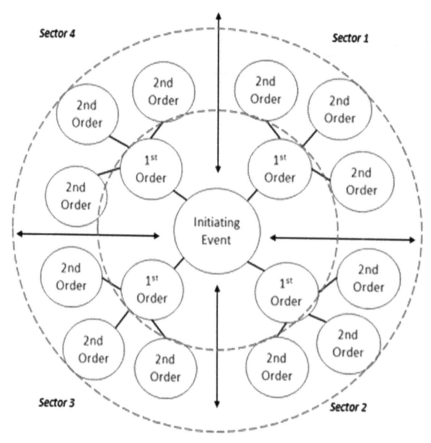

Figure 8.25   Futures Wheel.

Refer to the text as needed to develop your forecast. Use a futures wheel like the one below to record your data. You need to identify at least two, but no more than four '1st order effects,' at least one needs to be positive, and at least one needs to be negative in nature.

You have one hour to perform the exercise and document the results. Use your time wisely, and be prepared to provide a brief presentation explaining your thinking.

CHAPTER 9

Threat Finance

INTRODUCTION

Although *threat finance* may not have a significant bearing on Business Intelligence, it is a major enabling factor of crime and terrorism. Therefore, having a solid understanding of threat finance is essential to the all-source military, intelligence community (IC), or crime intelligence analyst. Threat finance includes the means and methods used by organizations to finance illicit operations and activities that challenge national and international securities. Intelligence efforts directed toward countering threat finance encompass threat organizations' processes and mechanisms used to finance their activities. The analytical approaches to find and disrupt them are equally varied. This chapter explores illicit funding and money-laundering (ML) schemes such as shell companies, donations from complicit and unwitting sources, extortion, kidnapping/human trafficking, counterfeiting, and fraud. It also looks at the more sophisticated and contemporary threat finance instruments which fall in the areas of market-based commodities or securities schemes or cybercrime.

Why Financial Institutions Should Fight Money-Laundering or Terrorist Financing

It is always critical for organizations to protect their reputation from adverse news events. No bank wants to be on the newspaper's front page or the lead item of a newscast, with the bank's name being associated with ML or terrorist financing (TF). Besides being a public relations nightmare, ML is a threat to the proper functioning of a financial system and potentially damages healthy revenue streams and company profits. Aside from the hefty-associated regulatory fines and possible jail time for willing participants, one must ask, 'what stockholder, business manager, or credit card owner wants it known that their bank is associated with terrorists and criminals?'

ILLICIT FUNDING AND MONEY-LAUNDERING SCHEMES

ML is the underlying technique of threat finance, and it takes on many guises. The most common of these is known as the 'laundry cycle.' The 'laundry cycle' has three phases (see Figure 9.1). These three stages are typically referred to as placement, structuring, and integration.

Placement

The placement phase is the first, and it characterizes the initial entry of the criminal proceeds into the financial system. Typically, this phase accomplishes two purposes: it allows criminal organizations to dispense (take off their hands) large amounts of illicit cash, separating the illicit

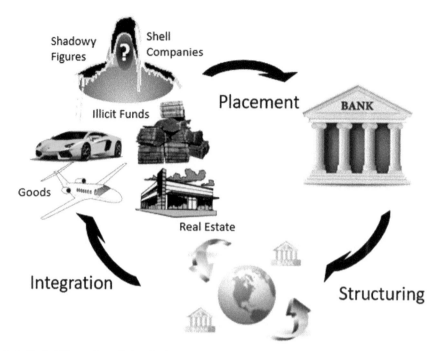

Figure 9.1   Typical Money-Laundering Cycle.

money from its origin by injecting these same funds into the legitimate financial system. In other words, moving funds away from direct association with the crime or other nefarious activity. During this phase, money launderers are most vulnerable to discovery by financial institutions because introducing large sums of money into the legitimate financial system can trigger electronic flags and raise suspicions.

Structuring

The next phase is the structuring phase (aka the layering phase). The structuring phase typically includes the transfer of illicit funds internationally and encompasses some of the more detailed characteristics of the ML cycle. Structuring is done through a sophisticated progression of layered financial transactions, whose purpose is to obscure the money trail to foil pursuit and expand the breaks that an auditor must overcome to associate the licit funds with the unlawful source activity.

Integration

The final phase is dubbed 'integration.' Just as the name implies, in this phase, the laundered funds come home to the criminals from what appears to be a legitimate source(s). At this point, the original criminal proceeds (cash) have been laundered through a structured process involving multiple monetary transactions, are now completely integrated into the financial system, and can be utilized for legitimate purposes.[1] The monies that began the cycle in the first phase (placement) are again made available to the criminal organization, but this time from what seems legitimate sources.

The following is an illustrated portrayal of a global ML scheme (see Figure 9.2). On February 10, 2011, the US Treasury Department, Financial Crimes Enforcement Network (FinCEN), issued a finding and proposed rule. According to the USA Patriot Act, the Lebanese Canadian Bank (LCB) was the financial institution of primary concern for ML. The basis of this finding stems

---

1   United Nations, United Nations Office on Drugs and Crime, *Money-Laundering*, 2018, www.unodc.org/e4j/en/organized-crime/module-4/key-issues/money-laundering.html, Retrieved May 31, 2020.

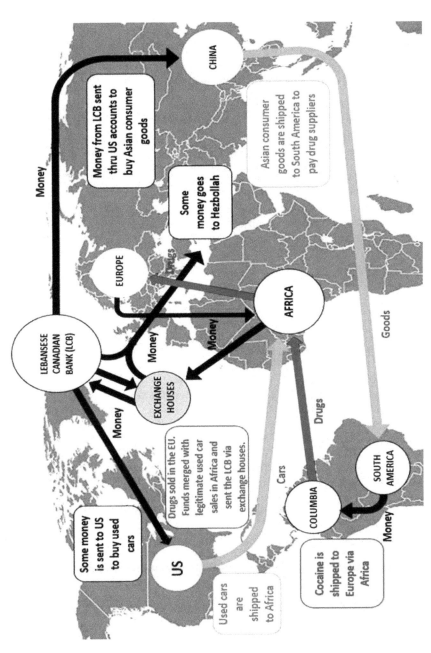

Figure 9.2 Money Laundering Scheme.

from, among other things, FinCEN's determination that LCB had been routinely used by drug traffickers and money-launderers operating in various countries in Central and South America, Europe, Africa, and the Middle East. FinCEN also determined that there was a reason to believe that LCB managers were complicit in the network's ML activities.[2]

What Is Being Done to Combat Money-Laundering

Following are the Financial Action Task Force (FATF) on ML recommendations; an increasing number of countries have stepped up their efforts domestically and in coordination with regional and international partners to combat ML. Many countries have drafted, and of those, many have already passed, new domestic legislation outlawing ML and enforcing stiffer penalties when laundered money is found to be supporting terrorist activity.

Though the volume of criminal and terror-stained financial accounts frozen internationally remains insignificant, the impact of interdicting these assets can be noteworthy if the appropriate accounts, businesses, or front organizations are shut down. Denying organized criminal groups (OCGs) and terror groups access to their preferred means of generating, laundering, and transferring money complicates their efforts to conduct their nefarious activities.

Constricting OCGs and terror groups in their favored operating environment and cracking down on their financing requires a disciplined focus on the critical nodes in the OCG/terror group's network financial and logistical support organizations. Alarmingly, many of these facilitating financial and logistical support organizations are not particular to any OCG or terror group.

TIPS/NOTES:

Key North American and Global Regulatory Bodies and Requirements Related to Anti-Money-Laundering (AML)

- **Financial Crimes Enforcement Network (FinCEN)** is the financial intelligence unit (FIU) for the United States. FinCEN has published a great deal of material on the relationship between fraud and ML that can be used to assist threat finance analysis. FinCEN also issued the Currency and Foreign Transactions Reporting Act of 1970, aka 'Bank Secrecy Act.'
- **US Bank Secrecy Act** affects any business that deals with a transaction or series of transactions for more than $10,000. If a customer buys an item such as a $17,000 boat with cash, the dealer has to report the sale.
- **Financial Transactions and Reports Analysis Centre of Canada (FINTRAC)** is Canada's FIU for all reporting entities, i.e., real estate sector, banking, securities dealers, money services businesses, accountants, and others. FINTRAC's mandate is to facilitate the detection, prevention, and deterrence of ML, TF, and other threats to national security.
- **Office of the Superintendent of Financial Institutions (OSFI)** is a federal Canadian bank regulator. The OSFI issued the AML guideline, B-8.
- **Financial Action Task Force (FATF)** – FATF was established by the G-7 Summit in Paris in 1989 to develop a coordinated international response to ML. FATF developed 40 recommendations that set out the national governments' measures to implement effective AML programs.
- **United Nations Convention against Transnational Organized Crime, Articles 6 and 7** – Article 6 requires State parties to criminalize ML, while Article 7 refers to measures to combat ML.

---

2   US Department of the Treasury, Financial Crimes Enforcement Network (FinCEN), *Manhattan U.S. Attorney Announces $102 Million Settlement Of Civil Forfeiture And Money Laundering Claims Against Lebanese Canadian Bank*, June 25, 2013, www.justice.gov/usao-sdny/pr/manhattan-us-attorney-announces-102-million-settlement-civil-forfeiture-and-money, Retrieved June 2, 2020.

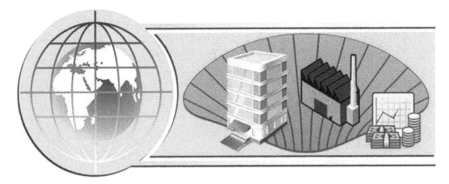

Figure 9.3   Shell Companies.

GLOBAL ML SCHEME EXAMPLE

Shell Companies

Shell companies are incorporated companies that possess no significant assets and do not perform any significant operations (Figure 9.3).

Licit and Illicit Purposes for Shell Companies

Shell companies can have legitimate business purposes. A few examples of legitimate shell companies are businesses that act as trustees for a trust; perhaps a company formed to create a partnership to provide limited liability for the partners. Another example might include a company used to immunize the rest of the business from the litigiously risky activities of one part (i.e., an energy company might spin a nuclear power plant off into a shell corporation to avoid possible litigation from environmental groups).

The use of shell companies is a common practice of ML schemes. The shell company purports to provide some service that would reasonably require its customers to pay with cash regularly to obscure the money trail (launder money). Some more common, less sophisticated examples are vending machine-based franchises, gambling casinos, street vendors, and many others.

Tools and Methods of Determining if a Shell Company Is Legitimate

Typically, an analyst endeavors to define just what the company does for its money when investigating a shell company to determine whether or not its purpose is above board. The more difficult it is to determine just what a company's business is, who its customers are, and how it provides its reported product or service, the higher the likelihood that the shell company has criminal purposes as its basis.

Another method to assess the legitimacy of a shell company is to determine if known criminals or state-sanctioned individuals are associated with the company's corporate structure or ownership. To aid analysts in this effort, the US Treasury Department, Office of Foreign Assets Control (OFAC), maintains a helpful tool called the Specially Designated Nationals (SDN) List (see Figure 9.4). The SDN List is an online compilation of entities and individuals who have been targeted under one or more of the US Treasury's sanctions programs.[3]

---

3   US Department of the Treasury, Specially Designated Nationals and Blocked Persons List (SDN) Human Readable Lists, May 27, 2020, www.treasury.gov/resource-center/sanctions/sdn-list/pages/default.aspx, Retrieved June 1, 2020.

Figure 9.4   Specially Designated Nationals List (SDN).

Donations from Complicit and Unwitting Sources

At its core, financing terrorism through charitable organizations is simply a variation of conventional criminal ML techniques. Terrorist groups most typically use charitable donations from complicit and unwitting sources to raise funds for their organizations. Terror group support networks employ facilitators based in the United States and countries worldwide to raise funds from their supporters and donors under the false pretenses of charity and outside of any tax-exempt charitable organization. The guise of a charitable organization permits them to operate, often for decades, unhindered and in plain sight.

Author's Note: No one thinks it happens in my town, but it does. I am a resident of Northern Virginia, so in 2002, a fundraising operation run by a terror group was uncovered a few miles from my front door; I could not help but take notice. As it happens, several charitable groups and business front organizations were run out of that 555 Grove Street, Herndon, Virginia address, and to my surprise, those organizations were indeed funding terror.

A Department of Homeland Security (DHS) operation (code-named 'Green Quest') targeted the cluster of organizations. The list included the Safa Group, SAAR Foundation, Success Foundation, and many more.

In March 2002, federal agents raided the organization's offices, 14 interlocking business entities, and the homes of eight of the group leaders associated with the SAAR Foundation looking for ties to the Al Taqwa Bank and the Muslim Brotherhood. Over 500 boxes of paper and computer files were confiscated, filling seven trucks. Investigations stemming from Operation Green Quest led to 70 indictments and $33 million in seized funds.

A 101-page affidavit revealed that leaders of the Safa Group knowingly supported the Islamic Resistance Movement (aka Hamas) and the Palestinian Islamic Jihad, both designated terrorist entities by the US government. The alleged financial ties reached back almost two decades between the Safa Group and other organizations in Florida and Texas, also under investigation for terrorist ties.

How to Determine if a Charitable Organization Is Legitimate

To determine whether or not a charitable organization falls under the category of tax-exempt, analysts consult the US Internal Revenue Service's (IRS) website.[4] This IRS tool allows one to enter the organization's name and see if the organization is tax-exempt or not. Other countries have similar tools. In the United Kingdom, one can consult the UK.gov website and search the national charity register.[5] However, not finding a charity's tax-exempt status is not a confirmation that it is

---

4   US Internal Revenue Service, *Tax Exempt Organization Search*, www.irs.gov/charities-non-profits/tax-exempt-organization-search, Retrieved June 27, 2020.

5   United Kingdom Government, *Search the Charity Register*, www.gov.uk/find-charity-information, Retrieved June 27, 2020.

www.charitynavigator.org

www.charitywatch.org

www.guidestar.org

BBB Wise Giving Alliance www.bbb.org

Figure 9.5 Nongovernment Charity Information Sources.

affiliated with a terror group. It is but the first data point and should make one suspicious. Further analysis and corroborating evidence must be obtained, such as multiple known ties to a terrorist organization.

Nongovernment Charity Information Sources

Other independent online websites exist which can provide additional related information about charitable organizations. Four of the more well-known websites are depicted in Figure 9.5. Charity Navigator rates charities based on their financial health, accountability, and transparency to help donors make informed decisions about their contributions. Charity Watch rates charities on specific criteria such as advice, articles, and other fundamental information open to the public. GuideStar maintains information on 501(c)(3) nonprofits.

Financial documents, such as the 990 data, assist analysts in evaluating an organization's legitimacy (see Figure 9.6). IRS Form 990 is required for all title 501(c)(3) nonprofit organizations. The 990 also discloses where and how an organization's donations are spent, including the earnings of top officers. Finally, BBB Wise Giving Alliance rates charities against 20 specific standards. These standards include governance and oversight, effectiveness, finances, solicitations, and other informational materials, which contribute to the charity's overall score.

Author's Note: Donations from Complicit and Unwitting Sources are discussed later in this chapter's More Sophisticated and Contemporary Threat Finance Instruments section.

Extortion

Extortion is obtaining property from another through the wrongful use of actual or threatened force, violence, or fear (Figure 9.7). Such coercive extortion is synonymous with *blackmail*, an older term used to indicate extortion.

Other Types of Extortion

Extortion 'under color of office' or 'under color of official right,' which is the wrongful taking by a public officer of money or property that is not due to them, whether or not the taking was accomplished by force, threats, or use of fear. Some legal jurisdictions outside the United States

Figure 9.6 IRS Form 990.

Figure 9.7 Extortion Is Characterized by Acts or Threat of Violence.

also refer to another type of extortion. Extortion under *color of office* fits well with the next topic, *Official Corruption*.

Author's Note: 'Color of Office' is a legal term. It describes an act by a public official or law enforcement officer done without authority under the pretext that they have an official right to do the act by reason of the officer's position.

Official Corruption

US jurisdictions typically refer to this type of extortion (under color of office) as a form of corruption. Extortion and official corruption are the grease that lubricates ML schemes and allows them to function alongside and sometimes leverage legitimate businesses.

> *Author's Note: In the United Kingdom, charities would not be in the Charity Commission's register if they haven't registered because their income is less than £5,000. In this case, the charity is considered 'excepted' from regulation by the England and Wales Charity Commission.*

Kidnapping and Human Trafficking

Organized kidnapping and human trafficking often go hand-in-hand and are considered the most heinous of the many threat finance generation schemes. Both crimes (kidnapping and human trafficking) routinely utilize ML schemes to disguise their funding streams from authorities. Of the two, organized kidnapping for ransom is addressed first (Figure 9.8).

Kidnapping for Ransom or Hostage Taking

Kidnapping for ransom, aka hostage-taking, is defined by the International Convention against the Taking of Hostages of 1979 as:

> *Any person who seizes or detains and threatens to kill, to injure, or to continue to detain another person to compel a third party, namely, a State, an international intergovernmental organization, a natural or juridical person, or a group of persons, to do or abstain from doing any act as an explicit or implicit condition for the release of the hostage.*[6]

Kidnapping for ransom is endemic in many countries. Numerous multinational companies and nongovernmental organizations (NGOs) operate in remote areas where kidnapping thrives, such as Colombia, Iraq, Mali, Mexico, and Nigeria. Employers have a duty of care: If they operate in these environments, it means they trust that the situation resolves peacefully, provided the abductors are paid. Surprisingly, the sheer volume and associated charges for resolving kidnappings have become so predictable that insurers sell kidnapping for ransom insurance coverage. The unfortunate outcome of this consistent financial throughput has been that these money transfers have been regulated and integrated into the insurers' and the kidnappers' business models.

Figure 9.8 Kidnapping and Human Trafficking Are All-Too-Common, Frequently Global Criminal Enterprise.

---

6 UN Secretary-General, International Convention against the Taking of Hostages, December 18, 1979.

Figure 9.9 Various Forms of Exploitation.

Human Trafficking

Human trafficking generally does not involve ransom exchanges. However, kidnapping is combined into the human trafficking business model as the final step of the recruitment phase. Human trafficking involves the recruitment, movement, or harboring of people for exploitation, such as sexual exploitation, forced labor, slavery, or organ removal. Victims can be of any age or gender and are trafficked by threat or use of force, fraudulent schemes, deception, or abuse of power. It can occur within a country or across borders. Human trafficking is therefore characterized by an act (recruitment, transportation, transfer, harboring, or receipt of people), specific means (threats or use of force, deception, fraud, abuse of power, or abusing someone's vulnerable condition) for exploitation (Figure 9.9).

EXAMPLE OF HUMAN TRAFFICKING

Inexperienced analysts can sometimes mistake human trafficking for something else. This trafficking scenario should help to reinforce the concept.

Scenario: Individuals take jobs as night cleaning staff at a large company in a different country with the promise of pay and benefits. Unfortunately, the jobs turn out to be cleaning sewers without proper tools under poor work conditions, and they do not receive a salary.

Criminal Act: Their recruitment and transportation to, and harboring in, a different country; **Means:** Deception and a false promise of proper working conditions; however, the purpose is labor exploitation for degrading work.

Counterfeiting

When counterfeiting is mentioned, most visualize fake 20 or 100 dollar banknotes like the money shown in Figure 9.10. However, the counterfeiting of software, ID cards and documents, CDs, DVDs, cigarettes, medicine, clothing, and other items has exploded in recent years. The advent of

Figure 9.10 Counterfeit Specialist Examining a Banknote.

three-dimensional (3D) printing, color copiers, and other advances in technology has been a significant catalyst for stimulating the worldwide forged products trade.

Who Are the Counterfeiters?

The involvement of rogue nations (e.g., North Korea) and OCGs in producing and distributing counterfeit currency and goods is well documented. These groups operate across national borders using a mix of legitimate and illicit businesses for manufacturing, exporting, importing, and distributing fraudulent goods, identification papers, and counterfeit currency.

Where Counterfeit Goods Are Manufactured

Much of the production of these fake items takes place in East Asia, but other production centers are based in Italy, Spain, and Portugal. Counterfeit product sales also serve as a convenient way for OCGs to launder money, and these forged products become one of the many-layered financial transactions that make up the ML process.

Fraud

Fraud is an umbrella term that refers to acts intended to swindle someone. In essence, it is the use of intentional deception for monetary or personal gain. Hundreds of thousands of people worldwide each year fall victim to it. Fraud always includes a false statement, misrepresentation, or deceitful conduct. The purpose is to gain something of value, usually money, by misleading or deceiving someone into believing something the perpetrator knows is false.

How Fraud Schemes Are Intertwined with Money-Laundering Schemes

Fraud is a crime that facilitates ML. In the context of ML schemes and TF, criminal activity related to fraud generates money that needs to be laundered, so where fraud exists, ML coexists. The following example illustrates the concept.

FRAUD AND MONEY-LAUNDERING EXAMPLE

- **Scenario:** A criminal ML organization purchases a stolen Ferrari SF90 Stradale (see Figure 9.11) from the car thieves for 100,000 dollars. The ML group then sells the vehicle to an unsuspecting buyer for the market price of $625,000 (FRAUD).
  Money from the fraudulent purchase is deposited in a bank and is now viewed as legitimate business revenue by banking authorities.
  This one transaction represents the obfuscation of hundreds of thousands of ill-gotten dollars as part of a multilayered ML scheme.

How Either Fraud or Money-Laundering Gets Overlooked During Terrorist Finance Investigations

In many financial institutions, separate departments try to protect a financial institution from ML and fraud. In these cases, the fraud group and the AML group do not communicate or work together on the ML and TF threats affecting their respective departments. However, the two departments (AML and Fraud) often have diametrically opposing goals.

The AML department works to comply with the AML regulatory requirements, whereas the fraud side of the house tries to protect the financial institution from monetary losses.

Additionally, the institution's senior leadership most probably views the two departments from very different lenses. Legally, the AML side must comply with the AML regulatory requirements, whereas the Fraud side tries to protect the organization from financial losses. Consequently, the Fraud group has a much easier time demonstrating value to the institution because it can measure in dollars ($) [or pounds (£)] the impact of its anti-fraud efforts on the company's bottom line. However, AML departmental efforts are frequently perceived as a legal compliance expense to the business organization. The benefits realized are not felt by the institution but rather by the financial system as a whole and society at large.

Figure 9.11   2020 Ferrari SF90 Stradale.

However, as demonstrated in the following example, banks and other financial institutions can profit significantly by synergizing their anti-fraud efforts with their AML resources.

A MORE CRAFTY FRAUD AND MONEY-LAUNDERING EXAMPLE

Scenario:

A hypothetical US bank customer has a credit card account with a credit limit of $10,000 and a zero balance. (The kind of credit card customer most banks desire.) The customer is the only name on the account, and his listed profession is 'self-employed real estate developer,' and making $300,000 annually.

Figure 9.12   ATM Transaction.

The customer makes a personal check payable to his credit card account of $50,000 via an automated teller machine (ATM) (Figure 9.12). This payment creates a positive credit balance of $50,000, which alerts banking authorities because it is highly unusual for a credit card account to have a considerable positive balance. Typically credit card account holders owe the bank money, not the other way around, and if there is a positive balance, it is generally negligible (e.g., a few dollars).

(Note: There were no regulatory issues associated with the transaction, and there were no automated banking 'red flags' triggered by this deposit. The 'sizeable positive credit card account balance' was the only indication of out-of-the-ordinary banking activity.) See the Tips/ Notes: Regulatory Banking Notifications dialog box that follows.

However, the size of a personal check creates a fraud alert because there is doubt that the check is good. The bank's Fraud Department calls the customer to determine what is going on. The customer says that he is traveling overseas for an extended period and wants to use the credit card to take cash advances because credit cards are not widely accepted in the destination countries. The Fraud Department accepts the response as 'reasonable' and waits for the check to clear, which it does in five business days.

The Fraud Department takes no further action because the money was deposited, so there was no risk of fraud or loss to the bank. The bank stopped asking questions and closed the case, but no one asked where the money came from or whether the transaction was reasonable for this customer based on his occupation, age, or past transactions.

Had the bank pulled the customer's account transactions for the past year, they might have found the following banking transactions consistent with ML:

Multiple transactions on the same day using different channels (phone, web, in-person), made from multiple locations – Activity, which suggests more than one person using the credit card.

High-velocity account transactions – over 100,000 attempted credit card transactions in one year, with about a fraction being approved. Assuming the number of observed transactions is roughly 100,000, it would require an average of over 17 transactions to take place every waking hour in the past calendar year. Quickly doing the math, the average person is awake 16 hours per day; therefore, one can use their credit card for 5,840 hours per year. Therefore it is not reasonable that one person could make this many transactions; this activity suggests more than one person is using the credit card.

ATM withdrawals attempted from foreign locations – ATM withdrawals in countries other than the customer's home of record are not always suspect. However, some countries have a signifi-cant OCG activity making them higher risk locations for ML/TF.

TIPS/NOTES: REGULATORY BANKING NOTIFICATIONS

- Banks must notify the government whenever they receive more than $10,000 in a single deposit.
- They must also report withdrawals of that size or anyone using that much cash to buy a negotiable instrument such as a cashier's check or a bank draft.
- This rule applies to American dollars and foreign currency worth more than $10,000.
- It also kicks in if the bank receives multiple payments from the same agent or individual over a year, adding up to more than $10,000.
- However, banks DO NOT have to report personal checks, regardless of the amount.
  - Withdrawal attempts made beyond the maximum per day amounts – Typically, a cardholder stops trying to withdraw money after being notified that the day's with-drawal limit has been met. Repeated attempts after the maximum per day limit are met also suggest that more than one person uses the credit card.
  - **ATM withdrawals attempted from foreign locations** – ATM withdrawals in coun-tries other than the customer's home of record are not always suspect. However, some countries are known to have a significant OCG, making them higher risk locations for ML/TF.
  - **Withdrawal attempts made beyond the maximum per day amounts** – Typically, a cardholder stops trying to withdraw money after being notified that the day's withdrawal limit has been met. Repeated attempts after the maximum per day limit are met also suggest that more than one person uses the credit card.

MORE SOPHISTICATED AND CONTEMPORARY THREAT FINANCE INSTRUMENTS

The more sophisticated and contemporary threat finance instruments include market-based com-modities, security schemes, or cybercrime, as illustrated in Figure 9.13. Security schemes and cybercrime are the latest emerging threats used by a sophisticated set of actors.

As in the topics discussed earlier, the practice underpinning many of these activities is ML or another process by which illicitly gained funds are concealed and made to appear legitimately sourced.

Figure 9.13   Sophisticated Threat Finance Instruments.

Security Schemes

Terror groups and criminal organizations use security schemes to launder their money, and they manage this task by avoiding the definitions used by financial regulatory bodies like the FATF. It should be noted that, while most jurisdictions treat certificates of deposit as securities, many do not. Also, only some jurisdictions treat bills of exchange as securities. The fact that certificates of deposit and bills of exchange are not defined as a 'security' alone does not mean gaps exist in the regulatory system. Still, it highlights the complexity of the terminology used to define these products.

The differing interpretations of security definitions create anonymity in security transfers. This anonymity provides easy transferability of bearer securities and presents a significant ML/TF vulnerability at all three stages of ML. Illicit assets can be placed in the security industry through the purchase of bearer securities. Once bearer securities have been issued, money launderers or terrorist financiers can hold these securities or transfer them to others without necessarily having to use financial institutions' facilities that would record a transaction that regulatory bodies might otherwise observe.

A SECURITY SCHEME EXAMPLE

Scenario:
Drug cartels want to move millions from one continent to another. Cartel operatives purchase bearer securities in one country that does not necessarily require that the owner of the security be registered with an issuer or a transfer agent. The operative boards a plane in one country, with the bearer securities, and flies to their destination. Once they arrive, they transfer the bearer securities by handing them over to a new owner, and no transfer record exists.

Note: The photo is of an actual $1,000 US Treasury, 30-year bearer bond issued in August 1977. Note: The US Treasury has not issued bearer bonds since 1986 (see Figure 9.14).

TIPS/NOTES:

For more information on other Security-Based ML, schemes go to the FATF publication: 'Money Laundering and Terrorist Financing in the Securities Sector' dated October 2009.

Figure 9.14   Sophisticated Threat Finance Instruments.

Cybercrime

For some, it is difficult to conceptualize how threat financial groups use cybercrime. However, using a few simplified instances of how TF and OCGs use cybercrime swiftly becomes apparent. Cybercrime is another tool or mechanism that TF and OCGs use to ply their trade. The terminology changes, yet the crimes are the same; for example, 'extortion' becomes 'ransomware,' 'human trafficking' is expedited by leveraging computer social networks to lure the victims into bondage, and TF donations are collected from fraudulent 'go fund me' websites. Cybercrime includes Dark Markets and other nefarious Dark Web schemes.

Dark Markets

Before one can understand just what *Dark Markets* are, *black markets* and *the Dark Web* need to be further clarified. Although they share nefarious purposes for existence, one has been around for ages; the other is truly unique to the 21st century.

Black Markets

Laypersons recognize black markets, or underground economies, are clandestine markets or series of transactions that have some aspect of illegality, such as smuggling or some other type of trade in illegal goods or services. Black markets have existed since antiquity. The British Museum contains 4,000year-old clay cuneiform tablets that record the secret black market trading tales of Assyrian smugglers and merchants, revealing some of their cunning plans to avoid paying taxes on their trade wares.[7]

The Deep Web versus the Dark Web

However, a modern variety of black markets exist as in an electronic version, and these illicit markets reside on the Dark Web. The World Wide Web (WWW) has been around for decades,

---

7   The British Museum, *Trade and contraband in ancient Assyria*, April 2, 2018, https://blog.britishmuseum.org/trade-and-contraband-in-ancient-assyria/, Retrieved June 30, 2020.

and the overwhelming majority of the world's population is familiar with what it is. Even Afghan shepherds can be found to have smartphones on their person who have web access. A similar fraction of the population can explain the *Surface Web*. However, a far lesser number can provide full details on just what the Deep Web is.

The Surface Web is accessible to anyone and everyone using the internet; though, the Deep Web content is hidden behind Hypertext Transfer Protocol (HTTP) forms. The noteworthy difference between the Surface Web and the Deep Web is that the content of the Deep Web, like Surface Web content, can be located and accessed by its direct Internet Protocol (IP) address. But the Deep Web content may require a password or other security access to get past public-facing website pages.

The Deep Web includes many common uses such as webmail, online banking, restricted access to social media pages and profiles, some web forums requiring registration for viewing content, and services that users must pay for, protected by paywalls. In essence, most web content resides in the Deep Web (see Figure 9.15).

The Dark Web occupies a small part of the web. The Dark Web is the portion of WWW that is not indexed to locate its content using web search engines.

The types of people who generally use Dark Markets are usually criminals, terrorist groups, drug dealers, or other types of people who do not want an auditable record of their dealings. The Dark Web consists of friend-to-friend peer-to-peer networks and large, popular networks like TOR, Freenet, I2P, and Riffle. The Dark Web uses the traffic anonymization technique of Onion routing.

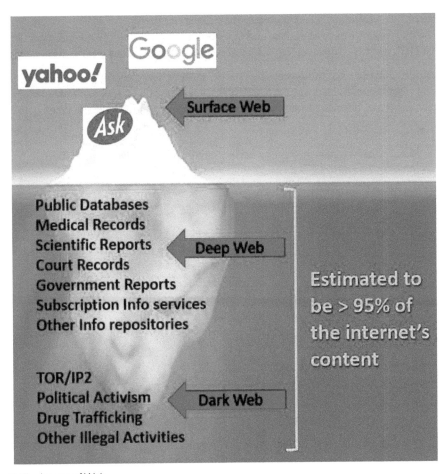

Figure 9.15 Layers of Web.

Figure 9.16 The Silk Road – Dark Market Website.

Dark Markets are essentially black markets that reside in the Dark Web. Examples of Dark Markets include the Silk Road, AlphaBay, and OpenBazaar. Both the Silk Road and AlphaBay were centralized Dark Markets. However, OpenBazaar is a decentralized Dark Market.

In a decentralized market, technology enables participants to deal directly with each other instead of operating within a centralized web exchange. Virtual markets that use decentralized currency or cryptocurrencies (e.g., Bitcoin, Monero) are examples of decentralized markets (see Figure 9.16).

Author's Note: Tor has a three-layer proxy node structure, like the layers of an onion (hence the name: Onion Sites!) (Figure 9.17).

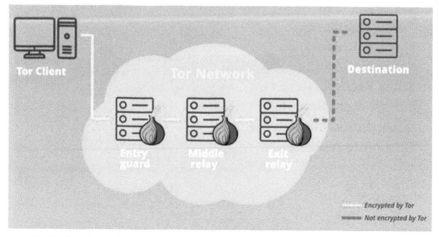

Figure 9.17   The Tor Network and Structure.

The Silk Road was the first major 'dark market.' The Silk Road was best known as a platform for selling illegal drugs. However, in October 2013, the Federal Bureau of Investigation (FBI) shut the website down.

Figure 9.18   AlphaBay – Dark Market Website.

Before being shut down by authorities in July 2017, AlphaBay was the most prominent Dark Market with over 200,000 users (see Figure 9.18). AlphaBay operated for over two years on the Dark Web. It sold deadly illegal drugs, stolen and fraudulent identification documents and network access devices, counterfeit goods, malware, and other computer hacking tools, firearms, and toxic chemicals throughout the world.[8]

OpenBazaar

OpenBazaar, a decentralized Dark Market, began in April 2016. Since that time, it has experienced substantial growth. Since the launch of OpenBazaar 2.0 in late 2017, the Dark Market's network has seen over 100,000 nodes created and 20,000 nodes with at least one listing. 'Nodes' refer to setting up the application (or app) and creating a discoverable profile (or store) that connects to other nodes on the network. OpenBazaar cannot be shut down or 'seized' the way Silk Road and other centralized Dark Markets have been. Some see decentralized Dark Markets as the future of this type of illicit activity (see Figure 9.19).

Innovations in Money Laundering

The tried and tested methods continue to serve as lucrative means to launder money; however, one of several emerging digital schemes is gaining traction. That scheme is digital currencies.

Digital Currencies

Common digital currencies include Bitcoin, Monero, Dash, Litecoin, et cetera. These digital currencies can be used to facilitate many forms of illicit financial activity online, such as online gambling, Dark Markets, and ransomware. So just what are digital currencies, and why do ML/TF organizations like them?

---

8   US Department of Justice, Office of Public affairs, *AlphaBay, the Largest Online 'Dark Market,' Shut Down,* July 20, 2017, www.justice.gov/opa/pr/alphabay-largest-online-dark-market-shut-down, Retrieved July 1, 2020.

Figure 9.19 OpenBazaar 2.0.

AlphaBay – Dark Market Website.

What Are Digital Currencies?

Answering the first question, *What are digital currencies*? Digital currency is essentially a record stored in a distributed database on the internet, in an electronic computer database, within digital files, or a stored-value card. Digital currencies display characteristics common to other currencies, but they do not have a physical form, such as banknotes and coins. Not having a physical form allows for nearly instantaneous financial transactions. Digital money can either be centralized, where there is a central point of control over the money supply, or decentralized, where the control over the money supply can come from various sources.

Why Do ML/TF Organizations Like Digital Currencies?

ML/TF organizations like digital currencies because they need a solid plan to handle their ill-gotten assets in a way that makes them appear legitimately acquired and, as a result, safer to spend. The ideal method that you are looking for is:

- **Liquid,** in that they want to liquidate and spend the proceeds conveniently, and digital currencies are incredibly liquid, and they can be moved anywhere in the world in minutes.

- **Untraceable,** in that these currencies can mask their digital trail; this capability is essential to avoiding detection. The goal of the ML/TF is to obscure as many links between the initial placement of funds and their final disposition. Digital currencies are less traceable than many digital transactions, especially in the short term, with few regulations in effect.

- **Efficient** ML usually results in additional costs, such as transactional charges from intermediaries, taxes paid as part of the integration process, or volatility (such as stock and currency declines). The ideal system minimizes these costs; as far as efficiency is concerned, digital currencies are only moderately efficient because they come with some level of risk. As shown in the stock value of Bitcoin over five years (see Figure 9.20).

- **Secure,** in that just because funds were earned through crime does not mean someone else should get to steal them from your organization. For the most part, ML or TF wants their assets kept inaccessible to authorities and other criminals alike.

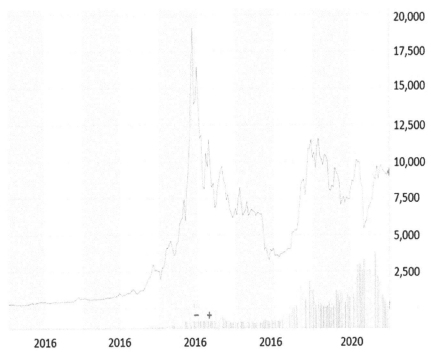

Figure 9.20   Volatility of Bitcoin Over Five Years.

CHAPTER SUMMARY

This chapter defined threat finance as an enabling factor of crime and terrorism. It included the means and methods used by organizations to finance illicit operations and activities that challenge both national and international securities. It described intelligence efforts directed toward countering threat finance encompasses the complex processes and mechanisms used by threat organizations to finance their activities and the analytical approaches to find and disrupt them.

This chapter explored illicit funding and money-laundering (ML) schemes such as shell companies, donations from complicit and unwitting sources, extortion, kidnapping/human trafficking, counterfeiting, and fraud. It also looked at the more sophisticated and contemporary threat finance instruments which fall in the areas of market-based commodities or security schemes, or cybercrime.

WHY FINANCIAL INSTITUTIONS SHOULD FIGHT MONEY-LAUNDERING OR TERRORIST FINANCING

It is always critical for organizations to protect their reputation from adverse news events. No bank wants to be on the newspaper's front page or the lead item of a newscast, with the bank's name being associated with ML or terrorist financing (TF). Besides being a public relations nightmare, ML is a threat to the proper functioning of a financial system and potentially damages healthy revenue streams and company profits. Aside from the hefty-associated regulatory fines and possible jail time for willing participants, one must ask, 'what stockholder, business manager, or credit card owner wants it known that their bank is associated with terrorists and criminals?'

ILLICIT FUNDING AND MONEY-LAUNDERING SCHEMES

ML is the underlying technique of threat finance, and it takes on many guises. The most common of these is known as the 'laundry cycle.' The 'laundry cycle' has three phases, and these three stages are typically referred to as placement, structuring, and integration.[9]

Placement

The placement phase is the first, and it characterizes the initial entry of the criminal proceeds into the financial system. Typically, this phase accomplishes two purposes: it allows criminal organizations to dispense (take off their hands) large amounts of illicit cash, separating the illicit money from its origin by injecting these same funds into the legitimate financial system.

Structuring

The next phase is the structuring phase (aka the layering phase). The structuring phase typically includes the transfer of illicit funds internationally and encompasses some of the more detailed characteristics of the ML cycle. Structuring is done through a sophisticated progression of layered financial transactions, whose purpose is to obscure the money trail to foil pursuit and expand the breaks that an auditor must overcome to associate the licit funds with the unlawful source activity.

Integration

The final phase is dubbed 'integration.' Just as the name implies, in this phase, the laundered funds come home to the criminals from what appears to be a legitimate source(s). At this point, the original criminal proceeds (cash) have been laundered through a structured process involving multiple monetary transactions, are now completely integrated into the financial system, and can be utilized for legitimate purposes.[10] At this point, the monies that began the cycle in the first phase (placement) are again made available to the criminal organization, but this time from what seems to be legitimate sources.

What Is Being Done to Combat Money-Laundering

Following are the Financial Action Task Force (FATF) on ML recommendations; an increasing number of countries have stepped up their efforts domestically and in coordination with regional and international partners to combat ML. Many countries have drafted, and of those, many have already passed, new domestic legislation outlawing ML and enforcing stiffer penalties when laundered money is found to be supporting terrorist activity.

Though the volume of criminal and terror-stained financial accounts frozen internationally remains insignificant, the impact of interdicting these assets can be noteworthy if the appropriate accounts, businesses, or front organizations are shut down. Denying organized criminal groups (OCGs) and terror groups access to their preferred means of generating, laundering, and transferring money complicates their efforts to conduct their nefarious activities.

Constricting OCGs and terror groups in their favored operating environment and cracking down on their financing requires a disciplined focus on the critical nodes in the OCG/terror group's network financial and logistical support organizations. Alarmingly, many of these facilitating financial and logistical support organizations are not particular to any OCG or terror group.

---

9 United Nations, United Nations Office on Drugs and Crime, *The Money-Laundering Cycle*, 2012, www.unodc.org/unodc/en/money-laundering/laundrycycle.html, Retrieved May 31, 2020.

10 United Nations, United Nations Office on Drugs and Crime, *Money-Laundering*, 2018, www.unodc.org/e4j/en/organized-crime/module-4/key-issues/money-laundering.html, Retrieved May 31, 2020.

Shell Companies

Shell companies are incorporated companies that possess no significant assets and do not perform any significant productive operations.

Licit and Illicit Purposes for Shell Companies

Shell companies can have legitimate business purposes. A few examples of legitimate shell companies are businesses that act as trustees for a trust, or perhaps a company formed to create a partnership to provide limited liability for the partners.

The use of shell companies is a common practice of an ML scheme. The shell company purports to provide some service that would reasonably require its customers to pay with cash regularly to launder money.

Tools and Methods of Determining If a Shell Company Is Legitimate

Typically, an analyst endeavors to define just what the company does for its money when investigating a shell company to determine whether or not its purpose is above board. The more difficult it is to determine just what a company's business is, who its customers are, and how it provides its reported product or service, the higher the likelihood that the shell company has criminal purposes as its basis.

Another method to assess the legitimacy of a shell company is to determine if known criminals or state-sanctioned individuals are associated with the company's corporate structure or ownership. The US Treasury Department, Office of Foreign Assets Control (OFAC), maintains a helpful tool called the Specially Designated Nationals (SDN) List to aid analysts in this effort. The SDN List is an online compilation of entities and individuals who have been targeted under one or more of the US Treasury's sanctions programs.[11]

Donations from Complicit and Unwitting Sources

At its core, financing terrorism through charitable organizations is simply a variation of conventional criminal ML techniques. Terrorist groups most typically use charitable donations from complicit and unwitting sources to raise funds for their organizations. Terror group support networks employ facilitators based in the United States and countries worldwide to raise funds from their supporters and donors under the false pretenses of charity but outside of any tax-exempt charitable organization. The guise of a charitable organization permits them to operate, often for decades, unhindered and in plain sight.

How to Determine If a Charitable Organization Is Legitimate

To determine whether or not a charitable organization falls under the category of tax-exempt, analysts consult the US Internal Revenue Service's (IRS) website.[12] This IRS tool allows one to enter the organization's name and see if the organization is tax-exempt or not. Other countries have similar tools. One can consult a UK.gov website and search the national charity register in the United Kingdom.[13] However, not finding a charity's tax-exempt status is not a confirmation that it is affiliated with a terror group. It is but the first data point and should make one suspicious. Further analysis and other corroborating evidence must be obtained, such as multiple known ties to a terrorist organization.

---

11 US Department of the Treasury, Specially Designated Nationals and Blocked Persons List (SDN) Human Readable Lists, May 27, 2020, www.treasury.gov/resource-center/sanctions/sdn-list/pages/default.aspx, Retrieved June 1, 2020.

12 US Internal Revenue Service, *Tax Exempt Organization Search*, www.irs.gov/charities-non-profits/tax-exempt-organization-search, Retrieved June 27, 2020.

13 United Kingdom Government, *Search the Charity Register*, www.gov.uk/find-charity-information, Retrieved June 27, 2020.

Nongovernment Charity Information Sources

Other independent (non-government) online websites exist which can provide additional related information about charitable organizations. Charity Navigator rates charities based on their financial health, accountability, and transparency to help donors make informed decisions about their contributions. Charity Watch rates charities on specific criteria such as advice, articles, and other fundamental information open to the public. GuideStar maintains information on 501(c)(3) nonprofits. Financial documents, such as the 990 data, assist analysts in evaluating an organization's legitimacy. The 990 also discloses where and how an organization's donations are spent, including the earnings of top officers. Finally, BBB Wise Giving Alliance rates charities against 20 specific standards. These standards include governance and oversight, effectiveness, finances, solicitations, and other informational materials contributing to the charity's overall score.

Extortion

Extortion is obtaining property from another through the wrongful use of actual or threatened force, violence, or fear. Such coercive extortion is synonymous with the term *blackmail*, an older term used to indicate extortion.

Other Types of Extortion

Some legal jurisdictions outside the United States also refer to another type of extortion. Extortion 'under color of office' or 'under color of official right,' which is the wrongful taking by a public officer of money or property that is not due to them, whether or not the taking was accomplished by force, threats, or use of fear.

Official Corruption

US jurisdictions typically refer to this type of extortion (under color of office) as a form of corruption. Extortion and official corruption are the grease that lubricates ML schemes and allows them to function alongside and sometimes leverage legitimate businesses.

Kidnapping and Human Trafficking

Organized kidnapping and human trafficking often go hand-in-hand and are considered the most heinous of the many threat finance generation schemes. Both crimes (kidnapping and human trafficking) routinely utilize ML schemes to disguise their funding streams from authorities. Of the two, organized kidnapping for ransom is addressed first.

Kidnapping for Ransom or Hostage Taking

Kidnapping for ransom, aka hostage-taking, is defined by the International Convention against the Taking of Hostages of 1979 as

> Any person who seizes or detains and threatens to kill, to injure, or to continue to detain another person to compel a third party, namely, a State, an international intergovernmental organization, a natural or juridical person, or a group of persons, to do or abstain from doing any act as an explicit or implicit condition for the release of the hostage.[14]

Kidnapping for ransom is endemic in many countries. Numerous multinational companies and nongovernmental organizations (NGOs) operate in remote areas where kidnapping thrives, such as Colombia, Iraq, Mali, Mexico, and Nigeria. Employers have a duty of care: If they operate in these environments, it means they trust that the situation resolves peacefully, provided the abductors are paid. Surprisingly, the sheer volume and associated charges for resolving kidnappings have become so predictable that insurers sell kidnapping for ransom insurance coverage. The unfortunate

---

14 UN Secretary-General, International Convention against the Taking of Hostages, December 18, 1979.

outcome of this consistent financial throughput has been that these money transfers have been regulated and integrated into the insurers' and the kidnappers' business models.

Human Trafficking

Human trafficking generally does not involve ransom exchanges. However, the act of kidnapping is combined into the human trafficking business model as the final step of the recruitment phase. Human trafficking involves the recruitment, movement, or harboring of people for exploitation, such as sexual exploitation, forced labor, slavery, or organ removal. Victims can be of any age or gender and are trafficked by threat or use of force, fraudulent schemes, deception, or abuse of power. It can occur within a country or across borders. Human trafficking is therefore characterized by an act (recruitment, transportation, transfer, harboring, or receipt of people), specific means (threats or use of force, deception, fraud, abuse of power, or abusing someone's vulnerable condition) for exploitation.

Counterfeiting

When counterfeiting is mentioned, most visualize fake 20 or 100 dollar banknotes. However, the counterfeiting of software, ID cards and documents, CDs, DVDs, cigarettes, medicine, clothing, and other items has exploded in recent years. The advent of three-dimensional (3D) printing, color copiers, and other advances in technology has been a significant catalyst for stimulating the world-wide forged products trade.

Who Are the Counterfeiters?

The involvement of rogue nations (e.g., North Korea) and OCGs in producing and distributing counterfeit currency and goods is well documented. These groups operate across national borders using a mix of legitimate and illicit businesses for manufacturing, exporting, importing, and distributing fraudulent goods, identification papers, and counterfeit currency.

Where Counterfeit Goods Are Manufactured

Much of the production of these fake items takes place in East Asia, but other production centers are based in Italy, Spain, and Portugal. Counterfeit product sales also serve as a convenient way for OCGs to launder money, and these forged products become one of the many-layered financial transactions that make up the ML process.

Fraud

Fraud is an umbrella term that refers to acts intended to swindle someone. In essence, it is the use of intentional deception for monetary or personal gain. Hundreds of thousands of people worldwide each year fall victim to it. Fraud always includes a false statement, misrepresentation, or deceitful conduct. The purpose is to gain something of value, usually money, by misleading or deceiving someone into believing something the perpetrator knows is false.

How Fraud Schemes Are Intertwined with Money-Laundering Schemes

In the context of ML schemes and TF, criminal activity related to fraud generates money that needs to be laundered, so where fraud exists, ML coexists. Fraud is a crime that facilitates ML.

How Either Fraud or Money-Laundering Gets Overlooked During Terrorist Finance Investigations

In many financial institutions, separate departments try to protect a financial institution from ML and fraud. In these cases, the fraud group and the anti-ML (AML) group do not communicate or work together on the ML and TF threats affecting their respective departments. Additionally, the two departments (AML and Fraud) often have diametrically opposing goals.

The AML department works to comply with the AML regulatory requirements, whereas the fraud side of the house tries to protect the financial institution from monetary losses.

Additionally, the institution's senior leadership most probably views the two departments from very different lenses. Legally, the AML side must comply with the AML regulatory requirements, whereas the Fraud side tries to protect the organization from financial losses. Consequently, the Fraud group has a much easier time demonstrating value to the institution because it can measure in dollars ($) [or pounds (£)] the impact of its anti-fraud efforts affect on the company's bottom line. However, AML departmental efforts are frequently perceived as a legal compliance expense to the business or organization. The benefits realized are not felt by the institution but rather by the financial system as a whole and society at large.

MORE SOPHISTICATED AND CONTEMPORARY THREAT FINANCE INSTRUMENTS

The more sophisticated and contemporary threat finance instruments include market-based commodities, security schemes, or cybercrime. Security schemes and cybercrime are the latest emerging threats used by a sophisticated set of actors.

The practice underpinning many of these activities is ML or another process by which illicitly gained funds are concealed and made to appear legitimately sourced.

Security Schemes

Terror groups and criminal organizations use security schemes to launder their money, and they manage this task by avoiding the definitions used by financial regulatory bodies like the FATF. It should be noted that while most jurisdictions treat certificates of deposit as securities, many do not. Also, only some jurisdictions treat bills of exchange as securities. The fact that certificates of deposit and bills of exchange are not defined as a 'security' alone does not mean gaps exist in the regulatory system. Still, it highlights the complexity of the terminology used to define these products.

The differing interpretations of security definitions create anonymity in security transfers. This anonymity provides easy transferability of bearer securities and presents a significant ML/TF vulnerability at all three stages of ML. Illicit assets can be placed in the security industry through the purchase of bearer securities. Once bearer securities have been issued, money launderers or terrorist financiers can hold these securities or transfer them to others without necessarily having to use financial institutions' facilities that would record a transaction that regulatory bodies might otherwise observe.

Cybercrime

Cybercrime is just a more contemporary tool or mechanism that TF and OCGs use to ply their trade. The terminology changes, yet the crimes are the same; for example, 'extortion' becomes 'ransomware.' 'Human trafficking' is still human trafficking. However, it advanced by leveraging computer social networks to lure the victims into bondage, and threat financial groups are enriched by donations collected on fraudulent 'go fund me' websites. Cybercrime includes Dark Markets and other nefarious Dark Web schemes.

Dark Markets

Before one can understand just what *Dark Markets* are, *black markets* and the *Dark Web* need to be further clarified. Although they share nefarious purposes for existence, one has been around for ages, and the other is truly unique to the 21st century.

Black Markets

Black markets have existed since antiquity.

The Deep Web versus the Dark Web

However, modern black markets exist as an electronic version, and these illicit markets reside on the Dark Web. The World Wide Web (WWW) has been around for decades, and the overwhelming majority of the world's population is familiar with what it is. Even Afghan shepherds can occasionally be found to have smartphones on their person who have web access. A similar fraction of the population can explain the *Surface Web*, but a lesser number can provide full details on the Deep Web.

The Surface Web is accessible to anyone and everyone using the internet; however, the Deep Web content is hidden behind Hypertext Transfer Protocol (HTTP) forms. The noteworthy difference between the Surface Web and the Deep Web is that the content of the Deep Web, like Surface Web content, can be located and accessed by its direct Internet Protocol (IP) address. But the Deep Web content may require a password or other security access to get past public-facing website pages.

The Deep Web includes many common uses such as webmail, online banking, restricted access to social media pages and profiles, some web forums requiring registration for viewing content, and services that users must pay for, protected by paywalls. In essence, the majority of web content resides in the Deep Web.

The Dark Web occupies a small part of the web. The Dark Web is the portion of WWW that is not indexed so that its content can be located using web search engines.

The types of people who generally use Dark Markets are usually criminals, terrorist groups, drug dealers, or other types of people who do not want an auditable record of their dealings. The Dark Web consists of friend-to-friend peer-to-peer networks and large, popular networks such as Tor, Freenet, I2P, and Riffle. The Dark Web uses the traffic anonymization technique of Onion routing.

Dark Markets are essentially black markets that reside in the Dark Web. Examples of Dark Markets include the Silk Road, AlphaBay, and OpenBazaar. Both the Silk Road and AlphaBay were centralized Dark Markets. However, OpenBazaar is a decentralized Dark Market.

In a decentralized market, technology enables participants to deal directly with each other instead of operating within a centralized web exchange. Virtual markets that use decentralized currency or cryptocurrencies (e.g., Bitcoin, Monero) are examples of decentralized markets.

The Silk Road was the first major 'dark market.' The Silk Road was best known as a platform for selling illegal drugs. However, in October 2013, the Federal Bureau of Investigation (FBI) shut the website down.

Before being shut down by authorities in July 2017, AlphaBay was the most prominent Dark Market with over 200,000 users. AlphaBay operated for over two years on the Dark Web. It sold deadly illegal drugs, stolen and fraudulent identification documents and network access devices, counterfeit goods, malware, and other computer hacking tools, firearms, and toxic chemicals throughout the world.[15]

OpenBazaar

OpenBazaar, a decentralized Dark Market, began in April 2016. Since that time, it has experienced substantial growth. Since the launch of OpenBazaar 2.0 in late 2017, the Dark Market's network has seen over 100,000 nodes created and 20,000 nodes with at least one listing. 'Nodes' refer to setting up the application (or app) and creating a discoverable profile (or store) that connects to other nodes on the network. OpenBazaar cannot be shut down or 'seized' the way Silk Road and other centralized Dark Markets have been. Some see decentralized Dark Markets as the future of this kind of illicit activity.

Innovations in Money Laundering

The tried and tested methods continue to serve as lucrative means to launder money; however, one of several emerging digital schemes is gaining traction. That scheme is digital currencies.

---

15 US Department of Justice, Office of Public affairs, *AlphaBay, the Largest Online 'Dark Market,' Shut Down,* July 20, 2017, www.justice.gov/opa/pr/alphabay-largest-online-dark-market-shut-down, Retrieved July 1, 2020.

Digital Currencies

Common digital currencies include Bitcoin, Monero, Dash, Litecoin, etc. These digital currencies can be used to facilitate many forms of illicit financial activity online, such as online gambling, Dark Markets, and ransomware. So just what are digital currencies, and why do ML/TF organizations like them?

What Are Digital Currencies?

Digital currency is essentially a record stored in a distributed database on the internet, in an electronic computer database, within digital files, or a stored-value card. Digital currencies display characteristics common to other currencies, but they do not have a physical form, such as banknotes and coins. Not having a physical form allows for nearly instantaneous financial transactions. Digital money can either be centralized, where there is a central point of control over the money supply, or decentralized, where the control over the money supply can come from various sources.

Why Do ML/TF Organizations Like Digital Currencies?

ML/TF organizations like digital currencies because they need a solid plan to handle their ill-gotten assets in a way that makes them appear legitimately acquired and, as a result, safer to spend. The ideal method that you are looking for is:

- Liquid, in that they want to liquidate and spend the proceeds conveniently, and digital currencies are incredibly liquid, and they can be moved anywhere in the world in minutes.

- Untraceable, in that covering up a digital trail is essential to avoiding detection. The goal of the ML/TF is to obscure as many links between the initial placement of funds and their final disposition. Digital currencies are less traceable than many digital transactions, especially in the short term, with few regulations in effect.

- Efficient, in that ML efforts usually result in additional costs, such as transactional charges from intermediaries, taxes paid as part of the integration process, or volatility (such as stock and currency declines). The ideal system minimizes these costs. As far as efficiency is concerned, digital currencies are only moderately efficient because they come with some level of risk.

- Secure, in that just because funds were earned through crime does not mean someone else should get to steal them from your organization. For the most part, ML or TF wants their assets kept inaccessible to authorities and other criminals alike.

Note: The practical exercise is not contained in the student text; the instructor has to print out and distribute the handout for this exercise.

PRACTICAL EXERCISE – USING FICTION TO EXERCISE CRITICAL THINKING SKILLS

Besides entertainment, movies based upon actual events also serve to inform the audience about a story, incident, or person. The best movies also can highlight important substantive themes relevant to understanding organized crime and terror finance.

The exercise facilitator will pass out a Student Guide. Read the movie (*The Infiltrator*, 2016) summary within (and watch the movie if you have not done so already), then answer the following questions to better visualize the organized crime connections in the story. Please, bear in mind that movies can oversimplify reality and perpetuate erroneous stereotypes.

Figure 9.21 Movie Poster for The Infiltrator.

CHAPTER 10

Open-Source Intelligence

INTRODUCTION

This chapter introduces, defines, provides some historical context, and presents proven methods for producing *open-source intelligence* (OSINT). Most common perceptions understand OSINT as data and information that is readily available to the public via the internet or other public sources. Although the web may be a valuable source, OSINT is not limited to what is discoverable using one's preferred search engine (e.g., Google, Yahoo, Dogpile, and so on). Sixty years ago, there were no commercial satellites, and 40 years ago, no search engines or data mining algorithms. Today open-source information is reinventing, redefining, and accelerating the intelligence community (IC) and how it finds, analyzes, and develops intelligence.

However, for hundreds of years, there has been publicly available information that complements and supplements the more traditional state-developed covert and classified intelligence sources, most often appearing in the form of newspapers and peer-reviewed scientific research papers.

Jane's information group is an example of a modern publicly available intelligence company that has evolved with the times. Janes originally began in 1898 when a little-known artist sketched warships and published a book, *Jane's All the World's Fighting Ships*. Janes is a multinational information company specializing in military, national security, aerospace, and transportation topics. Refer to Figure 10.1 for an early example of an exhibit from Jane's All the World's Fighting Ships.[1]

Today, Let us start with the US Military definition of OSINT and build our knowledge base from there. OSINT is intelligence developed from collecting and analyzing publicly available and open-source information not directly controlled by the US government. Analysts produce OSINT by systematically collecting, processing, and analyzing publicly available, relevant information in response to intelligence requirements.[2]

America's adversaries have long used open sources to exploit apparent weaknesses. The former Soviet Union found OSINT so lucrative that it established intelligence services and academic institutes dedicated to collecting open-source data. For example, assessments indicate the Soviets were first alerted to the existence of the stealth fighter and the signals intelligence satellite programs by exploiting open-source information (see Figure 10.2). Soviet operatives attended congressional hearings, examined major newspapers daily, extracted data from the publications of academic and

---

1 Sampson Low, Marston, *Jane's Fighting Ships 1906-07*, Edited by Fred T. Jane, 1906 and public domain in the United States.
2 Headquarters Department of the Army, Open-source Intelligence, Army Techniques Publication, ATP 2-22.9, July 10, 2012.

DOI: 10.4324/9781003241195-10

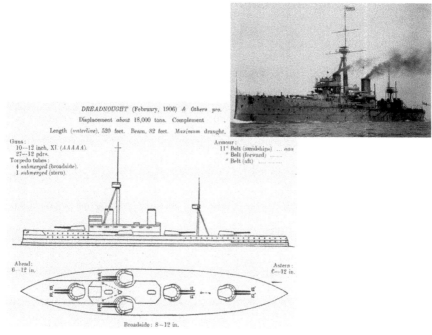

Figure 10.1   Diagrams of HMS Dreadnought from 1906.

Figure 10.2   Classified Stealth Fighter and Satellite Programs.

research organizations, and obtained information from technical journals. The Federal Bureau of Investigation (FBI) estimated that up to 90% of the information collected by the Soviets came from open sources.[3] There are no indications that present-day Russian intelligence services have changed collection methods from the Soviet era. If anything, their pursuit of open sources has become more aggressive. Figure 10.3 depicts some examples of commonly exploited publicly available open sources.

Adversaries are prudent to pursue open-source information. The US IC appreciates the consequence and application of OSINT and how it serves as an economy of force, provides added

---

3   Ballinger Publishing, *Sword and Shield: Soviet Intelligence and Security Apparatus*, Jeffrey T. Richelson, 1986.

Figure 10.3 Common Publicly Available Open Sources.

leverage and capability, and offers tips and cues to other technical or classified assets, thereby enhancing and corroborating disparate intelligence collected by other means.

Though OSINT is highly valued, in the present day, there can be too much of good thing, and information overload has become a genuine concern. Therefore, analysts introduce control measures (collection plans) into the collection process to filter and segregate open sources to limit the introduction of meaningless or deceptive data, constantly aware that adversaries can access the same information that friends and allies can find.

This chapter discusses *OSINT Collection Special Considerations, OSINT Applications, Open-Source Types, Basic Internet Query Language Search Practices,* and *OSINT Collection and Processing Techniques.*

OSINT COLLECTION SPECIAL CONSIDERATIONS

When planning and preparing for intelligence collection activities, there exist considerations common to most other intelligence collection activities, and then some are unique to OSINT collection. Special considerations include operations security (OPSEC), linguist requirements, and copyright and intellectual property.

Ghosting the Net

OSINT analysts must be vigilant when performing searches on the internet because everything is visible to those who know how to search for it. One's internet searches can potentially alert adversaries to what you are searching for and provide helpful counterintelligence. Effective misattribution is critical for successful online intelligence collection. Analysts may find it necessary to maintain a consistent identity, one other than your real identity, also known as a pseudonym or alias. Using a pseudonym (false identity) enables one to mask their true identity and protect the integrity of the parent organization. Still, it can often allow entry to websites that one could not otherwise gain access. This process is known as ghosting. Ghosting is an internet term often associated with using a false identity on dating apps and social networks and is painfully frowned upon if discovered. However, in OSINT collection, the practice is critical to maintaining good OPSEC.

Foreign Languages

The ability to gather and analyze foreign materials is critical in OSINT exploitation. Effective OSINT production necessitates having the capacity to translate, transcribe, and interpret foreign languages. However, developing a reliable and proficient linguist requires a great deal of time, both for training and gaining experience. This extended timeline often results in shortages of linguist personnel. Automated language translation software can help provide the capacity to meet language requirements and demands.

Software solutions cannot fully replace linguists. Though language translation software can significantly augment an organization's capability for translation when appropriately employed. Reliable automated translators exist for media broadcasts and internet sources to auto-translate into English. Analysts frequently use computerized translations to get the gist of a document, email, or media broadcast. Analysts decide whether the translation requires foreign linguist skills to perform a formal, more technical, or more comprehensive translation based on the raw machine translation.

Translation

Translation requires bilingual proficiency, and linguists must also read and comprehend the source language and write comprehensibly in English.

Transcription

Transcription entails both listening and writing proficiency in the source language, sometimes requiring more than language proficiency. The linguist often needs a technical understanding of the source material (e.g., aerospace engineering, nuclear physics, or biogenetics). Adequate technical knowledge of the subject matter and English language skills are critical for authoritative or direct translation from audio or video into English text.

Interpretation

Interpretation entails bilingual competence, the ability to hear and comprehend the source language, speak comprehensibly in English, and choose the equivalent expression in English that adequately conveys the meaning intended in the source language.

Copyright and Intellectual Property

Copyright is a form of protection for published and unpublished works and is legally protected based upon the host nation's laws. Copyrighted open sources include 'original works of authorship,' such as literary, dramatic, musical, artistic works, discoveries, inventions, and sometimes symbols and designs. US government and military intelligence organizations recognize the rights of copyright owners consistent with the mission. Unless US copyright law authorizes the usage, OSINT personnel cannot produce or distribute copyrighted works without the copyright owner's permission. US regulations call for OSINT personnel to forward intelligence products to the organization's legal authority to obtain an approval or a waiver of notice to the copyright holder, if necessary, for OPSEC considerations.

OSINT Applications

Business owners, military commanders, and government leaders employ OSINT in many of the same ways as other types of intelligence. OSINT can define the operating (or business) environment, evaluate threats or adversaries, and determine courses of action (COAs). There are hundreds of commercial-off-the-shelf (COTS) OSINT applications available today. Some of the more popular examples are shown in Table 10.1.

Table 10.1   COTS OSINT Applications

Name	Description
Twint	Twint is an advanced Twitter scraping and OSINT tool written in Python that doesn't use Twitter's API, allowing you to scrape a user's followers, following, Tweets, and more while evading most API limitations.
Ghunt	Ghunt is used to investigate Google emails and documents.
Pentesting Bible	Pentesting Bible assists those wanting to learn the skill of ethical hacking and how to perform online reconnaissance, windows/Linux hacking, attacking web technologies, and pentesting wireless networks. Resources for learning malware analysis and reverse engineering.
Photon	Photon is a speedy web crawler designed for OSINT collection activities.
Social Analyzer	Social Analyzer is an API, CLI, and Web application for analyzing and finding a person's profile across 400+ social media/websites (detections are updated regularly).

Note: *The table is purely for academic purposes and should not be considered an endorsement of any particular OSINT software application.*

Defining the Operating Environment

Whether it is a soldier crossing into enemy territory, a police officer patrolling a different section of town, or a business owner venturing into a new market sector, understanding the existing operating environment is crucial to success. OSINT personnel use public broadcasts, local media, social networks, internet searches, and data mining to collect weather conditions, road trafficability, identify popular government policies, programs, and local power brokers. Without regard to who the intended OSINT product users are (soldiers, law enforcement, or salesman), intelligence professionals want to know that people accept, appreciate, or buy into what is presented. To further illustrate the concept, refer to the three examples below:

- Military commander's concerns lie in whether locals see their troops as conquers or liberators;
- Law enforcement officials intend to increase foot patrols and police presence in a given neighborhood, and they want to know if citizens greet their officers as protectors of the peace and private property or oppressors; and
- Marketing and salespeople who are trying to determine if a new business can thrive in a specific locality. They must decide if a neighborhood location can return the productive results or reposition to a different neighborhood.

Evaluating Threats or Adversaries

Evaluating the threat is a formal step in the military's intelligence preparation of the battlespace (IPB), requiring the analyst to assess each significant threat in the area of operations (AO). The publicly available information and open sources can provide most of the information required to identify threat characteristics and provide possible information to inform threat models.[4]

Law enforcement might use OSINT to perform this task using Google Street View to find any graffiti on buildings or other structures or tattoos on pedestrians caught in the photos. Recognized graffiti and tattoos identify potential gangs in the area.

Whereas a business owner (e.g., Starbucks) may use publicly available tax records and aerial imagery to determine if there are competitors (e.g., Dunkin Donuts, Crispy Crème, or another Starbucks) located in the vicinity of where a new store is planned (see Figure 10.4).

---

4   Headquarters Department of the Army, Open-source Intelligence, Army Techniques Publication, ATP 2-22.9, July 10, 2012.

Figure 10.4 Using Aerial Imagery to Find Competitors.

Determining Courses of Action

Determining COAs is also a step in the military IPB process. Its purpose is to identify, develop, and determine likely threat COAs that can affect the accomplishment of the friendly mission. The end state of the IPB is to produce a set of COAs open to the enemy commander and identify those areas and activities that, when observed, distinguish which COA the threat commander has chosen. The products of the IPB process yield indicators that act as signposts for the commander, which signal and describe threat changes in strength, posture, and intent (e.g., the mood of the local people or potential for an insurgency).

Referring back to the law enforcement analogy, crime analysts would expect a similar outcome as in the military example. Crime analysts would flag public information indicators like no negative press coverage, perhaps an increase in positive news coverage, signs in shop windows indicating law enforcement discounts offered, and perhaps something as simple as citizens thanking officers for their service. These would all be indicators that assist in determining if a neighbor accepts or rejects their increased presence.

Business owners' OSINT task is far more straightforward. They can also use positive or negative press coverage of their business, aerial photographs of their competitor's parking lot, and many other public information indicators to gauge the community's response. However, the ultimate yardstick is the product sales tally sheets to indicate the success or failure of their commercial venture.

Author's Note: All open sources are frequently problematic and hard to differentiate as they all are subjective. Primary sources are not necessarily valued more highly than other types. From an intelligence perspective, no source type is more important, expert, greater governing authority, or superior. Each source must be weighed based upon its inherent merits. OSINT personnel are responsible for evaluating the source information to determine reliability and validity and assess for indications of deception and bias.

For example, from personal experience in Iraq (circa 2005), after Coalition Forces had taken control, it was observed that local television public service announcements were not being followed or believed by the Iraqi populace. The Iraqi populace's lack of credulity for public service announcements initially confused military leadership. This conundrum is because US citizens generally trust public service announcements (e.g., severe weather warnings, reports of dangerous criminals at large, or other public hazards) are considered authoritative sources. Further investigation determined that under the previous despotic Saddam Hussein regime, most local television programming consisted of pure propaganda and was considered untrustworthy for good reason (Figure 10.5). Alternatively, locals would get their news from more trusted sources, the second-, third-, and fourth-hand reports (rumors) originating from acquaintances found at the local 'suqs' (public markets).

Figure 10.5   Saddam Hussein.

OPEN-SOURCE TYPES

There are three types of open sources: primary, secondary, and authoritative sources.

Primary Sources

OSINT analysts categorize primary sources by their content (e.g., either public or private). These sources can be incomplete, disconnected, and difficult to analyze. Since they often originate from the author, primary sources may contain outdated meanings of familiar words, colloquialisms, and popular expressions (*e.g., thou hast turned my mourning into dancing…translation, you make me happy*).

Primary sources may include:

- Individuals and recording devices with direct knowledge (e.g., local inhabitants, remote surveillance devices, cell phones, doorbell cameras, and customer online testimonials and complaints).
- Creative works range from published literature and songs to expressive graffiti murals on walls and buildings.
- Original documents (specific passages or translations) include diaries, research journals, public speeches, personal letters, news camera footage, interviews, autobiographies, and public records.

Figure 10.6   Photo of the Soviet newspaper *Pravda*.

Secondary Sources

Secondary sources provide interpretations, content analysis, and citations (sometimes out of context) from primary sources. Secondary sources may also contain pictures, quotes, or graphics from primary sources. Some examples of secondary sources are textbooks, histories, media articles, encyclopedias, and commentaries.

Authoritative Sources

Authoritative sources come in the form of reported information from the political leaders, governments, or ruling parties. Once thought to be more accurate than primary and secondary sources, history has proven these also can be distorted by what the reporter (or the one being interviewed) selects to include or omit from the report (statement) or misrepresent based upon the biases of either party. One of the more egregious examples of inaccurate government-sponsored authoritative sources is the Soviet government-sponsored newspaper, *Pravda* (see Figure 10.6[5]). *Pravda*, meaning 'truth,' was an official publication of the Central Committee of the Communist Party between 1918 and 1991. However, those outside the Soviet bloc believed that *Pravda* was a purveyor of Communist theories and interpretations rather than an unbiased account of reality.

---

5   1941 *Pravda* Newspaper front page photo, photo ID: ПРАВДАобращениесталина.jpg, This work is in the public domain in Russia according to Article 1281 of Book IV of the Civil Code of the Russian Federation No. 230-FZ of December 18, 2006, and Article 6 of Law No. 231-FZ of the Russian Federation of December 18, 2006.

Figure 10.7   Analysts Must Assess the Reliability and Credibility from Any Source, Including Them Media.

EVALUATING OSINT

OSINT analysts, like all intelligence analysts, evaluate collected open-source information in terms of reliability and credibility of the actual material collected and the information source provider. The analyst might ask, 'Is the source an authority on the subject, or did they just look it up on the internet?' If the intelligence organization keeps reliability assessment records on a particular source, the analyst only refers to the source's reliability score. Whatever way the OSINT analysts assess the open-source information, the assessment process needs to be documented so that others can understand how the assessment was performed.

Information Reliability and Credibility

It is essential to assess and rate the reliability of open sources to recognize the objective and the factual material and detect any bias or deception. Ratings rely upon the subjective judgment of the information appraiser and the accuracy of previous information produced by the same source.

Analysts must assess the reliability and credibility of the collected open-source material independently of the information source to avoid bias. The three types of sources used to categorize, evaluate, and analyze received information are primary sources (sources having direct access to the information), secondary sources (sources that convey information through intermediary sources), and authoritative sources (sources that accurately reports the information), for example, a journalist interviewing a political leader or government official (Figure 10.7).[6]

---

6   Headquarters Department of the Army, Open-source Intelligence, Army Techniques Publication, ATP 2-22.9, July 10, 2012.

TIPS/NOTES: ALL SOURCES CAN BE BIASED

Secondary and authoritative sources, such as television media outlets, government press offices, commercial news organizations, political campaign staffs, research center publications, newspapers, periodicals, databases, and libraries, can intentionally or unintentionally add, delete, modify, or filter the information made available to the public. Analysts must validate all collected data by finding separate supporting (or refuting) evidence.

Even though nonauthoritative sources lack reliability and trustworthiness, they rarely stand apart from authoritative sources. Information provided by nonauthoritative sources generally does not support topics agreed to be factual and consistent in academia and other established subject matter experts.[7] Nonauthoritative sources omit referential citations or make tracing the underlying supporting information challenging and problematic to locate.

Nonauthoritative Sources

Nonauthoritative sources usually are inaccessible by the public, and they are unsubstantiated by multiple publicly available information sources. Examples of nonauthoritative sources include:

- Informal personal communications (e.g., letters to the editor and opinion articles) (see Figure 10.8).

- Information received via unverified email, hearsay (second-, third-hand, and others' comments), or strictly verbal statements solely (not written down or recorded).

- Unsupported documents from self-published online repositories (e.g., wikis, political sites, blogs, and advertisements).

Figure 10.8   Nonauthoritative Sources.

7   Headquarters Department of the Army, Open-source Intelligence, Army Techniques Publication, ATP 2-22.9, July 10, 2012.

EVALUATING SOURCES

When assessing sources of information to determine reliability and credibility, analysts consider the source's motive(s), authority, access, timeliness, identity, and consistency (MA2TIC).

- M – Motive. Why was the information published? (Is there a hidden agenda?)
- A – Authority. How much does the source know of the provided data's origin? (Is the source a subject matter expert or witness?)
- A – Access. Did the source have direct (or indirect) access to the incident or information? (Was the source an eyewitness, or did they hear about the event from someone else?)
- T – Timeliness. What is the date of the information? (Does the source have prior knowledge of an occurrence, and is the information not so dated to be irrelevant?)
- I – Identity. Who provided the information (e.g., a student, teacher, political organization, or reporter)?
- C – Consistency (internal and external). Does the information contradict administrative protocols and policies among local citizens? For example, a source has no rationale for obtaining restricted data that he reportedly collects from a controlled government facility during nonwork hours.[8]

BASIC INTERNET QUERY LANGUAGE SEARCH PRACTICES

A Keyword Search is the most basic and commonly used type of query and uses a minimal set of processing rules. The only mandatory requirement for this query is that the provided keywords must be applied against the available data resources to determine potential matches. This query language definition does not place any restrictions on the exact keyword matching algorithm. However, additional beneficial functionality is added by supporting phrases, Boolean operators, and parenthetical notation, as in this specification is commonly found in many public search services on the internet.[9]

> *Author's Notes: It is understood that Millennials, Generation -Xers, and other computer tech-savvy individuals may find the chapter topic Basic Internet Query Language Search Practices somewhat tedious. I have included the topic for those not tech-savvy. A brief section is included only to ensure everyone has a fundamental understanding of internet query language.*

Boolean Operators

Online search services utilize Boolean operators found in a keyword expression (for example, the search *'treaty OR verification'* would return metadata for items that match *either* 'treaty OR verification', while the search *'treaty AND verification'* would only return metadata for items that match *both*) (see Figure 10.9). The following paragraphs describe the behaviors of operators, where *Apple, Orange,* and *Banana* are substituted for arbitrary keywords, phrases, or groups.

Groups '( )'

A *group* uses a text expression and a parenthetical notation to regulate the order of precedence of a keyword query. The insertion of a particular text expression within parentheses requires

---

8   Headquarters Department of the Army, Open-source Intelligence, Army Techniques Publication, ATP 2-22.9, July 10, 2012.

9   US Department of Defense (DoD), Intelligence Community and Department of Defense Content Discovery and Retrieval Integrated Project Team, IC/DoD Keyword Query Language Specification, Version 1.1, March 2003.

that a subset of the keyword query expression be processed before the rest of the expression. The parenthetical notation allows increasingly complex Boolean operations. The following example illustrates the concept:

Ex. (Apple AND (Orange OR Banana))

When resolving an expression with multiple sets of parentheses, evaluate the innermost parentheses first, followed by the next innermost, and so forth. In the previous example, the innermost set of parentheses is '(Orange OR Banana).'

Phrase

A phrase is a collection of keywords separated by spaces and surrounded in single quotes such as 'Hello, Dolly.' The results contain the string (case-insensitive) within those quotation marks. For example, if the expression contained the phrase 'Hello, Dolly' in quotes as shown, the search service would only return exact matches to the phrase and not data that matched one or two of the keywords.

> *Example phrase search string results for 'Hello, Dolly'…The production of Hello, Dolly! is big and bright and brassy with Barbra Streisand taking center stage as Dolly Levi, the matchmaker with a mind to marry a crusty half-a-millionaire from Yonkers.*

OPEN-SOURCE INTELLIGENCE COLLECTION AND PROCESSING TECHNIQUES

To this point, this chapter described applications of OSINT, covered how to identify and categorize types of open sources and public information, and discussed how to evaluate open sources using the mnemonic, 'MA2TIC.' This section explains techniques for collecting and processing OSINT.

The Collection Plan

First, analysts develop a collection plan that provides a clear strategy and framework for acquiring and applying the OSINT. The sought-after open-source data must be directed explicitly toward answering predefined intelligence requirements. For example, a business analyst assigned an OSINT information requirement to determine if a specific population might support oil exploration near their town. It may be tempting to perform broad online searches to determine what, if any, environmental groups are associated with the town's population or other tangential research. However, a likely more effective approach would be to conduct an actual survey directly posing survey questions to the townspeople using social networks or other more specific open-source collection strategies. If one desires better confidence in their survey/research results, they need to be as specific as possible about their survey/research questions.

TIPS/NOTES:

* *Remember, if you are an analyst in the military, law enforcement, or part of the IC, the OSINT you develop would be a part of the intelligence you collect, process, and analyze.*
* *OSINT is only one intelligence source; it would likely be fused with other intelligence to produce a final intelligence product.*
* *Do NOT try to collect all the OSINT information that may be 'interesting or useful,' the sheer volume of information available through open sources can be overwhelming.*
* *Be careful to ensure that all OSINT collection tasks are legal and sanctioned (if a state-sponsored program).*

Open-Source Collection Tools

The next step is to identify a set of tools and techniques for collecting and processing open-source information. Again, the potential volume of information available may exceed your ability to handle it effectively. The advent of cable, online news, 24-hour news cycles, and near real-time information services have improved the quantity, quality, and timeliness of information obtainable from open sources. News services, television, electronic bulletin boards, online databases, blogs, social networks, along with a wide range of specialized publications available in full text, offer detailed information on the activities of the US government, the military services, and the private sector. The ubiquity of these open sources allows allies and adversaries access. Today, nations worldwide, including the United States, leverage open-source networks and news outlets to gain insights into the actions and motives of adversaries.

Aside from the more traditional open sources (e.g., scientific papers, textbooks, college courses, Freedom of Information Act, FOIA, requests, and so on), this chapter makes an effort to introduce more modern and trending open-source collection tools. These advanced open-source tools include, but are limited to:

* Google Dork Searches
* Email Breach Lookup
* Fact-Checking Websites
* Open-source Image Search
* Online Public Property Records Search
* Online Search Engines
* Social Media Search Tools
* Specific-Built Search Software
* Surveillance Camera Feeds
* Transportation Network Feeds (Aircraft, Boats, Vehicles)
* Username Search
* Visual/Clustering Search Engines

Passive Collection

Identification of web technologies used by the target, application platform, and other infrastructure details and identifying sensitive information (e.g., API keys, AWS S3 buckets, leaked internet credentials, and so on…) OSINT collection generally falls into two categories: passive collection and active collection. Passive collection (information gathering) often involves using a physical surveillance device or system, publicly available information (physical or online), online search engines, or specialized software to gather information about a target or satisfy information requirements. Online collection frequently requires identifying one or more internet protocol (IP) addresses, subdomains, ports, and services.

While online OSINT collection is much easier than manual collection methods, the perils of information overload are still substantial. More modern and automated passive solutions address the data overload problem using artificial intelligence, machine learning, and language processing tools to automate and selectively filter the data. The process prioritizes data sets and uses alerts that trigger based upon the OSINT collection plan's specific needs.

Author's Note: Although still used in the storylines of many television police dramas, most modern police departments and surveillance companies no longer use microphones connected by a wire to bulky batteries to eavesdrop on private conversations covertly. Instead, the ubiquitous nature of cell phones is leveraged.

A cell phone can easily be converted to a small area audio-video collection device and transmitted via the local Wi-Fi network to a remote location for observation and recording. Additionally, since everyone has a cell phone, it generally goes unnoticed by others involved in the conversation.

Active Collection

Unlike passive collection, the active collection uses an assortment of techniques to search for information aggressively. Most people are familiar with the more recognized methods of manually going through courthouse records, or perhaps 'wearing a wire' or the 'shirt-button' surveillance camera made famous by Hollywood police genres. Alternatively, several less well-known contemporary active collection methods exist that use automated web services that may not be as familiar to the layperson. The text focuses on instances of the more up-to-date OSINT collection methods.

Besides OSINT collection efforts pursuing data to satisfy intelligence requirements, there are multiple other reasons for using automated active collection devices. Cybersecurity professionals use this type of collection for network penetration testing or to provide network alerts.

Similarly, active OSINT collectors can use botnets to collect valuable information using traffic sniffing and keylogging techniques.

Common Automated OSINT Tools

While many readily available tools are available to OSINT collectors and cybersecurity specialists, some are free; others must be purchased or have associated usage fees. Be aware that these tools are just as accessible to adversaries (e.g., enemy states, terrorists, and criminal actors).

Online Search Engines

The most frequently used (and abused) OSINT tools are search engines (i.e., Google, Yahoo, Bing, DuckDuckGo).

Though these search engines are pretty efficient, the data on the web is much more diverse and spread out than most OSINT analysts fully realize. Large amounts of data like databases, files, and several web pages go under the radar because search engines cannot properly index them. Some exposed and non-indexed data are queriable. However, one can't use standard search engines. The data can be accessed using other lesser-known tools like 'Google Dorks.'

Google Dork Searches

Due to the regularity that typical, otherwise well-meaning, users negligently leave sensitive information exposed on the internet. There is often sensitive information exposed on the web, and there are cyber tools that OSINT collectors employ to find this unprotected sensitive information. There are unconventional search functions called 'Google Dork' queries, and Google Dork queries are search tools that identify sensitive information accessible but not intended to be exposed to the public.

Author's Note: Outside of cybersecurity vulnerability testing exercises. Google Dorking is an illegal activity. Hackers employ dork searches to access information for illegal purposes like identity theft, cyberterrorism, industrial and state-sponsored espionage. Cyber tools and training shall be provided if your organization is lawfully authorized to perform these types of queries. However, the specifics of Google Dorking are not covered in this text.

Google Dork searches utilize the same search query operators employed by information technology (IT) professionals and hackers routinely in their work. Typical operator examples include 'filetype,' which narrows search results to a specific file type, and site, which only returns results from a specified website or domain. Log files can also be accessed using Google Dorks, making it ideal for finding vulnerabilities and hidden information. A few typical Google Dork software applications include Sublist3r and Knockpy. These automated attack tools use customized query operators to locate vulnerable systems and sensitive information disclosures in public networks. The following is a list of some of the more common Google Dork search operators:

- *Filetype*: Defines a specific file type
- *Site:* Restricts search results to those websites in a given domain
- *Intext*: Locates particular text on a webpage
- *Ext*: Identifies the file extension
- *Intitle*: Retrieves web pages that have a specific text in their title
- *Inurl:* Retrieves web pages with specific text in their URLs

Fact-Checking Websites

Many of the fact-checking websites are free. They research everything from fake or incorrect news, urban legends, rumors, dubious photos and videos, articles, and claims made by public figures (e.g., Snopes). Unfortunately, many of these same 'fact-checking websites' are also politically biased. Multiple independent and reliable sources are needed to support (or deny) collected data and adequately vet the data. Ultimately, it is up to the OSINT analyst to assess the trustworthiness of the information.

Email Breach Lookup

Email breach lookup sites allow the user to determine if an individual email address was affected by one of several data breaches over the years. Upon entering an email address, the web service tells the user which breaches the email was associated with. Additionally, it gives a brief overview of the breach (e.g., BreachAlarm).

> *Author's Note: By now, a trend should have become apparent. First, there are a large and ever-increasing number of OSINT collection tools available. Next, only a few representative examples of each OSINT tool type are provided.*
>
> *These online tools come, go, or are acquired by others and merged into a newer OSINT tool suite under another name. Therefore, there is no guarantee that the particular tool(s) mentioned shall exist by the time of this textbook's publication. As a result, little effort is being spent to explain how each tool is used. There is adequate instruction available at the individual OSINT tool websites.*

Open-Source Image Search

Image search web services can search the web for images associated with a particular location or perform reverse image searches. The reverse search feature allows users to search by image and find out where that image is online (e.g., TinEye and Current Location).

Online Public Property Records Search

Most Americans are familiar with the information you can get from real estate sites (e.g., Realtor. com, Redfin, Trulia, and Zillow). These sites are helpful when investigating a particular property if the address is known. The public record web service can yield the particulars on the property, such as if it is currently for sale, size, number, and types of rooms. It may even provide photos of the interior and exterior. However, other web tools offer more extensive information, like the property owner's name, other residents at that location, assessed value, year built, and more; some examples include Melissa Lookups and BeenVerified.

Social Media Search Tools

People today put up a truly incredible amount of personal information on their social networking pages, and there are several search tools available to take advantage of this circumstance. Social media search tools, among other things, can download a user's friends list, check to see if two accounts follow one another, download a user's followers list. These tools include Twitter Search tools like *Tweatbeaver* and Facebook Search Tools like *NetBoot Camp* and *People Search*.

Specific-Built Search Software

Several types of specific-built search software are used primarily by law enforcement, cyber forensic investigators, and cybersecurity professionals to analyze OSINT. They are usually operating platform-agnostic (i.e., they run on Windows, Linux, OSX,…). OSINT personnel use the software to collect data and information from various sources and display them graphically. Using software specifically built for the task helps reduce analysis time, make connections, and uncover leads. Specific-built OSINT search software examples include *Hunchly*, *Sentinel Visualizer*, and *Lampyre*.

Surveillance Camera Feeds

There is an online web service that aggregates access to hundreds of surveillance cameras and public web cameras worldwide. The cameras are not 'hacked' and do not include surveillance cameras linked to personal computers, laptops, tablets, or other specialized types of cameras. These sites have cameras arranged by an assortment of groupings. Two examples of these amassed OSINT surveillance camera web services are Earth Cam and Insecam.

Transportation Network Feeds (Aircraft, Boats, Vehicles)

Some websites allow OSINT personnel to view live flight tracking and marine shipping traffic around the globe. Also, there are online tools that help determine if a vehicle is reported as stolen but not recovered. A few web services are Marine Traffic, Flight Radar 24, and VINCheck.

Username Search

A username search is a method of finding someone online. Employing the username and running a reverse lookup on the username may yield additional identifying and other bits of potentially related information about the person associated with the username.

> **TIPS/NOTES:**
> - Many people use the same username on multiple websites. For similar reasons, people reuse passwords and email addresses for every website, thereby avoiding the necessity for remembering separate screen names.
> - OSINT personnel can take advantage of this oversight to find all the websites associated with a particular username.
> - The other websites may contain other details related to the person associated with the username, like their name, address, employer, etc.

Tracing a username may not be as effective as other search techniques, but if the username is all that is available, it can be a start. Often used username search web services include Google Social Search, Usersearch.org, or PeekYou.

Visual/Clustering Search Engines

Visual/Clustering Search Engines are search engines designed to search for information online and visually display the clustered search results as groupings. A clustering engine allows interactive browsing through clustered web search results for a large population of users. Common examples include *Clusty, A9,* and *Accumo.*

> **TIPS/NOTES:**
> - Clustering analysis is the task of grouping a set of objects so that objects in the same group are more similar to each other than those in other groups.
> - Refer to Figure 10.10; notice the blue dots and the red dots 'cluster' around specific numbers on the X and Y axes.

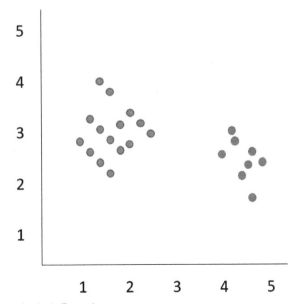

Figure 10.10 Clustering Analysis Example.

CHAPTER SUMMARY

The chapter introduced, defined, provided some historical context, and presented proven methods for producing Open-Source Intelligence (OSINT). The text pointed out that America's adversaries have long-used open sources to exploit apparent weaknesses. There are no indications that present-day Russian intelligence services have changed collection methods from the Soviet era.

Adversaries are prudent to pursue open-source information. The US intelligence community (IC) appreciates the consequence and application of OSINT and how it serves as an economy of force, provides added leverage and capability, and offers tips and cues to other technical or classified assets, thereby enhancing and corroborating disparate intelligence collected by other means.

Though OSINT is valued, in the present day, there can be too much of a good thing, and information overload is a genuine concern. Therefore, analysts introduce control measures (collection plans) into the collection process to filter and segregate open sources to limit the introduction of meaningless data, constantly aware that adversaries can also access information that can be found by friends and allies.

This chapter also discussed OSINT Collection Special Considerations, OSINT Applications, Open-Source Types, Basic Internet Query Language Search Practices, and OSINT Collection and Processing Techniques.

OSINT COLLECTION SPECIAL CONSIDERATIONS

When planning and preparing for intelligence collection activities, there exist considerations common to most other intelligence collection activities, and then some are unique to OSINT collection. These special considerations include operations security (OPSEC), linguist requirements, and copyright and intellectual property.

Ghosting the Net

OSINT analysts must be vigilant when performing searches on the internet, as everything is visible to those who know how to search for it. Effective misattribution is critical for successful online intelligence collection. Analysts may find it necessary to maintain a consistent identity, one other than your real identity, also known as a pseudonym or alias. Using a pseudonym (false identity) enables one to mask their true identity and protect the integrity of the parent organization. Still, it can often allow entry to websites that one could not otherwise gain access.

Foreign Languages

The ability to gather and analyze foreign materials is critical in OSINT exploitation. Effective OSINT production necessitates having the capacity to translate, transcribe, and interpret foreign languages. However, developing a reliable and proficient linguist requires a great deal of time, both for training and gaining experience. This extended timeline often results in shortages of linguist personnel. Automated language translation software can help provide the capacity to meet language requirements and demands.

Software solutions cannot fully replace linguists, but language translation software can augment an organization's capability for translation when appropriately employed. Analysts frequently use software-based translators to get the gist of a document, email, or media broadcast based on the raw machine translation. They then decide whether the translation requires foreign linguist skills to perform a formal, more technical, or more comprehensive translation.

Translation

Translation requires bilingual proficiency, and linguists must read and comprehend the source language and write comprehensibly in English.

Transcription

Transcription entails both listening and writing proficiency in the source language, sometimes requiring more than language proficiency. The linguist often needs a technical understanding of the source material (e.g., aerospace engineering, nuclear physics, or biogenetics). Adequate technical knowledge of the subject matter and English language skills are critical for authoritative or direct translation from audio or video into English text.

Interpretation

Interpretation entails bilingual competence, the ability to hear and comprehend the source language, speak comprehensibly in English, and choose the equivalent expression in English that adequately conveys the meaning intended in the source language.

Copyright and Intellectual Property

Copyright is a form of protection for published and unpublished works and is legally protected by the laws of the host nation. Copyrighted open sources include 'original works of authorship,' such as literary, dramatic, musical, artistic works, discoveries, inventions, and sometimes symbols and designs. US government and military intelligence organizations recognize the rights of copyright owners consistent with the mission. Unless US copyright law authorizes the usage, OSINT personnel cannot produce or distribute copyrighted works without the copyright owner's permission. US regulations call for OSINT personnel to forward intelligence products to the organization's legal authority to obtain an approval or a waiver of notice to the copyright holder, if necessary, for OPSEC considerations.

OSINT Applications

Business owners, military commanders, and government leaders employ OSINT in many of the same ways as other types of intelligence. OSINT can define the operating (or business) environment, evaluate threats or adversaries, and determine courses of action (COAs).

Defining the Operating Environment

Whether it is a soldier crossing into enemy territory, a police officer patrolling a different section of town, or a business owner venturing into a new market sector, understanding the existing operating environment is crucial to success. OSINT personnel will use public broadcasts, local media, social networks, internet searches, and data mining to collect weather conditions, road trafficability, and identify popular government policies, programs, and local power brokers. Without regard to who the intended OSINT product users are (soldiers, law enforcement, or salesman), intelligence professionals want to know that people accept, appreciate, or buy into what is presented.

Evaluating Threats or Adversaries

Evaluating the threat is a formal step in the military's intelligence preparation of the battlespace (IPB), requiring the analyst to assess each significant threat in the area of operations (AO). Publicly available open-source information can provide most of the information needed to identify threat characteristics to inform threat models.[10]

Law enforcement might use OSINT to perform this task using Google Street View to find any graffiti on buildings or other structures or tattoos on pedestrians caught in the photos. Recognized graffiti and tattoos identify potential gangs in the area.

---

10 Headquarters Department of the Army, Open-source Intelligence, Army Techniques Publication, ATP 2-22.9, July 10, 2012.

A business owner (e.g., Starbucks) may use publicly available tax records and aerial imagery to determine if there are competitors (e.g., Dunkin Donuts, Crispy Crème, or another Starbucks) located in the vicinity of where a new store is planned.

Determining Courses of Action

Determining COAs is also a step in the military IPB process. Its purpose is to identify, develop, and determine likely threat COAs that can affect the accomplishment of the friendly mission. The end state of the IPB is to produce a set of COAs open to the enemy commander and to identify those areas and activities that, when observed, distinguish which COA the threat commander has chosen. At the end of the military IPB process, the use of publicly available information and open sources yields indicators that act as signposts for the commander, which signal and describe threat changes in strength, posture, and intent (e.g., the mood of the local people or potential for an insurgency).

Referring back to the law enforcement analogy, crime analysts expect a similar outcome as in the military example. Analysts would flag public information indicators like no negative press coverage, perhaps an increase in positive news coverage, signs in shop windows indicating law enforcement discounts offered, and perhaps something as simple as citizens thanking officers for their service. These would all be indicators that assist in determining if a neighbor accepts or rejects their increased presence.

Business owners' OSINT task is far more straightforward. They can also use positive or negative press coverage of their business, aerial photographs of their competitor's parking lot, and many other public information indicators to gauge the community's response. However, the ultimate yardstick is the product sales tally sheet that indicates a commercial venture's success or failure.

OPEN-SOURCE TYPES

There are three types of open sources: primary, secondary, and authoritative sources.

Primary Sources

OSINT analysts categorize primary sources by their content (e.g., either public or private). These sources can be incomplete, disconnected, and difficult to analyze. Since they often originate from the author, primary sources may contain outdated meanings of familiar words, colloquialisms, and popular expressions.

Secondary Sources

Secondary sources provide interpretations, content analysis, and citations (sometimes out of context) from primary sources. Secondary sources may also contain pictures, quotes, or graphics from primary sources. Some examples of secondary sources are textbooks, histories, media articles, encyclopedias, and commentaries.

Authoritative Sources

Authoritative sources come in the form of reported information from the political leaders, governments, or ruling parties. Once thought to be more accurate than primary and secondary sources, history has proven these also can be distorted by what the reporter (or the one being interviewed) selects to include or omit from the report (statement) or misrepresent based upon the biases of either party. One of the more egregious examples of inaccurate government-sponsored authoritative sources is the Soviet government-sponsored newspaper, *Pravda*. *Pravda*, meaning 'truth,' was an official publication of the Central Committee of the Communist Party between 1918 and 1991. However, those outside the Soviet bloc believed that *Pravda* was a purveyor of Communist theories and interpretations rather than an unbiased account of reality.

EVALUATING OSINT

OSINT analysts, like all intelligence analysts, evaluate collected open-source information in terms of reliability and credibility of the actual material collected and the information source provider. The analyst might ask, 'Is the source an authority on the subject, or did they just look it up on the internet?' If the intelligence organization keeps reliability assessment records on a particular source, the analyst only refers to the source's reliability score. Whatever way the OSINT analysts assess the open-source information, the assessment process needs to be documented so that others can understand how the assessment was performed.

Information Reliability and Credibility

It is essential to assess and rate the reliability of open sources to recognize the objective and the factual material and detect any bias or deception. Ratings rely upon the subjective judgment of the information appraiser and the accuracy of previous information produced by the same source.

Analysts must assess the reliability and credibility of the collected open-source material independently of the information source to avoid bias. The three types of sources used to categorize, evaluate, and analyze received information are primary sources (sources having direct access to the information), secondary sources (sources that convey information through intermediary sources), and authoritative sources (sources that accurately reports the information), for example, a journalist interviewing a political leader or government official.[11]

Even though nonauthoritative sources lack reliability and trustworthiness, they rarely stand apart from authoritative sources. Information provided by nonauthoritative sources generally does not support topics agreed upon as factual and consistent with academia and other established subject matter experts.[12] Nonauthoritative sources omit referential citations or make tracing the underlying supporting information challenging and problematic to locate.

Nonauthoritative Sources

Nonauthoritative sources usually are inaccessible by the public, and they are unsubstantiated by multiple publicly available information sources.

EVALUATING SOURCES

When assessing sources of information to determine reliability and credibility, analysts consider the source's motive, authority, access, timeliness, identity, and consistency (MA2TIC).

- M – Motive. Why was the information published? (Is there a hidden agenda?)
- A – Authority. How much does the source know of the provided data's origin? (Is the source a subject matter expert or witness?)
- A – Access. Did the source have direct (or indirect) access to the incident or information? (Was the source an eyewitness, or did they hear about the event from someone else?)
- T – Timeliness. What is the date of the information? (Does the source have prior knowledge of an occurrence, and is the information not so dated to be irrelevant?)
- I – Identity. Who provided the information (e.g., a student, teacher, political organization, or reporter)?

---

11 Headquarters Department of the Army, Open-Source Intelligence, Army Techniques Publication, ATP 2-22.9, July 10, 2012.

12 Headquarters Department of the Army, Open-Source Intelligence, Army Techniques Publication, ATP 2-22.9, July 10, 2012.

- C – Consistency (internal and external). Does the information contradict administrative protocols and policies among local citizens? For example, a source has no rationale for obtaining restricted data that he reportedly collects from a controlled government facility during nonwork hours.[13]

BASIC INTERNET QUERY LANGUAGE SEARCH PRACTICES

A Keyword Search is the most basic and commonly used type of query and uses a minimal set of processing rules. The only mandatory requirement for this query is that the provided keywords must be applied against the available data resources to determine any potential matches. This query language definition does not place any restrictions on the exact keyword matching algorithm. However, additional beneficial functionality is added by supporting phrases, Boolean operators, and parenthetical notation, as this specification is commonly found in many public search services on the internet.[14]

Boolean Operators

Online search services utilize Boolean operators found in a keyword expression (for example, the search 'treaty OR verification' would return metadata for items that match either 'treaty OR verification,' while the search 'treaty AND verification' would only return metadata for items that match both). The following paragraphs describe the behaviors of operators, where Apple, Orange, and Banana are substituted for arbitrary keywords, phrases, or groups.

Groups '( )'

A group uses a text expression and a parenthetical notation to regulate the order of precedence of a keyword query. The insertion of a particular text expression within parentheses requires that a subset of the keyword query expression be processed before the rest of the expression. The parenthetical notation allows increasingly complex Boolean operations.

When resolving an expression with multiple sets of parentheses, evaluate the innermost parentheses first, followed by the next innermost, and so forth. In the previous example, the innermost set of parentheses is '(Orange OR Banana).'

Phrase

A phrase is a collection of keywords separated by spaces and surrounded in single quotes such as 'Hello, Dolly.' The results contain the string (case-insensitive) within those quotation marks. For example, if the expression contained the phrase 'Hello, Dolly' in quotes as shown, the search service would only return exact matches to the phrase and not data that matched one or two of the keywords

> Example phrase search string results for 'Hello, Dolly'... This production of Hello, Dolly! is big and bright and brassy with Barbra Streisand taking center stage as Dolly Levi, the matchmaker with a mind to marry a crusty half-a-millionaire from Yonkers.

OPEN-SOURCE INTELLIGENCE COLLECTION AND PROCESSING TECHNIQUES

This section explained techniques for collecting and processing OSINT. To this point, this chapter described applications of OSINT, covered how to identify and categorize types of open

---

13 Headquarters Department of the Army, Open-Source Intelligence, Army Techniques Publication, ATP 2-22.9, July 10, 2012.

14 US Department of Defense (DoD), Intelligence Community and Department of Defense Content Discovery and Retrieval Integrated Project Team, IC/DoD Keyword Query Language Specification, Version 1.1, March 2003.

sources and public information, and discussed how to evaluate open sources using the mnemonic, 'MA2TIC.' The following is a list of some of the more common automated open-source online collection tools:

- Online Search Engines
- Google Dork Searches
- Fact-Checking Websites
- Email Breach Lookup
- Open-Source Image Search
- Online Public Property Records Search
- Social Media Search Tools
- Specific-Built Search Software
- Surveillance Camera Feeds
- Transportation Network Feeds (Aircraft, Boats, Vehicles)
- Username Search
- Visual/Clustering Search Engines

PRACTICAL EXERCISE 1 – WHAT IS YOUR OPEN-SOURCE EXPOSURE?

PARTICIPANT'S GUIDE

The exercise participants perform a simplified open-source search task using one of their email address(es) or username(s). Take care to keep your personal information private. Meaning that you do NOT provide any personal information but your name and your email. Rest assured, both your name and your email are already on the net. The exercise results are **NOT to be** turned in to the instructor or shared with other students (*that is, unless you or they are willing to share them*). However, if your private information is already compromised, this exercise may reveal this fact.

If your career choice is a job in law enforcement or to be an intelligence analyst, you must have the ability to determine what your internet presence is.

INSTRUCTIONS

Give them a half-hour to read and complete the practical exercise or assign it as homework to review when class reconvenes.

Participants have an hour (in total) to perform, review, and discuss the results (longer, if a larger group, i.e., more than ten participants).

TASK

Using the instructions provided, a laptop, and access to the internet, perform open-source research using their own username(s) and/or email address(es). The goal is to find as much descriptive information on themselves using only your username and/or email address. Data types sought:

- Full name, age, gender
- Physical address(es)
- Names of others who may reside at that physical address
- Phone number(s)
- Personal photos
- Family or friend photos, addresses, phone numbers, email addresses
- Pictures of your car or motorcycle, license number(s)
- Other personal

Take notes of your findings and/or save the web pages where you found the specified information. You may be called to discuss your search activities afterward. At the end of the exercise, selected participants will explain the process they used, and the types of information found, not the specifics (e.g., their age, phone number, address, and so on).

PRACTICAL EXERCISE 2 – EXTREMIST OR CRANK?

PARTICIPANT'S GUIDE

Scenario Setup

Participants assume they are OSINT analysts working for the Department of Homeland Defense (DHS) and assigned to find information on a suspected homegrown violent extremism (HVE). Using only an online username and/or email address associated with a dark website called the 'The Anarchist's Blog' (Figure 10.11), The information collected supports an investigation to determine if the individual associated with the username/email address is a harmless blogger or a potential HVE.

TIPS/NOTES: PARTS OF AN EMAIL ADDRESS

To understand an email address, observe the elements of the fictitious email address JohnDoe@BlueBird.com. The essentials go from general to specific, from right to left.

- *Starting on the right, the '.com' end-element represents the top-level domain (TLD) for the email address. The TLD could also be .net, .org, .edu, etc. Each TLD signifies a type of entity. Common TLDs include:*
  - *'.com' is typically used by companies that engage in commerce.*
  - *'.org' is used by nonprofit organizations.*
  - *'.edu' is used by educational institutions.*
  - *'.net' is for network providers.*
  - *'.gov' is for governmental agencies.*
- *To the left of the TLD is the organization (e.g., Google, AOL, etc.).*
- *Further to the left is the '@' symbol followed by the username ('JohnDoe').*

Figure 10.11   The Anarchist's Blog.

Suggestions to Get Started

Use a social media website:

- disqus.com
- facebook.com
- soundcloud.com
- twitter.com
- instagram.com
- example.tumblr.com

Use a search engine:

- dogpile.com
- google.com
- bing.com
- duckduckgo.com
- yahoo.com

Use an email reverse lookup:

- thatsthem.com
- usersearch.org
- publicemailrecords.com

TIPS/NOTES: ONLINE SEARCHES

- *When doing open-source research on the internet, use multiple sources. One must use more than one website in your people searches since it is doubtful one would find everything on a single website.*
- *Granted, the internet is a useful open-source research tool. However, if a person you are researching has not been active online in some way, then it follows that their information might not easily show up.*
- *Additionally, if they have a common name (like John Smith), one would need other associated identifiers to ensure you have the correct person (e.g., age, gender, etc.).*

Author's Note: Be careful not to download any files, browser plugins, or applications onto your laptop while searching. It is probably best to do your searches in 'incognito' mode.

CHAPTER 11

Activity-Based Intelligence

INTRODUCTION

The underlying principles of intelligence, surveillance, and reconnaissance (ISR) used by state-sponsored military forces have changed little through the millennia; only the tools used have improved. In ancient times, a limited number of scouts would seek out massed enemy forces by looking for signs of enemy activity, which would indicate a large force positioned itself in a given area. Once the enemy army's location was known and confirmed, the scout's next mission was to determine 'intent.' The scouts would then maintain visual contact with the massed force for a while, search for high ground, or perhaps observe a chokepoint (e.g., river crossing or a mountain pass) to ascertain the army's direction of movement to determine their intent. The alternative would be to infiltrate the enemy force with spies.

A thousand years ago, it may have only taken one cavalry scout on a high mountain to warn of the Mongol horde's approach. A spotter in an observation balloon with binoculars could provide early warning of an impending enemy offensive in World War I's trenches. Today, the problem set is generally not massed troops crossing sovereign borders. The enemy is often a handful or a solitary terrorist planting an improvised explosive device (IED) on a convoy route or driving a large truck through a crowded urban market. It takes few ISR assets to locate and identify large formations of mechanized forces. Conversely, it requires several ISR platforms with various sensors and capabilities, often working in concert to find that single terrorist in an urbanized environment (see Figure 11.1).

The traditional intelligence process follows a cycle: Tasking, Collection, Processing, Exploitation, and Dissemination, abbreviated as 'TCPED.' The insurgent problem soldiers face in the Middle East and Afghanistan and the lone actor terrorist threat faced at home is ill-serviced by the often too slow and plodding TCPED intelligence method. The TCPED technique works well for producing serialized intelligence products on standing issues. However, *activity-based intelligence* (ABI) is a paradigm shift, and the practice of ABI can profoundly alter the way one thinks about approaching an intelligence problem.

Referring to Figure 11.2, using more traditional intelligence methods (e.g., monitoring target signatures), say one knew what an adversary's armored brigade formation looked like when massed for an attack. If the last location were known, the logical response would be to task ISR assets to monitor the target (e.g., enemy tank brigade). However, today's diverse assortment of sensor platforms and vast amounts of collected intelligence data is available and accessible. The emphasis has shifted to *discovering targets* and *searching for desired information* within massive data sets.

DOI: 10.4324/9781003241195-11

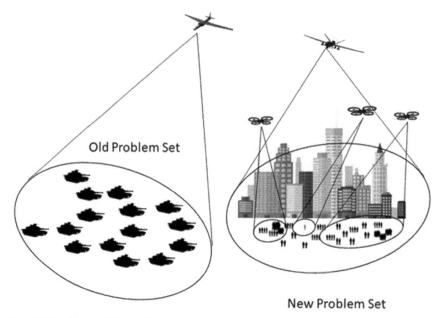

Figure 11.1   ISR Looking at Differing Problem Sets.

Figure 11.2   ABI versus Traditional Intelligence Processes.

At its essence, ABI is a multi-INT approach to activity and transactional data analysis to resolve **unknown-unknowns, develop intelligence, and drive collection.** ABI adapts to a multifaceted world with many threats exhibiting weak and nonpersistent signatures to enable a faster, better-informed intelligence collection and analysis process. Intelligence professionals use the ABI process to create knowledge and specialized collection strategies by:

- Using problem-focused dynamic workflows,
- Creating access to diverse data sets,
- Leveraging rapid data discovery techniques,

- Automating upstream processing of targeted,
- Utilizing untargeted and incidentally collected data ('unknown-unknowns),
- Applying state-of-the-art information technology (IT) and specialized analytics.[1]

The proliferation of human sources and automated tech-based intelligence collection sensors is literally and figuratively burying the intelligence community (IC) in terabytes of data. ABI uses computer-assisted problem-solving techniques and methodologies to assist intelligence analysis, making the analysis process more efficient and timelier. The superabundance of collected data has made it nearly impossible for the human analyst to conceptualize the selected activities needing targeting action. In plain terms, the analyst does not see the 'big picture.' The IC has a mind-numbing amount of critical data (aka 'big data') at their disposal collected and stored each second. In this warehoused or 'stored' state, the data are useless. However, when analyzed correctly, this massive analytical data set can help accelerate mission outcomes to address emerging security threats while enhancing the quality of the analysis in real-time.

By organizing large volumes of collected data, relevant patterns can be more readily recognized. Therefore, intelligence products extracted from the ABI process allow analysts to identify potential adversaries and their designated targets with less effort.

Thus, these identified suspect behaviors can be acted on before these potential threats become imminent.

WHAT IS 'BIG DATA,' ITS SIGNIFICANCE, AND HOW WE GOT HERE

Big data drive thousands of decisions in business, banking, advertising, and other aspects of our lives each day. But what is *big data* exactly, and how or why should it impact efforts in the realm of intelligence analysis?

Definition of Big Data

First is an explanation of the term 'big data.' Big data appear in the common lexicon around the turn of the century and describes large amounts of data. At its inception, it was a term used to identify data sets that were so large and unwieldy they were beyond the capacity of traditional database and analysis technologies. However, database technology eventually caught up, but big data keeps getting bigger.

Significance and How to Quantify Big Data

Aside from simply being a large amount of information, big data are now more precisely described by a set of characteristics. The IT sector commonly refers to these quantifying characteristics as the four 'Vs.' They are Volume, Velocity, Variety, and Veracity[2] (see Figure 11.3).

As persistent sensors hover over the planet, soaking up every movement and measurable aspect of the battlespace, the volume, variety, and complexity of the data are expanding exponentially. The IC has been dealing with data *volume* and *velocity* issues for decades. Still, the problem set has more recently expanded to include the sophistication of big data with *variety* and *veracity* added to the equation, as illustrated above.

---

1   Phalanx, Vol. 48, No. 4 (December 2015), pp. 8–13 (6 pages), Published By: Military *Operations Research Society, Operations Research Methods in Support of Activity-Based Intelligence*, Stephen R. Riese, Michael R. Etz and Scott D. Scherer, www.jstor.org‹stable›24910135, Retrieved May 16, 2022.

2   Dea, J. (2015), *What Are the Four V's of Big Data?* https://blog.intelex.com/2015/07/16/do-you-know-the-4-vs-of-big-data/, Retrieved November 14, 2016.

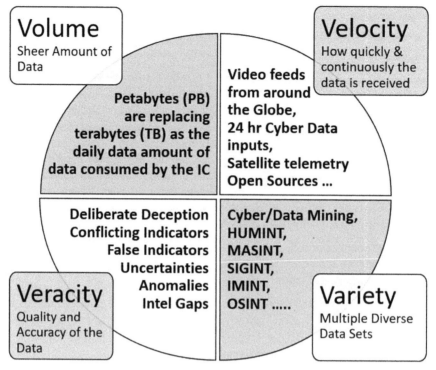

Figure 11.3   ABI Characteristics of Big Data.

HOW ABI WORKS

As discussed earlier, ABI is an analysis methodology that rapidly integrates data from multiple INTs (e.g., HUMINT, SIGINT, IMINT, and so on) tied to social interactions (in the form of human activity and events). These interactions are analyzed to ascertain relevant patterns, identify change, and characterize those patterns to drive collection and create a decisive advantage.[3]

> **TIPS/NOTES: QUICK REVIEW OF THE KEY POINTS OF 'HOW ABI WORKS'**
>
> *ABI is an analysis methodology which (see Figure 11.4 figure below):*
>
> 1. *Rapidly integrates data from multiple INTs (e.g., HUMINT, SIGINT, IMINT, and so on)*
> 2. *Around the interactions of people, events, and activities*
> 3. *To discover relevant patterns, determine and identify change, and characterize those patterns*
> 4. *To drive collection and create a decision advantage.*

3   Atwood, C. (2019). *Activity-Based Intelligence: Revolutionizing Military Intelligence Analysis* [online]. National Defense University Press. https://ndupress.ndu.edu/JFQ/Joint-Force-Quarterly-77/Article/581866/activity-based-intelligence-revolutionizing-military-intelligence-analysis/, Retrieved October 6, 2019.

Figure 11.4   How ABI Works.

The ABI methodology expedites analytic processes by applying automated real-time correlations between current collections and archived data sources. These data correlations establish a baseline understanding of the information, historical trends of activity, and anomalies identification. Four distinct data processes make up the ABI methodology, often described as pillars; they are data georeferencing at discovery, data integration before exploitation, sensor (data) neutrality, and lastly, sequence neutrality (see Figure 11.5).

TIPS/NOTES:

ABI analysis is a semi-automated process that assumes that one (or more) data sources (e.g., sensor data streams, intelligence/reporting databases, etc.) are available to provide georeferenced and temporally indexed data an analyst can perform relational searches.

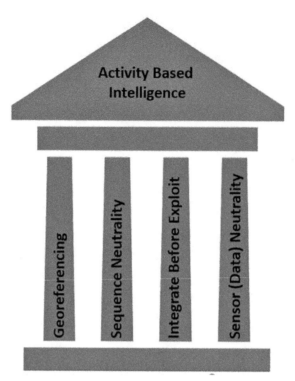

Figure 11.5 ABI's Four Processes.

Georeferencing

Georeferencing relates the internal coordinate system of a map or aerial photo image to a ground system of geographic coordinates. The associated geo-coordinates are typically stored within an image file, though many possible storage mechanisms exist. To georeference at discovery implies that all data sources are spatially and temporally indexed at the time of collection as part of the collection process. Up until recently, georeferencing was performed as a post-collection data process. The information is tied to a specific point in space and time by georeferencing the data as they are collected. The georeferenced information can then be used in the ABI process allowing the analyst to correlate, integrate, and cluster intelligence from multiple sources (e.g., HUMINT, SIGINT, MASINT, and so on) around a specific location and thereby enabling the discovery of entities, activities, transactions, and begin to relate them. The data, now preconditioned with the exact time and locational identifier, allow the analyst to better direct their efforts to associate other contextual information with the problem set, focusing their analysis. The ABI product displays a series of objects against various map backgrounds, visually providing limited supplementary information (using shape, colors, and labels) about the object and its connection(s) to other surrounding objects. However, when an object is selected, a virtually limitless amount of data can potentially be accessed from the connections transactions, such as those activities surrounding preparatory chemical weapon (CW) attack efforts (see Figure 11.6).

Sequence Neutrality

Sequence neutrality is the second pillar of ABI. Essentially, data obtained via the ABI process may not become relevant until the analyst acquires more data and can develop a recognizable pattern. Conversely, ABI processed data may reveal itself immediately upon collection. The major takeaway is that archived multi-INT data analyzed forensically may (or may not) be as or more important than data obtained in near-real-time (NRT). In truth, casually collected data may be just as or even more significant than data collected in a more deliberate and targeted fashion.

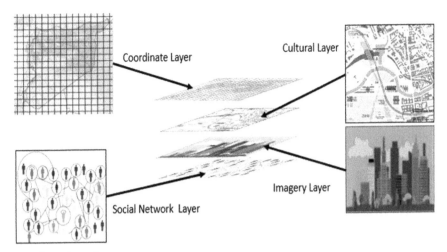

Figure 11.6   Georeferencing.

Integration Before Exploitation

The georeferenced data in the ABI environment allow *integration before exploitation*. With this pillar, exploitation is decoupled from the collection, and only relevant data are exploited. Georeferenced data sets are correlated at the first available opportunity before analysts begin to conduct full exploitation and analysis. The ABI methodology requires data sets to associate temporal/spatial relationships during integration providing context earlier than in the intelligence process than ever before. Before ABI, the IC/military ISR process only integrated selectively exploited and analyzed single-source information and at the end of the intelligence production process for select intelligence entities. Treating data in this fashion is called 'stove piping.' The ABI process initially provides analysts large volumes and more varieties of data, allowing them to observe how data converge, intersect, and overlap, thereby allowing them to identify and define relationships. These critical connections and associations enable the more significant data to be elevated and distinguished from the higher volume of data.

Sensor (Data) Neutrality

The last pillar of ABI is sensor (data) neutrality. Accepting all viable data sources in such a fashion so that no one source or piece of information has a value higher than another is the basis of the data neutrality approach. In other words, data sources that have an accompanying spatial component are equally viable. Following this methodology, a more significant share of available information is available to reinforce, enhance, or conversely question or discredit early indicators, and analytical hypotheses are less likely to be disregarded. However, analysts still must account for the confidence, reliability, and potential errors in the integrated data source acquired through the ABI methodology.

ABI EXAMPLE

Let us assume a military of a foreign adversary receives a HUMINT report from a high-placed source. The report indicates that a piece of prohibited equipment used in a weapon of mass destruction (WMD) production was transferred last month by an ocean freighter. The freighter was registered under a false flag and named the 'Adventure.' The freighter shipped the contraband to a rogue nation in violation of multiple UN treaties. In this case, the WMD contraband equipment was a P2 centrifuge used to process weapons-grade nuclear material.

Figure 11.7   Human Intel Example Regarding WMD Contraband Equipment.

*Following the ABI methodology, these data can be integrated earlier in the intelligence pro-
duction process. The HUMINT tip prods SIGINT and GEOINT analysts who perform routine
signal collections and review imagery separately. The tip prompts a more concerted effort to
recognize the communications intercepts and observe related activity in the days leading up
to the alleged weapons transfer to confirm or deny the transfer event. Suppose analysts had
not known the HUMINT information before the transfer event. In that case, they potentially
could have disregarded the activities as insignificant, and the associated WMD transfer would
not have been identified as such.*

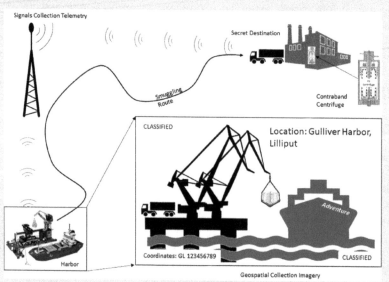

Figure 11.8   Representation of the P2 Centrifuge Shipment Path.

Observe Figure 11.8 and try to recognize the four pillars of ABI in the example:

1. **Data georeferencing at discovery** – *Routine imagery collection stored under geo-
   coordinates, date, and time allows retrieval after the fact.*
2. **Data integration before exploitation** – *Multiple sources (SIGINT, HUMINT, and IMINT)
   are correlated with associated coordinates.*
3. **Sensor (data) neutrality** – *No one source tells the whole story, but all the pieces, when
   assembled, display a comprehensive picture of what transpired.*
4. **Sequence neutrality** – *In this case, all the georeferenced ABI-related data (except the
   HUMINT tip) was archived in stored data sets until the HUMINT tip queued analysts to
   investigate further.*

Author's Note: In this example, the P2 centrifuge does not have a particularly recognizable collection signature. It was probably just packed in a shipping crate disguised and labeled as some other type of industrial machinery. Without the activity-based HUMINT tip, the illicit shipment would likely have gone unnoticed. However, since the needed information had already been collected and stored in a searchable format, it was available for later exploitation. The information was waiting to be 'discovered.'

The application of the ABI concept is not just limited to the 'georeferencing' parameter. ABI can also utilize other data cataloged beyond geo-coordinates such as internet proxies, locations (URLs), Twitter handles, online transactions, threat actor key terms, and internet-related data such as IP addresses connected to domains, phishing *emails delivering malware, and other online exploits blogged in the cyber domain* to further enrich the intelligence value of the final product for the end-user.

ABI's uniqueness is that it permits intelligence organizations to upscale search areas in multiple information domains (e.g., geospatial, temporal, internet, and so on), thereby accessing more data without increasing the number of analysts.

This upscaled multidomain search capability using diverse collection data sets allows the detection of more entities that lack clear recognition signatures or can suppress detection by more traditional collection platforms.

Author's Note: The IT sector adage of 'What goes on the internet never leaves' is true. The ability to expand data searches outside IC/Department of Defense (DOD) holdings can be a powerful tool.

ABI SUBDISCIPLINES

ABI's subdisciplines include forensic network analysis (FNA), big data triage, and activity forecasting. There is no requirement that analysts use all or any of the subdisciplines when performing ABI analysis. Due to the inherent uncertainties associated with new adversaries (e.g., new terror groups), there may not be adequate doctrinal indicators or signatures to apply ABI subdisciplines. Each ABI subdiscipline can be used to inform the other two subdisciplines.

Forensic Network Analysis (FNA)

Unlike the more common practice used to thwart or investigate computer network attacks, FNA, as it relates to ABI, seeks to operationally scrutinize selected networks to identify and categorize the component entities and their associated activities by spatially and temporally analyzing their constituent-related activities. FNA is used extensively in counterterrorism analysis.

Author's Note: Forensic Analysis (Definition) – The process of understanding, re-creating, and analyzing previous events.

Figure 11.9 illustrates the FNA process. For more detail on how a network analysis is performed, go to Chapter 6, Applications of Modeling in Analysis.

FNA Example

Big Data Triage

Big data triage is an automated process that uses various search techniques that continuously monitor large-volume data feeds. The triage monitoring scheme compares the data feed contents to specified indicators associated with locations of interest within specified timeframes. The monitored data feed can be from any source (HUMINT, OSINT, SIGINT, and so on). Monitoring the data over time can build patterns that can be later used to develop a pattern of life (POL) and distinguish normal, abnormal, elevated/reduced activity and activity-specific POLs (see Figure 11.10).

Activity Forecasting

Activity forecasting categorizes, defines, structures, and organizes to develop observational-based understandings that create entity/organization activity pattern definitions. The observations ultimately produce data-driven models that allow the analyst to forecast responses to stimuli and inform doctrinal and trend analysis efforts. See the example in Figure 11.11.

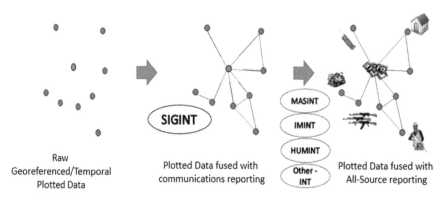

Figure 11.9   Forensic Network Analysis (FNA).

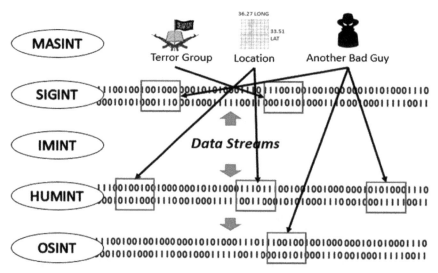

Figure 11.10   Big Data Triage.

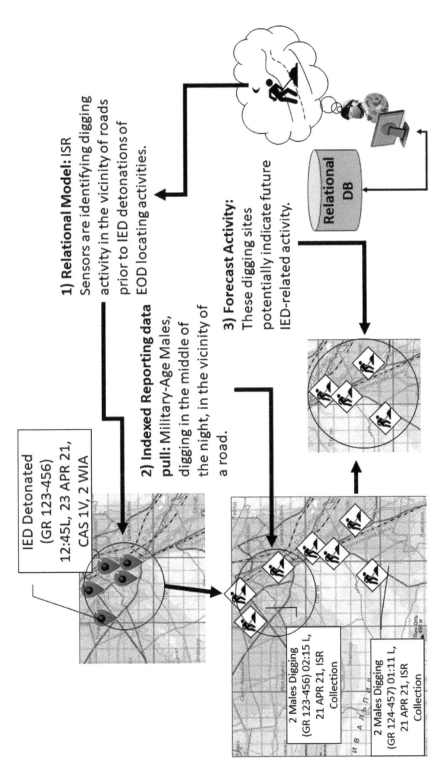

1) Relational Model: ISR Sensors are identifying digging activity in the vicinity of roads prior to IED detonations of EOD locating activities.

2) Indexed Reporting data pull: Military-Age Males, digging in the middle of the night, in the vicinity of a road.

3) Forecast Activity: These digging sites potentially indicate future IED-related activity.

Relational DB

IED Detonated (GR 123-456) 12:45L, 23 APR 21, CAS 1V, 2 WIA

2 Males Digging (GR 123-456) 02:15 L, 21 APR 21, ISR Collection

2 Males Digging (GR 124-457) 01:11 L, 21 APR 21, ISR Collection

Figure 11.11 Activity Forecasting.

ACTIVITY FORECASTING EXAMPLE

Multiple observations of military-age men digging on (or around) roads used by friendly troop convoys have been collected by ISR aerial platforms (drones). These sightings appeared to precede detonations or explosive ordnance disposal (EOD) IED demining operations.

The analyst runs a relational search looking for correlations between insurgent activity reporting and other mundane activity reporting from aerial sensors.

The analyst notices several reports of men digging in the vicinity of roads at various times of the day. Most of the digging done during daylight hours typically corresponds to legitimate road repair work. The analyst creates an activity model which might fit the recognized pattern. That pattern indicates that four reports of men digging on roads at night may forecast future IED activity.

METHOD

Because there is no specific ABI workflow, the four pillars may have to be exercised using various combinations and sequences as new information is collected. ABI also assumes that one (or more) data sources (e.g., sensor data streams, intelligence/reporting databases, and so on) are available to provide georeferenced and temporally indexed data that relational searches can be performed.

Generally, an analyst identifies and develops multiple alternative scenarios that reflect the activity they wish to locate and monitor. The next step is to identify or develop indicators that would only present themselves should a particular set of activity indicators materialize. Using the observed activity indicators, the analyst follows the following steps.

- *Who-Where-Who or Where-Who-Where?*
  - If an analyst knows *whom* they are looking for (the subject), then they would want to find *where* the subject is going [*e.g., identify where the entity (the who) is operating in a given area and who else they are operating with?*]
  - Similarly, if one knows *where* to look, one typically also knows how to find. More specifically, *who* is operating in the area [*e.g., identify who (what group/groups) has/have been operating in that area and where else they are operating?*]
- It is a simple iterative process, extending the analyst knowledge from a known point to *discover the unknowns.*
- The fundamental four pillars to be followed are:
  1. **Data georeferencing at discovery** – *Routine imagery collection stored under geo-coordinates, date, and time allows retrieval after the fact.*
  2. **Data integration before exploitation** – *Multiple sources (SIGINT, HUMINT, and IMINT) are correlated with associated coordinates.*
  3. **Sensor (data) neutrality** – No one source tells the whole story, but all the pieces, when assembled, display a comprehensive picture of what transpired.
  4. **Sequence neutrality** – *Georeferenced ABI-related data are archived in stored data sets until queued, prompting analysts to investigate further.*

(Note: Refer to the simplified demonstration provided above in the 'ABI Example.')

PRACTICAL EXERCISE

The ESRI® video *Activity-Based Intelligence – A Perilous Journey to Intelligence Integration*[4] provides an excellent example of how ABI is used and integrated into real-world intelligence products. Start the video at the 9-minute, 58-second mark.

---

4   ESRI® video, *Activity Based Intelligence – A Perilous Journey to Intelligence Integration*, narrated by Ben Conklin, www.esriuk.com/en-gb/industries/defence-and-national-security/segments/integrating-intelligence

The video is available online at URL: www.esriuk.com/en-gb/industries/defence-and-national-security/segments/integrating-intelligence.

> **TIPS/NOTES: QUICK REVIEW OF THE ABI PROCESS**
>
> *If you would rather not reread the chapter to internalize the lesson material, the first half of the ESRI® video 'Activity-Based Intelligence – A Perilous Journey to Intelligence Integration' (used in the Practical Example) contains a first-rate review of the ABI process.*

CHAPTER SUMMARY

The underlying principles of intelligence, surveillance, and reconnaissance (ISR) used by state-sponsored military forces have changed little through the millennia; only the tools used have improved. In ancient times, a limited number of scouts would seek out massed enemy forces by looking for signs of enemy activity, which would indicate a large force had positioned itself in a given area. However, *activity-based intelligence* (ABI) is a paradigm shift in the tradecraft, and the practice of ABI is changing the way analysts perceive and approach intelligence problems.

At its essence, ABI is a multi-INT approach to activity and transactional data analysis to resolve unknown-unknowns, develop intelligence, and drive collection. ABI adapts to a multifaceted world with many threats exhibiting weak and nonpersistent signatures to enable a faster, better-informed intelligence collection and analysis process. Intelligence professionals use the ABI process to create knowledge and specialized collection strategies by:

- Using problem-focused dynamic workflows,
- Creating access to diverse data sets,
- Leveraging rapid data discovery techniques,
- Automating upstream processing of targeted,
- Utilizing untargeted and incidentally collected data ('unknown-unknowns'),
- Applying state-of-the-art information technology (IT) and specialized analytics.

The proliferation of human sources and automated tech-based intelligence collection sensors is literally and figuratively burying the intelligence community (IC) in terabytes of data. ABI uses computer-assisted problem-solving techniques and methodologies to assist intelligence analysis, making the analysis process more efficient and timelier. The superabundance of collected data has made it nearly impossible for the human analyst to conceptualize the selected activities needing targeting action. In plain terms, the analyst does not see the 'big picture.' The IC has a mind-numbing amount of critical data (aka 'big data') at their disposal collected and stored each second. In this warehoused or 'stored' state, the data are useless. However, when analyzed correctly, this massive analytical data set can help accelerate mission outcomes to address emerging security threats while enhancing the quality of the analysis in real-time.

By organizing large volumes of collected data, relevant patterns can be more readily recognized. Therefore, intelligence products extracted from the ABI process allow analysts to identify potential adversaries and their designated targets with less effort. Thus, these identified suspect behaviors can be acted on before these potential threats become imminent.

WHAT IS 'BIG DATA,' ITS SIGNIFICANCE, AND HOW WE GOT HERE

Big data drive thousands of decisions in business, banking, advertising, and other aspects of our lives each day. But what is *big data* exactly, and how or why should it impact efforts in the realm of intelligence analysis?

Definition of Big Data

First is an explanation of the term 'big data.' Big data appear in the common lexicon around the turn of the century. This somewhat vague term is used to describe large volumes of data. At its inception, it was a term used to identify data sets that were so large and unwieldy they were beyond the capacity of traditional database and analysis technologies. However, database technology eventually caught up, but big data keeps getting bigger.

Significance and How to Quantify Big Data

Aside from simply being a large amount of information, big data are now more precisely defined by a set of characteristics. The IT sector commonly refers to these quantifying characteristics as the four 'Vs.' They are Volume, Velocity, Variety, and Veracity.[5]

HOW ABI WORKS

As discussed earlier, ABI is an analysis methodology that rapidly integrates data from multiple INTs (e.g., HUMINT, SIGINT, IMINT, and so on) around the interactions of people, events, and activities to discover relevant patterns, determine and identify change, and characterize those patterns to drive collection and create decision advantage.[6]

Georeferencing

Georeferencing relates the internal coordinate system of a map or aerial photo image to a ground system of geographic coordinates. Although many possible mechanisms exist, the relevant geo-coordinates are typically stored within a digital image file. To georeference at discovery implies that all data sources are spatially and temporally indexed at the time of collection as part of the collection process. Up until recently, georeferencing was performed as a post-collection data process. The information is tied to a specific point in space and time by georeferencing the data as it is collected. The georeferenced information can then be used in the ABI process allowing the analyst to correlate, integrate, and cluster intelligence from multiple sources (e.g., HUMINT, SIGINT, MASINT, and so on) around a specific location and thereby enabling the discovery of entities, activities, transactions, and begin to relate them. The data, now preconditioned with an exact time

5   Dea, J. (2015), *What Are the Four V's of Big Data?* https://blog.intelex.com/2015/07/16/do-you-know-the-4-vs-of-big-data/, Retrieved November 14, 2016.
6   Atwood, C. (2019). *Activity-Based Intelligence: Revolutionizing Military Intelligence Analysis* [online]. National Defense University Press. https://ndupress.ndu.edu/JFQ/Joint-Force-Quarterly-77/Article/581866/activity-based-intelligence-revolutionizing-military-intelligence-analysis/ Retrieved October 6, 2019.

and locational identifier, allow the analyst to better direct their efforts to associate other contextual information with the problem set, focusing their analysis. The ABI product displays a series of objects against various map backgrounds, visually providing limited information (using shape, colors, and labels) about the object and its connection(s) to other surrounding objects. However, when an object is selected, a virtually limitless amount of data can potentially be accessed from the connections transactions, such as those activities surrounding preparatory activities that precede chemical weapon (CW) attacks.

Sequence Neutrality

Sequence neutrality is the second pillar of ABI. Essentially, data obtained via the ABI process may not become relevant until the analyst acquires more data and can develop a recognizable pattern. Conversely, ABI processed data may reveal itself immediately upon collection. The major takeaway is that archived multi-INT data analyzed forensically may (or may not) be as or more important than data obtained near-real-time (NRT). In truth, casually collected data may be more significant than data collected in a more deliberate and targeted fashion.

Integration Before Exploitation

The georeferenced data in the ABI environment allow *integration before exploitation*. With this pillar, exploitation is decoupled from the collection, and only relevant data are exploited. Georeferenced data are correlated at the first available opportunity before analysts can begin to conduct full exploitation and analysis. The ABI methodology requires data sets to associate temporal/spatial relationships during integration providing context earlier than in the intelligence process than ever before. Before ABI, the IC/military ISR process only integrated selectively exploited and analyzed single-source information and at the end of the intelligence production process for select intelligence entities.

Sensor (Data) Neutrality

The third pillar of ABI is *sensor (data) neutrality*. Accepting all viable data sources in such a fashion so that no one source or piece of information has a value higher than another is the basis of the data neutrality approach. In other words, data sources that have an accompanying spatial component are equally viable. Following this methodology makes a more significant share of available information used to reinforce, enhance, or conversely question or discredit early indicators and analytical hypotheses less likely to be disregarded. However, analysts still must account for the confidence, reliability, and potential errors in the integrated data source acquired through the ABI methodology.

ABI SUBDISCIPLINES

ABI's subdisciplines include forensic network analysis (FNA), big data triage, and activity forecasting. There is no requirement that analysts use all or any of the subdisciplines when performing ABI analysis. Due to the inherent uncertainties associated with new adversaries (e.g., new terror groups), there may not be adequate doctrinal indicators or signatures to apply ABI subdisciplines. Each ABI subdiscipline can be used to inform the other two subdisciplines.

Forensic Network Analysis (FNA)

Unlike the more common practice used to thwart or investigate computer network attacks, FNA, as it relates to ABI, seeks to operationally scrutinize selected networks to identify and categorize the component entities and their associated activities by spatially and temporally analyzing their constituent related activities. FNA is used extensively in counterterrorism analysis.

Big Data Triage

Big data triage uses various search techniques to monitor large-volume data feeds continuously. The data feed contents are compared to specified indicators associated with locations of interest within specified timeframes. The monitored data feed can be from any source (HUMINT, OSINT, SIGINT, and so on). Monitoring the data over time can build pattern sets that can be later used to develop a pattern of life (POL) and distinguish normal, abnormal, elevated activity levels.

Activity Forecasting

Activity forecasting categorizes, defines, structures, and organizes to develop observational-based understandings that create entity/organization activity pattern definitions. The observations ultimately produce data-driven models that allow the analyst to forecast responses to stimuli.

CHAPTER 12

Trends in Intelligence Analysis

INTRODUCTION

This chapter begins by describing the present state of the problem sets faced by the intelligence analysis profession, more specifically referring to crime, business, terrorism, and military intelligence analysis. The text catalogs some of the more significant threats to modern society and western culture. These prominent threats to western culture (and by extension in varying degrees the whole world) include violent crime (both individual and organized), new weapons technologies, pandemics, and terrorism, specifically the lone actor threat. Following an explanation of modern analytical problem sets, there is a brief synopsis of the technological and analytical tradecraft improvements observed in the last several decades.

The text discusses some of the innovative analytical concepts and technologies used by intelligence professionals to counter these current and emerging threats and some adverse implications arising from using these technologies. These concepts and technologies are now in use (or soon to be in use) to augment and advance information processing and analytical tradecraft and bolster and facilitate the intelligence profession. These new concepts and technologies include persistent surveillance, activity-based intelligence (ABI), target modeling, autonomous targeting, data mining (DM), data thinning, data reduction, and new data initiatives, artificial intelligence (AI), machine learning (ML), and deep learning (DL), and using Bayesian statistics to improve intelligence products. This section only briefly touched upon ABI and target modeling because they have their own chapter devoted to the topics.

STATE OF THE INTELLIGENCE PROFESSION

Aside from the already unfathomable amount of open-source data available on the internet, the growing quantity of HUMINT sources, ground, air, and space sensors continues to soar. A decades-old and still climbing data proliferation wave generates incalculable data volumes that confound and saturate the intelligence community (IC), Department of Defense (DoD) planners, and business and law enforcement leaders. These listed organizations struggle with analytical processing and techniques to ensure that collected data remain useful, available, and exploitable.

Certain technological aspects of espionage, surveillance, and intelligence tradecraft have also progressed significantly in the last half-century. By that, I mean that spies are not just listening more often, and surveillance cameras are more sophisticated and efficient. I assert that novel sensors and science fields now exist that could not even be imagined as few as 25 years ago,

DOI: 10.4324/9781003241195-12

such as Lidar, ground-penetrating radar (GPR), infrared thermography (IRT), and many others. Intelligence sensor platforms (e.g., satellites and drone-based collection platforms) have advanced the most. Researchers even claim they are close to making significant breakthroughs in the science of reading minds.

What has not progressed so much is the actual analysis of the collected data. With the possible exception of relational databases and various other software innovations, analytical methods, and processes, for the most part, have changed little.

In parallel with the accrescent tsunami of data washing over the IC and DoD information technology (IT) networks, the warfighter and policymakers task intelligence analysts ever more heavily by requiring analysts to produce more products. Each of those products now requires more in-depth analysis. The days of providing intelligence products that only answer the "who," "what," "where," "why," and "how" are no longer considered adequate. Assessment results also need to address probability, reliability, and confidence factors. Each of these factors also needs to be quantified as a percentage, and in some cases, one or more alternative analyses are also required. Each alternative assessment developed requires the analyst to provide the same analytic rigor as the original analytic product required.

Old Way versus the New Way, Pretty Much the Same

One could argue that the analysis tradecraft has changed so little in the last 75 years that a well-seasoned World War II (WWII)-era intelligence analyst might be able to walk through a fictional time portal, sit down at a present-day intelligence analyst's desk, and do their job (see Figure 12.1). Granted, they would need to sit through a few days of software training and gain some 'buttonology' skills. Yet, once overcoming the technology familiarization hurdle, that WWII analyst would likely become a successful and valued addition to any military intelligence analytical team. They would still need a few months of adjustment to the new 21st-century terminology to overcome a heavy reliance on a technical dictionary. However, once the culture shock subsides, they would debatably become productive and valuable to the modern analytical team. This argument can be extended to business or crime analysis, as well. Some tools have changed. Relational databases now replace the old spreadsheets (matrixes) used by marketing or crime analysts years ago. However, most of the tasks and concepts are unchanged.

In the Loop Versus on the Loop

In recent years, the tools used to perform analysis have evolved. In other words, the tools (software versus pencil and paper) have changed, which means that only the tools and not the tradecraft has come a long way. Human analysts are holding up analytical progress because of this lack of progress in the analytic tradecraft. Collected data continues to pile up, and an ever-smaller fraction of data gets analyzed. The next crucial step for the intelligence analysis profession is to *take analysts*

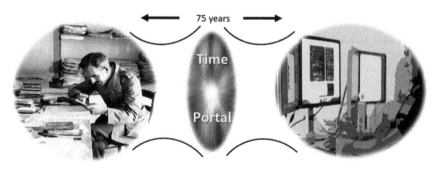

Figure 12.1   WWII versus Today's Intelligence Analyst.

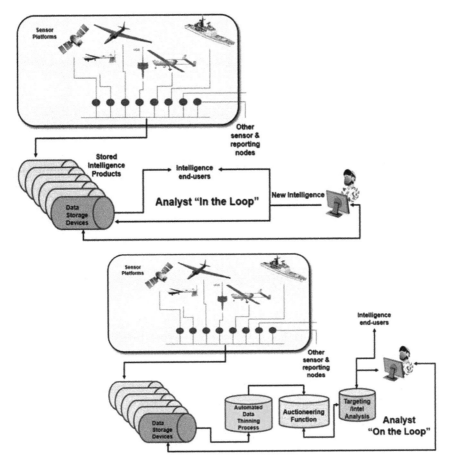

Figure 12.2   In the Loop versus On the Loop.

out of the loop and move them to a more observational position *on the loop*. So what does that mean? The following figures are provided to illustrate the concept of having an *analyst on the loop* versus having an analyst *in the loop* (see Figure 12.2).

Notice in the *analyst on the loop* analogy; the analyst acts as a gatekeeper controlling and contributing to the end user's flow of new intelligence from automated intelligence production sources. The in-the-loop illustration shows that the analyst is often an impediment to the flow of new intelligence. Since the analyst is the sole production source, the flow rate of new intelligence is controlled by how fast the analyst can produce it.

Multiple New Threat Weapons Technologies

In the last century, nuclear weapons introduced warfare to exponential levels of destruction. For decades after that, the world's foremost weapons programs focused on delivery systems for those atomic (and thermonuclear) weapons (e.g., ballistic, cruise, hypersonic missiles, extremely quiet nuclear submarines, and stealth long-range heavy bombers). Recently, high-powered lasers have entered the land, air, and space battlefields. Some minor advances in chemical and biological weapons also appeared, but the international arms convention prohibited their use in 1997.[1]

---

1   The chemical weapons convention (CWC) outlaws the production, stockpiling, and use of chemical weapons and their precursors. The treaty entered into force on April 29, 1997. There are 193 parties to the treaty. Four UN states are not party: Egypt, Israel, North Korea, and South Sudan.

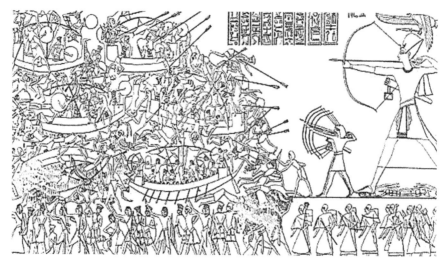

Figure 12.3   Sea Peoples Shown Being Defeated by Pharaoh Ramesses III.

High-profile use of fourth-generation nerve agents by Russia (Novichoks[2]) and North Korea (VX[3]), as well as the use of Sarin and mustard agents in Syria, demonstrated that the chemical weapons convention (CWC) was an unenforceable hollow document. Biological weapons, thanks to advances in gene editing, not only can kill in untold numbers, but soon their creators may have the ability to focus them to target and slaughter based upon a group's (or individual's) DNA signature.

Even with these phenomenal weapons advances, the most significant would have to be the development of supercomputers and quantum computing. These ultrafast thinking platforms hold the potential to push the superpower arms race to whole new levels and into another an ever-increasingly aggressive, unfamiliar, and dangerous phase.

Business, Terror Groups, Crime, and Corruption

The combination of business, crime, and corruption are as old as civilization. Early written history informs us that the ancient Egyptians punished corrupt judges with death by suicide. The Old Testament admonishes judges to avoid corruption in the book of Exodus 28:3: 'Take no rewards in a cause: for rewards make blind those who have eyes to see, and make the decisions of the upright false.' To see crime as a 'business,' one only has to look at modern-day Somali pirates, or perhaps their forerunners, the Barbary Pirates, Vikings, or the Sea Peoples of antiquity (see Figure 12.3[4]). Throughout history, pirates typically trade their ill-gotten goods to legitimate merchants (at least those with the appearance of legitimacy) who know or at least suspect that they are trading in stolen merchandise. Finally, we come to terrorism; terror has always been an essential component of piracy. Today, the distinguishing aspect that elevates terrorism to a category of its own is often its connection to a religion or ideology.

---

2   'Novichoks' is the name given to the controversial chemical weapons developed in the former Soviet Union between the 1970s and the 1990s. Designed to be undetectable and untreatable, these chemicals became the most toxic of the nerve agents, being very attractive for both terrorist and chemical warfare purposes.

3   North Korea used the nerve agent VX to assassinate the estranged half-brother of North Korea's leader Kim Jong Un, according to US State Department sources.

4   Wikimedia Commons, File: Medinet Habu Ramses III. Tempel Nordostwand Abzeichnung 01.jpg, Downloaded February 21, 2021.

Usama Bin Laden   Abu Musab al-Zarqawi   Abu Bakr al-Baghdadi   Qasem Soleimani

Figure 12.4   Former Terror Group Leaders.

Business

On the business side of world affairs, with world trade competition increasing and profit margins shrinking, commercial customers look ever harder to gain the slightest competitive advantage through business intelligence. Just a few of the business-based analysis examples provided in Chapters 3, 6, and 10 (targeted marketing, analytic modeling, and open-source intelligence) illustrate the real and substantial benefits of having a robust business intelligence presence at the corporate level.

Terror Groups

There has not been another attack on the United States equal to what transpired on September 11, 2001, and the mastermind of that attack, Al Qaeda leader, Usama Bin Laden (UBL), has been found and killed.

As shown in Figure 12.4, UBL's fate is also shared by other terrorist leaders. However, that has not stopped other terror groups (and individuals) from stepping up to don the terror leadership robes. Today, Al Qaeda has a new leader; though, he maintains a lower profile. ISIS has stepped into the top terror group slot, but for how long. Intelligence professionals worldwide persistently watch for the next terror group and their associated leadership, who want the top position.

Organized Crime

Transnational organized crime is not stagnant; in an ever-changing industry, crime adapts to market change agents and creates new forms of crime. Sources indicate that, as of 2009, global organized crime revenue was over $870 billion annually, and as of 2017, that number had risen to between $1.6 trillion and $2.2 trillion annually[5,6] (see Table 12.1[7]). Referring to the table, one quickly observes that counterfeiting ranks higher than drug trafficking. In 2018, counterfeiting was the most significant criminal enterprise in the world. Sales of counterfeit and pirated goods total $1.7 trillion for the year, more than drugs and human trafficking combined. Crime is escalating worldwide; in a time of government law enforcement belt-tightening, criminal organizations continue to work smarter and more efficiently, making the crime analysts' task that much more demanding and challenging.

---

5   Global Financial Integrity, *Transnational Crime and the Developing World, March 2017,* https://gfintegrity.org/report/transnational-crime-and-the-developing-world/, Retrieved May 16, 2020.

6   United Nations Office on Drugs and Crime, *Transnational Organized Crime: The Globalized Illegal Economy,* October 2011, www.unodc.org/toc/en/crimes/organized-crime.html, Retrieved May 16, 2020.

7   *Forbes* Magazine, Wade Shepard, *Meet the Man Fighting America's Trade War Against Chinese Counterfeits (It's Not Trump),* March 29, 2018, www.forbes.com/sites/wadeshepard/2018/03/29/meet-the-man-fighting-americas-trade-war-against-chinese-counterfeits/#3fab1e141c0d, Retrieved May 16, 2020.

Table 12.1   Estimated Global Revenue from Crime 2017

Transnational Crime	Estimated Annual Value (US$)
Drug trafficking	$426 billion–$652 billion
Small-arms and light weapons trafficking	$1.7 billion–$3.5 billion
Human trafficking	$150.2 billion
Organ trafficking	$840 million–$1.7 billion
Trafficking in cultural property	$1.2 billion–$1.6 billion
Counterfeiting	$923 billion–$1.13 trillion
Illegal wildlife trade	$5 billion–$23 billion
IUU fishing	$15.5 billion–$36.4 billion
Illegal logging	$52 billion–$157 billion
Illegal mining	$12 billion–$48 billion
Crude oil theft	$5.2–$11.9 billion
Total	**$1.6 trillion–$2.2 trillion**

Figure 12.5   Brazil, Paraguay, Argentina, Tri-Border Area.

The Dark Nexus

Businesses, terror groups, and criminal organizations not only have kept pace with technology, but they have leveraged and shared processes, practices, and skills from one to the others. This dark nexus synergizes the combined parts into a powerful adversary for law enforcement.

A stark and enduring example of this business, crime, terror, and corruption nexus is the tri-border area (TBA) of South America (see Figure 12.5). Nonindigenous mafias operating in the TBA include crime syndicates from Chile, China, Colombia, Corsica, Ghana, Libya, Italy, Ivory Coast, Japan, Korea, Lebanon, Nigeria, Russia, and Taiwan. Al-Qaeda, Hamas, Hezbollah, and other terror groups also operate in the TBA.[8]

---

8   US Department of Justice, National Criminal Justice Reference Service, *Terrorist and Organized Crime Groups in the Tri-Border Area (TBA) of South America*, July 2003, www.ncjrs.gov/App/Publications/abstract.aspx?ID=202323, Retrieved May 16, 2020.

Figure 12.6 The Overwhelmed Modern Analytical Workforce.

The alliance of crime, business, terror, and corruption is mutually beneficial. Criminal organizations provide safe havens for terror groups; terror groups provide arms and skills to criminal organizations (e.g., bomb-making skills); banks and businesses provide logistics and money-laundering services. These types of business, crime, terror, and corrupt state and business relationships appear and fade away, usually cropping up in opportune environments like civil wars and other violent conflicts. Still, despite regional law enforcement, United States, and Interpol efforts, weak governance (or total lack thereof) in the area has allowed it to thrive for decades in the TBA.

Technological progress only reinforces the demands for more intelligence, faster, higher quality, and more reliable intelligence products. Add the tsunami of data washing over today's analytical workforce. A workforce that has only increased marginally in size, skill, and efficiency over the last 75 years. One can now begin to visualize the daunting predicament of the modern-day intelligence analyst (see Figure 12.6).

Despite the daunting obstacles facing intelligence professionals, several promising methods and technologies are available now (or near future) to assist with shouldering the analyst's burden. Most intelligence texts dwell on historical intelligence failures without pointing out how to anticipate the calamity and avoid it. This chapter spends the minimum amount of text required to describe the numerous threats in order to provide a better opportunity for a more detailed explanation of potential remedying tradecraft methods and technologies to counter those identified threats. This chapter examines several threats to the homeland and national interest to gain insight and possibly more effective methods of identifying and impeding their actions. Starting with extremist terrorism, one of the more challenging analytical problem sets is the lone actor (aka lone wolf or lone offender).

THE LONE ACTOR PROBLEM SET

The lone actor can directly (or indirectly) be a problem set for business, crime, IC, or military intelligence analysts. The September 11, 2001 terror attack was not a 'lone actor' event, but the lone actor attack could have similar economic effects. Imagine for a moment, what would be the implications of a single individual with a biological agent at the New York stock exchange, US Congress, or a silicon valley manufacturing facility?

The lone actor formulates and commits violent acts alone, outside of any command structure, and without material assistance from any extremist–terrorist group. Lone actors may be influenced or inspired by an ideology or views of outside groups or ideologies and may perform acts of violence to support such groups or ideologies.

It is often difficult to tell whether an actor has received external assistance, and what appears to be a lone actor attack may have been carefully orchestrated from outside. The most significant danger lies in intelligence organizations concentrating a substantial portion of their terrorism collection efforts on the parent extremist–terrorist group. Hence, the lone actor's nefarious activities may go unnoticed until it's too late.

Let us construct a rudimentary model that designates a few more common associated characteristics to restate and better describe the lone actor problem set. For this purpose, the text uses information from the Federal Bureau of Investigation (FBI)'s Lone Offender Terrorism Report. The report pulls data from 52 lone offender terrorist attacks committed within the United States between 1972 and 2015.

Demographics and Characteristics

The study subjects varied broadly in age, race, relationship status, and educational background. Consistent with conclusions reached by both academic and government researchers studying targeted violence, the study found no evidence to support the existence of any meaningful demographic profile of a lone offender (actor).[9,10]

Potentially some females may have been involved in terror plots covered by the study; however, the trend consistently seen in studies of targeted violence is the overwhelming representation of male perpetrators. This study followed the trend in that all 52 subjects were male.

Most offenders were born in the United States ($N = 47$, 90%). Four offenders (8%) were naturalized citizens, and one offender (2%) was a legal permanent resident. Most offenders were white/Caucasian ($N = 34$, 65%), while the remaining 18 offenders (35%) were divided among five different racial groups, as shown in Figure 12.7.

More than half of the offenders ($N = 28$, 54%) were neither working nor attending school at the time of their attack. Of the 26 offenders who identified as religious, 13 were affiliated as Christian (50%), 9 as Muslim (35%), 1 as Jewish (4%), and 3 as belonging to another religion (12%). Seventeen offenders (33%) either stated they were not religious or no information was present to suggest the offender held any religious affiliation, and 19 (37%) had served in the military.

The youngest offender was 15 years old, the oldest was 88, with the distribution of ages displayed in Figure 12.7. The average age at the time of the attack was 37.7 years old. (Note: The chart does not sum to 100 due to rounding.) Radical Islamic violent extremists, who averaged 26.3 years of age at the time of their attack, were significantly younger than the other ideological groups ($N = 52$, $p < 15$).

The study looks at several other possible characteristics: prior criminal behavior and aggression, mental health and substance use, radicalization ideologies, attack methods, and others. However, none of these factors yielded clear and reliable indicators to point toward lone actor violent extremism, less one. The study cites that *obsessive behavior* is a generally reliable indicator.

Law enforcement investigative remarks noted that most offenders devote inordinate time to persistently seeking, sharing, or discussing information relating to a specific topic, grievance, or ideology. Subjects' repetitive fixated activities form the basis of the 'obsessive behavior' observation.

---

9   Federal Bureau of Investigation, US Department of Justice, James Silver, Andre Simons, Sarah Craun, *A Study of the Pre-attack Behaviors of Active Shooters in the United States between 2000–2013*, June 2018.

10 Routledge, Paul Gill, *Lone-Actor Terrorists: A Behavioural Analysis*, February 11, 2015.

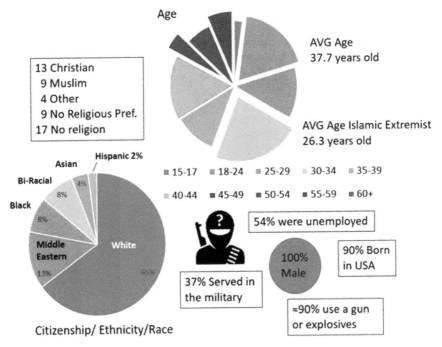

Figure 12.7   Lone Actor Demographics.

Explicitly, the study notes that more than half of the offender data set (*N* = 36, 69%) display fixations or obsessions. The basis of this finding comes from wide-ranging data collected from case files (e.g., offender behaviors, writings, online postings, or statements from bystanders).[11]

In summary, the Lone Offender Study acknowledges that no one characteristic or factor or a specific combination of factors causes an individual to engage in targeted violence. The study also notes that the research observations suffer from multiple other flaws. Among these shortfalls, researchers caution that due to the *small sample size of lone offender terrorism and the amount of variability between offenders, the addition of more cases could change the results of the current analysis.*

Constructing Analytical Models

As discussed in Chapter 6, analysts use models to guide collection activities and inform data processing and analysis algorithms. More often than not, data sources available to construct these models are inadequate. Such is the situation with the lone actor model.

For academic purposes and in the absence of better information, the text uses this study to form the basis for modeling lone actor behavior and demographics. However, to construct a reasonably conservative model of indicators (that is right more than wrong) for predicting the identity of lone actors, the analytical model uses a minimum standard of 'greater than 50%' is selected.

Figure 12.8 summarizes the Lone Offender Study demographics data exceeding the minimum standard. After constructing a profile of generally reliable indicators (and excluding less dependable factors), the next step is to identify sources and methods needed to collect or produce data sets containing these modeling indicators. In the following sections, Cameras Everywhere, the New Surveillance State, and The IoT, the text explores how observable indicators from the lone actor model help analysts identify and locate human targets.

---

11 Federal Bureau of Investigation, US Department of Justice, Behavioral Threat Assessment Center, *A Study of Lone Offender Terrorism in the United States (1972–2015)*, November 2015.

≈75% are White or
Middle Eastern

>99% are male

≈90% use a gun or explosives

≈75% are between
ages 18 to 44

≈90% are US born

Lone Actor

≈69% display
obsessive behavior

>50% unemployed

Figure 12.8   Predominate Demographic Characteristics.

CAMERAS EVERYWHERE, THE NEW SURVEILLANCE STATE

Persistent Surveillance

These days concept of *persistent surveillance* has come into its own, and high-tech observation is omnipresent. The US DoD defines *persistent surveillance* as a collection strategy that emphasizes some collection systems' ability to linger on demand in an area to detect, locate, characterize, identify, track, target, and possibly provide battle damage assessment and retargeting in near or real-time (see Figure 12.9).

Far more than just an eye in the sky, it is frankly everywhere. In addition to the more recognizable dedicated observation vehicles, such as military and commercial satellites and aerial platforms such as planes, balloons, and drones, the modern surveillance grid is integrated into society's very fabric. As noted previously, in Chapter 10 (*Open-source Intelligence*), persistent surveillance networks potentially contain:

- Private security CCTV
- Public street and doorbell cameras
- Personal computers
- Smartphones
- Personal assistants (e.g., Alexa and Siri)
- The Internet of Things (IoT) (e.g., TVs, refrigerators, coffee makers, and many others) are all continuously watching, listening, and tracking (see Figure 12.10 for an illustration of IoT).

Even though media sources are replete with stories of how tech companies listen to once thought to be private conversations of their customers, the typical layperson does not grasp how intrusively monitored their everyday lives are becoming.[12,13,14]

---

12 *The Guardian, Apple Contractors 'Regularly Hear Confidential Details' on Siri Recordings*, By Alex Hern, July 26, 2019, www.theguardian.com/technology/2019/jul/26/apple-contractors-regularly-hear-confidential-details-on-siri-recordings, Retrieved May 17, 2020.

13 The Verge, *Amazon's Alexa isn't just AI – Thousands of Humans Are Listening*, By Nick Statt, April 10, 2019, www.theverge.com/2019/4/10/18305378/amazon-alexa-ai-voice-assistant-annotation-listen-private-recordings, Retrieved May 17, 2020.

14 VRT NWS, *Google Employees Are Eavesdropping, Even in Your Living Room*, By Tim Verheyden, Denny Baert, Lente Van Hee, and Ruben Van Den Heuvel, July 10, 2019, www.vrt.be/vrtnws/en/2019/07/10/google-employees-are-eavesdropping-even-in-flemish-living-rooms/, Retrieved May 17, 2020.

NOTICE
SECURITY
CAMERAS
IN USE

The New Surveillance State

Figure 12.9   Persistent Surveillance.

> **TIPS/NOTES:**
>
> *The IoT is the network of physical mechanisms (things, e.g., appliances, tools, cell phones, baby monitors, and so on) that are embedded with sensors, software, and other technologies to connect and exchange data with other devices and systems over the internet.*

Erroneously, many people outside the IC conclude that government satellites are watching ordinary people. Granted, military and commercial satellites are far more numerous than only a few years ago. Despite how Hollywood productions may portray them to the contrary, a military space platform's principal purpose is to concentrate on militarily significant and national security target sets. Governments do possess satellites marginally capable of surveilling individuals but rarely use them for this purpose. The possible exception to this statement might be an individual who happens to be a high-value terrorist. However, aerial platforms (i.e., drones, small

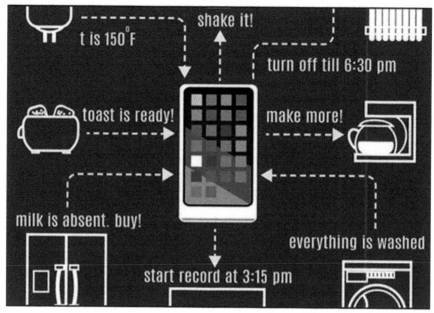

Figure 12.10   Internet of Things (IoT).

planes, and static balloons) that surveil the world's battlefields, these platforms are the true "eyes in the sky." Aerial platforms are also well-suited for spying on individuals, citizens, or criminals in densely packed urban areas. For more information on, or examples of, how aerial persistent surveillance platforms track and solve crimes in the United States, go to the YouTube video titled, *The Surveillance Firm Recording Crimes From Baltimore's Skies*,[15] located at URL address: *https:// youtu.be/wRa-AucbN6k.*

The Internet of Things (IoT)

Persistent surveillance features are incorporated into the component technology of the items we purchase routinely (e.g., cell phones, watches, TVs, and so on). These IoT surveillance mechanisms harvest the customer's data. National and local governments and commercial marketing leadership enable and leverage this surveillance technology for their purposes. The end purpose of the data harvesting may be as benign as the manufacturer trying to improve the customer experience by better understanding a customers' needs or refining a company's marketing strategy. However, the purpose can also be more nefarious, such as transforming customer data into cash flow by selling it to third parties, using the customer's data to secure more, or using one's data against an individual.

For example, a crime is committed, and law enforcement electronically interrogates local cell towers to determine if your mobile phone was in the vicinity at the time of the crime. Unbeknownst to you, you are now a suspect in a criminal investigation that your only connection to the crime was that you were nearby when it transpired. As a result of this circumstantial link to the crime scene, you might need to spend substantial sums of money to retain legal assistance or a private investigator to prove your innocence, or even worse, you may be convicted of a crime of which you are innocent.

---

15 Bloomberg YouTube Channel, *The Surveillance Firm Recording Crimes from Baltimore's Skies,* dated September 1, 2016, https://youtu.be/wRa-AucbN6k, Retrieved March 29, 2020.

TIPS/NOTES:

Monitoring cell phones is no longer a task only performed by computer geeks or nation-states. Below is a list of some of the monitoring activities readily accessible online, for free, or accomplished via a downloadable application:

- *Tracking GPS-enabled cell phones [Note: To accurately track (to within a meter) a cell phone via GPS only requires the cell to be GPS <u>equipped</u> and <u>enabled</u>. However, approximate tracking can be performed using cell towers in the vicinity.]*
- *Monitoring all the internet activities (e.g., purchase, emails, social network activities)*
- *Accessing:*
  - *Personal multimedia files*
  - *SMS traffic*
  - *Listening in on live and recorded calls*
  - *Recording ambient voice/sound (Note: This feature turns the phone into a listening device so that one can listen to whatever is going on in the immediate vicinity.)*
  - *Social chat traffic (e.g., WhatsApp, Facebook, Instagram, etc.)*

How the IoT Spies on the Public

Whenever a consumer purchases an item online, drives their automobile, makes a call, snaps a photo, or texts with a smartphone, a record is made of the activity. All these activity-related data are collected by the IoT and recorded to log files somewhere in the network cloud. If an intelligence analyst is familiar with how each IoT item stores its user activity log files, they can access them. The analyst can then utilize the files to track or build a *pattern of life* (POL). POL-related information on individuals or groups aids the analysis of the activities associated with individuals, groups, and adversary networks.

The example below is a brief demonstration of how intelligence analysts leverage the IoT to identify and locate bad guys.

EXAMPLE

Assume you are a human intelligence targeting analyst tasked with identifying and locating a high-value target (HVT) who happens to be an international terrorist. You don't have a name, location, or even the target's gender. All you have to go on is the online user name (Irhabi007) and a cell phone number. So, where does one start?

Using his cell phone and various proprietary (and sometimes classified) tracing software packages, one can access the phone's activity logs. With the activity log files, one can determine where Irhabi007 likely resides (using the phone's GPS data). One can also find multiple photos of the cell phone's user (it happens that this cell phone takes a selfie every time it starts up) and photos of possible associates (by accessing other stored images associated with the cell phone's cloud account) (see Figure 12.11).

Figure 12.11   Irhabi 007.

Author's Note: In Figure 12.11, the photo is that of Younes Tsouli (aka Irhabi 007), a convicted terrorist and Moroccan-born resident of the United Kingdom who, in 2007, was found guilty of incitement to commit acts of terrorism and sentenced to 16 years in prison. His crimes were carried out via the internet, where he was known by several pseudonyms based on variations of Irhabi 007; 'Irhabi' being the Arabic word for 'terrorist' and '007,' a reference to the well-known fictional British secret agent, James Bond.

Tsouli has been called the 'world's most wanted cyber-jihadist,' and his conviction was the first under British law for incitement to commit an act of terrorism through the internet.

Irhabi 007 was chosen as an example because he just so happened to be a terrorist who was tracked down and brought to justice partly based upon the information retrieved and exploited from his cell phone and online web presence.

ACTIVITY-BASED INTELLIGENCE (ABI)

Earlier, in the chapter introduction, it was demonstrated that the proliferation of human sources and automated tech-based intelligence collection sensors is literally and figuratively burying intelligence professionals in petabytes of data. Similarly, the previous chapter illustrated how ABI is a novel approach to assist analysts in making sense of all that data.

ABI is a multi-INT approach to activity and transactional data analysis to resolve unknown-unknowns, develop intelligence, and drive collection. ABI adapts to a multifaceted world with many threats exhibiting weak and nonpersistent signatures to enable a faster, better-informed intelligence collection and analysis process.

Using computer-assisted problem-solving techniques and methodologies, ABI helps intelligence analysis by making the analysis process more efficient and timelier. The superabundance of collected data has made it nearly impossible for the human analyst to conceptualize the selected activities needing targeting action. In plain terms, the analyst does not see the 'big picture.' The IC has mind-numbing amounts of critical data (aka 'big data') at their disposal collected and stored each second. Warehousing or placing data in a 'stored' data state renders it useless. ABI indexes massive stored data sets for efficient retrieval and accelerates production and real-time quality of intelligence analysis.

For additional detail on how ABI assists analysts in managing large data sets, refer to Chapter 11, Activity-Based Intelligence.

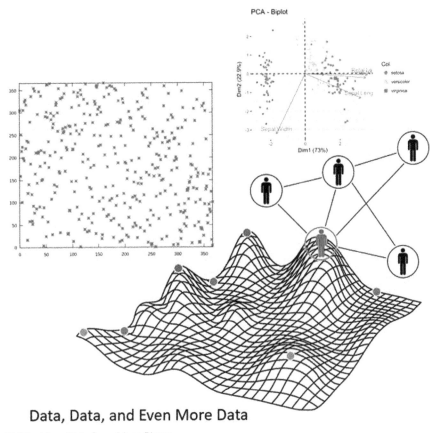

Data, Data, and Even More Data

Figure 12.12   More Data from More Places.

DATA, DATA, AND EVEN MORE DATA

As mentioned many times throughout the text, particularly in this chapter, modern intelligence analysis is increasingly more about storing, handling, and exploiting vast amounts of raw data using highly automated processes and cutting-edge technology. The following sections introduce the terminology: Data Management, Data Reduction, Data Thinning, DM, and Data Analytics. This chapter merely scratches these concepts' surface of how the IC, business, and crime analysts use them in the intelligence profession (see Figure 12.12).

Data Management

The term 'Data Management' is focused more on the attainment and processing of raw data. To the IT professional, some of the more common tasks attributed to the 'data management' task set are producing databases, creating historical backups, uploading data to data storage mediums, and assigning roles (or permissions) to others to access specific data files. These roles or permissions might also provide access to specific rows, fields, or data contained with a file (such as passwords). In the field of intelligence, data management also involves the 'preparation' (aka cleaning) of data before uploading it into a database. The following sections provide better descriptions of what the terms *attainment*, *processing*, *reduction*, and *thinning* of raw collected data mean to the intelligence analyst.

Data Attainment

Data attainment may entail collecting pixel data (imagery data) from an unmanned aerial vehicle (UAV) or satellite, radar data from a stationary ground sensor or ship at sea, then feeding via a data stream through a communications hub into a collections network. Just as easily, it could be a

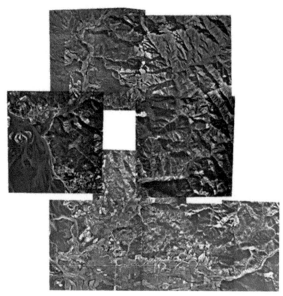

Figure 12.13   Digital Image Mosaic.

raw intelligence report being uploaded and transmitted by a human operator from anywhere on the planet. These data sets (e.g., pixels, temperature data, crop yield figures, commodity prices, and so on) are collected by the terabyte by government, business, academic, and private concerns, around the clock, all over the world, and stored in notebooks, spreadsheets, and vast complex data storage devices.

Tips/Notes: Data management is an administrative process that includes acquiring, validating, storing, protecting, and processing raw data to ensure the accessibility, reliability, and timeliness of the data for its end-users.

Data Preparation (or Processing)

However, these data sets, attained from various collection mechanisms, can rarely be stored in their raw collected forms or exploited by analysts without some level of preparation (aka data processing). These preparations/processes take many forms. Some as mundane as college students sorting data into columns and listing into a spreadsheet for sorting or when a data manager more rigorously sorts and files the data into a relational framework with fields in a database, to something much more complicated as taking the data streams from multiple satellite images, georeferencing the digital pixels, then combining the image data with other whole or fractional image data sets to create a combined image for an imagery analyst to exploit. This type of image processing is called mosaicing. An example of a digital image mosaic is shown in Figure 12.13.[16]

Author's Note: Image mosaicing is where multiple images (or portions of images) of the same area are processed and combined into a single (often larger) image. The resultant compound

---

16 US Department of the Interior, *Aerial Photo Mosaic of the Tillamook Basin, Oregon in 1967*, https://catalog.data.gov/dataset/aerial-photo-mosaic-of-the-tillamook-basin-oregon-in-1967, Retrieved December 6, 2020.

image uses complex-mosaicing algorithms to create the final image. The mosaic image pro-cessing technique is necessary when clouds partially obscure the area under observation or an inadequate number of images exist to observe the entire area of concern. In these cases, images from other dates that reveal the obscured or missing features are stitched together to create a final mosaiced image to provide a complete and unobscured fused image of the desired ground surface area.

Data Mining

DM (a term coined in the 1990s) is a modern computational/analytical process of discovering patterns in expansive data sets involving methods taken from the scientific fields of:

- AI, ML (human-like intelligence displayed by software and/or machines),
- Statistics (the numeric study of data relationships), and
- Database systems.

The DM's ultimate goal is to extract information from awkwardly large data sets and convert it into a more logical and comprehensible structure for further analysis (see Figure 12.14).

The process of 'digging' through data to discover hidden connections and extrapolate the data (i.e., predict future trends) has a long history as old as Aristotle, Newton, and the scientific method.

As analysts dig through the data, they explore data management concepts, data preprocessing techniques, analytics, data modeling, inference considerations, interestingness metrics, complexity considerations, data post-processing, and other aspects germane to 'mining' data. These DM concepts are merely mentioned in the text. However, there are many volumes dedicated to each concept should one desire to investigate further.

Data Analytics

Data analytics (DA) is an exercise that derives information value from data sets. DA examines data sets using a process that identifies trends and draws conclusions about the information contained. DA is combined with other dedicated processes, systems, and software to more effectively and reliably find these patterns and trends within the data at an ever-increasing pace.

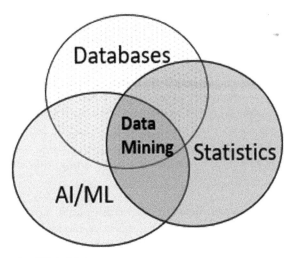

Figure 12.14   Components of Data Mining.

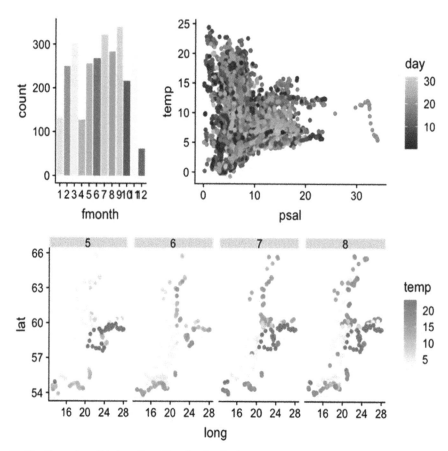

Figure 12.15 Examples of Various Data-Visualization Tools.

DA is a term broadly used to describe the application of 'mathematical procedures' to raw data sets. These procedures include basic counting tasks such as generating summary counts of 'events', creating reports with summary descriptive statistics, and application of 'data visualization' tools to create graphics that convey the 'information' in your data (see Figure 12.15).

'Analytics' also includes applying statistical modeling tools to predict future events based on historical data, 'clustering' or 'binning' similar units of analysis into distinct groups, to assess the effectiveness of marketing campaigns and similar 'interventions' on customer behavior.

....

Author's Note: In my experience, the best and most successful DA operations employed for intelligence purposes try to exploit/leverage the combined skills and talents of <u>data managers</u> and <u>data analysts</u>, often on the same team or in the same organizational unit.

Data managers unconsciously can identify patterns and trends in the raw collected data as they are categorized and grouped into the database sorting fields. Those data groupings often inform the logic-choices made by data analysts and thereby optimizing the data analysis.

....

While there is a high degree of overlap between the two disciplines, most people in the 'analytics' realm have extensive academic and other training in statistics, econometrics, operations research, and others. In contrast, those in the 'data management' field tend to exercise database modeling techniques, data sorting, performance tuning, data storage methods, and database architecture.

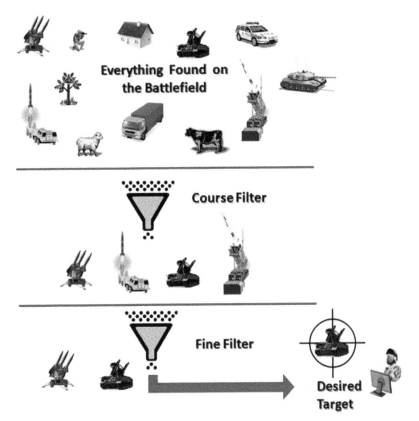

Figure 12.16   Visualizing Data Reduction.

Data Reduction

Data reduction transforms numerical or text-based digital information derived empirically or experimentally into a corrected, ordered, and simplified form. Stated more simply, it reduces multitudinous amounts of data down to the meaningful parts (see Figure 12.16).

Efficient data reduction activities endeavor not to exclude helpful data sets. This concept was stressed in the earlier section Constructing Analytical Models. In that section, a shallow threshold of >50% was chosen for example purposes. In practice, data reduction thresholds are higher to better exclude erroneous and spurious data from confusing the analysis outcomes.

An example of data reduction is terrain filtering. Terrain filtering is a standard intelligence analysis method that reduces redundant and useless data using a relatively nonautomated approach. The terrain filtering method used in imagery analysis is discussed in the following example.

EXAMPLE

It is desired to determine a potential adversary's (country: the 'XYZ Republic') surface-to-air missile (SAM) system locations. All reporting to date has been unable to provide an adequate targeting solution.

Though a small country in relation to Russia or China, the fictional XYZ Republic still represents a surface area of thousands of square miles. An uninitiated imagery analyst would regard this task as an insurmountable effort for a team of a dozen or more analysts.

So to avoid spending time and resources on studying the entire map of the XYZ Republic, to try and identify where the SAM batteries 'are,' the imagery analyst tries to eliminate the sections of the XYZ Republic where the SAM batteries 'cannot be located' (see Figure 12.17).

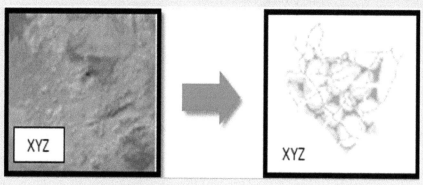

Figure 12.17   Reducing Potential Target Areas.

All-source analysis of the missile launch platform, support vehicles, and fire control limitations yields a reliable picture of the types of terrain and roads that can support the weapons' launch and logistical resupply. Further terrain analysis determines that the missile transporter erector launcher (TEL) can only move down improved roads with less than a 5% grade.

Using this information, the analyst will either import into a geospatial data layer or expose an existing terrain data layer that links elevation data to the image pixels. Using the elevation data and applying a filter to shade the terrain areas with a greater slope than 5%, a new overlay of the XYZ Republic appears.

In the figure on the right, the dashed lines and white area illustrate the roads and launch site capable zones that the SAM systems can successfully launch their missiles.

A quick geospatial analysis of the XYZ Republic's terrain elevation data determines that less than 500 square miles of the country fall in this category (for most applications, this exercise could quickly reduce potential target areas to a fraction of the original value).

Using data reduction in intelligence, surveillance, and reconnaissance (ISR) planning limits the number of sensors required to provide the most efficient collection coverage area and significantly expedites the search process to find desired target sets by looking only where the target sets can perform their mission.

Data Thinning

Data thinning is a subset of data reduction. Data thinning is one or more processes that remove unneeded or erroneous data points from the data input stream early in the acquisition process to reduce data volume before consumption in the analysis process. In a best-case scenario, data thinning transpires without reducing the data stream validity, reliability, or intelligence product output quality (see Figure 12.18).

Data attainment (collection) systems, along with the useful data for analysis and exploitation, may contain redundant data, nonfunctional data, erroneous data, nonstandard metadata reporting formats, and various other nonstandardized data collection stream variations that confuse and confound intelligence production operations adding to the task's complexity and reduce intelligence production volume, quality, and reliability.

Many automated data-thinning algorithms are used today for mapping and atmospheric modeling purposes; however, the strides these algorithms have made in enhancing computational processing speeds are sometimes offset by increased inaccuracies in the results. Attempts at

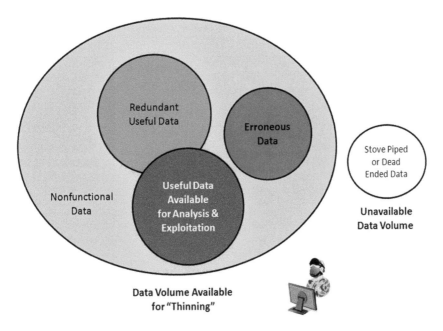

Figure 12.18 Visualizing the Data Thinning Task.

algorithms automating routine tasks like vehicle tracking have also met similar results; nominal or incremental improved output value from expensive processing of large amounts of data. However, because these automated algorithms are imperfect or can be universally applied should not preclude data thinning using other similar means. To date, there remain many skeptics on the acceptable level of automation and how the approach can best be applied.

An example of how data thinning could broadly be applied today would be writing data-thinning algorithms that could be made functional with a notional 60% correct output for any given collected data set. Complementary ML feedback processes could likely be designed and applied to these data-thinning algorithms to enhance the process further.

Stovepipes and Dead-Ends

Sensor platforms (e.g., highly classified satellites or ISR collection UAVs) are often stovepiped or dead-ended, meaning their sensor data can only report to their associated ground station or have to land first and then upload the sensor data before they can be analyzed and exploited for intelligence value. Both situations tend to exclude valuable sensor data from broader intelligence fusion processes.

Automating data reduction processes on a broad scale reduces unnecessary data collection and storage. Reducing unnecessary data collection saves collection time and reduces the cost of storing useless data. Unfortunately, many data collectors' default positions are to collect and store all data because the data may be of use someday, even if it is not useful today.

CURRENT US GOVERNMENT DATA INITIATIVES

From the beginning of this section, Data, Data, and Even More Data, we have discussed the present-day *Big Data* environment and how intelligence analysts function within that environment to collect, store, retrieve, process, exploit, and analyze data. Additionally, methods and tools used to assemble, organize, parse large data sets to support analysis have also been introduced. However, the text has directed little time toward initiatives to address the obstacles analysts face dealing with the Big Data environment in a meaningful way.

Historically the US government is on the cutting edge of technology (e.g., stealth aircraft, hypersonic missiles, nuclear submarines, and the internet). However, this same government often may lag years behind other governments and commercial best practices when implementing this new tech. For example, Americans (the Wright brothers) pioneered aviation. Still, the US military was slow to adopt airplanes and even had to borrow planes from their allies to fight World War I (WWI).

Author's Note: Many of these commercial IT initiatives are currently available for business and criminal intelligence analysts because business and crime data sets generally exist at a much smaller scale than US government data sets.

Multiple US government IT initiatives (available from commercial providers) are coming online to assist intelligence analysts with today's Big Data obstacles.

Of these many initiatives (and more coming every year), three of the more noteworthy have been selected for discussion. They are *JEDI, ICAM*, and *DCOI* (see Figure 12.19).

JEDI

JEDI (Joint Enterprise Defense Infrastructure) is a community effort to provide a unified data assimilation framework for research and operational use, for different components of DoD/IC networks, and for different applications, to reduce or avoid redundant work within the community and increase the efficiency of research and the transition from development teams to operations.

Figure 12.19   Government IT/Cloud Initiatives.

JEDI aims to offer the DoD a global network fabric by leveraging commercial "Infrastructure as a Service" and "Platform as a Service" capabilities.[17,18]

JEDI attempts to incorporate data reduction and data thinning into its design by increasing standardization. This cloud network exposes more useful data sources (reduced stovepipes) while removing redundant, erroneous, and no-functional data sources. JEDI includes enterprise-scale AI and ML projects that offer continuous feedback and task improvement.

ICAM/FICAM

ICAM (Identity, Credential, and Access Management) is a government IT initiative to make US government-maintained critical information sources safely available to public safety personnel to the greatest extent possible while protecting the information from improper access. FICAM is the federal version of ICAM. FICAM (federal identity, credential, and access management) applies ICAM policies, tools, and systems to federal agencies. By adopting ICAM/FICAM standardized policies, analysts can access more critical government data sources while minimizing the risks of identity theft and data breaches. ICAM/FICAM reduces the need for stovepiped and dead-end data sources.

DCOI

DCOI (Data Center and Cloud Optimization Initiative) is a US government initiative to consolidate and modernize IT infrastructure as part of the federal cloud computing strategy, Cloud Smart. This policy sets aggressive targets for agencies to optimize their data centers.

DCOI develops strategies to consolidate the US governments' inefficient IT infrastructure, optimizing existing facilities to achieve cost savings, and transition to a more efficient infrastructure, such as cloud services and interagency shared services.[19]

ARTIFICIAL INTELLIGENCE, MACHINE LEARNING, AND DEEP LEARNING

AI generally refers to a machines' simulation of human intelligence processes, including learning, reasoning, and self-correction. AI, ML, and DL are three different terms that need to be fully understood and used separately. In simplest terms, AI is the replication of human attributes or intelligence in machines, from unpretentious robots to complex computational networks. AI is the broader term of the three that encompasses ML and DL (see Figure 12.20). This text only introduces and scratches the surface of these concepts.

Artificial Intelligence (AI)

The concept of AI is transforming American life, with applications ranging from robotic doctors (medical diagnostics) and precision terraced irrigation projects (agriculture) to advanced manufacturing and driverless cars (autonomous transportation), national security, and defense. The pace of AI progress is rapid, and new technologies like autonomous systems, ML, and natural language processing continue to broaden the scope (see Figure 12.21).

AI is generally split into two broad categories: weak AI and strong AI. Weak AI denotes an AI system developed for a specific task. In contrast, a strong AI is one with comprehensive human

---

17 FedTech and StateTech, *DOD Sheds Light on Cloud Future With Its JEDI Project*, By Phil Goldstein, March 9, 2018, https://fedtechmagazine.com/article/2018/03/dod-sheds-light-cloud-future-its-jedi-project,   Retrieved   January 10, 2021.

18 JEDI Documentation, *What Is JEDI*, 2019, https://jointcenterforsatellitedataassimilation-jedi-docs.readthedocs-hosted.com/en/latest/overview/what.html, Retrieved January 10, 2021.

19 Sunbird, *What Is the Federal Data Center Optimization Initiative (DCOI)?* www.sunbirddcim.com/government-data-center-DCOI, Retrieved January 16, 2021.

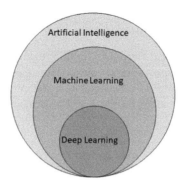

Figure 12.20   AI, ML, and DL.

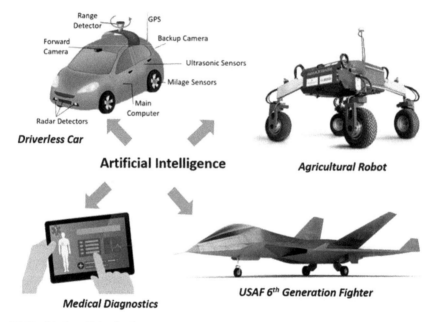

Figure 12.21   Modern AI Applications.

cognitive skills. Applications of weak AI are digital web services developed to solve customer service issues inform people about the latest news, live traffic updates, and weather forecasts. A typical more physical example of weak AI would be an assembly robot used in many modern factories of industrialized nations. However, strong AI examples are less common.

The strong AI example depicted in Figure 12.22 is the US Army's Modular Advanced Armed Robotic System (MAARS) unmanned ground vehicle (UGV) designed specifically for reconnaissance, surveillance, and target acquisition (RSTA) missions. As UAVs have become ubiquitous spies in the sky over today's battlefields, these UGVs are the new ground intelligence collectors, replacing infantry scouts on the modern battlefield. The MAARS UGV program explores the fundamental human-machine collaboration and interaction issues. As the MAARS' autonomy increases, human operators can exert less manual control of the vehicle and more time controlling vehicle swarms and directing the overall mission.[20]

---

20 *Signal* Magazine, *Combat Robot Ready for Limelight*, June 3, 2009, www.afcea.org/content/combat-robot-ready-lime-light, Retrieved December 16, 2020.

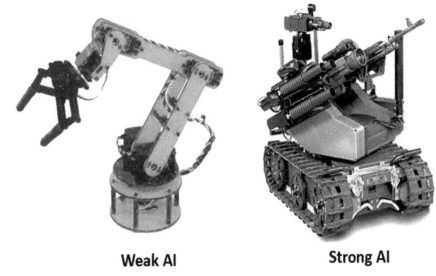

Weak AI   **Strong AI**

Figure 12.22   Examples of Weak and Strong AI.

Machine Learning (ML)

A representative application of ML is an AI that is utilized to learn and improve without reprogramming. ML concentrates on developing computer programs (algorithms) that access data and use them to learn for themselves. ML is often used to power recommendations or analytical engines that provide suggestions based on empirical data. Medical diagnostics is a typical application of ML.

An IC example of ML is the Defense Intelligence Agency's (DIA) Machine-assisted Analytic Rapid-repository System (MARS). MARS ingests and applies analytics to multiple infrastructure information sources in a database underpinning every aspect of global military operations. It gives planners, operators, and decision-makers direct access to critical insight and 50 times more data in an easy-to-use design.[21]

*Author's Note: (**Another definition of ML**) An AI discipline geared toward the technological development of human knowledge. ML allows computers to handle new situations via analysis, self-training, observation, and experience.*

MARS aims to make such gains possible by transforming current databases that house foundational military intelligence into a multidimensional, flexible, and rigorous data environment for the next century. This initiative's foundation is formed by advances in cloud computing, coupled with the promise of AI and ML.

The section began with a definition of ML, followed by a well-published application of how the IC (specifically the DIA) uses ML to provide more data faster to intelligence analysis end-users. However, many who started reading this section (and have no concept of ML) are likely to still be a bit fuzzy on the whole concept of ML. Therefore, to better understand what ML is, let us explain how ML works, followed by a basic ML example of how it can be applied to intelligence analysis.

---

21 Defense Intelligence Agency, *DIA's 'MARS' Project Achieves Key Milestone*, June 3, 2020, www.dia.mil/News/Articles/Article-View/Article/2206763/dias-mars-project-achieves-key-milestone, Retrieved December 16, 2020.

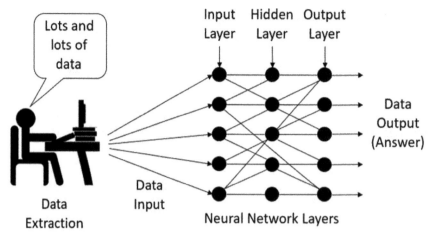

Figure 12.23   ML Neural Network.

How Machine Learning Works

ML is accomplished by humans interfacing with a machine (computer or neural network) and providing input(s) to produce an output (refer to Figure 12.23). A hefty portion of the complex data recognition, selection, and extraction is performed manually and input into an ML neural network. That input feeds one or more algorithms and produces an output. The ML output is generally much better (e.g., faster, more accurate, less biased, or more reliable) than what humans can produce on their own.

Author's Note: **Neural Network** *is a type of AI learning which models itself after the human brain. An artificial network of nodes organized into layers allows the computer to learn by incorporating new data via an algorithm. A simplified ML neural network has at least three layers:*

- *Input layer;*
- *Hidden layer; and*
- *Output layer.*

The following example describes how an intelligence analyst uses ML to perform a complex analytical task that might otherwise take many resources and a significant amount of time.

EXAMPLE

All-source intelligence analyst Jane Doe is looking for a specific SAM site called the Red Peregrin (fictitious name).

So how can Jane locate SAM sites using ML?

Following the four steps of ML:
- *Data Collection (aka 'Prepare');*
- *Data Preparation (aka 'Build');*
- *Training the Model; and*
- *Improve (aka 'Deploy' or 'Manage').*

1. Data Collection

The ML process begins with data collection (refer to Figure 12.24). Jane first goes over stacks of reports on where the SAM systems have historically been located (e.g., imagery and intelligence products, raw field reports). She may also review any doctrinal information available (e.g., operations manuals, test reports, or training materials).

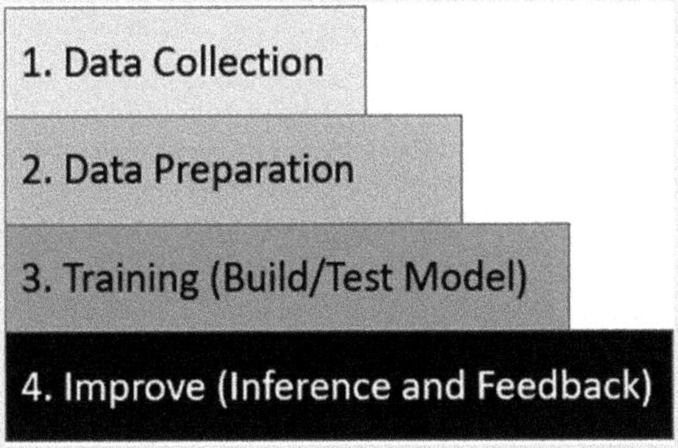

1. Data Collection

2. Data Preparation

3. Training (Build/Test Model)

4. Improve (Inference and Feedback)

Figure 12.24   Basic Steps of ML.

2. Data Preparation

After collecting the data, she prepares it using various techniques. These data preparation processes may include but are not limited to sorting, organizing, normalizing, removing extraneous, erroneous, and meaningless data (see Figure 12.25).

3. Training the Model

The data collected (once prepared) provide the foundational basis for the next step of model development and testing, also known as 'Training the Model.'

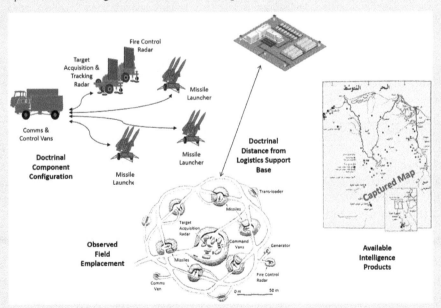

Figure 12.25   Examples of Potential Data Sources.

The analyst trains the model by running new data sets through the model and adjusting the model's algorithm to improve its predictive accuracy. For example, assume that the Red Peregrin SAM site could only be set up within 25 miles of its logistics base because of communications limitations. A Red Peregrin site was reported 35, 50, or even 100 miles from the nearest logistics base. The analyst would either have to adjust their model to the new distance or eliminate the 'distance between the SAM site and logistics bases' from the model because it is a derisory predictive parameter.

Once the model has been adequately trained to provide reliable results in a reasonable period (preferably more reliably and faster than a human can perform the task), it is ready for field testing.

4. Improve (Inference and Feedback)
Once in the operational environment, the ML process does not stop. Since most things change with time, your ML prediction model must also have the capability to change, or it will soon no longer be able to make predictions reliable. Once placed into the operational environment, the model must continuously be tweaked by continuous (or periodic) feedback or inference.

Author's Note:

- *The objective of this example is not to demonstrate how to develop models. For more information on developing analytical models, see Chapter 6 of this text.*
- *The purpose of the example is only to introduce the steps used in the ML process and illustrate them using an intelligence analysis use-case scenario.*
- *This example <u>analyst searching for a terrorist</u>.*
- *A far more sophisticated crime analysis model that exemplifies ML is used in Chapter 6, 'The AnyLogic Active Shooter Test Simulation.' In the simulation, Purdue University graduate students used ML to answer the question: Is 'run, hide, fight' effective in shooter situations?*

ML and Inference

ML inference is the process of feeding data points into an AI algorithm to calculate an output such as an arithmetic score. ML inference employs algorithms to make calculations based on the data characteristics, known as 'features.'

Deep Learning (DL)

DL is a subset of ML and AI and falls in the category of *strong AI*. DL takes ML to a higher, more complicated level. The term refers to a particular approach used to produce and train neural networks considered highly promising decision-making nodes. An example of a DL application is the highly automated systems used in self-driving cars. These cars can autonomously reorganize obstacles and use sensors and onboard analytics to facilitate situational awareness.

How Deep Learning Works

Input data are introduced to the DL process, and the data progress through several neural layers to compute an output. The subsequent few figures illustrate how DL works using a more visual description (see Figure 12.26).

The neural layers represent how the human mind functions. The input layer represents the senses (e.g., touch, taste, smell, sight, hearing), the output layer represents a response of some type (e.g., flip a switch, make a choice, fight or flight), and the 'hidden layers' abstractly represent our thoughts and decision processes. The following figures illustrate how DL functions and how DL differs from ML.

In Figure 12.26, the analyst provides a photo of a suspect along with a partial name, age, and ethnicity as inputs into a basic facial recognition ML algorithm. The ML algorithm then yields a selection of possible results to choose from.

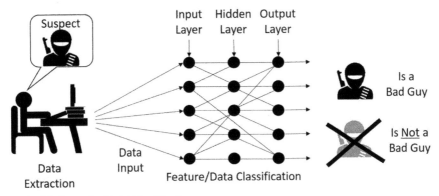

Figure 12.26 ML Example, Facial Identification.

However, in the DL example (unlike ML), there are numerous 'hidden layers,' additionally, only the *suspect photo* (without additional manual input data) provides all the required input data variables (see Figure 12.27). The DL algorithm(s) residing in the hidden layers performs the data extraction steps. The photo's pixels are broken down into numbers, and then the input variables are either standardized or normalized to be within the same range. The resultant bits of binary data are then fed into the recognition algorithm(s) residing at the various hidden layers.

The hidden layers artificially replicate human neural networks. In the example, the hidden layers constitute multiple layers of nonlinear processing used for image feature extraction and transformation. Each successive hidden layer uses the previous layer's output for its input. What a layer learns creates a hierarchy of concepts, and the accumulation of processed data travels through an ever more abstract and composite representation in the cognitive hierarchy. As the layers process data, the AI gains understanding.

TIPS/NOTES:

If interested in experimenting with ML using an open-source application, I recommend Amazon SageMaker.

SageMaker is a fully managed service that provides every developer and data scientist the capability to quickly build, train, and deploy ML models. SageMaker provides an inexpensive (and sometimes free) platform to introduce oneself to ML applications.

For more information, go to https://aws.amazon.com/sagemaker.

That means, for the facial image example, the input might be a matrix of pixels. The first layer might encode the edges of the eyes. The next layer might compare the arrangement or distance between the eyes. The next layer converts the nose and eyes' size and arrangement into an input comprehensible to the algorithm. The next layer might translate ear size or recognize that the image contains a face, and so on.

Author's Note: A true benefit of DL is that once the AI learns that 'eyes, nose, mouth, and ears' constitute a human face, the AI can apply that understanding to a different task. DL not only understands what something 'is,' but the AI also begins to learn 'why it is.'

The example (see Figures 12.27 and 12.28) presented is oversimplified and flawed in that the photo employed only provided an image of the suspect's eyes and part of a nose. Being charitable for the sake of argument and assuming that the 'eye region of the face' provides 50% of the identification factors required to meet the system's minimal facial identification standard, so the best one could hope for is a 50% confidence in the results. That said, the example does a fair job of explaining how DL and artificial neural networks function.

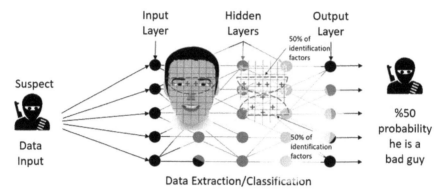

Figure 12.27   How DL Layered Networks Function.

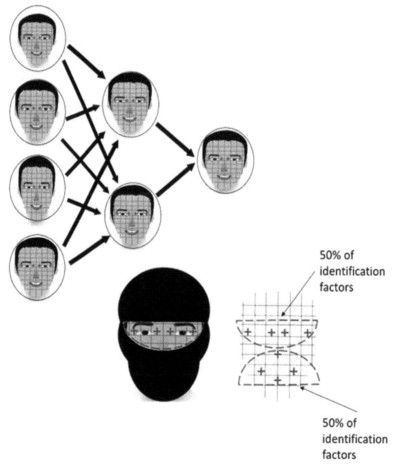

Figure 12.28   Description of What Takes Place in the Hidden Layers.

USING BAYESIAN STATISTICS TO IMPROVE INTELLIGENCE PRODUCTS

For intelligence analysis purposes, one could fill volumes on applying Bayes' equations to improve analytical products; however, that is not the goal of this section. But to that end, several footnotes are provided for further information on applying Bayesian theorems to improve analytical products.

This section explains Bayesian statistics and then focuses on where Bayesian statistics can best be applied in analysis, the associated pros, and cons, and walks through a simplified use-case example.

Bayesian Statistics

Created by Reverend Thomas Bayes over 200 years ago, 'Bayesian statistics is a mathematical technique that applies probabilities to statistical problems, and it provides people the tools to update their beliefs in the evidence of new data.' In the simplest terms, the analyst (e.g., business, intelligence, military, or crime) can arithmetically express the _probability_ of a _hypothesis_ (proposed event) occurring given specified _evidence_ (see Figure 12.29).

Bayesian Statistics Can Help

Intelligence is becoming increasingly complex, primarily because there is ever more information available. Nearer to the beginning of this chapter, the concept of 'placing the analyst on the loop' vice 'in the loop' was introduced to assist the analyst in handling today's information tidal surge. Bayesian statistics is a tool that can facilitate moving the analyst to the 'on the loop' state of affairs.

Reverend Thomas Bayes

The "Probability" of "H" given "E"

H: Hypothesis
E: Evidence

$$P(H\,|\,E) = \frac{P(E\,|\,H)\,P(H)}{P(E)}$$

Bayes' Theorem for Conditional Probabilities

Figure 12.29 Bayesian Statistics.

Using Bayesian statistics in ML or DL algorithms frees up analysts to do more analysis faster, with better reliability and less analytical bias.[22] Some applications where Bayes' theorems have been successfully tested when applied to intelligence analysis include:

- Assessing the credibility of sources, to include making separate judgments about the bits and pieces of evidence available[23,24];
- Deciding between competing hypotheses;
- Prediction of events.[25]

Author's Note: There are limitations to the use of Bayes' statistics. Like all statistical analyses, the variables and outcomes must be definable as possible outcomes or hypotheses.

EXAMPLE (DECIDING BETWEEN COMPETING HYPOTHESES)

Scenario: *You are a new intelligence analyst for the British government posted to the embassy in Warsaw, Poland, in 1939. Over the last week, multiple news stories have come in referring to attacks, shots fired, a few German civilian deaths, vandalism, and arson along the Polish Corridor and Polish-German border (Figure 12.30). The news reports included photos of several dead Polish soldiers (specifically dead men in Polish Army Uniforms). Along with these news stories, you have also listened to a radio report that an alleged 'Polish assault on Germany' has transpired. The report arrived from a German government news service at the Warsaw embassy. The report states that on the evening of August 31, a small group of soldiers wearing Polish uniforms seized the Gleiwitz radio station and broadcast a short anti-German message to the German public in Polish.*

Figure 12.30 The Polish Corridor.

22 US Central Intelligence Agency, Center for the Study of Intelligence, Jack Zlotnick, *Bayes' Theorem for Intelligence Analysis*, V16:2-43-52 (Spring 1972).

23 Proceedings of the Australian Security and Intelligence Conference 2011, J. Joseph and J. Corkill, *Information Evaluation: How One Group of Intelligence Analysts Go About the Task*, pp. 97–103 (2011).

24 US Central Intelligence Agency, Center for the Study of Intelligence, Jack Zlotnick, *Bayes' Theorem for Intelligence Analysis*, V16:2-43-52 (Spring 1972).

25 US Central Intelligence Agency, Center for the Study of Intelligence, *Bayesian Analysis for Intelligence: Some Focus on the Middle East*, Nicholas Schweitzer (July 2, 1996).

Task: *Your task is to provide an intelligence product for the British government in London regarding the veracity of the alleged 'Polish assault on Germany' report and the other recent German-Polish border incidents occurring over the last week (Figure 12.31). Besides the news reports, the only other data available to you are the German and Polish military order of battle numbers and disposition. The intelligence product should contain an assessed probability percentage. Use the Bayes' Theorem and show your work. You have three possible alternatives as to who is behind the attacks:*

- *Polish Forces*
- *German Forces*
- *Unknown Third Party?*

Figure 12.31   The Location of the Incidents on the Borders.

Given: As a new analyst (without the benefit of 70 plus years of hindsight), you feel based upon a gut feeling that there is a 30% chance that the Germans did it, a <u>60% chance the Poles did it,</u> and a <u>10% chance an unknown third party carried out the attacks.</u>

Note: You make these 'gut' assessments because of the news reports of dead bodies in Polish uniforms found at some locations and that most of the attacks were on German soil or German border facilities. The 10% figure originates from the fact that a third party is possible (however improbable); you assign a low probability value since you have no available supporting information.

According to the order of battle and multiple other sources, when war broke out, the Polish Army managed to mobilize about 1,000,000 men; at first glance, it is <u>a significantly large number</u>. However, that number represents troops located in marshaling areas scattered across Poland. Estimates vary, but it is a reasonable estimate that roughly <u>100,000 troops</u> were stationed along the German-Polish border on August 31, 1939. In reality, less than half of the Polish military had been mobilized by September 1, 1939.

Opposite the Poles, the Germans were poised to attack with numbers ranging from about 1,500,000 troops (German Sources) to 1,800,000 (Polish Government Official figure) (see Figure 12.32). Notice how the Polish forces are spread all along the border (even in areas with no opposing forces) and in-depth, whereas the German forces are concentrated for the attack.

Author's Note: Historians often cite the size of the Polish Army (1 million) at the outbreak of WWII as a significantly large number. They cite 3:1 comparisons with the US Army and American population in 1939. (The size of the US Army was 174,000, an additional 200,000 in reserves.) Also citing per capita arguments of 1 in 10 of the available male population being under arms. (This number is reached by taking the total Polish population of 35 million, assuming 50% are male, then assuming that approximately one-third are either too young or too old, leaving a 10 million eligible male population in which to draw upon.

A similar calculation using the 1939 US population of 131 million yields a resulting figure of 43 million eligible males to draw upon.

Solution: To begin the assessment, these are your data points. Hypothesis factors:
* Likelihood of Germans causing the attacks = 30%
* Likelihood of Poles causing the attacks = 60%
* The likelihood that it is an unknown third party?

Evidence factors:
* Number of Polish troops in the area = 100,000
* Number of German troops in the area = >1,000,000

You have no evidence in which to evaluate an unknown third party

Author's Note: Reportedly (according to Nuremberg Trial court documents), the Gleiwitz radio station incident and several other false flag attacks occurred along the Polish corridor in the days before the 1939 German invasion of Poland. SS attackers carried out these false flag attacks dressed in Polish uniforms to support 'Operation Himmler.'

The most notable attacks were on the German radio station, Sender Gleiwitz. The SS staged the attack on the night of August 31, 1939. Germany manufactured these attacks as a justification for the invasion of Poland, which began the following day.

Using the formula (Bayes' theorem), let's do the math.

The information you start your assessment with is the order of battle data. Polish forces in the area (100,000) and German forces in the area (>1,000,000)…so let us visualize that.

Based upon the order of battle data alone, it is ten times more likely that the German troops perpetrated the attacks because there are ten times as many Germans in the area (compared to Polish Forces). So first, relying only upon your 'gut instinct,' let's do the math (Figure 12.33).

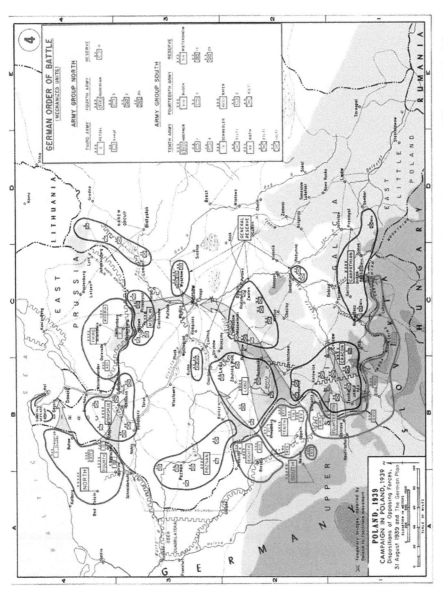

Figure 12.32   Polish and German Troops Dispositions along the Polish Corridor (Department of History, United States Military Academy).

*60% of 100,000 = 60,000 Poles or **60K***

*30% of 1,000,000 = 300,000 Germans or **300K***

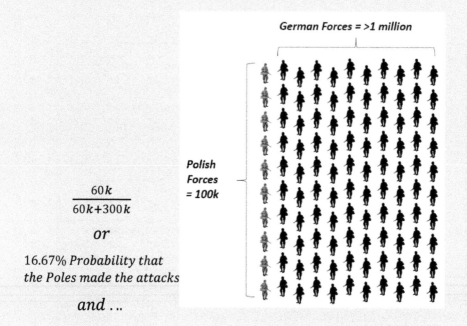

German Forces = >1 million

Polish Forces = 100k

$$\frac{60k}{60k+300k}$$

or

16.67% Probability that the Poles made the attacks

and ...

$$\frac{300k}{300k+60k} = 83.33\% \text{ Probability that the Germans made the attacks}$$

Figure 12.33   Conclusion Arrived At.

Therefore it is five times more likely that the <u>Germans</u> were behind the attacks. Note: You have no information available to evaluate the probability that a third party was involved properly.

Author's Note: Granted, this is an oversimplified probability assessment. However, it shows that one could apply Bayes' theorem and logically arrive at a defensible numerical assessment by using the numbers of soldiers in the area. Additionally, in not addressing the possible 'Unknown Third Party' alternative, the example points out that analysts often must (albeit reluctantly) respond to their customers that 'I have no answer' because there is not enough information to make an informed assessment.

Possible items for further class discussion: Without using historical hindsight, there were other logical and informational tidbits provided that one could have used to modify your initial hypothesis. A few of them are listed below:

- Things that don't fit from the German news reports:
  - Multiple bodies found dressed in Polish uniforms, but no prisoners? Therefore, no one to interrogate and validate that they were, in fact, Polish soldiers.
  - There were a few German civilian casualties and more alleged dead Polish soldiers?

- *It was well known in 1939 that the German Army was much larger and more modern than the Polish Army, so why would the Polish Army try to precipitate a war with a militarily superior adversary?*
- *If the Poles were secretly behind the attacks:*
  - *Wouldn't it make more sense for them to wear German (or another country's) uniforms or even civilian clothes to hide their Polish identity?*
  - *How is it that an inferior military force (the Poles) were able to, on multiple occasions, slip through a more densely dispersed army's forward lines and attack targets of opportunity in the enemy's rear?*
- *Because the Poles have to protect the entire border, they are spread thinly. However, the Germans are concentrated in preparation for invasion. So the troop ratio disparity may have been even more substantial than the figure we used (10:1).*

CHAPTER SUMMARY

This chapter began by describing the present state of the problem sets faced by the intelligence analysis profession, specifically referring to crime, business, terrorism, and military intelligence analysis. That was followed by listing some of today's more significant threats to modern society and western culture. These prominent threats to western culture (and by extension in varying degrees the whole world) include violent crime (both individual and organized), new weapons technologies, pandemics, and terrorism, specifically the lone actor threat. Following the explanation of analytical modern analytical problem sets, there is a brief synopsis of the technological and analytical tradecraft improvements observed in the last several decades.

The text discussed some of the innovative analytical concepts and technologies used by intelligence professionals to counter these current and emerging threats and some adverse implications arising from using these technologies. These concepts and technologies are now in use (or soon to be in use) to augment and advance information processing and analytical tradecraft and bolster and facilitate the intelligence profession. These new concepts and technologies include persistent surveillance, activity-based intelligence (ABI), target modeling, autonomous targeting, data mining (DM), data thinning, data reduction, and new data initiatives, artificial intelligence (AI), machine learning (ML), and deep learning (DL), and using Bayesian statistics to improve intelligence products. This section only briefly touched upon ABI and target modeling because they have their own separate chapter devoted to the topics.

STATE OF THE INTELLIGENCE PROFESSION

Aside from the already unfathomable amount of open-source data available on the internet, the growing quantity of HUMINT sources, ground, air, and space sensors, continues to soar. A decades-old and still climbing data proliferation wave generates incalculable data volumes that confound and saturate the intelligence community (IC), Department of Defense (DoD) planners, and business and law enforcement leaders. These listed organizations struggle with analytical processing and techniques to ensure that collected data remain useful, available, and exploitable.

Old Way Versus the New Way, Pretty Much the Same

One could argue that the analysis tradecraft has changed so little in the last 75 years that a well-seasoned World War II (WWII)-era intelligence analyst might be able to walk through a fictional time portal, sit down at a present-day intelligence analyst's desk, and do their job. Analytical tools have changed over the last 75 years, but analytical tradecraft has remained relatively constant.

In the Loop versus On the Loop

In the *in-the-loop analogy*, collected data pile up, and an ever-smaller fraction of those data get analyzed because the intelligence analyst creates a bottleneck. The next major step for the intelligence profession is to *take analysts out of the loop* and move them to a more observational position *on the loop*.

Multiple New Threat Weapons Technologies

In the last century, nuclear weapons introduced warfare to exponential levels of destruction. For decades after that, the world's foremost weapons programs focused on delivery systems for those atomic (and thermonuclear) weapons (e.g., ballistic, cruise, hypersonic missiles, extremely quiet nuclear submarines, and stealth long-range heavy bombers). Most recently, high-powered lasers have entered the land, air, and space battlefields. Some minor advances in chemical and biological weapons also appeared, but the international arms convention prohibited their use in 1997.[26] High-profile use of fourth-generation nerve agents by Russia (Novichoks[27]) and North Korea (VX[28]), as well as the use of Sarin and mustard agents in Syria, demonstrated that the chemical weapons convention (CWC) was an unenforceable hollow document. Biological weapons, thanks to advances in gene editing, not only can kill in untold numbers, but soon their creators may have the ability to focus them to target and slaughter based upon a group's (or individual's) DNA signature.

Even with these phenomenal weapons advances, the most significant would have to be the development of supercomputers and quantum computing. These ultrafast thinking platforms hold the potential to push the superpower arms race to whole new levels and an ever-increasingly aggressive, unfamiliar, and dangerous phase.

Business, Terror Groups, Crime, and Corruption

The combination of business, crime, and corruption are as old as civilization. Today, business intelligence is critical for companies to maintain an advantage in an increasingly competitive environment of shrinking profit margins. Today, the distinguishing aspect that elevates terrorism to a category of its own is often its connection to a religion or ideology. Transnational organized crime is not stagnant; crime adapts to markets and creates new forms of crime in an ever-changing industry. The alliance of crime, business, terror, and corruption is mutually beneficial and has created a dark nexus that synergizes the parts into a powerful adversary for law enforcement.

THE LONE ACTOR PROBLEM SET

The lone actor formulates and commits violent acts alone, outside of any command structure, and without material assistance from any extremist–terrorist group. Lone actors may be influenced or inspired by an ideology or views of outside groups or ideologies and may perform acts of violence to support such groups or ideologies.

It is often difficult to tell whether an actor has received external assistance, and what appears to be a lone actor attack may have been carefully orchestrated from outside. The most significant danger lies in intelligence organizations concentrating a substantial portion of their terrorism collection efforts on the parent extremist–terrorist group. Hence, the lone actor's nefarious activities may go unnoticed until it's too late.

---

26 The chemical weapons convention (CWC) outlaws the production, stockpiling, and use of chemical weapons and their precursors. The treaty entered into force on April 29, 1997. There are 193 parties to the treaty. Four UN states are not party: Egypt, Israel, North Korea, and South Sudan.

27 'Novichoks' is the name given to the controversial chemical weapons developed in the former Soviet Union between the 1970s and the 1990s. Designed to be undetectable and untreatable, these chemicals became the most toxic of the nerve agents, being very attractive for both terrorist and chemical warfare purposes.

28 North Korea used the nerve agent VX to assassinate the estranged half-brother of North Korea's leader Kim Jong Un, according to US State Department sources.

CAMERAS EVERYWHERE, THE NEW SURVEILLANCE STATE

Persistent Surveillance

These days concept of *persistent surveillance* has come into its own, and high-tech observation is omnipresent. The US DoD defines *persistent surveillance* as a collection strategy that emphasizes some collection systems' ability to linger on demand in an area to detect, locate, characterize, identify, track, target, and possibly provide battle damage assessment and retargeting in near or real-time.[29]

Far more than just an eye in the sky, it is frankly everywhere. The Internet of Things (IoT) (e.g., TVs, refrigerators, coffee makers, and many others) are all continuously watching, listening, and tracking.

Even though media sources are replete with stories of how tech companies listen to once thought to be private conversations of their customers, the typical layperson does not grasp how intrusively monitored their everyday lives are becoming.[30,31,32]

The Internet of Things (IoT)

Persistent surveillance features are incorporated into the component technology of the items we purchase routinely (e.g., cell phones, watches, TVs, and so on). These IoT surveillance mechanisms harvest the customer's data. National and local governments and commercial marketing leadership enable and leverage this surveillance technology for their purposes. The end purpose of the data harvesting may be as benign as the manufacturer trying to improve the customer experience by better understanding a customers' needs or refining a company's marketing strategy. However, the purpose can also be more nefarious, such as transforming customer data into cash flow by selling it to third parties, using the customer's data to secure more data, or using one's data against an individual.

How the IoT Spies on the Public

Whenever a consumer purchases an item online, drives their automobile, makes a call, snaps a photo, or texts with a smartphone, a record is made of the activity. All these activity-related data are collected by the IoT and recorded to log files somewhere in the network cloud. If an intelligence analyst is familiar with how each IoT item stores its user activity log files, they can access them. The analyst can then utilize the files to track or build a *pattern of life* (POL). POL-related information on individuals or groups aids the analysis of the activities associated with individuals, groups, and adversary networks.

DATA, DATA, AND EVEN MORE DATA

Modern intelligence analysis is increasingly more about storing, handling, and exploiting vast amounts of raw data using highly automated processes and cutting-edge technology.

---

29 US Department of Defense, Joint Publication 2-01, www.militaryfactory.com/dictionary/military-terms-defined.asp?term_id=4053, Retrieved January 16, 2021.

30 The Guardian, *Apple Contractors 'Regularly Hear Confidential Details' on Siri Recordings*, By Alex Hern, July 26, 2019, www.theguardian.com/technology/2019/jul/26/apple-contractors-regularly-hear-confidential-details-on-siri-recordings, Retrieved May 17, 2020.

31 The Verge, *Amazon's Alexa Isn't Just AI – Thousands of Humans Are Listening*, By Nick Statt, April 10, 2019, www.theverge.com/2019/4/10/18305378/amazon-alexa-ai-voice-assistant-annotation-listen-private-recordings, Retrieved May 17, 2020.

32 VRT NWS, *Google Employees Are Eavesdropping, Even in Your Living Room*, By Tim Verheyden, Denny Baert, Lente Van Hee, and Ruben Van Den Heuvel, July 10, 2019, www.vrt.be/vrtnws/en/2019/07/10/google-employees-are-eavesdropping-even-in-flemish-living-rooms/, Retrieved May 17, 2020.

Data Management

The term 'Data Management' is focused more on the attainment and processing of raw data. To the IT professional, some of the more common tasks attributed to the 'data management' task set are producing databases, creating historical backups, uploading data to data storage mediums, and assigning roles (or permissions) to others to access specific data files. These roles or permissions might also provide access to specific rows, fields, or data contained with a file (such as passwords). In the field of intelligence, data management also involves the 'preparation' (aka cleaning) of data before uploading it into a database. The following sections provide better descriptions of what the terms *attainment, processing, reduction,* and *thinning* of raw collected data mean to the intelligence analyst.

Data Attainment

Data attainment may entail collecting pixel data (imagery data) from an unmanned aerial vehicle (UAV) or satellite, radar data from a stationary ground sensor or ship at sea, then feeding via a data stream through a communications hub into a collections network. Just as easily, it could be a raw intelligence report being uploaded and transmitted by a human operator from anywhere on the planet.

Data Preparation (or Processing)

However, these data sets, attained from various collection mechanisms, can rarely be stored in their raw collected forms or exploited by analysts without some level of preparation (aka data processing). These preparations/processes take many forms. Some as mundane as college students sorting data into columns and listing into a spreadsheet for sorting or when a data manager more rigorously sorts and files the data into a relational framework with fields in a database, to something much more complicated as taking the data streams from multiple satellite images, georeferencing the digital pixels, then combining the image data with other whole or fractional image data sets to create a combined image for an imagery analyst to exploit.

Data Mining

DM (a term coined in the 1990s) is a modern computational/analytical process of discovering patterns in expansive data sets involving methods taken from the scientific fields of:

- AI, ML (human-like intelligence displayed by software and/or machines),
- Statistics (the numeric study of data relationships), and
- Database systems.

The DM's ultimate goal is to extract information from awkwardly large data sets and convert it into a more logical and comprehensible structure for further analysis.

Data Analytics

Data analytics (DA) is principally an exercise that derives information value from data sets. DA examines data sets using a process that identifies trends and draws conclusions about the information contained. DA is combined with other dedicated processes, systems, and software to more effectively and reliably find these patterns and trends within the data at an ever-increasing pace.

DA is a term broadly used to describe the application of 'mathematical procedures' to raw data sets. These procedures include basic counting tasks such as generating summary counts of 'events,' creating reports with summary descriptive statistics, and application of 'data visualization' tools to create graphics that convey the 'information' in your data.

'Analytics' also includes the application of statistical modeling tools to predict future events based on historical data, to 'cluster' or otherwise 'bin' similar units of analysis into distinct groups, or to assess the effectiveness of marketing campaigns and similar 'interventions' on customer behavior.

While there is a high degree of overlap between the two disciplines, most people in the 'analytics' realm have extensive academic and other training in statistics, econometrics, operations research, and others. In contrast, those in the 'data management' field tend to exercise database modeling techniques, data sorting, performance tuning, data storage methods, and database architecture.

Data Reduction

Data reduction transforms numerical or text-based digital information derived empirically or experimentally into a corrected, ordered, and simplified form. Stated more simply, it reduces multitudinous amounts of data down to the meaningful parts .

Efficient data reduction activities endeavor not to exclude helpful data sets. This concept was stressed in the earlier section Constructing Analytical Models. In that section, a shallow threshold >50% was chosen for example purposes. In practice, data reduction thresholds are higher to better exclude erroneous and spurious data from confusing the analysis outcomes.

CURRENT US GOVERNMENT DATA INITIATIVES

From the beginning of this section, Data, Data, and Even More Data, we have discussed the present-day *Big Data* environment and how intelligence analysts function within that environment to collect, store, retrieve, process, exploit and analyze data. Additionally, methods and tools used to assemble, organize, parse large data sets to support analysis have also been introduced. However, the text has directed little time toward initiatives to address the obstacles analysts face dealing with the Big Data environment in a meaningful way.

Multiple US government IT initiatives (available from commercial providers) are coming online to assist intelligence analysts with today's Big Data obstacles.

Of these many initiatives (and more coming every year), three of the more noteworthy have been selected for discussion: *JEDI, ICAM*, and *DCOI*.

JEDI

JEDI (Joint Enterprise Defense Infrastructure) is a community effort to provide a unified data assimilation framework for research and operational use, for different components of DoD/IC networks, and for different applications, to reduce or avoid redundant work within the community and increase the efficiency of research and the transition from development teams to operations. JEDI aims to offer the DoD a global network fabric by leveraging commercial 'Infrastructure as a Service' and 'Platform as a Service capabilities.'[33,34]

JEDI attempts to incorporate data reduction and data thinning into its design by increasing standardization. This cloud network exposes more useful data sources (reduced stovepipes) while removing redundant, erroneous, and no-functional data sources. JEDI includes enterprise-scale AI and ML projects and offers continuous feedback and task improvement.

---

33 FedTech and StateTech, *DOD Sheds Light on Cloud Future with Its JEDI Project*, By Phil Goldstein, March 9, 2018, https://fedtechmagazine.com/article/2018/03/dod-sheds-light-cloud-future-its-jedi-project, Retrieved January 10, 2021.

34 JEDI Documentation, *What Is JEDI*, 2019, https://jointcenterforsatellitedataassimilation-jedi-docs.readthedocs-hosted.com/en/latest/overview/what.html, Retrieved January 10, 2021.

ICAM/FICAM

ICAM (Identity, Credential, and Access Management) is a government IT initiative to make US government-maintained critical information sources safely available to public safety personnel to the greatest extent possible while protecting the information from improper access. FICAM is the federal version of ICAM. FICAM (federal identity, credential, and access management) applies ICAM policies, tools, and systems to federal agencies. By adopting ICAM/FICAM standardized policies, analysts can access more critical government data sources while minimizing the risks of identity theft and data breaches. ICAM/FICAM reduces the need for stovepiped and dead-end data sources.

DCOI

DCOI (Data Center and Cloud Optimization Initiative) is a US government initiative to consolidate and modernize IT infrastructure as part of the federal cloud computing strategy, Cloud Smart. This policy sets aggressive targets for agencies to optimize their data centers.

DCOI develops strategies to consolidate the US governments' inefficient IT infrastructure, optimizing existing facilities to achieve cost savings, and transition to a more efficient infrastructure, such as cloud services and interagency shared services.

ARTIFICIAL INTELLIGENCE, MACHINE LEARNING, AND DEEP LEARNING

AI generally refers to a machines' simulation of human intelligence processes, including learning, reasoning, and self-correction. AI, ML, and DL are three different terms that need to be fully understood and used separately. In simplest terms, AI is the replication of human attributes or intelligence in machines, from unpretentious robots to complex computational networks. AI is the broader term of the three that encompasses both ML and DL.

Artificial Intelligence (AI)

The concept of AI is transforming American life, with applications ranging from robotic doctors (medical diagnostics) and precision terraced irrigation projects (agriculture) to advanced manufacturing and driverless cars (autonomous transportation), national security, and defense. The pace of AI progress is rapid, and new technologies like autonomous systems, ML, and natural language processing continue to broaden the scope.

AI is generally split into two broad categories: weak AI and strong AI. Weak AI denotes an AI system developed for a specific task. In contrast, strong AI is an AI system with comprehensive human cognitive skills.

The strong AI example is the US Army's Modular Advanced Armed Robotic System (MAARS) unmanned ground vehicle (UGV) designed specifically for reconnaissance, surveillance, and target acquisition (RSTA) missions. As UAVs have become ubiquitous spies in the sky over today's battlefields, these UGVs are the new ground intelligence collectors, replacing infantry scouts on the modern battlefield. The MAARS UGV program explores fundamental human-machine collaboration and interaction issues. As the MAARS' autonomy increases, human operators can exert less manual control of the vehicle and more time controlling vehicle swarms and directing the overall mission.[35]

---

35 *Signal* Magazine, *Combat Robot Ready for Limelight*, June 3, 2009, www.afcea.org/content/combat-robot-ready-lime-light, Retrieved December 16, 2020.

Machine Learning (ML)

ML applies AI-generating systems to learn and improve without reprogramming. ML concentrates on developing computer programs (algorithms) that access data and use them to learn for themselves. ML is often used to power recommendations or analytical engines that provide suggestions based on empirical data. Medical diagnostics is a typical application of ML.

MARS aims to make such gains possible by transforming current databases that house foundational military intelligence into a multidimensional, flexible, and rigorous data environment for the next century. This initiative's foundation is formed by advances in cloud computing, coupled with the promise of AI and ML.

How Machine Learning Works

ML is accomplished by humans interfacing with a machine (computer or neural network) and providing input(s) to produce an output. A hefty portion of the complex data recognition, selection, and extraction is performed manually and input into an ML neural network. That input feeds one or more algorithms and produces an output. The ML output is generally much better (e.g., faster, more accurate, less biased, or more reliable) than what humans can produce on their own.

ML and Inference

ML inference is the process of feeding data points into an AI algorithm to calculate an output such as an arithmetic score. ML inference employs algorithms to make calculations based on the data characteristics, known as 'features.'

Deep Learning (DL)

DL is a subset of ML and AI and falls in the category of *strong AI*. DL takes ML to a higher, more complicated level. The term refers to a particular approach used to produce and train neural networks considered highly promising decision-making nodes. An example of a DL application is highly automated systems such as self-driving cars. These cars can autonomously reorganize obstacles and use sensors and onboard analytics to facilitate situational awareness.

How Deep Learning Works

Input data are introduced to the DL process, and the data progresses through several neural layers to compute an output.

The neural layers represent how the human mind functions. The input layer represents the senses (e.g., touch, taste, smell, sight, hearing), the output layer represents a response of some type (e.g., flip a switch, make a choice, fight or flight), and the 'hidden layers' abstractly represent our thoughts and decision processes.

The DL algorithm(s) residing in the hidden layers performs the data extraction steps. The resultant bits of binary data are then fed into the recognition algorithm(s) residing at the various hidden layers.

The hidden layers artificially replicate human neural networks. What a layer learns creates a hierarchy of concepts. Each successive hidden layer uses the previous layer's output for its input. What a layer learns creates a hierarchy of concepts, and each layer learns to transform its input data into an ever more abstract and composite representation in the hierarchy. As the layers process data, the AI gains understanding.

USING BAYESIAN STATISTICS TO IMPROVE INTELLIGENCE PRODUCTS

For intelligence analysis purposes, one could fill volumes on applying Bayes' equations to improve analytical products; however, that is not the goal of this section. But to that end, several footnotes are provided for further information on applying Bayesian theorems to improve analytical products.

Bayesian Statistics

Created by Reverend Thomas Bayes over 200 years ago, 'Bayesian statistics is a mathematical technique that applies probabilities to statistical problems, and it provides people the tools to update their beliefs in the evidence of new data.' In the simplest terms, the analyst (e.g., business, intelligence, military, or crime) can arithmetically express the *probability* of a *hypothesis* (proposed event) occurring given specified *evidence*.

Bayesian Statistics Can Help

Intelligence is becoming increasingly complex, primarily because there is ever more information available. Nearer to the beginning of this chapter, the concept of 'placing the analyst on the loop' vice 'in the loop' was introduced to assist the analyst in handling today's information tidal surge. Bayesian statistics is a tool that can facilitate moving the analyst to the 'on the loop' state of affairs.

Using Bayesian statistics in ML or DL algorithms frees up analysts to do more analysis faster, with better reliability and less analytical bias.[36] Some applications where Bayes' theorems have been successfully tested when applied to intelligence analysis include:

- Assessing the credibility of sources, to include making separate judgments about the bits and pieces of evidence available[37,38];
- Deciding between competing hypotheses;
- Prediction of events.[39]

PRACTICAL EXERCISE – LONE ACTOR (LONE WOLF) CLASSIFICATION

This exercise is designed further to acquaint students with the lone actor problem set. Additionally, the exercise familiarizes participants with the pros and cons of developing instructive models from study data.

Validating analytical models is a task that all analysts should understand and demonstrate proficiency. Fortunately, almost all the information is readily available online for this particular

---

36 US Central Intelligence Agency, Center for the Study of Intelligence, Jack Zlotnick, *Bayes' Theorem for Intelligence Analysis*, V16:2-43-52 (Spring 1972).

37 Proceedings of the Australian Security and Intelligence Conference 2011, J. Joseph and J. Corkill, *Information Evaluation: How One Group of Intelligence Analysts Go About the Task*, pp. 97–103 (2011).

38 US Central Intelligence Agency, Center for the Study of Intelligence, Jack Zlotnick, *Bayes' Theorem for Intelligence Analysis*, V16:2-43-52 (Spring 1972).

39 US Central Intelligence Agency, Center for the Study of Intelligence, *Bayesian Analysis for Intelligence: Some Focus on the Middle East*, Nicholas Schweitzer (July 2, 1996).

scenario. Additionally, the information provided comes from open sources, provided in a realistic untidy semi-organized format, similar to how it appears to intelligence analysts working in the profession.

Note: The practical exercise associated with this chapter is rather lengthy and is not included in the text. The instructor has to print it out from the Instructor Guide and provide you with a copy.

Glossary

Abscissa is the x-coordinate point: its distance from the y-axis, measured parallel to the x-axis (*for standard plane Cartesian coordinates*).

Activity-Based Intelligence (ABI) is an intelligence discipline where analysis and the subsequent collection focuses on activity and transactions associated with an entity, population, or area of interest.

Activity Forecasting is a subdiscipline of ABI that categorizes, defines, structures, and organizes to develop observational-based understandings that create entity/organization activity pattern definitions. The observations ultimately produce data-driven models that allow the analyst to forecast responses to stimuli and inform doctrinal and trend analysis efforts.

After-Action Review (AAR) is a professional discussion of an event focused on performance standards that enable soldiers to discover for themselves 'What' happened, 'Why' it happened, and 'How' to sustain strengths and improve weaknesses. An AAR's objective is to improve individual and collective task performance by providing immediate feedback about improving the training or tasks by providing positive recommendations related to observed shortfalls. The tool allows leaders and organizations to get the maximum benefit from every mission or task.

Alternate Futures Analysis (AFA) is a set of techniques used to explore dissimilar, more futuristic states developed by varying a set of key trends, indicators, drivers, or conditions. AFA Systematically explores multiple ways a situation can develop when there is high complexity and uncertainty. It is most useful when a situation is perceived as too complicated or the expected outcomes are too uncertain to trust a single outcome assessment.

Alternatives Analysis A diagnostic technique using rigorous analysis to explain events or data sets, select the best option, anticipate potential outcomes, or predict future trends.

Analysis of Alternatives (AoA) is a synonym for Alternatives Analysis. AoA is a business term used to describe a project management process in which key performance parameters (KPPs) (or metrics) are established or modified for each vendor provided an alternative. The AoA establishes and benchmarks metrics for cost, schedule, performance (CSP), and risk (CSPR) depending on customer needs. These metrics help compare the operational effectiveness, suitability, and life-cycle costs of other options to satisfy the acquisition/purchase requirements.

Analysis of Competing Hypothesis (ACH) is a structured analytical technique (SAT) that identifies, defines, and assesses alternative hypotheses by systematically listing them in a matrix and evaluating all associated evidence, focusing on what rejects rather than confirms hypotheses. A highly effective technique is when there is a large amount of data to absorb and evaluate.

Anticipatory Analytics is a systematic process that uses historical data/trends, machine learning, data mining, and modeling programs (like predictive analytics) using very robust and diverse data input and then folds this collected information into another algorithm that characterizes potential and imminent anomalies, identifies threats and opportunities, and compares the result to trending events and key events/potential catalysts. Anticipatory analytics factors in context, changing stakeholder/key player intent, possible reactions, and most significantly different alternative futures, ranging from probable to outlier outcomes.

Application Programming Interface Key (API key) is a unique identifier used to authenticate a user, developer, or calling program and is typically used to confirm a project with the API rather than a human user.[1]

Attribute is a characteristic feature of an entity that generally remains constant.

---

1   Google Cloud, 'Why and when to use API keys, Cloud Endpoints with OpenAPI,' https://cloud.google.com/endpoints/docs/openapi/when-why-api-key, Retrieved February 4, 2020.

Autonomous is an artificial intelligence (AI) construct that does not need help from people. Driverless cars illustrate the term 'autonomous' in varying degrees. Autonomy is ranked by levels. Level 0 autonomy indicates manual operation (or no autonomy), and Level 5 represents high autonomy (no human interaction required).

Anything beyond that would be called sentient. Despite the leaps that have been made recently in the field of AI, the singularity (an event representing an AI that becomes self-aware) is purely theoretical at this point.

AWS S3 Bucket is a public cloud storage resource available in Amazon Web Services (AWS) Simple Storage Service (S3), an object storage offering. Amazon S3 buckets, similar to file folders, store objects consisting of data and its descriptive metadata.[2]

Backcasting is an analytical process that defines a potential (desirable/undesirable) future (end-state). Then the analyst works backward to identify situations, policies, processes, and other items that connect the future to the present.

Battle Damage Assessment (BDA) estimates damage resulting from lethal or nonlethal military force application. Battle damage assessment is composed of physical damage assessment, functional damage assessment, and target system assessment.

Betweenness *(as it is used in social network analysis to determine a node's power)* is the number of links running through a player or the extent to which a node is directly connected only to those other nodes that are not directly connected, such as an intermediary, liaisons, bridges.

Big Data is a term used to identify data sets that were so large and unwieldy that they were beyond the capacity of traditional database and analysis technologies.

Big Data Triage, a subdiscipline of ABI, uses various search techniques that continuously monitor large-volume data feeds. The triage monitoring scheme compares the data feed contents to specified indicators associated with locations of interest within specified time frames. The monitored data feed can be from any source (HUMINT, OSINT, SIGINT,…). Monitoring the data over time can build pattern sets that can later be used to develop a pattern of life (POL) and distinguish normal, abnormal, elevated activity levels.

Boolean Operators, in the context of search engines, are conjunctions used to filter results by combining or excluding specific words and terms in queries (e.g., AND, OR, NOT, or AND NOT). Using Boolean operators significantly reduces or expands the number of items returned. Boolean operators save time by focusing on more *on-target* results appropriate to their needs and eliminating unsuitable or inappropriate responses.

Botnets are several internet-connected devices, each running one or more bots. Botnets can perform distributed denial-of-service attacks, steal data, send spam, and allow the attacker to access the device and its connection.

Buttonology is the necessary training required to start using a piece of software.

CARVER is an acronym that stands for 'criticality', 'accessibility', 'recoverability' (or recuperability), 'vulnerability', 'effect', and 'recognizability'. An assessment tool used to determine the criticality and vulnerability of US interests.

Closeness *(as it is used in social network analysis to determine a node's power)* is the numeric representation of the degree to which a node is near all other nodes within a network, including direct or indirect relationships. This power measurement reflects a node's access to information through the 'grapevine' of other nodes within the network. Closeness is calculated as the inverse of the sum of the shortest distance between each node and every other node within the network.

Clustering Analysis is the task of grouping a set of objects so that objects in the same group are more similar to each other than to those in other groups.

Collateral Damage Assessment (CDA) An analytical judgment derived by determining the amount and effects of collateral damage post-target engagement.

---

2   AWS Developers Webpage, What is Amazon S3? https://docs.aws.amazon.com/AmazonS3/latest/dev/Welcome.html, Retrieved February 4, 2020.

Confirmation Bias is the tendency of someone to believe or favor information that supports or confirms one's perspective or understanding of a subject, topic, or concept. Confirmation bias can easily lead the analysis process astray by disregarding/undervaluing critical evidence or focusing on or overvaluing misleading or erroneous information.

Consistent, means to be in agreement with other facts or with typical or earlier behavior, having the same principles or characteristics as something else. As used in ACH, it means the data or evidence is compatible with or supports one or more hypotheses.

CONUS (Continental United States) is the area of the United States of America located in the continent of North America.

Course of Action (CoA) Any sequence of activities that an individual, organization, or unit may follow.

Dark Web is the internet content that exists on darknets. These overlay networks use the internet but require specific software (e.g., Tor, I2P), configurations, or authorization to access. Typical web search engines cannot index the Dark Web because the websites do not have the necessary indexing terms in their source code.

Data Analytics (DA) is principally an exercise that derives information value from data sets. DA is the process of examining data sets to find trends and draw conclusions about the information contained. Increasingly data analytics is used with the aid of specialized systems and software.

Data Management is an administrative process that includes acquiring, validating, storing, protecting, and processing raw data to ensure its end-users accessibility, reliability, and timeliness.

Data Reduction is a process that transforms numerical or text-based digital information derived empirically or experimentally into a corrected, ordered, and simplified form. The basic concept is the reduction of multitudinous amounts of data down to the meaningful parts.

Data Thinning (a subset of Data Reduction) is one or more processes that remove unneeded or erroneous data points from the data input stream early in the acquisition process to reduce data volume before consumption in the analysis process.

Dauphin of France is a title given to the heir apparent to the throne of France. The term 'Dauphin' generally refers to the oldest son of the king of France.

DCOI (Data Center and Cloud Optimization Initiative) is a US government initiative to consolidate and modernize IT infrastructure is part of the federal cloud computing strategy, Cloud Smart. This policy sets aggressive targets for agencies to optimize their data centers.

Degree (*as it is used in social network analysis to determine a node's power*) is the number of links a node has to cross to reach other nodes within the network.

Delphi Method is a qualitative forecasting technique that uses a panel of experts who are given a situation and asked to make initial predictions based on a prescribed questionnaire. Experts develop written opinions individually, and these responses are analyzed, summarized, and submitted to the expert panel for further consideration. All these responses are anonymous so that others' opinions influence no member. This process is repeated until a consensus is obtained. Developed initially for forecasting military events, it has become a valuable tool in other areas.

Department of Defense (DoD) The DoD is headed by the Secretary of Defense, a cabinet-level head who reports directly to the President of the United States. Beneath the DoD are three subordinate military departments: the United States Department of the Army, the United States Department of the Navy, and the United States Department of the Air Force.

Department of Homeland Security (DHS) is a cabinet department of the US federal government with responsibilities in public security, roughly comparable to other countries' interior or home ministries. Its stated missions involve anti-terrorism, border security, immigration and customs, cybersecurity, and disaster prevention and management.

Devil's Advocacy is an analytical process best performed by an 'independent' agent (who is not part of the team that performed the original assessment). This analysis collects its own data/

evidence, which may be duplicative so that it arrives at the final assessment untainted by the initial analytical process.

Dumping is the act of charging a price lower than the typical value of a given product in a foreign market *(international trade definition)*.

Eigenvector Value *(as used in social network analysis to determine a node's power)* is an overall assessment of the node's importance based on centrality measures or measures of power, including the aspects of degree, betweenness, and closeness. The Eigenvector Value is a vector quantity that possesses a magnitude and a direction component.

Email Breach Lookup is a way to determine if your email address has been affected by a data breach. The *Have I Been Pwned* website allows one to enter their email address (without worrying about the security threat). The site does not ask for one's password or other personal data.

Emergency Action Plan (EAP) is a written document required by particular Occupational Safety and Health Administration (OSHA) standards. The purpose of an EAP is to facilitate and organize employer and employee actions during workplace emergencies.

Evaluation of Indicators is the process of creating a model that yields observables that can corroborate/confirm or invalidate/disprove a hypothesis, CoA, or specific data. Useful when performing ACH or monitoring multiple enemy/adversary CoAs or confirming a specific piece of data. It is particularly useful when looking for early warning indicators when the present environment is relatively static.

Extortion is obtaining property from another through the wrongful use of actual or threatened force, violence, or fear.

Extrapolation is to infer or estimate by extending or projecting known information.

Forecasting is the process of making analytical estimates of the future based on past and present data and is most commonly performed by analyzing trends.

Forensic Analysis is the process of understanding, re-creating, and analyzing previously occurring events.

Forensic Network Analysis (FNA) A subdiscipline of ABI that operationally scrutinizes selected networks to identify and categorize the component entities and their associated activities by spatially and temporally analyzing their constituent-related activities. FNA is used extensively in counterterrorism analysis.

Future Framing is the anticipatory analytical process where the analyst structures their 'question(s)' to identify and consider all direct/indirect factors that may impact current or future trajectories.

Futures Wheel is a visual aid or tool that helps the analyst imagine and document the forecasting exercise.

Georeferencing is when the internal coordinate system of a map or aerial/satellite photo image can be related to a geographic coordinate system. A georeferenced digital map or image has been tied to a known Earth coordinate system so that users can determine where every point on the map or aerial photo is located on the Earth's surface.

Global Positioning System (GPS) is a satellite-based radio-navigation system owned by the US government and operated by the US Space Force. One of many global navigation satellite systems (GNSS) provides geolocation and time data to a GPS receiver anywhere on or near the Earth. There is an unobstructed line of sight to four or more GPS satellites.

Google Dork Search is a search string that uses advanced search queries to find information not readily available on the websites. It is also regarded as illegal Google hacking activity, which hackers often use for cyberterrorism and cyber theft. A dork search can be used to locate devices connected to the internet. For example, the search string such as *inurl:'ViewerFrame?Mode='* can find public web cameras. Another useful dork search is the following *intitle:index.of,* followed by a search keyword. This can give a list of files on the servers. For example, *intitle:index.of mp3* provides all the MP3 files available on various types of servers.

You can use symbols or words to make your search results more precise.

Google Street View is a technology included in Google Maps and Google Earth that offers interactive views from positions along many streets globally.

Ground-penetrating Radar (GPR) is a geophysical sensor that uses radar pulses to image the Earth's subsurface.

Group *(for online searches)* is a text expression that uses parenthetical notation to regulate a keyword query's precedence order. The insertion of a particular text expression within parentheses requires that a subset of the keyword query expression be processed before the rest of the expression.

High Impact/Low Probability Analysis provides leadership and policy/decision-makers early warning that an event, perceived as unlikely, may transpire, accompanied by significant negative consequences.

High-Value Targets (HVTs) are targets the enemy commander requires to complete the mission successfully. The loss of HVTs would be expected to seriously degrade essential enemy functions throughout the friendly commander's area of interest.

Horizon Scanning Horizon scanning is a technique for detecting early indications of potentially significant developments through a systematic examination of potential threats and opportunities, focusing on novel technology and its effects on the issue at hand. The method calls for defining what is constant, what changes, and what always changes. It discovers new and unexpected issues and persistent problems and trends, including matters at the margins of current thinking that challenge past assumptions.

HUMINT is human intelligence (HUMINT), which is defined as any information gathered from human sources.

Hypertext Transfer Protocol (HTTP) is an application-layer protocol for transmitting hypermedia documents, such as HTML. It was designed for communication between web browsers and web servers, but it can also be used for other purposes.

IA *(CIA institutional acronym for intelligence assessment)* the IA is the longest form of current intelligence the CIA publishes. CIA regularly posts IAs to its classified webpage hosting the *World Intelligence Review electronic* (WIRe) for senior policy and security officials throughout the US government. Many items from the WIRe are available to major US military commands.[3]

Inconsistent, the reverse of consistent, disagrees with other facts or with typical or earlier behavior, having principles or characteristics that differ from something else. As used in ACH, the data/evidence is incompatible with or does not support one or more hypotheses.

Indicator is a marker of accomplishment/progress. A specific, observable, and measurable accomplishment or change that shows your logic model's progress toward achieving a specific output or outcome.

Infrared Thermography (IRT) is a sensor that detects thermal radiation in the long-infrared range of the electromagnetic spectrum (roughly 9,000–14,000 nanometers or 9–14 μm) and produces images of that radiation.

Infrastructure as a Service (IaaS) are online services that provide high-level APIs used to dereference various low-level details of underlying network infrastructure like physical computing resources, location, data partitioning, scaling, security, backup, etc.

Intelligence Community (IC) the US IC comprises 18 *(with the recent creation of Space Force)*[4] separate government intelligence agencies that work separately and together to conduct intelligence activities to support the United States' foreign policy and national security. Member organizations of the IC include intelligence agencies, military intelligence, and civilian intelligence and analysis offices within federal executive departments.

---

3   US Central Intelligence Agency, Products Webpage, www.cia.gov/offices-of-cia/intelligence-analysis/products.html, Retrieved April 6, 2019.

4   ExecutiveGoV, *John Ratcliffe on Space Force Becoming Part of US Intelligence Community*, By Jane Edwards, www.executivegov.com/2020/12/john-ratcliffe-on-space-force-becoming-part-of-us-intelligence-community,   Retrieved January 10, 2021.

Intelligence, Surveillance, and Reconnaissance (ISR) is the term that describes the primarily military process of reconnaissance and surveillance with intelligence production and dissemination. ISR is a continuous, recursive operation focused on collecting relevant information to analyze and create intelligence to inform the commander's visualization and support the operational cycle.

Internet of Things (IoT) is the network of physical mechanisms (*e.g., appliances, tools, cell phones, baby monitors,…*) embedded with sensors, software, and other technologies to connect and exchange data with other devices and systems over the internet.

Internet Protocol (IP) Address is a numerical tag assigned to each device connected to a computer network that uses the IP for communication. An IP address serves two principal functions: host or network interface identification and location addressing.[5]

Interpolation is when one estimates a value situated within two known values in a sequence of values.

Joint Effort for Data assimilation Integration (JEDI) is a community effort to provide a unified data assimilation framework for research and operational use for different components of DoD/IC networks and different applications, to reduce or avoid redundant work within the community and increase the efficiency of research and the transition from development teams to operations. JEDI aims to offer the DoD a global fabric by leveraging commercial 'Infrastructure as a Service' and 'Platform as a Service capabilities.'[6,7]

Keystroke Logging, often referred to as keylogging, is recording the computer keystrokes. Generally, the person using the keyboard is unaware that their activities are being monitored, and data can then be retrieved by another person monitoring the keylogging program.

Keyword is a single search string (containing uppercase or lowercase letters or numeric digits with no whitespaces) such as 'test' or 'hello.'

Lidar, which stands for light detection and ranging, is a remote sensing method that uses light in a pulsed laser to measure ranges from the sensor platform to the Earth.

Linchpin Analysis is an SAT-based upon known data or information (or data with at least a high probability of certainty), anchoring the analytical argument. A flexible SAT is intended to minimize mistakes and promote clarity even with complex issues containing multiple variables and uncertainty.

Linear Regression is an algebraic calculation used to find a linear relationship between two variables. Linear regression performs the task of predicting a dependent variable value (y) based on a given independent variable (x). This regression technique finds a linear relationship between x (input) and y (output). Hence, the name is linear regression.

MARS is an acronym for Machine-assisted Analytic Rapid-repository System. MARS ingests and applies analytics to multiple infrastructure information sources in a database underpinning every aspect of global military operations.[8]

MAARS is an acronym for Modular Advanced Armed Robotic System. MAARS is an unmanned ground vehicle (UGV) designed explicitly for reconnaissance, surveillance, and target acquisition (RSTA) missions to increase the security of personnel manning forward locations.

Measure of Effectiveness (MOE) is an indicator used to measure a current system state, with change indicated by comparing multiple observations over time.

Measure of Performance (MOP) is an indicator used to measure an action associated with task accomplishment.

---

5   DARPA, DOD Standard Internet Protocol, RFC 760, Information Sciences Institute, January 1980.

6   FedTech and StateTech, *DOD Sheds Light on Cloud Future with Its JEDI Project*, By Phil Goldstein, March 9, 2018, https://fedtechmagazine.com/article/2018/03/dod-sheds-light-cloud-future-its-jedi-project, Retrieved January 10, 2021.

7   JEDI Documentation, *What Is JEDI*, 2019, https://jointcenterforsatellitedataassimilation-jedi-docs.readthedocs-hos ted.com/en/latest/overview/what.html, Retrieved January 10, 2021.

8   Defense Intelligence Agency, DIA's 'MARS' Project Achieves Key Milestone, June 3, 2020, www.dia.mil/News/Articles/ Article-View/Article/2206763/dias-mars-project-achieves-key-milestone, Retrieved December 16, 2020.

Money-Laundering is the processing of criminal proceeds to disguise their illegal origin.

MSHARPP is an acronym for mission, symbolism, history, accessibility, recognizability, population, and proximity. It is an assessment tool used to determine the criticality and vulnerability of US interests.

Network Cloud is generally used to describe data centers available to many users over the internet. Network resources (e.g., processing, storage, routing) are distributed over multiple locations from central servers, thereby providing higher bandwidth, computing capacity, efficiency, and reliability.

Neural Network is a type of AI learning which models itself after the human brain. An artificial network of nodes organized into layers that allows the computer to learn by incorporating new data via an algorithm.

Normative, pertains to giving directives, rules, standards, or norms; standardizing, controlling, regulating, prescriptive, normalizing, or regularizing.

Normative Modeling is a process where observations of behaviors and activities are performed and collected. From these observations, a model is created as the basis for judging deviations in behavior or predictions of future trends or potential outcomes.

Occupational Safety and Health Administration (OSHA) is an agency of the United States Department of Labor. Its purpose is to ensure safe and healthful working conditions for working men and women by setting and enforcing standards and providing training, outreach, education, and assistance.

Onion Routing is a routing technique used for anonymous communication over a computer network. In Onion networks, layers of encryption encapsulate messages comparable to the layers of an onion.

Open-Source Intelligence (OSINT) is intelligence developed from the overt collection and analysis of publicly available and open-source information not under the US government's direct control. OSINT is derived from the systematic collection, processing, and analysis of publicly available, relevant information in response to intelligence requirements.[9]

Operations Security (OPSEC) is a term derived from the US military. It is an analytical process used to deny an adversary information that could compromise the secrecy and/or the operational security of a mission.

Order of Battle is the disposition of military forces ready for combat. It can be expressed as a tabular collection of units, size, commanders, equipment, and their positions in a theater of operation.

Ordinate is the y-coordinate of a point: its distance from the x-axis measured parallel to the y-axis (*for standard plane Cartesian coordinates*).

Overfitting is the production of an analysis that corresponds too closely or exactly to a particular data set. In modeling, overfitting implies that the model may fail to fit additional data or predict future observations unreliably.

Pattern of Life (POL) is a method of surveillance used explicitly to record or understand a subject's behaviors. This observation method is typically done without the knowledge or consent of the subject. Motivations for collecting POL data include security, targeting, marketing, espionage, scientific research, traffic analysis, and other legitimate and nefarious purposes.

Peoples' Liberation Army (PLA) PLA is the acronym for the Communist People Republic of China's (PRC) army.

People's Liberation Army Marine Corps (PLAMC) is the marine force of the People's Republic of China (PRC) and one of five major branches of the PLA Navy (PLAN). It currently consists of two 6,000-man brigades.

Persistent Surveillance is a collection strategy that emphasizes some collection systems' ability to linger on demand in an area to detect, locate, characterize, identify, track, target, and possibly provide battle damage assessment and retargeting in near or real-time.

9   Headquarters Department of the Army, Open-Source Intelligence, Army Techniques Publication, ATP 2-22.9, July 10, 2012.

Phrase (in online searches) is a collection of keywords separated by spaces and surrounded in single quotes such as '*Hello, Dolly.*' The results contain the string (case-insensitive) within those quotation marks. For example, if the expression contained the phrase '*Hello, Dolly*' in quotes as shown, the search service would only return exact matches to the phrase and not data that matched one or two of the keywords.

Platform as a Service (PaaS) is a cloud computing service category that allows customers to develop, run, and manage applications without the complexity of building and maintaining the infrastructure typically associated with developing and launching an application.

Prediction Markets (also known as predictive markets, information markets, decision markets, or 'cloud sourcing') are exchange-traded markets created for trading the outcome of events. Prediction markets are a cutting-edge quantitative/qualitative analytical process that applies economic theory for the ideas behind prediction to tackle real-world issues, including intelligence analysis problem sets.

Predictive Analytics is an analytical process that uses historical data/trends, machine learning, data mining, and modeling programs to predict the future. As mentioned earlier, the basis of predictive analytics is the hypothesis that past events tend to recur cyclically. However, predictive analytics is somewhat limited in that the historical data/trends input is not comprehensive.

Qualitative Forecasting (*or backcasting*) is a subjective technique based on consumers' and experts' opinions and judgment, appropriate when past data is unavailable. It is usually applied to intermediate or long-range decisions.

Quantitative Forecasting (*or backcasting*) is a more objective technique used to forecast future data as a function of past known data. It is appropriate to use when past numerical data is available and reasonable to assume that some patterns are expected to continue. This method is usually applied to short- or intermediate-range decisions.

Red Team Analysis is a contrarian analysis approach that performs three general types of tasks: (1) provides decision support, (2) critically reviews existing plans/analysis, and (3) provides a hypothetical Devil's Advocate (threat) perspective.

Scalar Quantity is a quantity that has only magnitude, not direction.

Selfie is a self-portrait digital photograph, typically taken with a digital camera or smartphone, held in hand or supported by a selfie stick. Selfies are often shared on social media via social networking services such as Facebook, Twitter, Snapchat, and Instagram.

Shell Company is an incorporated company that possesses no significant assets and does not perform any significant operations. The shell company purports to provide some service that would reasonably require its customers to pay with cash to facilitate money laundering on a regular basis.

Society for Worldwide Interbank Financial Telecommunication (SWIFT) SWIFT is an organization founded in Brussels in 1973 to establish standardized processes for financial transactions.

STP Marketing Process is the business version of target-focused analysis that is more commonly referred to as a 'marketing analysis.' It is a three-step approach where 'S' stands for segmenting, 'T' for targeting, and the 'P' for positioning. Post-marketing 'customer surveys' and 'analysis' of those surveys are implied steps and generally are not called out as part of the STP process.

Structured Self-Critique is a systematic method used to identify weaknesses in ones' analysis.

Target Effects is the cumulative result of actions taken to attack targets and target systems by lethal and nonlethal means. These effects can be primary (effects that are the direct result of targeting actions) or secondary (effects that are indirectly the result of targeting).

Target-focused Analysis is a methodology that attempts to align or 'focus' all aspects of the intelligence process (Plan, Collect, Process, Analyze, Disseminate) towards one objective and optimize the entire process.

Target Materials (TM) are standardized products that capture graphic and textual presentations of target intelligence and other information. These may come in the form of target graphics (soft or hardcopy imagery) annotated with pertinent information, titling, and other reference data or textual descriptions of target information (e.g., collateral damage concerns, target significance) and/or geospatial features that outline or depict key aspects of a target/target area.

Threat Assessment is the practice of determining the credibility and seriousness of a potential threat, as well as the probability that the threat may become a reality.

Threat Finance is an enabling factor of crime and terrorism. It includes the means and methods used by organizations to finance illicit operations and activities that challenge national and international security.

TOR is free and open-source software for enabling anonymous communication. The name is derived from the acronym for the original software project name 'The Onion Router.'

Traffic Sniffer, also known as a packet sniffer, is a computer program or piece of computer hardware that can intercept and log traffic that passes over a digital network or part of a network. As data streams flow across the network, the sniffer captures each packet and, if needed, decodes the packet's raw data, shows the values of various fields in the packet, and analyzes its content according to the appropriate request comments or other specifications.

Trend Impact Analysis (TIA) is a simple quantitative forecasting approach that extrapolates historical data into the future while considering unprecedented future events. This method permits an analyst to systematically examine the effects of expected future events that affect the extrapolated trend. The events can include technological, political, social, economic, and value-oriented changes.

Underfitting is when a model cannot adequately capture the model's foundational data set's complete structure. An underfitted model typically is missing functional terms or has gaps in its primary (training) data set, causing some output parameters or terms to appear incorrectly or not at all. Such models tend to have poor predictive performance.

Web Crawler is a search engine known as a spider, spiderbot, or just a crawler. An internet bot that systematically browses the World Wide Web, typically operated by search engines for web indexing purposes.

Index

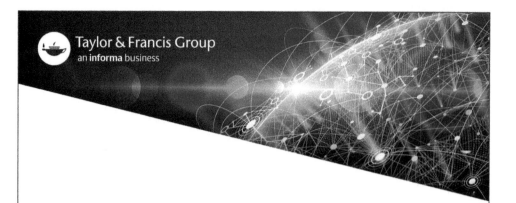